AF782342

Interdisciplinary Insights on Fraud

Interdisciplinary Insights on Fraud

Edited by

Aurora A.C. Teixeira, António Maia,
José António Moreira and Carlos Pimenta

CAMBRIDGE
SCHOLARS
PUBLISHING

Interdisciplinary Insights on Fraud,
Edited by Aurora A.C. Teixeira, António Maia,
José António Moreira and Carlos Pimenta

This book first published 2014

Cambridge Scholars Publishing

12 Back Chapman Street, Newcastle upon Tyne, NE6 2XX, UK

British Library Cataloguing in Publication Data
A catalogue record for this book is available from the British Library

Copyright © 2014 by Aurora A.C. Teixeira António Maia,
José António Moreira, Carlos Pimenta and contributors

All rights for this book reserved. No part of this book may be reproduced, stored in a retrieval system, or transmitted, in any form or by any means, electronic, mechanical, photocopying, recording or otherwise, without the prior permission of the copyright owner.

ISBN (10): 1-4438-5656-8, ISBN (13): 978-1-4438-5656-0

TABLE OF CONTENTS

INTRODUCTION

AURORA A.C. TEIXEIRA

"Do you know, Watson," said he, "that it is one of the curses of a mind with a turn like mine that I must look at everything with reference to my own special subject. You look at these scattered houses, and you are impressed by their beauty. I look at them, and the only thought which comes to me is a feeling of their isolation and of the impunity with which crime may be committed there."
— Arthur Conan Doyle,
Sherlock Holmes: The Complete Novels and Stories, Volume I

Fraud is a complex and transnational phenomenon. It severely undermines the profitability, reputability, and legitimacy of individuals, organisations and states wherever it occurs. It is especially damaging to countries in times of crisis. Given the scarcity of resources and the urgent need for economic growth, fraud can be extremely costly and devastating. Indeed, the draining of resources that results from fraud, regardless of its type and scope, amplifies the costs of running businesses, thus weakening their competitiveness.

Due to its complexity, no single lens or perspective is sufficient to apprehend its causes and ramifications. Fraud should therefore be analysed through a myriad of lenses, involving a wide range of disciplines. In short, an interdisciplinary approach should be adopted.

The aim of this volume is to provide an interdisciplinary insight into fraud, departing from the premise that a proper understanding of the phenomenon of fraud is required in order to be able to undermine it. Such an understanding demands both a clarification of its definition and a proper analysis of its diverse types and scientific perspectives.

Structure of the book

The thirteen chapters selected for the present book address fraud from a transversal and interdisciplinary perspective (see Figure 1). The book contextualizes the phenomenon (Chapter 1 and 2), offers a wide diversity of empirical approaches to fraud – tax fraud (Chapters 2, 4 and 5), fraud related with copyright infringement (Chapter 6), academic fraud (Chapter 7), and white collar crime (Chapter 8) -, as well as putting forward methods – econometric (Chapter 9), simulation (Chapter 10) and statistical (Chapter 11) - for predicting and thus helping to prevent fraud. It further proposes some strategies for action to cope with fraud and fraudsters (Chapter 12) and recover the assets stolen through these scams, most notably through money laundering (Chapter 13).

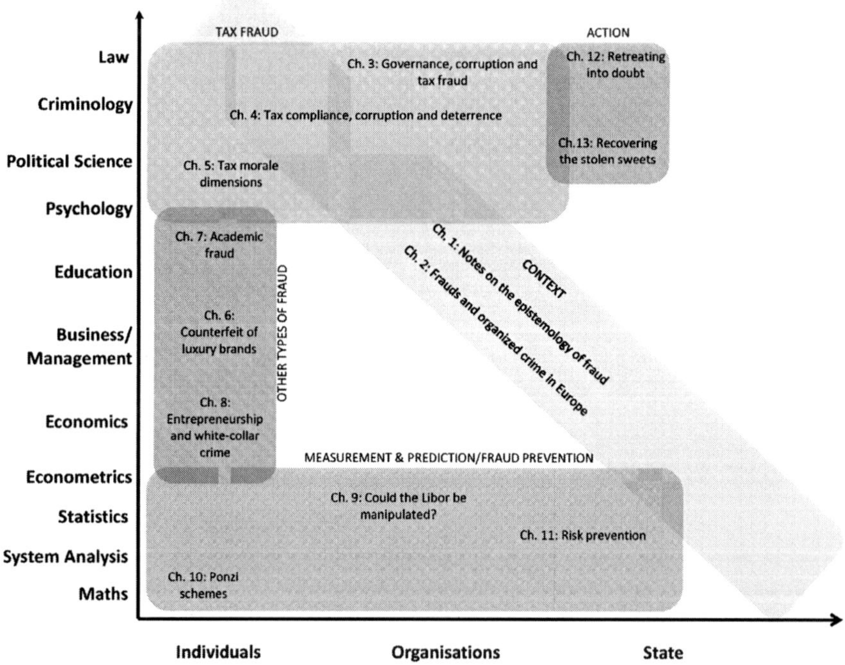

Figure 1: Organisation and structure of the book

Content of the book

In Chapter 1 ('Notes on the epistemology of fraud'), Carlos Pimenta and Óscar Afonso go deep into the multidimensional phenomenon and concept of fraud, evidencing that in this field "interdisciplinarity is weak", although it is "institutionalized and operational". Contrasting with the relevance and concern that fraud posits to societies, the authors establish that educational and research institutions seem to underestimate and ignore it. Specifically, they argue that "[r]esearch into fraud as a wholly social phenomenon is very incipient and education is not training new staff properly", emphasizing that "[p]revention and fight against fraud are too fragmented compared to the need to fight for a more ethical society". Finally, they assert that a proper analysis of fraud requires the contributions of various subject areas (e.g., Psychology, Social Psychology, Anthropology, Sociology, Economics, Management, Political Science, Law, Criminology, History, Geography, Mathematics, Social Network Analysis, Systems Security) and the integration of individual, institutional and social dimensions.

The multidimensionality of fraud is also highlighted by Jean-François Gayraud in his chapter dedicated to 'Frauds and Organized Crime in Europe'. Still barely explored by scientific research, organized crime "is a phenomenon of powers… with a capacity of strategic autonomy away from subordination to other forms of powers (state, economic, financial or media powers)" that "provokes a transformation, often silent and invisible, of the institutions and of the political, economic or social systems". Gayraud provides evidence on some geographical areas – Mexico, Japan, Turkey, the East Coast of the USA, Canada (Quebec) or France – where a large part of the economy is doped with drug money, industry markets criminalization, and "high corruption" (control and corruption of politicians and senior officials by mafia groups). According to the author the only possible path for a successful fight against organized crime in Europe encompasses fundamental knowledge and pedagogy, the existence of a credible judicial system, and adequate criminal intelligence mechanisms.

A successful fight against fraud in general demands indeed fundamental knowledge most notably regarding the diversity of approaches to and types of fraud. Glória Teixeira and Ary Ferreira da Cunha (Chapter 3) establish both a parallel and distinction between corruption and tax fraud, emphasizing that corporate and public governance can learn a lot from each other on how to curb corruption and tax fraud. The authors stress that both corruption and tax fraud pose a significant obstacle for societies, interacting in a vicious circle, in which corruption diminishes social trust, making people much less likely to promote welfare, and more likely to evade taxation. This latter "significantly hampers the ability of the State to obtain the income it needs in order to provide for public goods and services such as justice, security, education or health".

The two following chapters also address the issue of tax fraud but focusing now on the perspective of tax compliance (Chapter 4) and morale (Chapter 5). Daniela Wilks and Luís Pacheco highlight that tax evasion is a particularly serious problem in times of economic austerity, concluding that trust in authorities and their capacity to deter and punish tax evaders are interrelated and both are important in securing tax compliance. The intrinsic motivation to comply with fiscal duties or tax morale is analysed by Cristina Sá, António Martins and Carlos Gomes, who conducted a factor analysis and identified religiosity, trust in government and democracy, trust in public institutions and political participation as the main tax morale dimensions of Portuguese citizens. They further point out that an improvement in the quality of public services and a better relationship between taxpayers and public authorities can promote tax morale and taxpayer compliance.

Using also individuals as the unit of analysis, Neuza Silva and Aurora Teixeira (Chapter 6) study the determinants of the intention to purchase counterfeit luxury brands by university students. The authors discuss how the inappropriate use of a brand, namely by counterfeiting its products, has compromised and destroyed its value for producers and consumers. Such a phenomenon is particularly acute in the luxury market which has observed considerable growth in the last decade, accompanied by the growth of counterfeit luxury goods. It is demonstrated, through econometric estimations, that integrity and a strong belief that the law should be obeyed are the characteristics that best distinguish individuals that do not intend to buy counterfeit luxury products from those that do.

The attitudes of university students are the focus of Chapter 7. Filipe Almeida, Ana Seixas, Paulo Gama, Paulo Peixoto and Denise Esteves deal with the phenomenon of academic fraud, which has drawn increasing attention from researchers As with fraud in general, academic fraud remains a phenomenon whose boundaries are not yet clearly understood, to a large extent due to a lack of consensus regarding its conceptual frontiers and the absence of any clear and comprehensive tool with which to assess it. The authors seek to understand the types, practices and the reasons which cause or prevent academic fraud in Portugal. They conclude that the majority of the students considered fraud to be a frequent practice, revealing a culture of tolerance towards academic misconduct that neither legitimises nor encourages its denunciation. It is further shown that the perceptions and attitudes of the students varied according to the type of fraud in question and the subject they were studying.

Departing from Baumol's contention of white-collar crime as 'destructive entrepreneurship', in Chapter 8, José Cruz translates the theoretical groundings of the model of personality traits applied to entrepreneurial inclination into a model to study white-collar crime inclination/intentions. He argues that if the positive relationship between entrepreneurial intentions and white-collar crime intentions is not rejected, it is possible to establish that institutions and the contextual "rules of the game" (e.g., regulatory framework, the efficiency of the judicial system) matter and should be shaped so as to reduce the attractiveness of unproductive entrepreneurship (i.e., white-collar crime) and to encourage productive entrepreneurship. Additionally, if the influence of perceived social norms is not rejected, social context also becomes relevant in the choice between productive and unproductive entrepreneurship.

Different variants of white-collar crime – financial markets manipulation (Chapter 9), Ponzi Schemes (Chapter 10) and public procurement-related fraud (Chapter 11) – are the focus of the three chapters dedicated to the measurement and prediction of fraud. In Chapter 9, Marius-Cristian Frunza presents an econometric study of the times series of submitted rates by the banks involved in the LIBOR. Providing real case evidence on scandals surrounding some infamous banking institutions (e.g., Bankia, J.P. Morgan Chase & Co., HSBC, Barclays, and Citibank), he assesses the influence of banks on the final LIBOR figures and evaluates the possible impact of their misrepresentation. The author shows that, even though after 2008, under the hypothesis of a bank acting alone, changes in LIBOR rates would have been limited, an organized approach from at least four financial institutions could result in a significant manipulation of the LIBOR.

Mário Cunha, Hélder Valente and Paulo Vasconcelos (Chapter 10) introduce a computational approach to assess the behaviour of a fund under a Ponzi scheme. The mathematical modelling and numerical simulation describe the mechanics of this type of scams, going beyond the simplistic explanation that its sustainability depends only on rapid (exponential) growth of the number of customers and investors. Furthermore, it explores the numerical simulation of Ponzi schemes, allowing for fast evaluation of funds showing unrealistic performances. The authors demonstrate the usefulness of simulation techniques in the detection of unsustainable patterns, being a tool likely to be of interest to financial regulators and investors.

Prediction of business failure is of major interest also in contracts between public institutions and private companies. Leonardo Sales (Chapter 11) selected credit scoring models, which are based on the statistical consideration of the company's characteristics to calculate its probability of becoming a defaulter, as a tool in the prevention of defaults. The author shows for the case of Brazil the feasibility of using multivariate statistical techniques for the prediction of problems by government administrators with their suppliers. Sales argues that for administrators it is interesting to know their suppliers and the risks they offer to execute the services under their responsibility, increasing therefore the efficiency of public procurement processes.

The two final chapters address action-based strategies for fighting and curbing fraud and crime, namely that related to money laundering. Michelle Gallant, in her chapter 'Retreating into Doubt: Tainted Finance, Civil Devices and the Rule of Law', draws principally on developments in select common law jurisdictions, particularly Canada, to offer a critical appraisal of modern civil tools aimed at criminal finance. Gallant states that some jurisdictions, notably the United Kingdom, in order to recover assets tainted by crime, rely on the process of civil recovery while the Canadian province of Alberta relies on restitution and compensation regimes. According to the author, "a degree of reliance on civil tools holds some promise" as they facilitate the actual taking or forfeiture of property. Specifically, they offer a degree of efficiency that criminal instruments – encumbered by the weighty exigencies of the prosecutorial process – do not. It is, however, in Gallant's viewpoint, of great importance to monitor that reliance. Jeffrey Simser, in Chapter 13 ('Recovering the Stolen Sweets of Fraud and Corruption'), recognizes, as Gallant does, that recovering assets "is a challenging enterprise". Simser reviews a number of techniques used by criminals to advance fraudulent or corrupt schemes. One of such techniques is money laundering where assets are transformed, through movement and transactions, from dirty money to apparently clean money. According to the author, there are opportunities as we look for better ways to prevent and deter fraud and corruption and as we seek to dispossess criminals of their loot and make victims whole.

Acknowledgements

The present volume resulted from a careful selection of the top quality articles, focusing on the issue of fraud, presented in the first international conference organized by OBEGEF (Observatory of Economics and Management of Fraud). This conference, entitled 'Interdisciplinary Insights on Fraud and Corruption', was held in Porto (Portugal) on 13-15 September 2012 - http://www.obegef.pt/i2fc/index.html.

The editors are sincerely grateful to the reviewers of the chapters for their insightful comments and suggestions that have significantly contributed for the quality of the present book, and the authors of the chapters for their efforts in putting together and account for such comments and suggestions.

PART I –

CONTEXT

CHAPTER ONE

NOTES ON THE EPISTEMOLOGY OF FRAUD

CARLOS PIMENTA AND ÓSCAR AFONSO

Introduction

When in 1939 Edwin Sutherland created the concept of "white collar criminality" (1940) and identified it "as a crime committed by a person of respectability and high social status in the course of his occupation" (1983, 7), he was underpinning fraud as the main topic of the then-young field of Criminology and as a social problem to be studied. He effectively recognized the importance of this matter when he noted that:

> "the financial cost of white collar crime is probability several times as great as the financial cost of all the crimes which are customarily regarded as the «crime problem»" (1983, 9),

adding that these crimes are echoed "in politics" and "violate trust and therefore create distrust, and this lowers social morale and produces social disorganization on a large scale" (1983, 10). A reality that is self-reproduced because it is rooted in society itself, as he explained with his theory of differential association.

If, at the time, fraud was an important social fact, it has become so much more some decades later, taking several forms, with disparate manifestations, increasing repercussions and complexity as a result of globalization. The last two decades of the 20th century and the early years of the 21st have brought fraud to the forefront.

Several sciences have increasingly come to focus on fraud as a topic of study. Firstly, Law, since it should anchor social relations in legal standards and fight against fraudulent behaviour. Then, Criminology and other sciences have to apply their knowledge to fight and prevent fraud: Risk Analysis and Internal Control operate as a specialization of Management against fraudulent behaviour; the non-observed economy is assumed as a field of study in Economics; Auditing, a traditional instrument to detect irregularities in the operation and accounting reports of institutions, specializes in Forensic Accounting; Psychology analyses the behaviour of "communities of fraudsters"; Forensic Sciences have to include proof of economic-financial fraud in their field of work; Systems Analysis has to strongly respond to security issues. In short, the first trend consisted in a specialization within the existing sciences and techniques.

Nevertheless, a second trend was being forged at the same time based on intersections among fields or spheres of knowledge. Taking the company as the focal point, Management, − action and reflection, positive and normative, aiming to optimize the resources of institutions – came to generate Fraud Management, the meeting point for diverse spheres of knowledge and practices, such as Accounting, Auditing, Law, Criminal Investigation, Mathematics and Psychology. The degree of interdisciplinarity is weak, but institutionalized and operational, as shown by the deployment of the international association, ACFE – Association of Certified Fraud Examiners (ACFE 2012), and other similar institutions.

Fraud today

It has long been known that fraud is complex and that "fraud has become a challenge to the security of the State." (Pons and Berche 2009, 13).[1] The resolutions of international institutions and bilateral and multilateral agreements on fraud or some of its manifestations (e.g., corruption and tax fraud) uphold this. It is also a common observation that "the defrauder is a professional" and that "fraud enriches in a complex world." (2009, 17).[2] More and more sectors are being affected by fraud and the interconnection between autonomous, yet closely related, realities increases (e.g., types of black-market economy, fraud, money laundering, corruption, financing of election campaigns). Society is more aware that there is a relation between the quality of life of communities and the ability to prevent and fight fraud.

The recent subprime crisis, the slump of which we are still experiencing, has put many of these aspects in the spotlight. Although the concealed nature of fraud reduced its visibility, despite the many warnings, the violent crisis and the intensity and nature of fraud has brought this matter to the forefront. Some authors, especially Gayraud (2011; Gayraud and Thual 2012), explain the systemic relationship between crises, international organized crime and fraud. Several authors, economists (Kindleberger and Aliber 2011; Galbraith 1990) and others (de Saint Victor 2012; Ernst-Vintila et al. 2010), have shown that the "economic-financial" crises should increasingly be studied by other social sciences, and that to overcome the crisis, one has to fight conflicts of interest, fraud and crime, as well as state deregulation.

Structure of the text

The next section (II) specifies the meaning of fraud, which is required due to the polysemy of the term, the variety of involved components and the use of a wider definition in this work. Moreover, fraud unfolds in multiple manifestations that reflect a layered diversity of manifestation (individual, institutional and social) and of implementation processes. This brief analysis highlights the hypothesis that we are facing a complex phenomenon. The following section (III) draws attention to the divide between the critical importance of this theme for societies worldwide today and the low priority it is given in teaching and research, highlighting the need for further scientific work in this area. Finally, the last section (IV) presents a proposal that intends to provide the required impulse for scientific research on fraud to be conducted in new ways, given the phenomenon's complexity, the links between its various layers and its inherent interdisciplinarity. The proposal is relevant to the action to be taken, and is realistic and achievable, despite the expected difficulties.

Multidimensional phenomena

The concept of fraud

Everyone agrees that armed robbery is not fraud. Things are indeed what they seem. There is no pretence. The same can be said of the production and trafficking of drugs. If activities are prohibited by law, they must be done covertly, but no attempt is made to make drugs seem what they are not. In these two situations, as in many others, it is easy to say that these activities (in this case, illegal) cannot be classified as fraud.

It is easy to say what is not fraud, but harder to say what is. This is why there is a myriad of definitions with many commonalities, but various nuances and differences (Pimenta 2009, 11-16)

However, there is ample room for consensus. For example, if in a company there is asset misappropriation without the company being aware of it, having evaded records and controls, it is a fraud. The same can be said of tax evasion by creating shell companies and issuing false invoices. Swindling is also not what it seems. Many other situations have the particular feature of involving deception: rigging election results, selling fake works of art, disseminating counterfeit currency, tampering with management data in a political organization in order to reveal non-existent financial efficiency, using personal data of others obtained by electronic means. In corruption, too, results are forged in a covert manner.

Many other situations are dubious. Is counterfeiting a fraud? Is selling fish that is illegally caught a fraud?

Let us drop the borderline cases.

Although there are many cases of fraud, and they are part of common knowledge terminology, in this paper, we are interested in economic-financial fraud, which generates benefits or harms income and wealth.

Thus, we can say that fraud is any intentional act by persons, individual or collective, perpetrated with deception that causes, effectively or potentially, advantages for someone or damage to others and which violates either good social practices or the law.

This definition, which we will adopt in the scope of this analysis, casts two doubts that need to be clearly addressed.

Why "effectively or potentially"? The intention of this dual reference is to cover those situations in which information was falsified but did not result in either benefits or harm because the agreed situation did not take place (e.g., false information on an illness when filling out a health insurance policy).

Why "good social practices or the law"? Why add the diffuse sense of "good social practices" to the positive quality of the law? Firstly, the subjectivity of the classification is not only present in these "social practices". The law also provides for them, for example, the case of substantiated factual evidence that is not conducive to a judicial ruling for formal reasons; the fact that many frauds are victimless crimes (from a legal standpoint), not resulting in legal proceedings; and the existence of social and institutional leniency in regard to a conduct that infringes the rules of law, but "which everyone does". Secondly, there is no reason for handling different, materially identical situations on an equal footing, because the State deliberately or inadvertently did not legislate properly. A typical example are tax havens – which in 2010 soaked up between US\$21 x 10^{12} and \$32 x 10^{12} of global private wealth (Henry 2012) –, while, at the same time, many laws are created to prevent tax evasion, and a vast majority of citizens have no access to these mechanisms. Thirdly, changes in social representations, ideologies and ethical concepts over the cycles are particularly interesting for the studies we propose elsewhere in this paper.

Splits and readings

A frequent mistake made when studying fraud is to consider it as an isolated act, as a relationship between an individual and wealth, ignoring that all frauds are a social relationship and are part of a vaster process, whether from a social standpoint, in general, or an economic and criminological standpoint, in particular.

We will later analyze some aspects of this fraudulent process. Our major concern here will be to accurately define some of the terms used.

We are still a long way from having full knowledge of fraud to be able to categorically label it as a complex process and to measure the value of its complexity even less. We can, however, categorically state that it does not have a single cause, that it can be viewed in a lot of ways (multidimensionality), and that it has at the same time many elements of reference (multireferentiality), the necessary, but not sufficient, features of complexity.

Fraud depends on individual behaviour, on interpersonal relationships and on institutional contexts. It depends on the institutions (e.g., State, market, companies, family), on their existence and functioning. It depends on social representations, risk perception and related emotions, and on the collective feeling in relation to ethical behaviour. It depends on the interpenetration between what is legal and what is illegal:

> "there are no longer two parallel worlds, the legal and the illegal, but a world of business which is increasingly penetrated by organized crime" (Véry and Monnet 2008, 180).[3]

These logical findings have been confirmed by a number of empirical studies on some types of more measurable frauds: perception of corruption, tax evasion.

We are still far from understanding the multiplicity of perspectives and views, but we can choose the *non-observed economy* to reflect the macro-dimension of society and economic activity, *social disintegration* to observe the interpersonal and inter-institutional relationships, and *ethical degeneration* to express individual options, obviously embedded in a society.

What we call ethical degeneration is the social weakening of the effective moral norms, which are not uniform in a society, differ by community, and sometimes are stable over long periods of time and sometimes change in short periods of time (Katz 2011, 39-57; Polanyi 2000).

If there are difficulties in objectively examining the development of moral norms, this can be partly overcome by using quantifiable indicators as social representations: "generally speaking, representations inspire and frame human conduct" (Ernst-Vintila et al. 2010, 517).[4]

We have to admit there may be a positive relationship between fraud, particularly economic-financial fraud, and ethical degeneration.

What we call social disintegration are the disruptions of consensus, and combined actions of life and its reproduction. This is a general term to refer to a wide variety of relationships among people, individuals and groups, institutional procedures, ideologies, beliefs and feelings. Several studies have shown a relationship between the Hofstede indicators (http://geert-hofstede.com) and certain types of fraud, between levels of social cohesion and probability of fraud, between social notions of time and fraudulent practices.

Because:

> "intuitively, we understand that an atomised society, where people are distanced from each other, in which they do not communicate or gather together, cannot function as well as another society in which the citizens develop community ties, participate in public life, and gather for a range of purposes, from sports and recreational events, to unionistic or political ones" (Almeida 2011, 9),[5]

Sociologists have used the concept of negative social capital, in quantifiable terms, to gain deeper insights into fraud, particularly in the analysis of corruption (Sousa (Org.) 2009, 93-125).

We have to admit there may be a positive relationship between social disintegration and fraud, in general, and economic and financial fraud, in particular.

Adopting the terminology of the OECD (2002), the non-observed economy includes all economic activities not considered in the aggregate national accounts. This difference between economic activities and national accounts results from the characteristics of the activities.

There is a strong identity between the underground economy and fraud. By definition, it is essentially tax fraud, assuming the definition of fraud presented before. For this reason, we can say that there is a close relationship between the underground economy and economic and financial fraud, in that they have a common share and because an environment of greater tax evasion increases the probability of there being other types of fraud.

In its diversity, the illegal economy (Napoleoni 2009) is rarely fraud, yet there is a close relationship between its variation and the dimension of economic and financial frauds. As we have mentioned, there are different borderlines. First, because it reflects a certain level of permissibility and control of the activities prohibited by law and, second, because some illegal activities contribute directly to some frauds, including corruption and money laundering. Finally, because there is a close relationship between these activities and international organized crime, on the one hand, and between the latter and fraud processes, on the other. In some periods of history, international crime, including mafias, specialized only in certain illegal activities, but not today. Drug trafficking currently supports international economic crime (Queloz 2002; Cretin 2007; Gayraud and Thual 2012), but it is an activity among many.

The relationship between fraud and the informal economy is much more elusive. It depends on the situation. It can either indicate types of occupational fraud, as a means to increase social cohesion, or show the overlapping of different modes of production that result from stabilizing social customs.

Finally, some words on *money laundering*. Regardless of its possible particulars and different legal definitions (Silva et al. 2009), we can say that it is the social concealment of the origin of economic values (Braguês 2009).

The reference to this category in the terminological accuracy of the components making up the fraud process is different from the ones mentioned before. Money laundering is a phase in the circulation of wealth and income associated to fraud and the non-observed economy. There are feedback effects between money laundering and fraud, and this is relevant in the concept of complexity.

From the normative point of view, there is today an association between terrorism and money laundering. This is a highly controversial relationship (Kane and Wall 2004; Vittori 2004; Dupuis-Danon 2005), both because of the amounts involved and of the actual financing of terrorism. Some authors (Gayraud) uphold that this is a fictitious relationship that led only to a diversion of resources in the fight against fraud. Nevertheless, we cannot deny the close relationship between the non-observed economy and fraud, on the one hand, and money laundering, on the other. Similarly, the States have, over the years, made life easier for money laundering by setting up tax havens, implementing deregulation and free movement.

In short, fraud is a multidimensional and multireferential social process, processed in different layers of the social structure, with dynamic and different times of reproduction and changes, with feedback effects. Its integrated reading alone can provide us with a more accurate contextualized understanding of the phenomenon. The intersection of spheres of knowledge is a prelude to a more effective fight in the prevention and detection of fraud.

Reality and Ignorance

The fraud reality

We can say that fraud has always existed. Historical references prove it. However, since fraud is a process of social relationships, we cannot establish a continuity that supersedes the periods of continuing social dynamics and does not take into account the disruptions in social organization.

Even though Adam Smith and many of his followers did not establish a relationship between businesses and fraud – if he had some concerns regarding the deterioration of social behaviours those concerns were related to the workers (Walraevens 2011; Smith 1983) – such a relationship was always present in capitalism. It changed its shape with capitalism and assumed new dimensions and features with the financialization of the economy after the 1980s, at a time when neoliberal theses and the abandonment of controls and regulation were strengthened.

While this is not the place to present a history of fraud and of the categories previously associated to it, it is nonetheless important to recall some data that show the relevance of this reality today. The inventory is not exhaustive, which would be impossible to do, but it does show some of the most significant references.

According to ACFE data, occupational fraud against companies represents, in the USA, between 5% and 7% of their revenues (ACFE 2012, 2010, 2008, 1996, 2006, 2004, 2002). It may be higher in many other countries. The World Bank estimates that corruption of members linked to the State is of about $1 x 10^{12}$ US dollars, 1.6% of the world GDP in 2010. To this must be added bribery in international business transactions (OECD / World Bank 1012) and corruption in sports. We have elsewhere referred to the estimated amounts in tax havens. Money laundering of criminal origin represented $1.6 x 10^{12}$ US dollars in 2009 (UNODC 2010). The average shadow economy in EU countries is estimated at 18.4% of GDP this year (Schneider 2012).

If we were to include the illegal economy, which is impossible to calculate, it would strengthen the catastrophic image that the previous numbers already bring to mind. We will only mention that the estimated profits from transnational organized crime are of about 35×10^{10} US dollars a year (Gayraud and Thual 2012, 155).

Trends of evolution

The costs underlying all these illegal activities must be added to the values above: prevention costs and the costs of the consequences of these situations.

As evidenced by several empirical studies on corruption, we know that fraud negatively impacts on domestic investment, foreign investment and the product, government expenses and the quality of public services, competition, international trade, employability and wages. It challenges the key values of society and democracy itself. Fraud in financial business and tax fraud underlie the current sovereign debt crisis in the EU.

However, the consequences of fraud and economic crime, in particular, are much more wide-ranging. First, fraud, economic crime and some criminogenic behaviour in the USA have strongly contributed to the current international economic-financial crisis. Gayraud (2011) shows this clearly, postulating that all economic-financial crises are political crises, and that crime is always present. Basing his considerations on some important economists, which we will refer to ahead, he shows that:

> "The criminogenic environment which led to the crisis of the savings banks first and to subprime afterwards, can be summed up in three words: deregulation, de-supervision and decriminalization. These are the three Ds at the core of the crisis." (Gayraud, 2011, 230).[6]

Given this conflict of interest-filled context, the speculative business environment in which "the profits are privatized and the losses socialized",[7] marked by the asymmetry of information and misselling (the ethically questionable practice of a salesperson misrepresenting or misleading an investor about the characteristics of a product or service) (2011, 203-205), has boosted the exponential growth of frauds, detonating the international financial crisis.

Second, the context mentioned above, the difficulties facing companies and States, the restrictive policies regarding privatization packages and the divestiture of State sovereignty, have paved the way for capital of criminal origin to penetrate the legal companies, to gain greater influence over international economic crime in the business world and greater political control (de Saint Victor 2012; Gayraud and Thual 2012).

These penetrations are operated in myriad ways, sometimes to solve cash-flow problems and, at the same time or subsequently, to participate in companies until they are controlled. These capital crime penetrations buy out privatized, often strategic companies. They support and fund electoral campaigns, they corrupt officials, use offshores, control new and small States without authority, as well as kleptocratic countries. Moreover, they "manage human resources" outside the world of crime that may be of use in the future.

The experience of the economic management of mafias in some countries and sectors is a micro-view of the dangers that such control of business by economic criminality poses to the future of mankind. Europe is today a particularly sensitive region (Gayraud 2012; Napoleoni 2009).

Third, the progression of organized economic crime and the generalization of fraud are cumulative. The tendency to deteriorate is done in many ways, but we will limit ourselves to metaphorically recalling Gresham's law: "The bad capitalism removes the good capitalism; the bad capitalists remove the good capitalists." (Gayraud 2011, 229).[8]

If a company is not open to corruption in a public tender for a major work and another company is, which is more likely to grow economically? If these two companies want to export to a country where corruption is a prerequisite for penetration, which is more likely to have any chance? If a company meets its tax obligations and another company evades them, which one is more likely to show a higher profit rate? If a company promotes industrial espionage, will it be more likely to attract the new market share or the company that suffers industrial espionage? If a company grappling with cash-flow problems has to turn to credit and another company resorts to money laundering, which company will have less costs in obtaining cash? In short, those behaving contrary to the "good trade practices" are the most likely to win over the competition and expand their business.

Admittedly, the "misbehaving" company runs the risk of being penalized for an unlawful act, which can end a successful career. This is a fact. However, having taken place in white-collar crime territory (Santos 2001) these risks are smaller. If economic crimes were to be decriminalized, the amount to be returned would always be a small part of what was earned. All we would have to do is include it as a business risk. The analysis of money-related convictions in the USA in the past thirty years proves this.

Insufficient training

Training on the nature, detection and prevention of fraud should be in place just by reason of its social relevance. Unfortunately, this is not the case:

> "Economists receive no training about fraud risk, incidence, or mechanisms (beyond the conventional wisdom that it was trivial, a distraction during the debacle). Lawyers receive no fraud training. (…) The average new accountant receives no meaningful training about fraud and no training at all about fraud control" (Black 2005, 247).

The same can be said in relation to the directly correlated facts mentioned previously. For economists, honesty is *ceteris paribus*. The economic reality is not a part of the social one (Polanyi 2000) and they do not examine whether markets are self-regulated or not. They admit they are. It is, therefore, not surprising that the social representations presented by management students defend the *status quo* (Ernst-Vintila et al. 2010, 521).

Insufficient research

Research on the problems of fraud also seems to be at a far distance from the relevance of the phenomenon.[9]

Having selected the twenty-four keywords related to fraud, corruption and bribery, money laundering, non-observed economy, tax evasion, cyber fraud, to refer to specific cases of fraud that we have examined so far, and criminology, a general term, we found that between 2000 and 2011 there were 9715 articles registered in the *Scopus* database that contain at least one of the keywords. This number has increased year after year, from 377 in 2000 to 1411 in 2011. The two journals with the most articles are the *Journal of Business Ethics* (176) and *Crime Law and Social Change* (145). By nationality of authors, the USA (34.2%), the United Kingdom (12.1%) and Australia (4.2%) represent more than half of the articles.

The Table below shows the result of a more detailed analysis by discipline (Economy, Management, Psychology, Anthropology, Geography, Accounting and Law) and by journals in top or intermediate positions in the ranking:[10] percentage of articles that mention at least one of the keywords in relation to the total number of articles published by discipline and level of journals.

Table 1: Frequency of references to fraud by discipline

Subject area	Journal ranking	# Journals	Min (%)	Max (%)
Accounting	Top	3	0.8	3.4
	Middle	-	-	-
Economy	Top	3	0.3	0.5
	Middle	3	1.0	2.3
Management	Top	3	0.5	1.4
	Middle	3	1.3	1.7
Law	Top	3	0.7	2.6
	Middle	3	0.0	6.2
Anthropology	Top	2	0.0	2.1
	Middle	3	0.0	0.5
Geography	Top	3	0.0	0.5
	Middle	2	0.0	0.2
Psychology	Top	3	0.0	2.0
	Middle	4	0.0	1.7

Note: See Appendix 1.

Criminology journals have much higher percentages (between 0.8% and 50%), but the use of general keywords means that this information is not comparable with the remaining disciplines.

In short, whereas fraud is a social reality of great concern, educational and research institutions underestimate and ignore it, particularly those that are responsible for training technical members who will be more likely to take positions that require an ethical attitude, to promote the detection and prevention of fraud.

Whereas international economic criminality has a worldwide decision-making centre and conditions that facilitate criminal cooperation, the institutions likely to fight against it are predominantly split by countries, referring to the tree but ignoring the forest. Experts are hived-off in their specific areas, treated in a disciplinary way. Research into fraud as an entirely social phenomenon is very incipient and education is not training new professionals properly. Moreover, totally different terminologies used to interpret the same reality hinder a common understanding.

Although universities and other research institutions are not responsible for overcoming some of these segmentations, they are nevertheless responsible for addressing the matter and disseminating it in a professional and integrated manner.

Interconnecting spheres of knowledge

Interdisciplinarity: object and methodology

From what we have said above, we can easily conclude that the study, prevention and fight against fraud are too fragmented compared to the need to fight for a more ethical society. This fragmentation finds more unity within fraudulent people and institutions, and in permissive and boosting factors of fraud.

A more unified and complete study of the fraud process is a significant contribution to reducing the said fragmentation on two complementary levels. First, it would increase scientific knowledge and strengthen unity within a scientific community that is often dispersed and hived-off. Additionally, it would increase the likelihood of a more appropriate public opinion, all the more so when the media serve the cause. Second, it would provide tools for analysis and action to enhance the capacity for detection and prevention. This prevention must be understood in a micro and macro-social sense. This epistemological work is highly pragmatic.

This interconnection between fields of knowledge does not arise spontaneously. Counter-trends are greater than those for the start-up of such a venture, despite some positive developments, as we have already mentioned.

We propose that there are three key vectors in such a project.

First, the focus of study is economic-financial fraud as a systemic element of the entire social reality.

When doing science, the focus of study is not the ontological reality, but an epistemological construction thereof, maintaining ties as strong as the literalness and realism of the study to be undertaken (Pimenta 2012, Chap. III). In our case, the core of the object of study is *economic-financial fraud as a process*. A social process that only assumes real meaning when part of a whole (Godin 1997) that reproduces itself.

Every economic-financial fraud reflects, within its specificity, the entire social reality of which it is an integral element: the mode of production and its organization, social-political structure, various social representations, existing ethical and philosophical concepts, and structure of individual and institutional social relationships. In its specificity, every fraud is unique. At a given historical moment, every fraud, as a reflection of the social whole, shares common patterns with other frauds.

While the process of economic-financial fraud is a limiting factor of the object of study, its entirety (as a fraud, as a crime) expands it. The two ensuing vectors, and the methodology of the project, help pinpoint this tension.

Second, we need to articulate in a structured whole the micro and macro dimensions of the economic-financial fraud process, the interaction of the different social layers, with their own times, taking into account at least the non-observed economy, money laundering, social disintegration and ethical degeneration.

What has been said about these various groups shows that we face parts of the process that make up economic-financial fraud, which allows us to address the individual, institutional and social dimensions, always present in every event. It also sheds light on the circulation of income and wealth upstream and downstream of the fraud, in a strict sense.

There is a very good chance that the actual investigation into fraud in the contexts we have identified needs to consider other moments in the process, but these are sufficient and limit the starting point, which is a crucial moment for interconnections among spheres of knowledge.

Third, the two vectors mentioned are only feasible if interdisciplinary dynamics are in place. The integration of individual, institutional and social aspects, including the economic and political, requires contributions from various disciplines: Psychology, Social Psychology, Anthropology, Sociology, Economics, Management, Political Science and Law. Since fraud is a type of crime and is strongly linked to a "criminogenic society" (Dias and Andrade 1997), the contribution of Criminology is invaluable. Since the scientific object should reflect the ontological reality and the reading should be integrated and evolutionary, the presence of History is indispensable. According to some authors (Gayraud and Thual 2012), the association of fraud to organized crime and the importance of territory in its characterization would further the involvement of Geography.

The dark figure[11] of crime, the imagination that surrounds it, the proof that a fraud exists long before it comes to light, if it ever does, makes the phenomenon difficult to quantify, yet quantification is important as shown by various general works (Schneider 2004; Blanc et al. 2008) and specific works (Torgo and Lopes 2011; Gonçalves 2010; Schneider 2008; Del Monte and Papagni 2007). Mathematics is an auxiliary science that has to be present.

An analysis that integrates the individual and the social in an interconnected way requires, today, the use of tools such as the Social Network Analysis (Knoke and Yang 2008). The use of computer networks in the pursuit of fraud also requires specialists with expertise in this area, particularly in Systems Security.

A small final clarification is required. Why consider economic-financial fraud as the object of study and not fraud, which seems to be a more integrating epistemological reality? The difficulties that accompany the processes of interconnecting disciplinary, scientific and philosophical spheres of knowledge suggest that the object should be strongly delineated. Fraud is a too broad a concept. The experience accumulated in the cyclical dynamics of economy and society suggests a methodology strictly associated to economic-financial fraud.

Difficulties

Despite its increasing relevance, interdisciplinary difficulties are well known.

The main interdisciplinary difficulty probably lies in the fact that it unsettles the established powers. The hiving-off of scientists in their disciplinary area and, within it, in a specific theme, is a relatively consolidated situation, a controlling set of social relationships, a certain position in the teaching or research institution to which it belongs. It supports a certain social recognition, possibly mediatisation. This hiving-off and recognition facilitate access to funding. Participation in an interdisciplinary project is a risk to that stability, all the more so because final results are more uncertain and new competition has to be tackled.

It is essentially for this reason that institutions with a vast "geographical density" of disciplines and varied themes are, at the same time, so defensive and retroactive in relation to interdisciplinarity.

To this difficulty in correlating powers is added the greatest uncertainty of an interdisciplinary project. All those who have specialized in ethical problems are aware of a possible range of research topics and are likely to add information to some of them. The same applies to whoever studies the deviating behaviour or dynamics of investment in the economic cycle. When such scientists gather around the process of economic-financial fraud, the horizon of outcomes is yet to be built. At the outset, the joy of findings can be huge, but may be shadowed by major risks.

Finally, there is a set of epistemological difficulties, namely the fact that it is impossible for every scientist to properly know in advance some of the sciences involved, the weight of a previous disciplinary reading that delimits the "consciousness possible" when interconnecting different fields of knowledge, the difficulty in understanding the participants since they are marked by profound terminological differences, and resistance to changing reference paradigms. Quite apart from the existence of some disciplinary paradigms which tend to invade and dominate other sciences such as those from History (Godin 2003, 8) and Economics (Maki 2009).

These are difficulties, not deterrents. They are risks, but also the possibility of breakthroughs, the ultimate aim of every scientist. The project design can minimize some of the difficulties.

The research project

Economic cycles are a traditional topic in Economics. Even in the strict field of that science it is common to consider parameters reportable to Social Psychology, as Keynes does (Keynes 2010). Almost all authors focus their attention on economic variables, but they recognize that there are "exogenous variables" that also influence the process (Schumpeter 2008, 13). Some of these exogenous variables are all the more important in some models, such as the analysis of the relationship between the "economic cycle" and the "political cycle", the political-economic cycles.

Frauds also appear here and there, virtually by accident, in various works – see, for example, Schumpeter (2008, 154), but they also figure prominently in other works. For example, Galbraith (1990), who "reviews the great speculative episodes of the last three centuries. As already observed, common features recur" (Galbraith 1990, 12), and point to the extreme brevity of the financial memory:

> "In consequence, financial disaster is quickly forgotten. In further consequence, when the same or closely similar circumstances occur again, sometimes in only a few years, they are hailed by a new, often youthful, and always supremely self-confident generation as a brilliantly innovative discovery in the financial and larger economic world. There can be few fields of human endeavour in which history counts for so little as in the world of finance. Past experience, to the extent that it is part of memory at all, is dismissed as the primitive refuge of those who do not have the insight to appreciate the incredible wonders of the present." (Galbraith 1990, 13)

He adds a second factor "contributing to speculative euphoria and programmed collapse is the specious association of money and intelligence" (Galbraith 1990, 13). A set of clichés and false associations means that "*financial genius is before the fall*" (Galbraith 1990, 17).

Kindleberger and Aliber (2011), for example, dedicate chapter 7 (in the 2005 edition, this latter edition had not been issued yet) to fraud: "Bernie Madoff: frauds, swindles, and the credit cycle". The interconnection between cycle and fraud is significant:

> "Swindles, fraudulent behaviour, defalcations, and elaborate hustles are part of a life in market economies (...). Corrupt behaviour is part of virtually every economy. The number of transactions that appear to overstep both moral and legal norms increases in euphoric periods (...). Fraudulent behaviour increases in economic booms" (Kindleberger and Aliber 2011, 121; 123; 141)

"Reduced regulation" (Kindleberger and Aliber 2011, 127) also contributes to this situation.

In short, Economics and Criminology are already drawing closer as regards the relationship between social cycle and economic-financial fraud, which is a good starting point for interdisciplinary work, given the importance assumed by these disciplines in the project.[12]

However, the intersecting points are not limited to this. Regardless of the causes, phases and nature of the economic cycle, crisis plays a central role. The use and meaning of the concept of crisis are different depending on the social science, even though they converge in some points. In all sciences, it means a breakdown; in all sciences, terminology overlaps; and all sciences can use similar analytical tools. This is what accounts for the widespread use of the Catastrophe Theory (Thom, 1989).

Moreover, sweeping political, economic, criminological, ideological and ethical changes have occurred for short periods of time during the economic-social cycles. They are a good testing ground for inventorying events that may be an interdisciplinary field of study.

In short, the causal relationships between economic-social cycles and economic-financial fraud, based on the assumption that we are dealing with a complex reality, is a good key objective for our proposed project.

A close relationship between Criminology, Law, Economics and History, cloaked unpretentiously as collective learning, seems to be a good backbone for an array of other social sciences, already mentioned above.

Conclusion

Our proposal is to broaden our knowledge and understanding of economic-financial fraud to increasingly operationalize the fight against it. To this end, we opted for linking the macro and micro readings and dealt with fraud as a social process interconnected with many other dynamics.

Interdisciplinarity, which does not detract from specialization, is, on the contrary, how it should be pursued. The delimitation of the object of study and the understanding that there is, at least at the outset, a hard core of disciplines involved may reduce the difficulties of the project.

There are many ways one can do this. However, they all have to be assumed by the institutions, inevitably international institutions and, in respect to operation, rely on the development of networks of interconnected spheres of knowledge.

Interconnecting this institutionalization with an educational project may give it consistency.

Appendix 1

List of journals considered:

Subject area	Journal ranking		Journals
Accounting	Top	3	- Journal of Accounting and Economics - Accounting Review - Journal of Accounting Research
Economy	Top	3	- American Economic Review - Econometrica - Journal of Political Economy
	Middle	3	- European Economic Review - Scandinavian Journal of Economics - Canadian Journal of Economics
Management	Top	3	- Review of Financial Studies - Journal of Finance - Journal of Financial Economics
	Middle	3	- Journal of Financial Services Research - Journal of Accounting and Public Policy - Fiscal Studies
Law	Top	3	- Harvard Law Review - Columbia Law Review - Yale Law Journal
	Middle	3	- American Journal of International Law - Journal of Criminal Law & Criminology - Journal of Law and Society
Anthropology	Top	2	- Journal of Anthropological Sciences - Cultural Anthropology
	Middle	3	- Journal of Anthropological Research - Cultural Studies - Anthropolie
Geography	Top	3	- Economic Geography - Progress in Human Geography - Journal of Economic Geography
	Middle	2	- Australian Geographic - Landscape Research
Psychology	Top	3	- Research in Organizational Behavior - Organizational Research Methods - Journal of Applied Psychology
	Middle	4	- Psicothema - Theory & Psychology - Journal of Psychology - Psychology Crime & Law

We also consider the following journals on Criminology:
Top:

- Crime and Justice
- Criminology
- Journal of Quantitative Criminology

Middle:

- Crime Media Culture
- Social & Legal Studies
- Journal of Forensic Psychiatry & Psychology

Bibliography

ACFE. 1996. *1996 Report to the Nation.* Nashville: ACFE.

—. 2002. *2002 Report to the Nation. Occupational Fraud and Abuse.* Nashville: ACFE.

—. 2004. *2004 Report to the Nation. Occupational Fraud and Abuse.* Nashville: ACFE.

—. 2006, *2006 Report to the Nation. Occupational Fraud and Abuse.* Nashville: ACFE.

—. 2008. *2008 Report to the Nation on Occupational Fraud & Abuse*: ACFE.

—. 2010, *2010 Report to the Nation on Occupational on Fraud and Abuse*: ACFE.

—. 2012, *2012 Report to the Nation on Occupational on Fraud and Abuse*: ACFE.

Almeida, J. 2011, *O Essencial sobre o Capital Social.* Lisboa: Imprensa Nacional - Casa da Moeda.

Bauer, A. 2010, La globalisation du crime. *Pouvoirs* 132 (1): 5-16.

Black, W.K. 2005, *The best way to rob a bank is to own one how corporate executives and politicians looted the S&L industry.* Austin: University of Texas Press.

Blanc, M., M. Ouimet, and D. Szabo. 2008, *Tratado de Criminologia Empírica.* Lisboa: Climepsi Editores.

Braguês, J.L. 2009, O Processo de Branqueamento de Capitais. In *Working Papers - OBEGEF*: Edições Humus & OBEGEF. http://www.gestaodefraude.eu.

Brytting, T., R. Minogue, and V. Morino. 2011, *The anatomy of fraud and corruption.* Surrey: Gower.

Cretin, T. 2007, Mafias. *Une criminalité accomplie, une lutte qui l'est moins* 407 (9): 153-165.

de Rosa, A.S., E. Bocci, and C. Bulgarella. 2010, Économie et Finance durant la crise financière mondiale : représentations sociales, métaphores et figures rhétoriques dans le discours des médias de l'automne 2008 au printemps 2010. *Les cahiers internationaux de psychologie sociale* Numéro 87 (3): 543-584.
de Saint Victor, J. 2012, Crise des dettes souveraines et essor des mafias. *Études* 416 (3): 319-329.
Del Monte, A., and E. Papagni. 2007, The determinants of corruption in Italy: Regional panel data analysis. *European Journal of Political Economy* 23 (2): 379-396.
Dias, J.F., and M.C. Andrade. 1997, *Criminologia. O Homem Deliquente e a Sociedade Criminógena.* Coimbra: Coimbra Editora. Original edition, 1984.
Dupuis-Danon, M.-C. 2005. La difficile traque du financement du terrorisme et du blanchissement d'argent sale. *Problèmes Economiques* (2880).
Ernst-Vintila, A., S. Delouvée, and M.-L. Rouquette. 2010, La crise financière de 2008 : menace collective ou défi individuel ? Une analyse de la pensée sociale mobilisée en situation de crise. *Les cahiers internationaux de psychologie sociale* Numéro 87 (3): 515-542.
Fernandes, F.S. 2013, *À Minha Maneira. Como Salazar resolveu o grande escândalo financeiro do estado Novo*. Lisboa: Matéria-Prima Edições
Galbraith, J.K. 1993, *A Short History of the Financial Euphoria*. London: Penguin Books.
Galli, I., B. Bouriche, R. Fasanelli, et al. 2010, La représentation sociale de la crise économique dans quatre pays européens. *Les cahiers internationaux de psychologie sociale,* 87 (3): 585-620.
Gayraud, J.-F. 2011, *La Grande Fraude. Crime, Subprimes et Crises Financières*. Paris: Odile Jacob.
—. 2012, A fraude e a criminalidade organizada na União Europeia / La fraude et la criminalité organisée dans l'Union Européenne. In *Working Papers - OBEGEF*: Edições Humus & OBEGEF. http://www.gestaodefraude.eu.
Gayraud, J.-F., and F. Thual. 2012, *Géostratégie du crime*. Paris: Odile Jacob.
Godin, C. 1997, *La Totatlité. Prologue. Pour une Philosophie de la Totalité*. Seyssel: Édition Champ Vallon.
—. 2003. *La Totalité 6*. Seyssel: Édition Champ Vallon.
Gonçalves, N. 2010, *Economia Não Registada em Portugal.* Porto: OBEGEF & Húmus.

Henry, J.S. 2012, *The Price of Offshore Revisited. New estimates for "missing" global private wealth, income, inequlity, and lost taxes*: Tax Justice Network.
Hodgkinson, P. 1997, The Sociology of Corruption - Some Themes and Issues. *Sociology* 31 (1): 17-35.
Hofstede, G. "Geert Hofstede", http://geert-hofstede.com.
Kane, J., and A. Wall. 2004, *Identifying the Links between White-Collar Crime and Terrorism*: NW3C.
Katz, F.J. 2011, *Questionando as teorias da dependência e da financeirização. O Brasil na encruzilhada do desenvolvimento do capitalismo*. São Paulo: Editora Plêiade.
Keynes, J.M. 2010, *The General Theory of Employment, Interest, and Money*. Adelaide: eBooks@Adelaide. Original edition, 1936.
Kindleberger, C.P., and R.Z. Aliber. 2011, *Manias, panics, and crashes a history of financial crises*. 6ª ed ed. Houndmills: Palgrave Macmillan. First edition, 1978.
Knoke, D., and S. Yang. 2008, *Social Network Analysis*. Los Angeles: Sage.
Lascoumes, P., and V. Le Hay. 2010, Tolérances de la fraude et relations de confiance. In *Les Français, des Européens comme les autres ?*, edited by D. Boy: Presses de Sciences Po.
Maki, U. 2009, Economics Imperialism. Concept and Constraints. *Philosophy of the Social Sciences* 39 (3): 31.
Mota, F.T. 2007, *Alves dos Reis - Uma História Portuguesa*. Cruz Quebrada: Oficina do Livro.
Napoleoni, L. 2009, *O Lado Obscuro da Economia*. Lisboa: Presença.
Ngai, E.W.T., Y. Hu, Y.H. Wong, et al. 2011, The application of data mining techniques in financial fraud detection: A classification framework and an academic review of literature. *Decision Support Systems* 2011: 559-569.
OECD. 2002, *Measuring the Non-Observed Economy - A Handbook*: OCDE.
OECD / World Bank. 1012, *Identification and Quantification of the Proceeds of Bribery*. Paris: OECD / StAR.
Pimenta, C. 2009, Esboço de Quantificação da Fraude em Portugal. In *Working Papers - OBEGEF*: Edições Humus & OBEGEF. http://www.gestaodefraude.eu.
—. 2012, Interdisciplinaridade nas ciências sociais.(Beta version of a book).
Polanyi, K. 2000, *A Grande Transformação. As Origens da Nossa Época*. 10 ed. São Paulo: Campus. Original edition, 1944.

Pons, N. 2010, Économie criminelle: vieilles ficelles et ruses insolites. *Pouvoirs* 132 (1):29-40.

Pons, N, and V. Berche 2009, *Arnaques. Le Manuel Anti-fraude*. Paris: CNRS Editions.

Queloz, N. 2002, Criminalité économique et criminalité organisée. *L'Économie politique* 15 (3): 58-67.

Ramamoorti, S. 2008, The Psychology and Sociology of Fraud: Integrating the Behavioral SciencesComponent Into Fraud and Forensic Accounting Curricula. *Issues in Accounting Education* 23 (4): 521–533.

Santos, C.M.C. 2001, *O Crime de Colarinho Branco (Da Origem do Conceito e sua Relevância Criminológica à Questão da Desigualdade na Administração da Justiça Penal)*. Coimbra: Coimbra Editora.

Schneider, F. 2004, The Size of the Shadow Economies of 145 Countries all over the World: First Results over the Period 1999 to 2003. *IZA - Discussion Paper* (No. 1431): 64.

—. 2008, Money Laundering and Financial Means of Organized Crime: Some Preliminary Empirical Findings. *Paolo Baffi Centre Research Paper* 2008 (17): 30.

—. 2012, Shadow Economy and Corruption in Portugal and in other OECD Countries: What can be done? In *Interdisciplinary Insights on Fraud and Corruption*. Porto: OBEGEF - Observatório de Economia e Gestão de Fraude.

Schumpeter, J.A. 2008, *Business Cycles. A Theoretical Historical and Statistical Analysis of the Capitalist Process*. Chicoutimi (Québec). Original edition, New York Toronto London : McGraw-Hill Book Company, 1939.

Silva, L.N., G.S.M. Bandeira, & [av]. 2009, *Lavagem de dinheiro e injusto penal análise dogmática e doutrina comparada Luso-Brasileira*. Curitiba: Juruá.

Smith, A. 1983, *Riqueza das Nações*. Translated by L. C. Aguiar. 2 vols. Lisboa: Fundação Calouste Gulbenkian. Original edition, 1776.

Sousa (Org.), Luís de. 2009, *Ética, Estado e Economia. Atitudes e Práticas dos Europeus*. Lisboa: Imprensa de Ciências Sociais.

Specht, M. 2010, Les représentations sociales des risques à l'origine des risques de crise. *Les cahiers internationaux de psychologie sociale* Numéro 87 (3): 393-422.

Sutherland, E.H. 1940, White-collar criminality. *American Sociological Review* 5 (1): 1-12.

—. 1983, *White-collar crime the uncut version*. New Haven: Yale University Press.

Thom, R. 1989, *Paraboles et catastrophes entretiens sur les mathématiques, la science et la philosophie, Champs*. Paris: Flammarion.

Torgo, L., and E. Lopes. 2011, Utility-Based Fraud Detection. In *Twenty-Second International Joint Conference on Artificial Intelligence*. Barcelona, Espanha.

UNODC. 2010, *Crime and Instability - Case Studies of Transnational Threats*: UNODC.

Véry, P., and B. Monnet. 2008, Quand les organisations rencontrent le crime organisé. *Revue française de gestion* 183 (3): 179-200.

Vittori, J.M. 2004, The Business of Terror: Al-Qaeda as a Multi-national Corporation. In *Conferencia Anual do Institute of National Security Studies (INSS)*. Washington: Pentágono.

Walraevens, B. 2011, Corruption des travailleurs et éducation dans les sociétés selon Adam Smith. *Cahiers d'économie Politique / Papers in Political Economy* 60 (1): 11-44.

Wells, J.T. 2007, *Corporate Fraud Handbook. Prevention and Detection.* 2 ed. 1 vols. New Jersey: John Wiley & Sons, Inc.

Notes

[1] Original citation: “la fraude est devenue un enjeu de la sécurité de l’État”

[2] Original citation: "le frauder est un professionnel (...) la fraude s’enrichit dans un monde complexe"

[3] Original citation:

> “il n’existe plus deux mondes parallèles, le légal et l’illégal, mais un monde des affaires de plus en plus pénétré par le crime organisé”

[4] Original citation: “en générale, les représentations inspirent et encadrent les conduites humaines”

[5] Original citation:

> “intuitivamente percebemos que uma sociedade atomizada, em que as pessoas estão afastadas umas das outras, em que não comunicam nem se agregam, não pode funcionar tão bem como outra sociedade em que os cidadãos desenvolvem laços comunitários, participam na vida pública, e se associam para os mais diversos fins desde os desportivos e recreativos, aos sindicais ou políticos.”

[6] Original citation:

> “L’environnement criminogène qui a conduit d’abord à la crise des caisses d’épargne, puis au subprime peut se résumer en trois mots: dérégulation, désupervision, décriminalisation. Ces trois D sont au cœur de la crise”

[7] Original citation : “les bénéfices sont privatisés et les pertes socialisés”

[8] Original citation: “le mauvais capitalisme chasse le bon capitalisme; les mauvais capitalistes chassent les bons capitalistes”

---

[9] Empirical data in this section was collected by Aurora Teixeira, to whom we are grateful. The interpretation of the data is of our responsibility.

[10] Taking into account the ISI Web of Knowledge Impact Factor 2010 for each science, top journals are those with the higher impact factor, whereas journals in intermediate positions are those with an average impact factor.

[11] The dark figure of crime is a term usually employed by criminologists and sociologists to report the level of unreported or undiscovered crime, which calls into question the reliability of official crime statistics.

[12] The strength of the evidence and the studies on fraud serve to establish a close relationship between the crises of 2007 with fraud, but less is known of the situation in other major previous crises, such as the one of 1929/33. We must rebuild this story. In Portugal the biography of Alves dos Reis (Mota 2007) should be re-examined and expanded with the research centred on the 1930s (Fernandes 2013).

CHAPTER TWO

FRAUD AND ORGANIZED CRIME IN EUROPE: IN THE ICE-COLD WATERS OF ORGANIZED CRIME

JEAN-FRANÇOIS GAYRAUD

Introduction

The reality that will be called into question is often concealed or ignored. As a matter of fact, this reality is tough. But how can a certain *reality* be recognized? Just because it is, at the same time, "unbearable and inevitable" as the French philosopher Clément Rosset[1] taught. And what can be noticed? Since the end of the Cold War and the beginning of a chaotic age of globalization, the *natural state* of organized crime has changed profoundly. Europe is not an exception to the general movement. However, we are faced with the great challenge of observing this *qualitative* transformation. The standard image of the "iceberg" remains the most relevant: as a matter of fact, regarding organized crime, the most important is not what is visible to the naked eye but what remains buried, hidden from closer analysis.

The examination of what organized crime has become will, in this short essay, deal with *three phases*: first, "organized crime as a strategic-level threat" will be considered; then "what organized crime is not in France: an anecdotal threat"; and finally, it will be necessary to consider "what will organized crime become in the future: its new horizons".

At every stage in our analysis, we will constantly wonder about the very nature of "organized crime", which, because of its history and the preconceived ideas it raises, obstructs more than enlightens our understanding of today's major criminal developments.

What has organized crime become: a strategic-level threat

We will approach the question from four angles, those of *diagnosis, blindness, changes* and specificity of the *mafias*.

Diagnosis: an insidious and fatal disease

Organized crime has been for a long time a rather *marginal and peripheral* matter, that only deserved the journalistic handling of "news in brief" (sensational and sporadic[2]), and state handling by exceptional repressive actions. Those days are gone or at least should be gone. Today, organized crime can be found at the very heart of contemporary societies, becoming a matter of geopolitical[3] and macroeconomic dimensions; a much more complicated and fatal question than terrorism itself, a phenomenon of uncertain description and of conversely proportional lethality compared to the political media passions created.

That is why it is essential to analyze these contemporary criminal phenomena with different approaches - different paradigms - from those of sociology or journalism, even from those of classical criminology. It is necessary to change the viewpoints, thinking about the geopolitical and geo-economic[4] ways of crime. So, the key-concepts to consider contemporary crime have to be those of the *territories* (of crime), of the *forces* (of crime) and of the *flows* (of crime). Organized crime actually provokes a *transformation*, often silent and invisible, of the institutions and of the political, economic or social systems. From a tactical matter it has mutated into a threat of *strategic* level. This qualitative jump is understandable as long as the four basic *characteristics* of contemporary organized crime are known. These specifications have an effect particularly on the European space.

First characteristic, big criminal organizations are *poly-criminal*, that is to say, they do not have any specialty, they are able to put a lot of time and effort into every criminal business prospect and do so with pragmatism and opportunism. They act with a pure predatory logic. As soon as an opportunity appears, those sophisticated criminal groups invest in it. Whatever the matters are, traditional activities or newly invented economic or financial crimes, a single criminal body can, simultaneously or sequentially, run a racket, traffic drugs, sell fake goods, fix on-line sports bets, etc.. Contrary to the generally accepted idea, conveyed by the media and most criminology studies, criminals do not have a specialty or a fixed job: they go from one activity to another, only considering the cost/benefit profit. Hence, attention should be paid less to a kind of criminal activity and more to the professionals of crime themselves, who make real careers within more or less structured groups.

Second characteristic, big criminal organizations are mostly *territorial ones*. They show a real ability to take root in a geographic space and to create their own biotope. These logics of territorial appropriation and of the definition of a true vital space are conclusive because they explain the power of those groups. A reversal of the sovereignties can be observed when criminal power is superseding legal power. This hold is particularly strong in places where the mafias act ruthlessly, being criminal entities do not show the sociology of simple gangs but the sociology of secret societies[5]. This created competition among the different powers is widely invisible, except to the populations subject to them and forced to compromise daily. In those criminalized territories, every public or private institution henceforth becomes porous - according to different paces and evolutionary paths - to criminal penetration.

However, these criminal territories do not remain stuck but are booming in accordance with identified mechanisms[6]. For instance, the way, at very fast geopolitical rate - in this case, half a century - the four Italian mafias (the Cosa Nostra from Sicily, the Ndrangheta from Calabria, the Camorra from Campania, the Sacra Corona Unita from Puglia[7]) and the Albanian-speaking gangs[8] as well, have been spreading all over Europe, is perfectly known. In the end, entire stretches of land in the European territory are today deeply criminalized and therefore nearing *collapse;* when they are not directly State structures. Are not Italy and Spain on the way to collapse under the conjugated and sometimes concerted weight of organized crime and of white-collar criminality? How many mafia or criminal states take shelter within geographical Europe? Yet this territorial collapse is poorly known because it is silent. It is also a global phenomenon redrawing the world map, ignoring classification and classical carvings. This geography/mapping of the criminal territories is essential for the understanding of the complex new way of the world. The territorial roots of a criminal entity can be easily deciphered in terms of some signs - the most vivid being a trivial but essential offense: racketeering. The development of extortion is a strong criminal marker because, beyond its obvious economic function, it is also symbolic of a local government statement: the one who takes taxes - legally or illegally - asserts himself *de facto or de jure* master of the house and tax payers are his vassals.

Third characteristic, these organizations are particularly *unsinkable* - resilient, physicists or psychologists would say - that is to say, on the one hand, highly adaptive in the face of economic and social policy changes and, on the other, highly resistant to repression. Thus, States more often fail to eradicate than to regulate. Confronted with the five Families of the American Italian Mafia in New York, the FBI says, *mezzo voce,* that they simply "mow the lawn, as they cannot uproot the weeds"; even when, in front of the cameras, the Federal Security officially proclaims after each wave of arrests, "the end of the last godfathers and mafia families"! The series of large judicial operations - in countries where these exist! - may give the appearance of decline or repeated failures of the criminal entities. Experience shows that they develop a real ability to regenerate and continue to expand.

Finally, the fourth characteristic, these organizations manage *financial flows of a macroeconomic magnitude* that can therefrom deeply influence the political, economic and social life of most countries. They have a turnover sometimes higher than the GDP of some small countries. These financial masses give them not only real social wealth, but also an as strong but discrete politico-social power. Thus, the 150/180 billion euro annual turnover cumulated by the four Italian mafias ridicule any budget of most law enforcement agencies. In many countries such as Italy or Albania, the first industry is the industry of organized crime not only in its handling of specific criminal activities but also in legal activities covering up laundering structures as well.

Those four particularities explain why these major criminal entities have become real global *powers*. Organized crime cannot be analyzed in terms of social *marginality*. It is a phenomenon of *powers*. And powers with a capacity for strategic autonomy away from subordination to other forms of powers (state, economic, financial or media powers). To the point, furthermore, of disrupting the system of traditional elites by incorporating them. Real *criminal bourgeoisies*[9] are thus created. The concept of "criminal bourgeoisie" is an extension of the concept of "mafia bourgeoisie" systematized by the Italian historian Umberto Santino. What can be seen indeed? The criminal world does not live - and in fact has never really lived - apart from the legal elites but within their close proximity. Increasingly important fringes of the ruling classes have relationships, not only occasional but ongoing or systemic, with the criminal sphere. It has thus existed since the beginning of the mafia in Italy, a link, an intricacy, sometimes a symbiosis, between respectable elites and criminal spheres. Members of the Italian mafia have always built close and permanent relations with the political, economic, social, media and sporting elites, who do not belong to those criminal entities but are related to them in a system of mutual assistance and reciprocal services. The description of these intricacies cannot be summarized in simple patterns. All configurations are available: inappropriate relationships, more or less explicit malignant agreements, crossed instrumentalizations, reciprocal favours, etc.. One only needs count the depth and the durability of these compromising connections, and the contamination. We should however give the concept of criminal/mafia bourgeoisie a wider meaning than that given by the judges and the humanities in Italy. This concept can certainly designate the criminalization of segments of the legal elites collaborating with organized crime, but also, in reverse, this same concept could designate the gentrification/legalization of the higher layers of organized crime: a form of "internalization" of the illegal elites towards the legal world.

This diagnosis would be incomplete without recalling an essential element. Organized crime always advances via two channels such as *corruption* and *intimidation*. Both techniques are furthermore entangled. Intimidation often precedes and explains the corruption phase: often, "gold" is accepted to escape "lead."

Blindness: the time of the criminal roots

But this *diagnosis* is struggling to gain ground. Organized crime is indeed subject to a continuous work of burial. In a word, blindness. Blindness is the most dangerous pathology in the so-called information and communication society, as it has been diagnosed by Martin Heidegger in 1954: ".../ but a still greater ill than blindness is delusion. Delusion believes that it sees, and that it sees in the only possible manner, even while this belief robs it of sight."[10]

Europe has offered brilliant proofs of it during the first four decades of its constitution. The big market is built into the total oblivion of criminal realities, allowing large organizations to make a mockery of the national borders, to spread across the continent, thus being handed an unexpected space for action. The Brussels awakening was as late and as shy at the turn of the 21st century (European Arrest Warrant, Europol, Frontex, etc.). Similarly, the European Union, as a good ally of NATO, has agreed to bring to power in Kosovo, the Kosovo Liberation Army (KLA or UCK), actually a mere appendix of the mafia clans, giving rise ultimately to a gangster State. The blindness is such that the report by the member of the Council of Europe Parliamentary Assembly, Dick Marty, denouncing this situation, has been carefully hidden by the media and the embassies, as it bothered the official version, cleverly maintained since the beginning, of a democratic fairy tale.[11]

Delusion is not blindness. Blindness is the result of an objective inability to see while delusion is a more subtle mechanism becoming a subjective inability to see: it is neither more nor less than a form of denial of the reality. Psychoanalysts perfectly know of this affliction called unconscious repression or scotomization. Philosophy itself, from Martin Heidegger to Clément Rosset, teaches that the nearest is always the most incomprehensible; that light sometimes blinds more than it enlightens. It is probably the writer Edgar A. Poe, who best described that strange paradox in his short story, *The Purloined Letter*. And, in general, faced with a serious criminal phenomenon, human beings and institutions as well tend to repel it vigorously to protect themselves, and that being of course illusory. This distance takes clearly identified forms via three types of discourse according to a well-established timeline.

In the beginning, there is the first period of brutal denial, of indignant or disgusted, even mocking negation using the themes of: "it does not exist, it is a fantasy, an invention, a simplification, etc.".

Then, when reality becomes too obvious, the discourse of denial is necessarily less vindictive and moves to another register: "this is well known and less serious than described, you are exaggerating". After the denial, relativization arises, often sardonic. However, the relativistic rhetoric is often masked. Thus, in order to subtly convey this relativism consisting in explaining that "it was worse before" or that "it is not worse than yesterday" (*nothing new under the sun*), this criminal reality is placed in a long history (since the Middle Ages for example) in order to dissolve the unbearable present times in an ancient genealogy. History no longer serves to understand the present thanks to the past, but to intimidate by crippling the disturbing analysis. The diversion of the historical discourse becomes a tool of the police of thought. All the French people who were surprised by the criminal deviations in Marseilles for a generation, cannot avoid the famous mantra "Marseilles is not Chicago in the 1930s", hammered in the media until they can hear no more. There are countless State sociologists, prefects, mayors, prosecutors, who, ordered to explain or to justify this criminal chaos, respond with a confused historical summary, sometimes spreading over a century. Because the longer the criminal summary, the deeper the dilution of reality will be.

Finally, in a much more insidious way because it is diffused, there comes the phase of "spectacularization": crime becomes a commercial product (movies, books, video games, songs, etc.) and definitely fits into the social economic fabric, the social imagery and the symbolic order, by its power of seduction and financial weight.[12] Thus, entertainment and consumerism ultimately trivialize crime. Is this not the famous "society of the spectacle" described by Guy Debord in 1967? The spectacular ideology works in full effect as it is now permanently integrated - the "integrated spectacle"[13] - into the system to the point of becoming invisible and unsurpassable.

This final stage of denial by sensationalism leads to a brief mention of the role played by a "peripheral" to the "spectacle" ideology, just as pernicious in this work of burial of criminal realities: the libertarian/liberal doxa. The fundamentalists of a deregulated liberalism - *the laissez-faire, laissez-passer,* absolutist version - since the 1980s, want to make believe that crime does not (almost) exist in the financial and economic markets; or, if it does exist, crime is anyway absorbed ("laundered") by the self-stabilizing and infallible properties of those markets. The same Ayatollahs of the free and unhindered markets often engage secretly, via the major media they control, intense propaganda in favour of the liberalization of drugs; is it really a coincidence?

But the question of blindness is crucial because the time of blindness is also the time of criminal rootedness: rootedness in territories, in minds and in manners. And the more blindness lasts, the deeper and the more insurmountable it may become.

The media sphere plays a key role in these blindness phenomena because of its dominant position. Besides the "real reality", there is the "media reality": and what the media cannot, or do not want to, take into account, does not really exist anymore. Yet, it is undeniable that the media world - because of its operating mode - misunderstands the discrete and invisible realities. This explains the permanent overexposure of terrorism - a noisy hot criminal reality, spontaneously generating images - and the underexposure of common crimes, discrete and complex by their nature (illegal insider trading, corruption, mafia rootedness, etc.). The more mature criminal entities have long since learnt that their survival depends primarily on their ability to stay under the media radars - "the grey zone" of air traffic control. They simply retract the periscope to work in the silence of the deep seabed. An "incident" arouses the attention of the media and political and judicial reactions may follow. Advertising often makes the beginning of the end.

The man in the street is not the only one to be so affected. A large fringe of the intellectual and academic elites has long been actively involved. And the refusal to study the crime is particularly noticeable in France, the only country in the West still refusing to accept criminology as an academic discipline. Besides, denial is not only an *attitude* or an overcautious *reflex.* It is also a *school* of thinking that does not tell its name but whose heavy corpus yet exists. This school - with its masters and disciples - is dominated by inevitably "critical" sociologists who are, for decades, dissolving the concept of crime - there is only "deviancy" or "situations of problems" - who assert that insecurity is a stinky, smelly fantasy and interpret the explosion of crime figures and of delinquency as a triple media, statistical and political artefact. The great French priests of this superstition[14] have long drawn meditative academic benefits from this denial whose philosophical groundings borrow from moral relativism and cultural liberalism.[15] The form of this refusal is usually expressed by two well-functioning devices intended to dissolve the very notion of "organized crime": first, by considering in an absolutist way its definition in the name of "deconstruction", then placing it in a long history to trivialize as we already noted.[16]

Mutations: new criminal "patterns"

In order to capture macroeconomic and geopolitical changes that organized crime imposes, three examples will illustrate our discussion.

First, in the political territorial field, with the case of Mexico. This country has faced since the early 2000s a real *criminal insurgency* ranging from *criminal armies* to largely corrupted and inefficient public authorities: probably an unprecedented historical phenomenon. Since 2005, approximately 8,000 to 10,000 Mexicans die every year - not to mention countless "missing people" - in a complex conflict not between the State and the drug cartels according to a simplistic interpretation, but in a kaleidoscopic and scalable way among segments of the State, the local authorities and the cartels within complex alliances. In the end, entire sections of the Mexican territory are now in the hands of the cartels: a large part of the economy is doped with drug money and the elites are durably compromised. This conflict is more an asymmetrical warfare than a classical anti-criminal policy and it metastasizes from all over Central America to the United States. For many small American States, the combined threat of the drug cartels and of the mega gangs of the Maras is a quasi-existential challenge. For the USA, the major strategic question of the 21st century will not be the super power of China, nor the nuclear Iran, but the stabilization of a great neighbour that, for the moment, is turning into a chaotic, anomic and dysfunctional territory. The Rio Grande will be more important than the Durant line historically marking the border between Afghanistan and Pakistan. But the United States were distracted by a long and illusory war "against terrorism"! This chaos projects from the early 1990s in West Africa and Sahel which became a place of both drug transit and laundering of profits.

Then, in the economic field, with construction and cement industries. Wherever large criminal organizations - in particular mafia groups - are present, this sector is no longer governed by the law of supply and demand, but by an "invisible and criminal hand" that mechanically has three effects: a raising of costs for the tax payers or consumers, a denial of social rights for those companies' employees and, finally, provisions of poor quality, that explain for example why during earthquakes houses are falling like houses of cards. The criminalization of the construction and cement markets is well documented for Japan, Turkey or the East Coast of the USA for half a century, and is explained by the former presence of real mafia groups rooted in these countries. However, what are we pretending to rediscover recently in Canada? Quebec is shaken since 2011 by the revelations of a parliamentary committee, known as Charbonneau, providing clear evidence of the widespread control of this sector by the mafia families that have corrupted a significant number of politicians and senior officials.

Finally, in the environmental field. The preservation of the environment can no longer be satisfied with nice prevention policies or incentives to citizens or consumers. Among the great destroyers of nature, there are today highly organized criminals. All reports of the UNODC show that about 80% of the loss of protected species or illegal deforestation is due to transnational and organized criminal groups. Who pollutes rivers, fields and streams in Campania or Columbia if not the Camorra and the drug cartels?

Mafia specificity: the word, the thing

The etymology and origin of the word "mafia" are obscure. For Sicily, historians and linguists hesitate between a matrix coming from either the Arab occupation or from the Spanish occupation, without giving the word a clear meaning. Inexplicably, the word is also present in the North of Italy, for example in Florence, where a "via Mafia" can be found, or even more strangely, in the Indian Ocean with an island named "Mafia" off Tanzania. Regardless the mystery of the origins, the word spread in Sicily from the mid-19th century. A successful play in Sicilian dialect *I mafiusi della Vicaria* written in 1863, popularized the word in its present meaning. However, the title only uses the word "mafia", the plot tells about everyday life in the prison of Palermo, of an organized group of criminals forming a secret society called "Camorra", imposing harsh laws on other inmates. At that time, in fact, all over the Italian Mezzogiorno, the terms Camorra/Camorrist refer to these sects of dreaded criminals. In Sicily, from the 19th century, the words "mafia" and "Camorra" become synonymous.

Like the word itself, the origins of the mafia as a criminal reality are also discussed and often mythologized. These legendary origins - so historically wrong - of the mafia are found in its imagery and etymology. The word and the thing Sicilian Mafia would be the result – say, of two legends - of the story of opposition to foreign occupation. Resistance to the French presence first: during the Sicilian Vespers, the slogan of the crowd in Palermo in 1282 - *Morte Alla Francia! Italia Anela !* (Death to France, Italy trembles!) gave birth to an eponymous organization. Resistance later to the Italians from the North in the 19th century, with the legendary corporation of the redressers of wrongs, the *Beati Paoli* whose slogan would have also given rise to the word: *Mazzini Autorizza Furti, Incendi, Avvelenamenti* (Mazzini authorizes theft, fire and poison).

Officially, the word appears for the first time in 1865 in a report by the prefect of Palermo highlighting the worrying power of this criminal organization. However, as soon as it becomes popular, the word mafia starts to suffer from polysemy revealing a fundamental debate. Using the same word, some designate a group of Sicilian criminals, organized as a secret society while others describe - in a more mundane way and far from the criminal world - a mere specificity of the insular culture consisting in pride, strength, glory, courage and virility. For over a century, these two contradictory meanings of the word crystallized and opposed two radically different grids of interpretation of the mafia phenomenon. As proclaimed by the famous anthropologist from Palermo, Guiseppe Pitrè, "real mafia" is just a typical behaviour of the brave Sicilian soul and not the criminal conspiracy described by parts of police and justice authorities. Advocates of the cultural thesis (sub-mafia culture) thus deny the existence of a formal and hierarchical criminal organization, conscious of itself, called "mafia", considering that it is an invention that reflects racism of Italians from the North, who want to criminalize a misunderstood and rebellious Mezzogiorno. This misunderstanding has become passionate over the decades and is useful to the Sicilian secrete organization, as they divert this Sicilian discourse and thereby can perfect out of sight their work of concealment.

In this debate, the investigation of baron Leopold Franchetti, *Condizioni politiche e administrative della Sicilia* (1877) - like elsewhere the book by baron Turrisi Colonna, *Pubblica sicurezza in Sicilia* (1864) – revealed a sharp perspicacity showing the existence of a real criminal organization called Mafia, having tight and decisive relationships with the local elites. We would have to wait for the investigations of the Sicilian judges in the 1980s (Falcone, Borsellino, etc.) to rediscover those forgotten truths.

The debate was finally settled in the 1980s, when the anti-mafia judges from Palermo, gathering the testimonies of mafia members who became "collaborators of justice" by interest (the "repentant/penitent" Buscetta, Calderone, etc.), provided definitive proof of the existence of a mafia organization, ancient, formal and hierarchical with a system of affiliation and rituals. Previously, in the United States in the 1960s, the repentant Joe Valachi had made similar revelations concerning the American Italian Mafia. The history of the mafia both in Italy and in the USA is thus historically a long story of denial and then a late awakening. Ironically, the spectacular statements of the collaborators also show that the proper noun "mafia" is an improper noun. Mafia members use in fact the term *Cosa Nostra* ("Our thing"; "The thing of ours"), a revealing word with a strong social link. But this proper noun revealed improper, becoming in the late 20th century a common noun, some would even say a common place. In current language, it becomes synonymous with "criminal" or "organized crime" or even with dubious association. Everything has become "mafia". This trivialization of the meaning is harmful because it makes the specificity of the Sicilian entity disappear. Above all, from the Sicilian laboratory, and strict criteria, it is possible to change this particular case into a criminological concept. It is indeed interesting to identify the criminological originality of a limited number of criminal organizations that can be described as "mafias" with the image of the Sicilian Cosa Nostra. Some of them are indeed more than bands or gangs. As Cosa Nostra, these are ancient and resilient secret societies with a mythological and legendary device, deeply territorialized, entangled in the history and the societies that gave them rise, able to ensure within their birth territories not only order and specific standards but also sovereignty, comparable and sometimes stronger than the one of the State. Unlike ordinary crime, a mafia does not work on the outskirts of a society but within its social and political heart, in symbiosis with it, in a complex system of interactions and entanglements.

Throughout the world, about ten criminal entities deserve to belong to this criminological category, constituting a kind of aristocracy of organized crime. Such are the Chinese Triads, the Yakuza in Japan, the Turkish Maffya and the Italian-American mafia (or Cosa Nostra). And Europe is not forgotten with a strong mafia density embodied by five entities: Cosa Nostra in Sicily, the Ndrangheta in Calabria, the Sacra Corona Unita in Puglia, the Camorra in Campania and the Albanian-speaking mafia in Albany and Kosovo. The mapping of the European mafias would be incomplete without the exogenous mafia entities that managed to settle there via their diasporas, such as the Chinese Triads and the Turkish Maffya.

European mafias just like their counterparts in other continents are in clear geographical expansion, showing a great ability to adapt to modernity. They have long since spun off their birth area. Now, in most European countries, a real *mafia question* is emerging because of the political, economic and financial power of these organizations. Mafias take the crime out of the ghetto of the news by giving it a macroeconomic and geopolitical dimension. Blindness is still deep, governments and the media world being more apt at perceiving the passing lights of terrorism than the corrosive clandestine nature of organized crime. A beginning of awareness is apparently surfacing, with the creation in the European Parliament in 2012 of a special committee for "organized crime, corruption and money laundering", known as the "anti-mafia commission" and chaired by members Sonia Alfano and Rosario Crocetta.

Mafia realities obviously cannot summarize alone the topic of crime (organized or white-collar) in Europe. However, they constitute the heart of it since they are raising genuine existential questions for some territories on the continent. It is also necessary to note the specific place occupied by the "mafia thing" in contemporary imagination. Few words indeed benefit from such popularity and global broadcasting. It is sufficient to be convinced, to observe the amount of queries about this keyword in major search engines (hundreds of millions). The entertainment industry has gripped the mafia brand, transforming it into a lucrative business, with feature films, television series, songs, video games, etc., specialized around this theme, the role of which is obviously not to inform but to entertain and delight, sometimes to the point of resembling a questionable propaganda. The "society of the spectacle" enjoys criminal and mafia shows.

What organized crime is not in France: an anecdotal threat

France is uncomfortable with the question of organized crime. And this discomfort lies in its political history. France being built around the State, French authorities cannot tolerate that a piece of its territory can escape its *imperium*. Facing a sustained criminal dispute, the French State has historically reacted in two ways.

Most of the time, with force. Thus, when under the Ancient Regime organized crime, nestled in "Cours des Miracles", tried to impose opposite legal power in the heart of Paris, it was immediately swept away, giving birth to the modern police with the creation of the General Lieutenancy of Police. But sometimes, public power, still watered with Hegelian philosophy and centralizing, also responded with blindness and healing, as has been the case since the 1980s. And thus it is on three major fronts:

First of all, the so-called "*criminality of the districts*" intimately linked to the history of immigration since the 1960s. It was not until the early 2000s that, at last, the idea that criminal "gangs" could exist in these suburbs of relegation and not just isolated and hyper active criminals, painfully surfaces. The denial has several explanations and origins: the desire to not "stigmatize", to use the usual newspeak; the tint of racist contempt for perpetrators, judged in the childhood of criminality, far from the performance of the traditional underworld; and finally, a profound ignorance of the gestation of criminal realities. How long will it take to admit that some of these gangs have already taken the higher level of organized crime? This criminality is the source of two major events, particularly fatal for the country's future. On the one hand, it is largely the cause of the "urban violences", recurring since the 1970s, in fact, resembling *criminal riots*, emerging with more and more closely spaced maturities, in a quasi-judicial impunity. On the other hand, it explains the formation of lawless areas, real *criminal ghettos* in the suburbs of an increasing number of large and small cities.

Then, the *organized foreign crime* coming from Central Europe and the Balkans, which impacts on crime statistics, is important, if we consider for example, such serious offenses as burglary or procuring. Without even mentioning the case of the Italian mafias in France, a subject which is still a rather strange taboo.

Finally, reference should be made to the *Corsican* and *Corsican-Marseilles criminality* which has undergone profound changes since the 1980s. This is an important and old question that, since the beginning of the fifth Republic, impacts significantly behind the scenes, away from the eyes of the citizens and parts of French political life. Corsican criminality today raises three major problems beyond mere criminal and judiciary contingencies.

First, Corsican organized crime has deep *roots* in Corsica itself, dividing the territory into an almost feudal system. Until recent years, the North was held by a gang called "Sea breeze" ("Brise de mer") and the South by Jean-Jé Colonna and his associates, not to mention the Filippedu family. The restructuring in progress of which the "settlings of scores" (homicides among those criminals) are only one symptom, will lead to a new distribution of those criminal fiefdoms. The financial and military power of organized crime strikes the island with an awe that often relegates the State to a secondary role.

Then, this organized crime was able to develop thanks to the *incompetence of the State.* The effect of diversion caused by the anti-terrorism efforts has been much evoked. But this diversion created by the fight against nationalism (the FLNC and avatars) does not explain everything. Some politicians and government officials sometimes developed "wicked pacts" with the Underworld less because of "reasons of State" than of "personal reasons" (corruption, etc.) giving it until recently considerable possibilities of negotiation and even total impunity. Let us remember that the "Sea breeze" was, until quite recently, called a "myth" by high State authorities. Is it possible to fight what is not supposed to exist? And do not think these facts belong to ancient history.

Finally, Corsican organized crime has a *strategic depth* abroad: in South America, particularly in Brazil, and Central America, and above all in Africa. There, it is surprising how great members of Corsican organized crime were able to transform a major country like Gabon, a historical epicentre of "France Africa" (*Françafrique*) for half a century, into a new judiciary, fiscal, economic and criminal paradise. The domination of a country by organized crime is moreover not unusual in history. We can recall the Cuba of Fulgencio Batista under the influence of the Italian American mafia. The parallel with Cuba is all the more relevant as the decreased *French connection*[17] had known how to launder its profits in Cuba and build productive relationships with the Italian American mafia who bought heroin refined in Marseilles.[18]

Today, after the assassination of the iconic figures of Corsican organized crime, Richard Casanova and Robert Feliciaggi, the case of Michel Tomi[19] deserves special attention. He embodies a truly global power across three continents, between France, Africa (Gabon at the top) and South America.

Finally, it would be regrettable to mask the fact that France has experienced since the 1980s, the invisible yet profound phenomena of "high corruption". Some so-called political and financial affairs - involving commercial intermediaries, top politicians, senior government officials and real gangsters under the guise of P2 type delinquent Masonic lodges -, harshly enlighten the background of French democracy. The book written by Pierre Péan under the uplifting title "The Briefcase Republic"[20] perfectly evokes these serious abuses, deeply affecting the integrity of French Institutions. The main character of the book is a certain Alexandre Djouhri. France has thus suffered a dangerous phenomenon similar to a comet tail of the "SAC" (Civic Action Service[21]) in its most troubled version, wondering even if France has not experienced some form (fortunately diminished) of " Deep State" as analyzed by Peter Dale Scott for other countries.[22] To the point that the penal standards usually applied to common law crimes, gangs, crime syndicates, can perfectly fit the crime of French elites. At the same time, the requirements of the law cannot fully account for all its subtlety, the nature of this criminalization in a part of the French elites. In fact, it goes beyond a simple organizational process, a more worrying situation if any. In Naples, residents have thus understood that the Camorra Families are more than a criminal entity: they form a system. And it is also the name the Neapolitans give to these mafia clans: *O' systemo.*

What organized crime will become tomorrow: its new horizons

It is necessary at this point to explain *why* organized crime has a bright future ahead, both in Europe and in the rest of the world; then, what are its *new spaces and actors;* and finally, how to identify a possible *start.*

A bright future for organized crime

The post-cold war *context* is particularly favourable to the expansion of organized crime. Let us mention - without having enough time to fully develop - the six *criminogenic factors*:

1. *Balkanization or fragmentation of the world.* We have gone since 1945 from about 40 states to 200 today, many of which are "Potemkin states" of empty power, fragile and vulnerable to organized crime forces. Organized crime naturally feeds on these too many protective borders - judiciary paradises - and on these lacks of power. The battles of wills are reversed between verticality (the States), as many as they are anaemic, and horizontality (organized crime), rich, transnational and fluid.

2. *Globalization* that allows free circulation of all material, immaterial or human flows. Criminal flows hide within transnational, economic and financial flows, without any major risks. Thus, the free trade agreements develop cross-border exchanges in a fast and fluid manner, which is paradoxical to the principle of control. So, since the NAFTA came into effect in 1994, between the United States, Canada and Mexico, the volume of drugs crossing the Rio Grande border toward the North has significantly increased. Only 3% or 4% of the (millions) of trucks, not including the cars, crossing the border are checked: the probability of a seizure remains very low[23]. The interception of criminal flows has many things in common

with "collateral damage" (to use a military term) or a light "operational risk" (to use an accounting term) rather than the possibility of a real neutralization of a criminal phenomenon. European borders suffer the same reality.

3. *Commodification and financialization:* everything is trade, everything is profit, so everything can make crime and criminal misappropriation. As the empire of trade and finance extends, the one of crime mechanically finds new opportunities of predations.

4. *The diversion effec*t caused by the "war against terrorism". Since the 1990s, the counter terrorist fight, a phenomenon that experienced spectacular growth following 9/11/2001, has redirected law enforcement and intelligence resources from the fight against crime (organized or white-collar) to "terrorism".[24] It is a "windfall" with deep and lasting consequences. The "diversion effect" can also lead to ambiguous and inconsistent situations, revealing profound contradictions in the implementation of counter-crime policies. Thus, in Afghanistan, after 2001, the global war against terrorism and the occupation of the countries by the NATO forces, have been concomitant with the explosion of opium production. And this is more than a correlation: it is a clear causal link. Let us not forget that the allies of the American and NATO forces have been the main drug traffickers.

5. *The dogmatic deregulation of the markets.* Deregulation is criminogenic in that it creates incentives and crime opportunities, having played a major role in the triggering of the great financial crises since the 1980s, including the subprime crisis[25]. Examples of financial crises with high crime density abound since the 1980s: "Yakuza recession" in Japan; bankruptcy of the US savings banks (savings and loans); etc. The bankruptcy of the European banking systems in the wake of the subprime crisis - Ireland; Spain; Greece; Slovenia; etc. - is also explained by an accumulation of what bankers and economists euphemistically call "non-performing loans", a great part of which are actually totally fraudulent loans. The deregulation born of laws (*de jure*) or of the expansion of new information technologies (*de facto*) produces effects the existence of which is not always suspected. Thus, the development of high frequency trading in the 1990s revolutionized the operation of markets by weakening them and making frauds and financial manipulations almost invisible. Has such an upheaval been considered?[26]

6. Finally *the consequences of the financial crisis.* The crisis will permanently support organized crime for two reasons. First, since 2008, thousands of financial and industrial companies find themselves bled dry; without access to dwindling bank credit, they are therefore turning to the

"shadow banking" of organized crime which can launder and thus buy large parts of the economy. This process is particularly strong in Italy, a country whose economy is largely dependent on a tight fabric of SMEs and SMIs.[27] This phenomenon is crucial insofar as the fight against money laundering is today a pathetic worldwide failure. The UNODC states in a 2011 report[28] that only 0.2% of the 1600 billion dollars laundered in the world can be picked up by regulation authorities or law enforcement agencies![29]

Then, the highly indebted States have engaged in austerity policies and therefore rapidly decreased the budgets of the police and justice services. Increasingly wealthy criminal organizations are facing public administrations struggling for the sanctuarization of their budgets.

New actors: hybridizations

Among the new actors, the question is not to enumerate such or such entities but to identify the emergence of new figures - typical ideals. A fearsome pattern emerges: the hybrid. We thus see the convergence of actors and criminal models that until now lived in relatively distinct worlds. The criminal apartheid is over. So we identify two crucial hybridizations for the future, but only mentioned briefly for lack of time.

On the one hand, the so-called terrorist entities and predators of common law groups. On the other, white-collar criminals and organized crime. It is easy to note an emergence of "white-collar organized crime". As such, the actuality of the banking and financial life, from the vogue of deregulation that started in the 1980s, offers numerous examples of this evolution.

The hybridizations in question are not only those of groups but also of methodologies. The identification and neutralization of these hybrid entities are a real challenge. This dual task is made more difficult by both the very nature of these entities, but also by their ability to defy the administrative divisions sneaking into institutional interstices.

Ancient or unrecognized: towards white-collar organized crime

The criminal world described so far deals principally with a familiar "underworld", the one referred to in French slang under the picturesque terms of "Milieu" or "Mitan" and in North America under the name of "organized crime". This traditional and comfortable representation of crime, dominant in the media world and fiction, developed in opposition to that of white-collar crime. For a century, our view of the criminal world is mostly structured around these two concepts. But is this dual analytical grid still useful? Let us even dare a more disturbing question: has it ever been totally relevant? Should we not today go beyond this somewhat short-sighted approach? In order to see more clearly it is necessary to go back to basics.

For a long time, criminals usually known in the 19th century as those who made crime a way of life and career, have been wrongly perceived as functioning in a rather isolated and unorganized way, associating only occasionally. This is a wrong view of crime, as the European Middle Ages had already seen, since structured and sustainable groups of criminals do indeed associate. Until the day when the French sociologist Gabriel Tarde[30] and later North American criminology developed the concept of *organized crime*, as a result of the works of the Chicago Crime Commission (1919). This independent commission had in view an incomparable subject of study: the powerful Irish and Italian American gangs. A new criminal reality had given birth to a new concept. The concept of organized crime was then defined with four characteristics: the modest social background of its members (the poor districts); the acquisitive and violent nature of its crimes (drug, robbery, homicides,…); its organizational, associative and entrepreneurship ability, with a view to stability and durability; and finally, a self-awareness of belonging to a group based on a specific identity. This concept, often criticized, to the point of denying any empirical and theoretical soundness, is sometimes confused with that of "criminal organization", a semantic shift, which serves to shift the analysis to the institutional dimension of the crime. Though tautological, the best definition of organized crime is actually "crime committed by criminal organizations".[31] However, the concept of organized crime is relatively ambiguous. That is why the distinction, as proposed by James O. Finckenauer, between "organized crime" (*strictly speaking)* or "criminal organization" and "crime that is organized" or "network" covers, with all the subtlety, the totality of usual and structured criminal behaviours.[32] The border, however, is more temporal and psychological than physical. An unpunished, in duration, network will naturally tend to institutionalize and formalize the relationships of its members. The network is, then, only a step on the way to rooting and structuring. Similarly, a network becomes a formal organization as much as a result of what it does in the duration, as of the idea of what it subjectively *is* or *is not*.

Until then, however, the world of crime is still understood as a social undergrowth. The socially dangerous come from the lower or working classes[33]. The dangerous classes are working classes, mainly "blue-collar" ones. Until the day when, during the interwar, the American sociologist Edwin S. Sutherland proposed a radical change in perspective, modifying our conception of the world of crime.[34] He showed that the political, economic and financial elites - the "white-collar" workers - could also commit crimes. So, "white-collar" crime as opposed to "blue-collar" organized crime presents three characteristics: principally, the higher social origin of its perpetrators (the *upper world* elites); the non-violent nature of the crimes, committed in connection with the exercise of their legitimate occupations; the very low social and judicial visibility of these crimes (disregarded or not repressed, nor socially perceived as dangerous). He harshly criticized the fact that his predecessors were primarily concerned with *street crimes* and, hence, the arrested and convicted criminals, dealt with by the justice system. His perspective was doubly revolutionary: on the one hand, it changed the view focused on the elites, and, on the other hand, and this aspect of his thinking has often been forgotten or overlooked, it removed from an argument the supporters of the social and economic explanation of crime.

Despite his developments, the concept of white-collar criminality, as it was developed by criminologists, has a failure, because it induces a skewed view of crime by the elites. Emphasizing its social origins (*upper classes*), it erases its, sometimes central, characteristics, those that can be observed in the world of organized and/or traditional criminal organization: the crime habit and/or the professionalization and especially the organization.

This dual notion is latent particularly in William K. Black, a criminologist who analyzed the crisis of American savings banks (*savings and loans*) in the 1980s.[35] In Europe, some textbooks on criminology (forgotten today) also proposed a typology of the varieties of organized crime, including *white-collar crime*.[36] The famous criminologist, Jean Pinatel, proposed in 1975 a strange distinction between two main types of organized crime: first, "organized crime within the criminal world" defined as "the activities of professional criminals (…) that can take for an acquisitive aim, some forms of violence, cunning and vice"; secondly, "organized crime outside the criminal world" exactly identified as being the "activity of white-collar criminals". Better yet, and it seems that the commentators have forgotten again this corrosive aspect of his thinking, Edwin H. Sutherland also made the white-collar crime a form of organized crime: "*White-collar crimes are not only deliberate; they are also organized*"[37]. For this sociologist, there is no fundamental difference between some criminals of the upper world and some of the lower world. Previously, the Dutchman William Bonger already spoke in 1905, in his thesis entitled *Crime and economic conditions*, of a crime of the propertied classes that could be durable, systematic and organized.[38]

However, the contemporary works about criminality of the elites do not often mention this organized dimension, even though the post-cold war context, that of globalization, brings to this crime and to others elsewhere, an effect of historical breath. Economic and financial crimes are studied but the crucial point of the radical changes of their perpetrators remains ignored. Yet, the initiators of these crimes have deeply mutated. Moreover, we do not see why the financial and economic world managers would be less able to associate and organize than "common" criminals of the lowlands. Would "managers" have an instinctive reluctance to apply to their criminal deviancy the managerial procedures they learnt during their studies? Under consideration, in fact, the business world continuously offers examples of this organizational capacity in the field of criminal entrepreneurship. We recall two examples. The first one refers to a pre- or infra-criminal situation of financial predation. Speculation against the Greek sovereign debt and euro was initiated in 2010 by a group of leaders of large American *hedge funds*, during a formal dinner, gone down in history as the *idea dinner*, the existence of which has not been denied[39]. The predation of the markets was less spontaneous than conceived and strategically thought.

The second one explicitly reports systematic criminal fraud: the BBCI[40] scandal. For a generation, a globalized bank had led, since its origins, a wide range of crimes (dirty money laundering, from drug trade in particular, fictitious loans, forgeries, etc.) making an international bank a broad financial "pyramid". The misappropriated funds could be counted in billions of dollars and, for the biggest part, have never been found. Even the great crimes committed in Wall Street, since the beginning of the deregulation in the 1980s, belong to that organizational scheme: Enron, Madoff, the tricks of *mortgage lenders*, in the subprime crisis, etc.. In Europe, the case of the Libor is emblematic, having experienced two long-lasting superimposed frauds: an institutional one to the benefit of the bank as a "legal person" and a "private one" to the benefit of the employees of these same banks in terms of personal enrichment.[41]

From the crime analysis point of view, it is now necessary to leave the ruts borrowed by the concepts of *organized crime* and *white-collar crime*. We must go one step further in order to report actual criminality in a realistic way, no longer stuck in narrow and short-sighted categories. With the globalization and the financialization of the economy, we observe in the business world, an unexpected form of what we propose to call a "white-collar organized crime" (WCOC). That world includes "criminals who are organized" with the meaning of a professional network, and probably, "white-collar criminal organizations" as well. White-collar criminal gangs do exist without however being necessarily aware of their existence, unlike their blue-collar counterparts.

In Italy, there are what criminologists call "business committees"[42], bringing together political and economic leaders, dubious intermediaries (*faccendiere*) and more or less displayed as mafia representatives. These committees have dominated the Mezzogiorno since the 1970s but, today, they have soared at national level. This is shown by, for instance, the "affairs" called "P3" or "P4" in Italy, remembering the famous "P2 lodge". The main purpose of the presence of mafia clans in these "business committees" is to evict any kind of competition, creating "invisible barriers", while officially claiming a neoliberal or even ultraliberal discourse.

If the theoretical and demonstrative report can look sceptical, the changing of police practices should, however, provide food for thought. In the USA, since the outbreak of the subprime crisis and the failure of the repression of the massive frauds which provoked it, the FBI is now using control techniques previously reserved for "organized crime" to unmask Wall Street fraudsters: wiretapping, trackers and indicators. The harshness of the target (illegal insider trading, giant scams, etc.) requires investigators to adopt the methods previously reserved for "gangsters" and "mafia members". Does not the evolution of the tool teach us something essential about the nature of the target?

However, the perimeter of the concept of "white-collar organized crime" far exceeds the single world of business. Its applications are wider. We shall only outline the acquisitive crime State, led by senior officials and politicians. The higher form of this level of predation comes from kleptocratic political regimes, a form of institutional organization, widespread in the world today, particularly in weakened states or *failed states* such as Somalia or mafia states like Montenegro, Kosovo or Bulgaria. The state structure is neutralized from the inside and made captive by an - exogenous or endogenous - criminality, becoming a system, operating in competition or collaboration with the world of traditional organized blue-collar crime.

Despite appearances, these definitional questions are not only formal. The definition given to organized crime is an important issue because it affects the degree of attention that will be paid by State, public opinion and media, and ultimately determines the level of political and repressive mobilization. The work of characterization is always important and founding[43]. Giving a wrong name or not being able to name in fact amounts to ignoring or denying a criminal reality. Philosophy is a powerful aid: words always precede things; and history of the mafia in Italy taught us that the best way to not deal with a criminal problem is still to deny it a fair and accurate qualification for its emergence, its revelation. For, as has already been said, the essential characteristic of criminal phenomena (organized common law crimes or white-collar crimes) is their furtiveness, especially when it comes to crimes that are by nature invisible (trafficking; economic and financial crimes) and/or committed by perennial entities naturally seeking discretion in order to escape from repression. Only a correct concept can make a reality emerge, because words precede things. The public and policy-makers can discover the new power of white-collar crime phenomena - up to the stage of their organized criminality - only if analysis reveals them (using the photographic meaning of the word). As long as an exact concept does not emerge, a criminal reality can easily remain hidden to the understanding of the public, and more importantly, of the law enforcement agencies. Intellectual invisibility precedes physical invisibility. Intellectual visibility is the first step toward action. The quality of the observation determines the precision and accuracy of the repression. When the thought is no longer blind, the action ceases from straying.

New areas: contaminations

Organized crime is investing in new areas. Let us mention three:

- by seizing *entire States*; what are Montenegro or Kosovo[44] if not mafia States?; and emphasis should be given to the question of "pirate or parasite States" that are the tax and banking havens which have obviously not disappeared but are laundered by the international community through a list system (white, grey or black...). The European Union should also examine the more or less criminal nature of some of its present or future members.
- by investing in the very heart of state sovereignties through the control of prisons. Prison gangs exist all over the world.
- finally, by investing in cyberspace, an unregulated universe, inherently. This cyberspace is a very vulnerable area to criminal entities, due to its main features: transnational, fluid, furtive and opaque. All major offenses that were committed in the past in the real world are now moving there in whole or in part.

The start: head out of the sand

In the chaotic post-cold war, organized crime represents a real *strategic challenge* beyond the courts of law enforcement and judicial organs. Sustainable successes against organized crime in Europe will not be achieved unless three conditions are fulfilled. First, through permanent efforts to develop both fundamental knowledge and *pedagogy*, in order to overcome blindness. What is ignored, denied or relativized cannot be fought. And here, the work of academics and parliamentary inquiries is essential to serve as a stimulus for both policy-makers and public opinion. Then, through the existence of a *credible* judicial system. To face professionals of crime, *real incapacitation* is an essential element. The *certainty* of a sanction - as already stated by Beccaria in the 18th century - is crucial. Finally, by giving priority to intelligence work[45]. It is necessary to leave the logics of strictly reactive working methods, the downstream ones, to the benefit of pro-active, intellectual and operational methods based on anticipation. Criminal Intelligence is the future for the fight against organized crime.

Notes

1 Clément Rosset, *Le réel et son double,* Folio essais, 1984; *Le principe de cruauté*, Les éditions de minuit, 1988; *L'école du réel*, Les éditions de minuit, 2008.

2 Louis Chevalier, *Splendeurs et misères du fait divers*, Perrin, 2004.

3 On a geopolitical approach to crime: Jean-François Gayraud et François Thual, *Géostratégie du crime*, Odile Jacob, 2012; Xavier Raufer, *Géopolitique de la mondialisation criminelle. La face obscure de la mondialisation*, Presses Universitaires de France, 2013.

4 What the author is trying to invent throughout his books, published in France by Editions Odile Jacob and CNRS.

5 Jean-François Gayraud, *Le monde des mafias, géopolitique du crime organisé*, Odile Jacob, 2005. Italian translation: *Divorati Dalla Mafia, Geopolitica del terrorismo mafioso*, Elliot, 2010. Spanish *translation: El G9 de las mafias en el mundo. Geopolitica del crimen organizado,* Ediciones Urano, 2007.

6 Jean-François Gayraud, *Le monde des mafias, géopolitique du crime organisé,* op. cit.

7 On this expansion of Italian Mafia: Francesco Forgione, *Mafia Export, Comment les mafias italiennes ont colonisé le monde*, Actes Sud, 2010.

8 On the expansion of the Albanian mafia: Xavier Raufer, *La mafia albanaise*, Favre, 2000.

9 About this cardinal evolution: Jean-François Gayraud et François Thual, *Géostratégie du crime*, Odile Jacob, 2012; Jacques de Saint Victor, *Un pouvoir invisible. Les mafias et la société démocratique XIX-XXe siècle*, Gallimard, 2012;

Roberto Scarpinato, *Le retour du prince. Pouvoir et criminalité*, La contre allée, 2012.

[10] *What is called thinking?* by Martin Heidegger, Harper Collins Publishers, 2010.

[11] «Inhuman treatments of people and illicit trafficking in human organs in Kosovo»: assembly.coe.int/asp/apfeaturesmanager/defaultArtSiteVoir.asp?ID=964.

[12] On this: Jean-François Gayraud, *Showbiz, people et corruption*, Odile Jacob, 2009.

[13] Guy Debord, *Commentaires sur la société du spectacle*, Gallimard, 1992.

[14] Laurent Mucchielli, Eric Fassin, etc.

[15] On this question, we read with profit the work by the philosopher Jean-Claude Michéa, in particular: *Les mystères de la Gauche*, Climats 2013.

[16] These two perspectives are highly legitimate and necessary when performed in good faith and with measurements. However, they are pathetic when they have the ultimate objective (i.e., for granted) to deny the reality of crime (white-collar, organized, etc.). Knowledgeable books and lectures, by the dozen, spend their time rehashing these two «tricks» within the meaning of magic. But are these illusionists aware that they are the «useful idiots» of the criminal elites?

[17] Name given by the Americans to a network of Corsican gangsters settled in Marseilles and its surroundings, who declined in the 1960s until they were dismantled in the early 1970s, heroin produced in Turkey and South Asia, which was then sold in the U.S. by the Families of the American Italian mafia.

[18] This episode - which blurred the French-American relations for a few years (Nixon / Pompidou) - has been a fine example of denial. Before the dismantling of the laboratories by the superintendents Le Moël and Morin, the French police long denied the existence of laboratories on the French Riviera.

[19] About this «godfather»: Jacques Follorou et Vincent Nouzille, *Les Parrains corses,* Fayard, 2009

[20] Pierre Péan, *La République des mallettes, Enquête sur la principauté française de non-droit,* Fayard, 2012. And our book: *Showbiz, people et corruption*, Odile Jacob, 2009, pages from 71 to 73.

[21] The SAC was in the 1960s and the 70s the militia of the French Gaullist party: a part of it used real criminals and so became criminalized.

[22] *American War Machine*, Editions Demi-Lune, 2012. His definition of the *deep state*: «a powerful coalition of the forces, having similar aims and gathering networks of Intelligence services, of police and legal official authorities, of organizations that resort to illegal but authorized violence, and of mafia groups having international connections.».

[23] In this case, the probability is further reduced by the reality of border controls: corruption and intimidation of Mexican policemen and customs officers by the cartels are such that few people dare to be vigilant.

[24] For a discussion of both this concept and that of «war against terrorism»: Jean-François Gayraud et François Thual, *Géostratégie du crime*, op.cit..

[25] Jean-François Gayraud, *La grande fraude. Crime, subprimes et crises financières*, Odile Jacob, 2009.

[26] Jean-François Gayraud, *Trading de haute fréquence : quels enjeux pour la sécurité nationale ?*, Centre des hautes études du ministère de l'Intérieur (CHEMI), unpublished, 2013. The author is writing a book on this theme in 2013 for Editions Odile Jacob.
[27] Examples abound. Thus «il giornale di Calabria» of March 23rd, 2013, reports the following: «a Calabrian magistrate terminated the investigation of cocaine trafficking linked to the «Ndrangheta» clan Mancuso: 41 people were referred to the Court to face these facts on June 19th 2013. But, on May 10th, six people were tried under the abridged procedure («rito abbreviate»): they are the Board of Directors of the Banca di credito Sanmarinese. The bank is accused of having agreed, to confront the financial crisis, the deposits by Vincenzo Barbieri, a cocaine 'broker', related to the Mancuso clan and killed in March 2011.»
[28] *Estimating Illicit Financial Flows Resulting from Drug Trafficking and Other Transnational Organized Crimes.*
[29] Investment in the legal economy serves several purposes. The first reason is economic: profit. The operation makes it possible to enjoy quietly the proceeds of crime or to enhance it if the investment is appropriate. The second reason is strategic: control of territory. The property of an economic activity - SMEs, bank, etc. - provides a social and political power over employees and more widely a whole customer base of obligees in all spheres of society. There is also a symbolic mobile: laundered money brings respectability and social status.
[30] *La philosophie pénale*, Elibron Classics, 2006.
[31] About this point, James O. Finckenauer, op. cit.. On this distinction, read also: Ko-lin Chin, *Heijin. Organized Crime*, Business, and Politics in Taiwan, Easr Gate Book, 2003.
[32] «organized crime», «organizing crime» and we could add to this typology, according to the categories of transformation the crime operates on the society, «crime organizer/organizing».
[33] Of course, we borrow the term from the major book by Louis Chevallier, *Classes laborieuses et Classes dangereuses,* Paris, Hachette, 1984.
[34] The essential work: Edwin H. Sutherland, *White collar Crime. The Uncut Version*, Yale University Press, 1983. The first edition dates from 1949. But the unredacted version (due to the proceedings from industrials implicated in the book) was not published until 1983. Edwin H. Sutherland starts using the expression in 1937. The sociologist had discerning predecessors such as Charles R. Henderson and Albert Morris. He was also heavily influenced by contemporary Thorstein Veblen with *The Theory of the Leisure Class* in 1912; translated in French, *Théorie de la classe de loisir,* Gallimard, 1970.
[35] *The Best Way To Rob a Bank Is to Own One*, Austin, University of Texas Press, 2005.
[36] Traité de droit pénal et de criminologie, Tome III Criminologie, par Jean Pinatel, Paris, Dalloz, 1975. And for the following quotations.
[37] Edwin Sutherland, op.cit..
[38] William Adrian Bonger, Henry P. Horton, *Criminality and Economic conditions*, Whitefish (Montana), Kessinger Publishing, 2008.

[39] Susan Pulliam, Kate Kelly and Carrick Mollenkamp, «Hedge Funds Try Career Trade Against Euro», Wall Street Journal, 26 février 2010
[40] Jean-François Gayraud, «Un loup déguisé en agneau. Une banque criminelle : la BCCI», Histoires ordinaires de fraudes, Paris, Eyrolles, Éditions d'Organisation, 2011.
[41] For proof, this document of the Financial Services Authority: www.fsa.gov.uk/static/pubs/final/barclays-jun12.pdf
[42] Jacques de Saint Victor, *Un gouvernement invisible. Les mafias et la société démocratique* XIXe-XXe *siècle*, Gallimard, 2012.
[43] This question of qualification is well-known to mafia specialists. Since the 19th century, it explains why some mafia organizations have escaped any form of repression, strengthening their power thanks to this impunity related to the limitations of the liberal constitutional State. For further information about legal qualification, read: Alain Papaux, *Essai philosophique sur la qualification juridique: de la subsomption à l'abduction*, Bruxelles, Bryulant, 2003.
[44] We read with interest the investigation by Pierre Péan, Kosovo, *Une guerre « juste » pour un Etat mafieux,* Fayard, 2013.
[45] François Farcy et Jean-François Gayraud, *Le renseignement criminel*, Cnrs éditions, 2012.

PART II –

DIVERSITY OF APPROACHES TO FRAUD

CHAPTER THREE

GOVERNANCE, CORRUPTION AND TAX FRAUD: WHAT CAN THE PRIVATE AND THE PUBLIC SECTORS LEARN FROM EACH OTHER?

GLÓRIA TEIXEIRA
AND ARY FERREIRA DA CUNHA

Introduction

In this paper, we survey the contribution of public governance to corporate governance and of corporate governance to public governance, specifically regarding the issues of corruption and tax fraud. We take a guided tour through the OECD's (2004) "Principles of Corporate Governance" and compare how they stand against the guidelines of the Independent Commission on Good Governance in Public Services (2004), "Good Governance Standard for Public Services". We have chosen the issues of corruption and fraud because of the limitations of time and space we were given, but – to be entirely honest – also because we are more familiar with these two concepts than with other related concepts. We have elected the "Principles of Corporate Governance" and the "Good Governance Standard for Public Services" because they are two widely known international references on corporate and public governance, respectively, which have some interesting parallels between them.

We will look for similarities and contrasts in both references with regard to their aptitude to combat corruption and fraud – both in terms of their theoretical (in)compatibility and the (a)symmetry of recommended policies – and we will offer some suggestions for policies in one of the fields that could be adapted to work in the other.

Corruption and Tax Fraud

What is Corruption?

There is no consensual definition of corruption in the literature (Gardiner, 2002). Legal definitions also vary and do not grasp the phenomenon as a whole, preferring to create a multitude of concepts, and even the more developed international treaties on the matter, such as the Merida Convention, do not define corruption.

Hence, for the purposes of this paper, we will adopt a working definition of corruption as "abuse of a resource, power or position inherit to his or her role as a public or private agent, through an act or omission that involves the violation of the duties invested on to him or her, with the purpose of conferring, enlarging or anticipating an advantage, or of avoiding, reducing or differing a disadvantage, for him or herself, and/or for individuals with whom he or she is linked through ties of private-regarding influence".

This working concept is not intended to be surgical, but it seems to add a little something to that used by the Portuguese Department of Criminal Investigation (DCIAP): "misuse of power for purposes other than for which it was granted. That is, the use (abuse) for private purposes of a power received by delegation" (https://simp.pgr.pt/dciap/denuncias/). This definition is also very close to that which has been used by Transparency International, one of the leading NGOs in the fight against corruption: "corruption is the abuse of entrusted power for private gain".

To these very general approaches, the notion we adopted adds the inspiration of one of the best known definitions of corruption which highlights the causes of this abuse:

> "Behaviour which deviates from the normal duties of a public role because of private-regarding (family, private-click paste), pecuniary or status gains, or violates rules against the exercise of certain types of private-regarding influence" (Nye, 1967: 416).

It has the advantage of including corruption both in the public and the private sectors, to cover situations where there is no pecuniary gain or increase in social status (Gardiner, 2002: 26) and to understand that corruption can refer to both obtaining advantages and evading disadvantages.

With this definition we move away from a concept of corruption decisively linked to the breach of legal rules – even if we believe it is always against legal principles. Those definitions laid down by the law can work well when dealing with corruption in bureaucracy, whose duty is often the mere enforcement of provisions, but it is inadequate to deal with political corruption, which often involves the creation, amendment or repeal of rules (Warren, 2004). If we think of the regulatory power of public administration, it becomes self-evident that the possibility of corruption may occur upstream to the violation of rules.

Finally, the definition highlights the agency relationship between citizens or shareholders and public servants or managers; viewing corruption as a violation of the duties that result from this relationship for those who have custody of the powers and resources that are entrusted in them. This is what some call the agency model of corruption (Carr, 2009; Klitgaard, 1988; Rose-Ackerman, 1975). But we will come back to this later on.

What is Tax Fraud?

Although tax fraud is a complex issue and the difference between tax fraud and tax avoidance is not always easy to determine in practice (Teixeira, 2008), the OECD has been able to propose a definition that now has wide acceptance among its member countries (with the notable exceptions of Luxembourg and Switzerland).

> "[Tax fraud is] an act, attempted act or failure to act by any person that is intended to violate a legal duty concerning the accurate reporting, determination or collection of a tax" (OECD, 2003: 11).

Tax fraud is certainly against the interest of the State and of the public in general, but it may be harder to establish if it is against the interest of the individuals and institutions that try to evade taxes.

Shareholders never like taxes. But it is not as if payment is voluntary, so the choice is not really between complying and not complying, but between complying and taking the chance of been caught.

Dahmi and al-Nowaihi (2007) claim that evading taxes can have a return of between 91% and 98.5%, and yet, most taxpayers do not evade taxes. Since the tax evader would get, on average, over 90% of the value he evaded, evading taxes seems like a very profitable venture, so why don't people do it [even] more often? Part of the reason might have to do with our negativity bias, the effect which explains how, after we have established a certain position that becomes our reference point, we start valuing our losses much more than our gains. Furthermore, it could also have to do with the fact that individuals assess the risk of tax evasion weighted with concerns of civil and criminal liability, as well as damages to their self-image, and the risk getting caught represents for their reputation and credibility regarding friends, relatives or co-workers.

Similarly, institutions and the people who run them should also consider all forms of potential liability, and the risks for their reputation and credibility regarding consumers, suppliers, investors and creditors.

All things considered, we believe tax evasion is not, in the long run, in the best interest of most institutions and therefore not in the best interest of most shareholders. But even if this is not the case, which might be more likely if the shareholder structure is composed heavily of short-term investors, the interests of the public and State defined by legal norms that design taxes should prevail if ever in conflict with the shareholders' interest.

In this sense, tax fraud can be an agency issue, where agents do not follow their principal's best interest, as they are pushed by other private interests; or it can it be a matter in which there is conflict between shareholders and stakeholders, in this case, the State, as a legal representative of the general public. In either case, corporate governance sides with the law, as we shall see.

The Relevance of Fighting Corruption and Tax Fraud

In different ways, both corruption and tax fraud pose a significant obstacle for the communities in which they grass. Corruption hampers competitiveness and efficiency in both private and public sectors: draws talent to rent-seeking occupations (Ni and Van, 2003: 3); diminishes productivity (Lambsdorff, 2003); works as a secret, unpredictable and regressive tax that raises the cost of investment, promotes the substitution of labour for leisure (Abed, Gupta and Alonso-Terme, 2002: 12; Becker, 1965; Myint-U, 2000: 48; Shleifer and Vishny, 1993; Toerrell, 2007: 12; Wei, 1997); lowers foreign and domestic investment (Bardhan, 1997; Mauro, 1995; Tanzi and Davoodi, 1998); promotes bad investments and higher military budgets (Gupta, Mello and Sharan, 2001; Mauro, 1997; Tanzi and Davoodi, 1997); and lowers the ability to preserve human capital (World Bank, 1997). Corruption also affects development (Sen, 1999); it is tied with higher infant mortality, lower weight in new-borns, lower literacy rates and higher drop-out rates in primary schools (Gupta, Mello and Sharan, 2001); and it promotes an unequal distribution of income (Li, Xu and Zou, 2000).

Furthermore, we must not forget the violated norms and duties most likely exist to protect some kind of legitimate interest. It can be economic (decisions in competition issues), environmental (logging permits), political (electoral frauds), social (misused attributed social subsidies), or of any other nature.

Finally, corruption diminishes social trust (Rothstein and Uslaner, 2005: 42), which makes people less likely to promote welfare, and more likely to evade taxation (Rothstein, 2005). It pushes firms and individuals to the non-registered economy, where they can hide corrupt money not subject to taxation.

But what about tax fraud? As taxes constitute the main source of revenue for public entities in most countries, tax evasion significantly hampers the ability of the State to obtain the income it needs in order to provide for public goods and services such as justice, security, education or health. The more people evade taxes the harder it becomes to spot and prosecute them, and the easier it becomes for citizens to rationalize evasion, lowering the psychological costs of crime. After all, if I pay a substantial amount in taxes but see little personal or societal benefits in doing so – be it because the State has low efficiency, high corruption or because most people evade taxes – there is a breach in the reciprocity rule implicit in the social contract and rationalizing a breach becomes much easier.

To obtain more income the State has to increase rates, so those who comply suffer a heavier tax burden, furthering social inequality. The higher the tax rate, the bigger the incentive not to comply with fiscal norms, the smaller the incentive to trade leisure for work, the smaller the incentive to invest, innovate and produce wealth.

In a time of great pressure on governments and businesses to perform, it is arguably today more important than ever to curb corruption and tax evasion, promoting social justice, economic growth and financial equilibrium.

Some may say that tax fraud and corruption are chronicle illnesses that some have and others do not. It is true that the level of corruption in the past influences current levels of corruption – what some call hysteresis (see Gunardi, 2008). But economic history shows us otherwise: countries like Botswana, Georgia, Colombia, Sweden, Hong Kong, Singapore or even Portugal haven shown, in different time periods and very different contexts, that it is possible to fight corruption and fraud with the right strategy (Doig & Riley, 1998; Fombad, 1999; Hoggart, 2004; Rothstein, 2011; Sundell, 2012; Tanzi, 1998: 586; World Bank, 2012).

Governance

What is Governance?

There are abundant definitions of governance (Rhodes, 1996), but this only increases the importance of understanding what the word means. It derives from κυβερνάω, which means *to steer*.

Much in this sense, the common denominator of most governance definitions stresses that governance describes formal and informal ways through which power is exercised (Michalski, Miller and Stevens, 2001; Williamson, 1996).

But power can be used in many ways: some good, some bad. So the relevance of governance as a field of research depends much more on identifying and promoting good governance than merely on describing influxes of power. The question then arises: what is *good governance*?

We usually see as being *good* all things that fulfil their mission, that are what they are meant to be. In this sense, a good knife is the one that cuts; but if even with manmade objects it can be hard to understand the purpose of things, it becomes harder to perceive the aim of complex social phenomena. However, hard questions are many times the ones worth asking. So what is the purpose of governance?

Tirole (2001: 4) defines corporate governance as "the design of institutions that induce or force management to internalize the welfare of stakeholders", and a focus on the citizens' well-being is paramount for public governance scholars and experts (Lynn, Heinrich, and Hill, 2001). Hence, the problem of governance is a problem of agency (Shleifer and Vishny, 1997).

In a way we find clearer, Canada's Institute on Governance (2002) says "governance determines who has power, who makes decisions, how other players make their voice heard and how account is rendered". In this, we see two kinds of power (sovereign/ownership power and decision-making) and two kinds of responsibility (towards third-parties and towards shareholders).

Governance: An Agency Problem

Mitnick (1973) said there is an agency relationship whenever a party, which can be comprised of one or more agents, acts on behalf of another party, which can also be comprised both by a single principal or a multitude of them. The Oxford English Dictionary presents us with three meanings for the expression "on behalf of". It can mean "in the interest of a person, group or principle", "as representative of" or "on the part of; done by".

In the corporate world, shareholders invest managers with the duty and necessary powers to act in their interest. In the political world, citizens entrust politicians with the duty to act in their interest and represent them.

The problem with agents is that their interests and therefore their agendas might not be the same as those of the principals, as they are rational self-interested individuals (Buchanan and Tullock, 1962). There is room for this to happen mostly because there are information asymmetries between managers and shareholders as between public servants – who are in a sense managers of *res publica* – and citizens – who in the same wide meaning own the *res publica*.

These information asymmetries lead to moral hazard, which happens as agents take undue action because the costs are not borne by them, and adverse selection, which happens as agents try to compete to acquire and maintain their status as agents by concealing flaws and hiding damaging information (Shapiro, 2005). Moral hazard may lead agents to shirk and just lead a quiet life (Bertrand and Mullainathan, 2003); or lead agents to use the power and position with which they were entrusted by the principal for private gain, thus committing an act of corruption; or it can even make managers try to avoid taxation if that can help them crunch better numbers.

Governance is therefore about two things:

I. Aligning incentives of private and public "managers" by reducing these asymmetries through increases in transparency and the establishment of mechanisms for direct and indirect supervision over management, regulation of its decision-making and account-providing procedures, and enforcement of internal and legal norms and standards that deter infraction.

II. Ensure that public and private agents pursue public interest, by incorporating the demands of different stakeholders or at least respecting the rule of law and legally established rights and duties.

Given the definition of corruption described above, it is clear how, through these two channels, good governance provides an adverse ecosystem to corruption and tax fraud.

Governance Matters

Companies with good governance are more profitable and more dynamic (Balasubramanian, Black and Khanna, 2010; Bertrand and Mullainathan, 2003; Ngobo and Fouda, 2012). Bernard Black compared corporate governance indicators from Russian companies to their market value and found a strikingly strong correlation:

"A one-standard-deviation improvement in governance ranking predicts an 8-fold increase in firm value; a worst (51 ranking) to best (7 ranking) governance improvement predicts a 600-fold increase in firm value" (Black, 2001: 2131).

Core, Holthausen and Larcker (1999) found that firms with weaker governance had greater CEO compensations and worse performances.

Fauver and Fuerst (2006) show that employee representation on the boards of big German companies was correlated with firm efficiency and market value by providing a "credible channel for the flow of information to the highest levels of the firm" and "employee representation on the board provides workers and unions credible information about firm strategy and profits that should reduce work halts and strikes" (Fauver and Fuerst, 2006: 703).

Better corporate governance also has encouraging effects on external capital flow (Shleifer and Vishny, 1997: 738), share prices (Black, Jang, and Kim, 2006) and, more to the point, the probability of the firm committing fraud (Chen, Firth, Gao and Rui 2006; Uzun, Szewczyk and Varma, 2004).

Consistent with these findings, Faber (2005) shows that companies caught manipulating financial statements have poorer governance characteristics and that firms that improve their governance after being caught present higher stock market performances, even after controlling for earnings performance.

As for the impact of better public governance on tax evasion, Feld and Freyer (2007: 102) argue that "citizens are willing to honestly declare income even if they do not receive a full public good equivalent to tax payments as long as the political process is perceived as fair and legitimate. Moreover, friendly treatment of taxpayers by the tax office in auditing processes increases tax compliance". They further add that "tax compliance in Switzerland is shaped by direct democracy establishing a fiscal exchange relationship between taxpayers and the state" (Feld and Freyer, 2007: 116).

On the other hand, good public governance has been found to be positively and significantly associated with public sector efficiency (Hwang and Akdede, 2011); and Rajkumar and Swaroop (2008) show that public spending has little impact on health and education outcomes in poorly governed countries.

Corporate Governance and Public Governance

Separated Twins

For most of their existence, Corporate Governance and Public Governance have been little more than acquaintances. Certainly, some authors have addressed governance as a whole but their focus was much more on building an economic theory of governance than on arbitrage and exploring the potential of applying strategies that are typical of one branch to the other branch. And of course a few other researchers have discussed the role of the State in promoting better corporate governance (Coglianese et alia, 2004; Stulz, 2005).

But our point is that, with a few notable exceptions, each field has developed its own methods and approaches to curb corruption and prevent fraud, without paying much attention to the strategies used by the other to achieve similar goals.

At least since the rise of the New Public Management movement, some three to four decades ago, many economists and public management theorists have promoted the idea that the public sector would gain in terms of quality, efficiency and cost-control if some of the approaches of corporate governance were put in place, especially in state-owned companies, but with an expanding trend to other kinds of public organizations, including public institutes and agencies (Hood, 1991; Hart, 1995; Clatworthy *et alia,* 2000).

But research has mostly been focused on promoting results-oriented governance, flexibility and accountability and not quite on these other concerns. More ironically, most studies that try to compare public to private performance fail to show significant if any differences in favour of private management (Jackson, 2001).

For long it seemed like the private sector was the only one capable or willing to share positive experiences. Ironically, results-oriented governance may be linked to higher pressure on executives to corrupt public officials and managers from other firms or to twist accounting rules and evade taxes (Ordóñez, Schweitzer, Galinsky and Bazerman, 2009). And though the public sector is still generally regarded as inefficient, many public sector institutions from Singapore to Sweden are competitive and efficient in the pursuit of their respective missions.

It was not until recently that some authors (Anwar and Sam, 2006b; Frey and Benz, 2005; Yener, 2011) have explored the possibility that the public sector might have some interesting approaches to governance as well.

Principles of Corporate Governance

Many academics and institutions have made their own lists of corporate governance principles, summarizing what they think to be the most important acquisitions of decades of experience and research on the matter - Spanhove and Verhoest (2007) counts at least thirteen international public governance codes. Among these, the OECD Principles of Corporate Governance is perhaps one of the most widely accepted standards guiding governments, stock exchanges, investors, corporations and other parties.

These principles are exposed and analysed in OECD (2004) and have the following headings:

"I. The corporate governance framework should promote transparent and efficient markets, be consistent with the rule of law and clearly articulate the division of responsibilities among different supervisory, regulatory and enforcement authorities. (…)

II. The corporate governance framework should protect and facilitate the exercise of shareholders" rights. (…)

III. The corporate governance framework should ensure the equitable treatment of all shareholders, including minority and foreign shareholders. All shareholders should have the opportunity to obtain effective redress for violation of their rights. (…)

IV. The corporate governance framework should recognize the rights of stakeholders established by law or through mutual agreements and encourage active co-operation between corporations and stakeholders in creating wealth, jobs, and the sustainability of financially sound enterprises. (…)

V. The corporate governance framework should ensure that timely and accurate disclosure is made on all material matters regarding the corporation, including the financial situation, performance, ownership, and governance of the company. (…)

VI. The corporate governance framework should ensure the strategic guidance of the company, the effective monitoring of management by the board, and the board's accountability to the company and the shareholders" (OECD, 2004: 17-24).

This set of principles is used to tackle agency problems arising from the divide between ownership and control which may, among other problems, derive into forms of corruption; and ensure that stakeholders' interests are taken into account, such as the State and its interest in collecting due taxes, or the public's interest in having transparent and efficient markets.

In different terms, corporate governance tries to align two kinds of power, sovereign/ownership and decision-making, and to balance two kinds of responsibilities, towards shareholders and towards stakeholders.

The strategies upheld by these principles may include:

I. Supervision of firms by public institutions; legal regulation of corporate practices and business sectors; enforcement of rules by courts or sector specific agencies; voluntary self-regulatory codes and standards; clear, effective and explicit attribution of powers and responsibilities, both within the institution and between institutions responsible for supervisory, regulatory and enforcement authorities, resulting in transparent decisions.

II. Capacity of shareholders to make informed decisions, regularly participate and vote in general shareholders meetings and namely concerning fundamental corporate changes, electing and removing members of the board.

III. Rules that avoid conflict of interests, insider-trading and abusive self-dealing, including wide discloser of interests by managers; rules that make less onerous the participation in decision making for all shareholders, including minor and foreign owners.

IV. Mechanisms to ensure informed participation of stakeholders, including employee presence on boards and works councils; protection of whistleblowers and establishment of confidential procedures that allow for unethical or illegal behaviour to be reported, namely through a ombudsman; protection of creditor rights.

V. Regular disclosure of relevant information regarding the situation of the firm, including its financial and operating results prepared and disclosed according to international accounting standards, the firm's objectives, major owners and their voting rights, selection criteria, remuneration, benefits and retirement schemes of board and key executives, related party transactions, foreseeable risks, issues regarding employees and other stakeholders, governance structure and policies; and regular external audits.

VI. A board structure that comprises non-executive members; two-tier boards that separate management and supervision, with this second board being responsible for guiding corporate strategy, monitoring managerial performance and return for shareholders, preventing conflicts of interest, balancing competing demands, selecting, compensating, monitoring and removing managers; align executive and board remunerations with longer term interests, and overseeing to the compliance with legal impositions, including tax laws and financial reporting systems; an additional statutory body for audit purposes.

Principles of Public Governance

There are also a number of public sector principles of good governance set out by academics and governance institutions. Among these, perhaps one of the most influential is the "Good Governance Standard for Public Services". This standard establishes a set of six principles on public governance:

"I. Good governance means focusing on the organisation's purpose and on outcomes for citizens and service users (…)

II. Good governance means performing effectively in clearly defined functions and roles (…)

III. Good governance means promoting values for the whole organisation and demonstrating the values of good governance through behaviour (…)

IV. Good governance means taking informed, transparent decisions and managing risk (…)

V. Good governance means developing the capacity and capability of the governing body to be effective (…)

VI. Good governance means engaging stakeholders and making accountability real". (Independent Commission on Good Governance in Public Services, 2004: 5).

Here we can also see that the main goal of public governance is to tackle the two problems we described earlier. The first being the divide between popular sovereignty and decision-making, which may, among other problems, derive into forms of corruption; and the second consisting of ensuring that stakeholders' interests are taken into account.

Given the fact that there is much wider overlapping between citizens and stakeholders than the one between shareholders and stakeholders, it could be thought that there is no need to consider other stakeholders and ensure only forms of popular participation and popular accountability. But we think differently, as we believe non-citizen residents or even neighbouring and allied nations are stakeholders in many decisions we make and in such an interdependent world their interests should not be simply ignored.

Future generations are also a key stakeholder in social security, education or environmental reforms. "Administrative stewardship refuses to hear only the voice of what Chesterton (1986, 251) called 'the small and arrogant oligarchy of those who merely happen to be walking about'" (Heclo, 2002: 692).

Pressure groups, non-governmental organizations and other social partners are useful to ensure a two-way flow of information between the part of the electorate they represent and decision-makers (Fauver and Fuerst, 2006).

To fulfil these principles, the following strategies may be put in place:

I. Comparison of efficiency, quality and satisfaction between similar organizations; give specific responsibilities to non-executive directors to ensure this information is brought to the attention of management and used in decision-making.

II. Ensure different bodies, representative of distinct sensibilities, scrutinize and challenge proposals developed by the executive, provide advice, make judgment, regulate the scale and pace of change the organization can handle, and are directly involved in strategy formulation from the early stages; separate supervision from execution; publish job descriptions and establish sets of powers and responsibilities for each body and body member.

III. Make values intrinsic to the actions of all public servants in their daily lives by involving them in establishing standards for ethical behaviour; talking openly about conflicts of interest that may arise and how they can be dealt with; reducing inequality among users; making the organization more transparent; promoting good relationships within the organization, with the public and with other organizations; establish formal and informal communication channels that allow information to flow between the public, service users, management and staff.

IV. Establish independent bodies, officers or advisers that have the authority and status to challenge governance practices; register potential conflicts of interest among decision-makers and exclude from influencing or taking part in the decision of those with conflicting interests; document and register different risks and assure they are managed by specific officers; obtain, treat and assess relevant information for decision-making; undertake regular internal and external audits and try to gain assurance on the effectiveness of different aspects of management.

V. Make selection criteria public and the *résumés* of appointed public servants easily accessible; develop a sustainable human resources policy by continually reviewing the range of expertise needed and available, so that recruitment and training can fill in the gaps, and avoid over-dependence on a few individuals.

VI. Open decision-making procedures to the public – through public consultations, petitions and *referenda,* for example – and assess how dialogue with stakeholders and feedback from account providing impacts decision making; work with civil society organizations to promote participation in designing, implementing and evaluating policy; implement a "360-degree" feedback mechanism from a sample of stakeholders; assess and publish information on how the public views the organization and to which extent it is upholding sound principles of governance.

What can we learn from each other?

Although there is no point-by-point overlap, as we observe and compare side-by-side the principles and strategies of sound corporate and public governance, the points in common are far more visible than the differences. This is not surprising, since we have shown both models are built with significant contributions from the agency theory.

It is striking that some strategies born in public governance have made their way into the corporate mind-set – like the establishment of an ombudsman, the policy of registering and publishing conflicts of interest or the idea of establishing checks and balances through a separation and interdependence of power.

The opposite obviously also occurred, specifically regarding the focus on the assessment of performance, on the value created, the use of internal and external audit mechanisms, and risk management techniques.

There are also some common strategies whose ownership is harder to determine, like use of regular financial and operational reports that are designed to enhance transparency and accountability, or the use of mechanisms for participation of stakeholders in strategic decision-making and supervision.

Despite the lack of research on the topic we pointed out earlier, it is clear some strategies of corporate governance have passed to public governance, and that some of those used in public institutions are now put in practice in private firms and even third sector organizations. But is there something missing?

Anwar and Sam (2006), Frey and Benz (2005) and Yener (2011) argue that corporate governance inputs have gained substantial interest, which have led the public sector to import some good habits from the corporate world; however, there is a lack of interest in public governance approaches that can make significant contributions to corporate governance.

Drawing from the successful Singaporean experience, Anward and Sam (2006) point out five measures to curb corruption that can be exported to corporate practice: setting up independent committees to spot investigate and mitigate ethical issues, increasing the penalties for violations, having strong political leadership to inculcate the incorruptible virtue, promotion of excellence in service, and paying competitively to agents.

This deserves a few comments. First, only fairly large institutions would be able to maintain a commission with full-time staff investigating ethical issues, many of which ought to be left for the police to look into. Second, penalties for most serious forms of unethical behaviour are defined by criminal and labour law and corrupt agents should be subject to trials with due procedure and not to moral harassment as the authors seem to suggest. Plus, there is little evidence that harsher penalties work as deterrents, and much more evidence to the fact that increased likelihood of being caught works as a deterrent (Nagin, 2012).

Strong political leadership in fighting corruption and fraud, promoting excellence in service, and paying competitively to public servants are three important practices against corruption, as multiple studies acknowledge (Äijälä (2001); Mookheriee and Png, 1995; Schacter and Shah, 2001).

Yemer (2011: 2) argues "that corporate governance can gain from realigning managers' compensation with the practice prevalent in the public sector – namely, fixed compensation not dependent on pay-for-performance", that there are "advantages of relying on the basic democratic idea of division of power in corporate governance", discusses "how rules of succession prevalent in the political sphere can be applied so as to devise better governance rules", and proposes that "corporate governance can be improved by relying on institutionalized competition in core areas of the firm".

The first point is controversial: traditional approaches say humans are marginal thinkers and so flexible compensations are better suited at delivering results (Anward and Sam, 2006), but it can also be argued that only some tasks are suitable for performance measurements and agents will multitask by putting effort only on these; and that it makes no sense to have politicians deciding the criteria for their own evaluation. Frey and Benz (2005) had on this point that materialistic motivators crowd-out intrinsic motivation, make individuals eager to fight for earnings and not dedicate energy to productive activities, and select agents with lower intrinsic motivation. For these reasons, there should be at least caution in implementing pay-for-performance systems.

Division of power is already achieved in current corporate governance, but much less strictly, as some corporate governance experts do not even go as far as stating that the CEO and Chairman should not be the same person. The same could be said of audit commissions, which are a relative rarity and could offer the same independence merits as courts of accounts in public governance. Frey and Benz (2005) express very similar concerns.

As for terms of succession, Yemer (2011) recalls that political institutions usually try to avoid that some figures in management cling to power by enforcing restricted terms of office, re-election restrictions and rotation mechanisms.

There are many reasons one could state for this: long tenure can enhance information asymmetries and create over-dependence on certain individuals, it can be blocking newcomers with fresher ideas but less status, and it may create or be the result of ties between management and supervision and in practice bypass formal limitations to management powers (Ferejohn, 1986).

On the other hand, higher rotation and short accountability cycles can remove from key positions the most able person for the job, discourage longer periods of research and long-term policy thinking, make struggles for succession occur more often and be detrimental to the board's morale, or make agents keen on making everyone happy come re-election instead of making the best decisions (Bó and Rossi, 2011).

Corporate governance has taken a conservative approach to this matter, focusing on the necessity of ensuring a sustainable human resources policy, but usually not making these limitations statutory. Frey and Benz (2005) share very similar views.

Finally, Yemer (2011) proposes institutionalized competition, with limitations to privileged shares and non-voting shares, open applications and elections mandatory for key positions.

Yemer's proposals are not trouble-free, but strike us as reasonable, and useful to implement at least in some cases. Privileged shares and non-voting shares are a violation of the general principle that if you bear equal risk you should be allowed equal opportunities to have control and return from your investments, but they are sometimes necessary to ensure key investments, and very difficult to eliminate once implemented.

As for open applications and elections, they decrease the confidentiality of the procedure, and some would say outsiders are unlikely to be selected because shareholders know that an outsider will have asymmetric information compared to their peers and middle managers, but they increase the pool of competitors and may refresh businesses with cross-pollination of ideas.

Besides the already mentioned ideas, Frey and Benz (2005) propose ways of fostering intrinsic motivation in the corporate world using public governance strategies.

First, the authors explain the need for democratic participation within corporate institutions, and its value in creating support, loyalty to the office and trust in the leadership.

Pink (2010) argues that maximizing profit for shareholders might not be a good intrinsic motivator, as it may fall short as an emotional catalyst.

But as corporate social responsibility grows, the notion that companies can be agents for good in the communities around them can be part of this intrinsic motivation mechanism, which makes agents into stewards. This offers us another insight on how shareholders can win from the integration of stakeholders' interest in corporate governance mechanisms.

These conclusions on the value of democratic participation may also be valid for public governance at multiple levels of government, and they can be key to improve trust and thus curb tax fraud (Hammar, Jagers and Nordblom, 2009).

Second, they propose extensive agent selection processes. These can be linked to Yener's (2011) proposal of institutionalized competition with election for key positions as it is the norm for political agents, but it also relates to the practice in traditional bureaucracy of having long batteries of multidisciplinary tests. Hard and long selection processes, which we can still see in EU bureaucracy and in many armed forces, would promote self-selection, attracting people with love for the challenge and dismissing those unwilling to engage and have a long-term commitment to the cause. They also preserve institutional culture, and identification of the selected individuals with the institution they now belong to. Thus, these hard and long procedures may be golden opportunities to select the right individuals and to create a value-oriented culture. But we will come back to this last point later.

Third, they argue for "autonomy within rules". The idea is that the powers of agents working in the private sector are usually defined in much looser terms, and this may lead to situations where the power of the powerful seems unrestricted and even above the law. In fact, many bookkeeping scandals were only possible because CEOs instructed employees to commit crimes, showing an astonishing level of ascendency over those around them.

Finally, Frey and Benz propose the corporate world should find inspiration in public practice by conceding titles and orders which bring status and recognition outside the organization, by generalizing them or linking them to quantitative performance. Creating prestigious awards celebrating long-term excellence can signal role models for public and private service.

Having said this, we must look into some additional ideas to bridge good corporate and public governance practices.

First, although still underdeveloped and typically experimental, governance practices that try to foster values which translate into ethical behaviour look promising. The Committee on Standards in Public Life (2001) endeavoured to codify the ethical principles that should guide all those who serve the public in any way. It set out the following principles: selflessness, integrity, objectivity, accountability, openness, honesty, and leadership. Heclo (2002: 692) states that more than "impartiality, efficiency, non-partisanship, rationality, public service, and fiduciary responsibility" the true spirit of public administration is stewardship.

It may seem that promoting stewardship, let alone selflessness, is an impossible task in a world of self-interested human beings. There is some reason behind this, of course, but all too often we ignore the power of intrinsic motivation over the sticks and carrots of extrinsic motivation (Deci and Ryan, 1985). Among these intrinsic motivators, researchers found autonomy, competence and relatedness. This last motivator is consistent with a need for purpose outside ourselves (Pink, 2010).

Promoting stewardship consists in fostering a genuine care for public good among people that decided to serve the public in the first place with their work, which does not seem that hard. It aims at the core of the public agency problem and, if successful, can have powerful effects on the way agents perceive their work and are motivated to not be corrupted.

This requires political and managerial will, as suggested by Anwar and Sam (2006b). But public governance practice would also win in further fostering dialogue with the public they serve, not only as a feedback mechanism – or may we say *feedforward* mechanism – but also as a constant reminder that they have a mission with a higher purpose. The same could be said about involving agents in drafting ethical standards of procedure that detail how agents should use their powers. This may also be a way not only of promoting better service but also keeping alive the spirit of public administration. And as we have seen with Benz and Frey (2005), both public and corporate governance can benefit from more participation.

Secondly, although in public institutions law must concede all the powers – and so the power structure is often much more clear and transparent than in the private sector – there seems to be at times much confusion about the responsibilities, especially in political institutions. This makes it possible for agents to avoid accountability by passing the blame up or down the stream of power (Hood, 2010).

Some corporate governance experts, like Dayton (2001), make governance seem mostly about the ideal distribution of powers and responsibilities. Only clear powers and responsibilities allow for useful accountability, efficient supervision and enforcement.

This is especially vital in cases where the misuse of power occurred through an omission of that use. If someone actively violated the law, it can be spotted and dealt with, but if, as in many cases, everyone ignored the threat until it was imminent, then it becomes harder to determine who should have done what without a clear definition of responsibilities. The cracks in the control mechanism increase the asymmetries of information, and thus moral hazard.

If responsibilities are laid down in a sensible manner they can be key to better governance. First, responsibilities should be aligned and proportional to powers, which means agents should not be held accountable for doing things they had no control over; i.e., if you are responsible for supervising spending but not for expenditure, you should not be held accountable for overspending, but for the failure to monitor expenditure or to take appropriate action. Second, they should acknowledge decisions are taken within complex environments with imperfect information about past events, the current situation and the full implications of all alternative courses of action. And finally, they should be specific enough to be controllable but comprehensible enough to be meaningful.

Third, it is at least curious to find such a big emphasis on minority rights in the principles of corporate governance, and much more timid statements from public governance. Institutions, whether public or private, should provide for equitable treatment principles, and in democratic systems, public institutions even more so. This means not only recognizing these minorities the same rights, but also removing unreasonable barriers to the representation and participation of less numerous or less well-funded factions. Democracy, as a government *of the people*, is only real when it involves the participation and representation *of all the people*, or it can become just a form of delegated oligarchy.

Fourth, usually citizens are in their country for the long run, and it is harder to diversify your "citizenship portfolio" than to diversity your investments, so they might be more likely to vote responsibly and ask for accountability than some shareholders.

In a survey of the literature (Li, 2012), firm performance seems to be tied with large shareholders that, unlike small owners, have the incentive to monitor management. This makes us think that corporate governance mechanisms should also look into the structure of ownership more attentively and see what statutory mechanisms could prevent principal abuse without entrenchment (Waterman and Meier, 1998).

Our fifth and final point for consideration is that not much attention has been given to the remuneration of politicians as a public governance issue. As managers of *res publica,* politicians have a conflict of interest when they decide on their own remuneration. A solution where remunerations are established, or at least suggested, by an independent body would tackle political corruption, both by avoiding excessive salaries, privileges and compensations, and by avoiding populist salaries that select for either corrupt or rich politicians – or both.

Concluding remarks

We believe this paper has shown that corporate and public governance have much to learn from each other on how to curb corruption and tax fraud. They have done so in the past, as corporations established checks and balances in their governance, but that same republican principle can be extended by institutionalizing competition inside the firm for some positions, by limiting mandates, or subjecting top leaders to periodical challenges to their rule. Similarly, public governance has endeavoured to mimic the private sector by establishing performance assessments and audit mechanisms, but it could establish remuneration committees to avoid conflicts of interest, and it is ironic that it can still learn a few lessons on the protection of minorities from corporate governance.

It is easy to see how corporate governance is a shareholders' choice, as they can directly promote governance changes; but so is public governance a citizens' choice – and to extend corporate governance as well – as they can demand legal changes in political institutions, and in corporate regulation, which matter greatly for good governance (Doidge, Karolui and Stulz, 2007).

There is still a long way to go for research on governance and its implications on corruption and fraud. Even if some principles on governance can be established and asserted with significant confidence, many of the strategies we discussed are controversial.

But the challenge is not just to keep these ideas coming, criticize, inquire, analyze, probe and test them; but also to ensure that the bridges between research and policy, and corporate and public governance are kept open, wide and with a smooth two-way traffic.

References

Abed, G. and S. Gupta (eds.) 2002, *Governance, Corruption & Economic Performance*, Washington: International Monetary Fund

Anward, S. and C-Y. Sam 2006, "Singaporean Style of Public Sector Corporate Governance: Can Private Sector Corporations Emulate Public Sector Practices?", *New Zeeland Journal of Asian Studies*, 8 (1), 41

Äijälä, K. 2001, *Public Sector: An Employer of Choice? Report on the Competitive Public Employer Project*, Paris: OECD Publishing

Balasubramanian, N., B. Black and V. Khanna 2010, "The relation between firm-level corporate governance and market value: A case study of India", *Emerging Markets Review*, 11 (4), 319
Bardhan, P. 1997, "Corruption and Development: A Review of Issues". *Journal of Economic Literature*, 35 (3), 1320
Becker, G.S. 1965, "A Theory of Allocation of Time." *The Economic Journal,* 75 (299), 493
Bertrand, M and S. Mullainathan 2003. "Enjoying the Quiet Life? Corporate Governance and Managerial Preferences". *Journal of Political Economy*, 111 (5), 1043
Black, B. 2001, "Does Corporate Governance Matter?: A Crude Test Using Russian Data", *University of Pennsylvania Law Review*, 149 (6), 2131
Black, B., H. Jang and W. Kim 2006, "Does Corporate Governance Predict Firms" Market Values? Evidence from Korea", *Journal of Law and Economics,* 22 (2), 366
Bó, E.D. and M. Rossi 2011, "Term Length and the Effort of Politicians", *Review of Economic Studies*, 78 (4), 1237
Bordignon, M. 1993, "A Fairness Approach to Income Tax Evasion", *Journal of Public Economics*, 52 (3), 345
Bruno, V. and S. Claessens 2010, "Corporate Governance and Regulation: Can There Be Too Much of a Good Thing?", *Journal of Financial Intermediation,* 19, 461
Buchanan, J. and G. Tullock 1962, *The Calculus of Consent*, Ann Arbor: University of Michigan Press.
Carr, I. 2009, "Corruption, the Southern African Development Community Anti-corruption Protocol and the Principal-Agent-Client Model", *International Journal of Law in Context,* 5 (2), 148
Chen, G., M. Firth, D.N. Gao, and O.M. Rui 2006. "Ownership Structure, Corporate Governance, and Fraud: Evidence from China." *Journal of Corporate Finance*, 12 (3), 424
Clatworthy, M.A., H.J. Mellett, and M. Peel 2000, "Corporate Governance under "New Public Management": An Exemplification", *Corporate Governance: An International Review*, 8 (2), 166
Coglianese, C., T.J. Healey, E.K. Keating, M.L. Michael 2004, *The Role of Government in Corporate Governance,* Cambridge: Harvard University
Committee on Standards in Public Life 2001, *The Seven First Reports: A Review of Progress. Committee on Standards in Public Life*, London.

Core, J.E., R.W. Holthausen, and D.F. Larcker 1999, "Corporate Governance, Chief Executive Officer Compensation, and Firm Performance". *Journal of Financial Economics*, 51 (3), 371

Crocker, K.J. and J. Slemrod 2005, "Corporate Tax Evasion With Agency Costs", *Journal of Public Economics*, 89 (9-10), 1593

Dahmi, S. and A. al-Nowaihi 2007, "Why People Pay Taxes? Prospect Theory versus Expected Utility Theory", *Journal of Economic Behaviour and Organization*, 64 (1), 171

Dayton, K.N. 2001, *Governance is Governance*, Washington: Independent Sector

Deci, E.L. and R.M. Ryan 1985, *Intrinsic Motivation and Self-Determination In Human Behavior,* New York: Plenum

Doig, A. and S. Riley 1998, Corruption and Anti-Corruption Strategies: Issues and Case Studies from Developing Countries. In United Nations, *Corruption and Integrity Improvement Initiatives in Developing Countries,* New York, NY: United Nations Development Programme, 45

Doidge, C., G.A. Karolyi and R.M. Stulz 2007, "Why do Countries Matter so Much for Corporate Governance?", *Journal of Financial Economics*, 86 (1), 1

Erickson, M., M. Hanlon and E. Maydew 2006, "Is there a link between executive compensation and accounting fraud?", *Journal of Accounting Research,* 44 (1), 113

Faber, D.B. 2005, "Restoring Trust After Fraud: Does Corporate Governance Matter?", *The Accounting Review*, 80 (2), 539

Fauver, L. and M. Fuerst 2006, "Does Good Corporate Governance Include Employee Representation? Evidence from German Corporate Boards", *Journal of Financial Economics*, 82 (3), 673

Feld, L. P. and B.S. Frey 2007, "Tax Compliance as the Result of a Psychological Tax Contract: The Role of Incentives and Responsive Regulation", *Law and Policy*, 29 (1), 102

Ferehohn, J. 1986, "Incumbent Performance and Electoral Control." *Public Choice*, 50(1), 5

Fombad, C.M. 1999, "Curbing corruption in Africa: some lessons from Botswana's experience", *International Social Science Journal,* 51 (160), 241

Frey, B.S. 1997, *Not Just For The Money: An Economic Theory of Personal Motivation,* Cheltenham: Edward Elgar.

Frey, B.S. and M. Benz 2005, "Can Private Learn From Public Governance?", *The Economic Journal,* 114 (507), 377

Gardiner, J. 2002, Defining Corruption. In A.J. Heidenheimer and M. Johnston (eds.), *Political Corruption: Concepts and Contexts*, New Brunswick: Transaction Publishers

Garratt, B. 2003, "Thin on the Top: Why Corporate Governance Matters and How to Measure and Improve Board Performance." London: Nicholas Brealey Publishing

Gunardi, H.S. 2008, *Corruption and Governance Around the World. An Empirical Investigation,* Groningen: University of Groningen.

Gupta, S., L. de Mello and R. Sharan 2001, "Corruption and Military Spending", *European Journal of Political Economy*, 17 (4): 749

Hammar, H., S. Jagers and K. Nordblom 2009, "Perceived Tax Evasion and the Importance of Trust", *Journal of Socio-Economics*, 38 (2), 238

Hart, O. 1995, "Corporate Governance: Some Theory and Implications". *The Economic Journal*, 105 (430), 678

Heclo, H. 2002, "The Spirit of Public Administration." *Political Science and Politics*, 35 (4), 689

Hill, C.J. and L.E. Lynn Jr. 2004, "Governance and Public Management: An Introduction", *Journal of Policy Analysis and Management*, 23 (1), 3

Hoggard, S. 2004, "Preventing Corruption in Colombia: The Need for an Enhanced State-Level Approach", *Arizona Journal of International and Comparative Law,* 21, 577

Hood, C. 1991, "A Public Administration for all Seasons?" *Public Administration*, 69, 3

—. 2010, *The Blame Game: Spin, Bureaucracy and Self-Preservation In Government*, Princeton: Princeton University Press.

Hwang, J. and S.H. Akdede 2011, "The influence of Governance on Public Sector Efficiency: A Cross-Country Analysis." *The Social Science Journal*, 48 (4), 735

Independent Commission on Good Governance in Public Services 2004, *The Good Governance Standard for Public Services*. London: Office for Public Management and Chartered Institute of Finance and Accountancy

Institute on Governance 2002, *Define Governance*, http://iog.ca/en/about-us/governance/governance-definition

Jackson, P.M. 2001, "Public Sector Added Value: Can Bureaucracy Deliver?" *Journal of Public Administration*, 79 (1), 5

Kleper, S. and D. Nagin 1989, "The Anatomy of Tax Evasion", *Journal of Law, Economics and Organization*, 5 (1), 1

Klitgaard, R.E. 1988, *Controlling Corruption*, Berkley: University of California Press

Lambsdorff, J.G. 2003, "How Corruption Affects Productivity", *Kyklos*, 56, 457
Lazonick, W. and M. O'Sullivan. 2000. "Maximizing Shareholder Value: A New Ideology for Corporate Governance", *Economy and Society*, 29 (2000), 12
Le Grand, J. 2010, "Knights and Knaves Return: Public Service Motivation and the Delivery of Public Services". *International Public Management Journal*, 13 (1), 56
Li H., Lixin C. X. and Heng-fu Z. 2000, "Corruption, Income Distribution, and Growth", *Economics and Politics*, 12 (2): 155-181.
Li, Y. 2012, *Ownership Structure and Corporate Performance*. Montreal: Concordia University.
Mauro, P. 1995, "Corruption and Growth", *Quarterly Journal of Economics*, 110 (3), 681
—. 1997, "Why Worry About Corruption?" *Economic Issues*, Washington, DC: International Monetary Fund, 6, 16p.
Michalski, W., R. Miller, and B. Stevens 2001, "Governance in the 21st Century: Power in the Global Knowledge Economy and Society", In OECD, *Governance in the 21st Century*. Paris: OECD Publishing
Mookherjee, D. and I.P.L. Png 1995, "Corruptible Law Enforcers: How Should They Be Compensated?", *The Economic Journal*, 105, 145
Myint-U, T. 2000, "Corruption: Causes, Consequences and Cures." *Asia-Pacific Development Journal*, 7, 33
Nagin, D.S. 2012, "Imprisonment and Crime Control: Building Evidence-Base Policy", In R. Rosenfeld, K. Quinet and C. Garcia (eds.), *Contemporary Issues in Criminological Theory and Research: The Role of Social Institutions*. Belmont: Wadsworth
Ngobo, P. V. and M. Fouda 2012, "Is "Good" Governance Good for Business?: A Cross-National Study in African Countries", *Journal of World Business*, 47 (3), 435
Nye, J.S. 1967, "Corruption and Political Development: A Cost-Benefit Analysis." *American Political Science Review*, 61 (2), 417
OECD 2001, *Citizens as Partners*, Paris: OECD Publishing
—. 2003, *Improving Access to Bank Information for Tax Purposes: The 2003 Report*, Paris: OECD Publishing
—. 2004. *OECD Principles of Corporate Governance*, Paris: OECD Publishing
Ordóñez, L.D., M.E. Schweitzer, A.D. Galinsky and M.H. Bazerman 2009, "Goals Gone Wild: The Systematic Side Effects of Overprescribing Goal Setting." *Academy of Management Perspectives*, 23 (1), 6

Osterloh, M. and B.S. Frey 2004, "Corporate Governance for Crooks. The Case for Corporate Virtue", In A. Grandori (ed.), *Corporate Governance and Firm Organization*, Oxford: Oxford University Press.

Pink, D. 2010, *Drive: The Surprising Truth About What Motivates Us*, New York: Riverhead Books

Pollitt, C. 2003, *The Essential Public Manager*, Maidenhead and Philadelphia: Open University Press

Rajkumar, A.S. and Vi. Swaroop 2008, "Public Spending and Outcomes: Does Governance Matter?", *Journal of Development Economics*, 86 (1), 96

Rhodes, R.A.W. 1996, "The New Governance: Governing without Government." *Political Studies*, 44 (4), 652

Rose-Ackerman, S. 1975, "The Economics of Corruption." *Journal of Public Economics*, 4(2), 187

—. 1978, *Corruption: A Study In Political Economy*. New York: New Academic Press

Rost, K.I, E. Osterloh, M. and B.S. Frey 2010, "The corporate governance of Benedictine abbeys What can stock corporations learn from monasteries?", *Journal of Management History*, 16 (1), 90

Rothstein, B. 2005, *Social Traps and the Problem of Trust: Theories of Institutional Design*, Cambridge: Cambridge University Press

—. 2011, "Anti-Corruption: The Indirect "Big Bang" Approach", *Review of International Political Economy*, 18 (2), 228

Rothstein, B. and E.M. Uslaner 2005, "All For All: Equality, Corruption and Social Trust", *World Politics*, 58 (1), 41

Schacter, M. and A. Shah 2001, *Look Before You Leap: Notes For Corruption Fighters*, Policy Brief No. 11. Ottawa: Institute On Governance.

Sen, A. 1999, *Development as Freedom*. New York: Anchor Books.

Shapiro, S.P. 2005, "Agency Theory", *Annual Review of Sociology*, 31(1), 263

Shleifer, A. and R.W. Vishny 1993, "Corruption", *Quarterly Journal of Economics*, 108 (3), 599

Shleifer, A. and R.W. Vishny 1997, "A Survey of Corporate Governance", *Journal of Finance*, 52 (2), 737

Slemrod, J. 2007, "Cheating Ourselves: The Economics of Tax Evasion", *Journal of Economic Perspectives*, 21(1), 25

Sousa, L. 2010, "Anti-corruption Agencies: Between Empowerment and Irrelevance", *Crime, Law and Social Change,* 53 (1), 5

—. 2011, *Corrupção,* Lisboa: Fundação Francisco Manuel Dos Santos and Relógio D"Água

Sousa, L. and J. Triães 2008, *Corrupção e Os Portugueses - Atitudes, Práticas, Valores,* Lisboa: Edições Rui Costa Pinto

Spanhove, J. and K. Verhoest 2007, *Corporate Governance vs. Government Governance: Translation or Adaptation,* https://lirias.kuleuven.be/bitstream/123456789/125531/1/eiasm_paper_spanhoveandverhoest.pdf

Stoker, G. 1998, "Governance as Theory: Five Propositions", *International Social Science Journal,* 50 (155), 17

Stulz, R.M. 2005, "The Limits of Financial Globalization", *The Journal of Finance*, 60 (4), 1595

Sundell, A. 2012. *Legalize It: An argument for formalizing petty corruption when state capacity is low.* http://www.qog.pol.gu.se/digitalAssets/1364/1364834_2012_2_sundell.pdf

Tanzi, V. 1998, "Corruption Around the World: Causes, Consequences, Scopes, and Cures." *International Monetary Fund Staff Papers,* 45 (4), 754

Tanzi, V. and H. Davoodi 1997, *Corruption, Public Investment, and Growth,* http://www.imf.org/external/pubs/ft/wp/wp97139.pdf

Tanzi, V. and H. Davoodi, 1998, "Roads to Nowhere: How Corruption in Public Investment Hurts Growth", *Economic Issues,* International Monetary Fund, 12

Teixeira, G. 2008, "A Fraude e o Princípio da Transparência". *Ciência e Técnica Fiscal*, 422(2), 25

Teixeira, G. 2012, *Manual de Direito Fiscal*, 2.ª ed., Coimbra: Almedina

Teorell, J. 2007, *Corruption as an Institution: Rethinking the Nature and Origins of the Grabbing Hand.* http://www.qog.pol.gu.se/digitalAssets/1350/1350653_2007_5_teorell.pdf

Tirole, J. 1986, "Hierarchies and Bureaucracies: On the Role of Collusion in Organizations." *Journal of Law, Economics and Organization,* 2(2): 181-214.

—. 1992, "Collusion and the Theory of Organizations." In Jean-Jacques Laffont (ed.). *Advances In Economic Theory: Sixth World Congress,* Vol II, Econometric Society Monographs, No. 21, Cambridge: Cambridge University Press.

—. 2001. "Corporate Governance," *Econometrica*, 69 (1), 1

Turley, S. and M. Zaman 2004, "The Corporate Governance Effects of Audit Committees", *Journal of Management and Governance*, 8 (3), 305

Uzun, H., S. H. Szewczyk, and R. Varma 2004, "Board Composition and Corporate Fraud", *Financial Analysts Journal*, 60 (3), 33
Warren, M.E. 2004, "What Does Corruption Mean in a Democracy?" *American Journal of Political Science*, 48 (2), 328
Waterman, R.W. and K.J. Meier 1998, "Principal-Agent Models: An Expansion?", *Journal of Public Administration Research and Theory*, 8 (2), 173
Wei, S-J 1997, *Why Is Corruption So Much More Taxing Than Taxes? Arbitrariness Kills,* NBER Working Paper No. 6255, Cambridge: National Bureau of Economic Research
Williamson, O.E. 1996, *The Mechanisms of Governance.* New York: Oxford University Press
World Bank 1997, *Helping Countries Combat Corruption: The Role of the World Bank*, Washington: World Bank
—. 2006, *A Decade of Measuring the Quality of Governance: Governance Matters 2006,* Washington: World Bank
—. 2012, *Fighting Corruption in Public Services: Chronicling Georgia"s Reform,* Washington, DC: World Bank
Xu X. and Yan W. 1999, "Ownership Structure and Corporate Governance in Chinese Stock Companies", *China Economic Review*, 10 (1), 75
Yener, D. 2011, "Public Governance Towards Corporate Governance", *International Journal of Governance*, 1 (3), 1

CHAPTER FOUR

TAX COMPLIANCE, CORRUPTION AND DETERRENCE: AN APPLICATION OF THE SLIPPERY SLOPE MODEL

DANIELA C. WILKS AND LUÍS PACHECO

Introduction

Tax evasion has been a common problem in some countries with damaging consequences to national budgets. Attitudes towards taxes reflect attitudes towards governments and tax evasion can be the only means available to citizens to express their disapproval (Lewis, 1982). Many citizens are skeptical about how governments manage and spend their taxes. Such doubts are heightened when there are reports of corruption and in times of fiscal imbalances and harsh measures to reduce public debt. Where governments take measures to increase tax collection, citizens may be more reluctant to comply under pressure of tight personal and domestic budgets. As a result, revenues may deteriorate or diminish.[1] Tax evasion diminishes overall tax revenue, and the lost revenue leads to higher tax rates to make up for the loss.

Tax evasion is considered to be an illegal act in developed countries. Tax evasion in Portugal is a criminal offence that can lead to prison. However, exploiting tax loopholes and dishonestly misreporting income on a tax return may not be considered crimes and are in any case difficult to detect.

Traditionally the main policy approach to tax evasion in Portugal has been through deterrent sanctions such as tax audits, fines and 'naming and shaming' by means of a black list. This approach has not been successful. Although figures for compliance are difficult to obtain, it is known that these are some way below par and the shadow economy is estimated to be about 25% of GDP (Afonso and Gonçalves, 2009; The Economist, 2010).

It is thus important to understand what informs attitudes towards tax compliance. Trust, perceptions of fairness and corruption have consistently been identified as playing a crucial role in tax compliance (e.g., Torgler, 2003, 2004; Wenzel, 2003a). Where governments are seen to be fair, not corrupt and treat citizens with respect, taxpayers will tend to trust them and show more willingness to comply (e.g., Feld and Frey, 2007). Several other factors have been identified as contributing to compliance namely the sanctions used to enforce it. However, research findings have been inconsistent regarding the use of deterrence power to discourage evasion (Kirchler and Wahl, 2010). According to the slippery slope framework (Kirchler, 2007; Kirchler, Hoelzl, and Wahl, 2008; Kirchler and Wahl, 2010; Muehlbacher and Kirchler, 2010), trust in authorities as well as deterrence measures deployed by them increase tax compliance even though the type of compliance is clearly discrete. Power increases enforced tax compliance and trust increases voluntary tax compliance.

The current paper attempts to contribute to the understanding of the effect of trust and deterrent power on compliance intentions within the slippery slope framework using a Portuguese sample. To the best of our knowledge, this is the first empirical test of this framework in Portugal. Results allows us to conclude that trust in authorities and their capacity to deter and punish tax evaders are interrelated and both are essential in securing tax compliance.

The paper is structured as follows. First, a literature review on the determinants of tax compliance is presented. This is followed by a description of the research method and procedure used in the study. Results are then presented and discussed in the current Portuguese context.

Literature review

The traditional view of tax compliance behaviour is that it is largely contingent on coercion: the assumption being that unless citizens are forced to declare and pay taxes they will not do so (Andreoni et al. 1998; Torgler, 2008). According to this view, tax authorities should focus on deterring evasion through tax audits and penalties for noncompliance. Although incentives and responsive regulation play a role in tax compliance (Feld and Frey, 2007), empirical studies have not found a statistically significant relationship between behaviour and the threat of punishment (Feld and Frey, 2002; Kirchler et al., 2008). Furthermore, research exists which shows that the deterrent effect of audits and fines is not strong and research findings have been so far inconclusive. Some studies have found that the threat of fines is slightly more related to tax compliance than the threat of audit, while other studies find no relation between fines and tax compliance although some relation between audit probabilities and tax compliance (Kirchler et al., 2008; Slemrod et al., 2001).

Considering the low probability of tax audits, the above approach to tax evasion cannot by itself account for high compliance rates (Alm et al., 1992). Several other factors have been identified. Justice, either procedural or distributive, has been found to influence compliance (e.g., Murphy and Tyler, 2008; Tyler, 2006; Wenzel, 2003a). Where governments are seen to be fair and not corrupt, citizens tend to trust them and show more favourable attitudes towards compliance (e.g., Braithwaite, 2003, 2007; Frey, 2003; Tyler, 2006).

Perceived treatment by tax authorities has also been pointed out as playing an important role in compliance (Feld and Frey, 2002, 2007), and the effectiveness of taxpayer service programs has also been found to be associated with compliance (Alm et al., 2010). The main conclusion seems to be that a willingness to comply with tax authorities is related to the degree of satisfaction with public services. Also, mutual respect between tax authorities and taxpayer has been found to play an important role in compliance as well as the extent of political participation and civil rights (Kirchler et al., 2008). The case of Switzerland is often cited to show that involvement in political decisions by the public is negatively associated with evasion (Pommerehne and Weck-Hannemann, 1996). An intrinsic motivation to pay taxes ("tax morale") has been advanced as a possible explanation for high rates of compliance (Torgler, 2002; Wenzel, 2003b). In this scenario, citizens pay taxes out of a sense of social responsibility and respect for the law.

There is a significant body of literature that shows that trust plays an important role in compliance behaviour in different settings. The main conclusion seems to be that where taxpayers are treated as trustworthy they reciprocate by way of compliance (Feld and Frey, 2002; Tyler, 1997). Trust thus appears actually to foster compliance. For example, political trust increases support for a variety of tax-cutting initiatives (though only among liberals) (Rudolph, 2009), and trust in tax authorities is positively related to tax compliance (e.g., Torgler, 2003).

The extent to which people trust authorities may partly depend on dispositional factors (Mulder et al., 2007). However, external factors count: in the wake of recent events, taxpayer levels of trust in governments seem to have reached an all-time low. The 12th Edelman Trust Barometer shows the steepest decline in trust in governments in its history across all the countries surveyed. Only 29 percent of respondents viewed government as credible and, of the 26 countries surveyed, Portugal scored fifth lowest for trust in government, considered by citizens as the nation's least trusted institution.

Trust is related with perceptions of corruption. In this respect, a recent European Commission survey on corruption (European Commission, 2012) revealed that 57% of Europeans believed that bribery and the abuse of power for personal gain were widespread amongst national politicians. The same report indicated that corruption was a serious concern in Portugal, where almost all respondents (97%) believed that corruption was a major problem in the country and was getting worse. According to a published report on the effectiveness of structures for preventing and fighting corruption in Portugal, the current EU/ECB and IMF-imposed austerity measures have exacerbated anxieties regarding perceived endemic corruption.

To sum up, previous studies have consistently found that where governments are seen to be fair and not corrupt, citizens tend to trust them and show more favourable attitudes towards tax compliance. On the other hand, sanctions used to enforce compliance also influence taxpayer behaviour although the degree of deterrent effect is dependent on other factors and their effect is so far inconclusive. Recent surveys indicate that in Europe the levels of trust are fairly low.

A study on Portuguese perceptions of the causes of tax evasion (Tavares and Iglesias, 2010) revealed that the origins are seen as two-fold: the justice of the tax system and the control of tax evasion. According to the authors, the Portuguese distinguish between two different causes of tax evasion. Firstly, there is global thinking regarding the equity of the taxation frame, characterized mainly by negative beliefs and values; secondly, citizens maintain that control and vigilance of tax evasion is ineffective. The paper concludes that evasion is due to widespread discontent with the tax system and its lack of effective measures of deterrence. Perceived injustice induces evasion and lack of control makes it possible.

The slippery slope framework

On the assumption that tax compliance is based on trust in authorities as well as their power of deterrence, Kirchler (2007) and Kirchler et al. (2008) developed the so-called slippery slope model, according to which the attitudes of the tax authorities towards taxpayers affect compliance.

Tax collection can be augmented either by increasing public trust in tax authorities or by increasing their deterrence power. Trust is here defined as a "general opinion of individuals and social groups that the tax authorities are benevolent and work beneficially for the common good" (Kirchler et al., 2008, p. 212) and includes a perception of fairness. Power is defined as a general perception of deterrence capability and in this way incorporates subjective evaluations concerning the ability of authorities to detect and deter tax evasion.

The framework conceives two distinct forms of tax compliance, namely voluntary and enforced compliance. The former is based on trust in tax authorities and citizen good will in paying taxes, whereas the latter depends on the power of tax authorities to forestall evasive intent. In this latter case, if deterrence power increases and citizens lack trust in authorities they will tend to weigh up the gains and costs of evasion and decide to pay their taxes only where such costs are seen to exceed possible benefits. However, use of excessive deterrence power by authorities generates a feeling of distrust and reduces cooperation, while trust generates more trust. Trust increases and power decreases voluntary compliance, whereas power increases enforced compliance.

To summarize, the slippery slope framework consists of three dimensions: (1) trust in tax authorities; (2) power of tax authorities, and (3) tax payments. Tax payments are assumed to be influenced by the twin determinants of trust and power. The main aim of this study was to analyze the influence of trust and deterrence power on tax compliance within this framework. It was hypothesized that:

- intended evasion would be lower and intended compliance would be higher in conditions of high trust (authorities perceived as fair and trustworthy) and high power (draconian deterrence, frequent audits and heavy fines) (hypothesis 1);
- intended compliance would be lower and intended evasion would be higher in conditions of low trust (authorities perceived as untrustworthy) and low power (authorities perceived as ineffectual) (hypothesis 2);
- voluntary compliance would be higher in conditions of high trust and low power (hypothesis 3);
- voluntary compliance would be lower in conditions of low trust and high power (hypothesis 4);
- enforced compliance would be higher in conditions of low trust and high power (hypothesis 5);
- enforced compliance would be lower in conditions of low trust and low power (hypothesis 6).

Method

Sample

The sample comprised 330 undergraduate and master's degree students in economics and business administration of two universities. Fifty-two per cent were females. The mean age was 23 years (SD = 1.11). Concerning income, 36% reported an average monthly net income equal to or below € 500, 30% an income between €500 and €1000, and the rest above €1000.

Students were invited to participate in a research project on tax compliance attitudes and were all volunteers. Questionnaires were distributed during class time from February to March 2012. The participation rate was 100%.

Instrument

This study used Kirchler and Wahl's (2010) questionnaire, translated into Portuguese by one of the authors and back-translated into English by the other author to ensure that the wording used reflected the original English items, and was then cross-checked. The translation was further tested on a sample of twenty students. The procedure followed the author guidelines as follows.

Respondents were asked to read the description of a hypothetical country (Varosia) and imagine themselves living and working in that country in which they had to pay taxes. Factors such as the size and population of Varosia were adjusted to fit with current data on Portugal to allow identification with the home country. The description varied according to the conditions and words indicating these differences were in bold. There were therefore four types of questionnaires combining low vs. high trust in authorities, low vs. high power of authorities, which were randomly distributed.

In the low trust condition, the text stated that the Varosia tax authorities were highly untrustworthy, authorities were not service-oriented and were perceived as being corrupt. The text of the high trust condition stated that the tax authorities were highly trustworthy, acted in service-oriented ways, and were not perceived as corrupt. In the low power condition, tax authorities were described as highly ineffective in detecting tax evasion and in the high power condition tax authorities were described as working efficiently.

After reading the description of Varosia, respondents answered three items on their general intention to pay taxes in Varosia (intended tax compliance) (e.g., "How likely will you be to pay your taxes completely honestly?"; 1= very unlikely to 7= very likely). Furthermore, respondents answered a set of items regarding voluntary compliance (e.g., "When I pay my taxes in Varosia as required by the regulations, I do so because to me it's obvious that this is what you do") and enforced compliance (e.g., "When I pay my taxes in Varosia as required by the regulations, I do so because I know that I will be audited"; 1= strongly disagree to 7= strongly agree). To assess intended evasion, five short items asked respondents to indicate how they would behave in situations where they were able to evade taxes with an extremely low probability of detection. A specimen item was: "You could intentionally declare restaurant bills for meals you had with your friends as business meals. How likely would you be to declare those restaurant bills as business meals?"; 1= very unlikely to 9= very likely).

Finally, respondents were asked to indicate their net income on a 5 item-scale: < €500; €500-1000; €1000-1500; €1500-2000; > €2000.

Results

Explanatory Factor Analyses were conducted on the items of trust, power, intended compliance, voluntary compliance, enforced compliance, and tax evasion intention scales. For each scale a Varimax rotation extracted one factor with eigenvalues greater than 1, and the Cronbach's alpha coefficient indicated a very good internal reliability. Negative items were reverse-scored and a global mean score was computed for each scale. Correlations suggested significant correlations between the variables except, as might be expected, for enforcement and intended compliance, and enforcement and voluntary compliance. Table 1 presents the descriptive statistics, Cronbach's alpha coefficients and correlations among the study variables.

Following Wahl et al. (2010), a two-way MANOVA was conducted to check manipulations of power and trust with power (high power: authorities perceived as effectual; low power: authorities perceived as ineffectual) and trust (high trust: authorities perceived as trustworthy and not corrupt; low trust: authorities perceived as untrustworthy and corrupt) as independent factors, and the responses on trust and power scales as dependent variables. Findings showed a significant interaction effect between power and trust for trust manipulation, $F(1,326) = 17.54$, $p < .001$, partial $\eta 2 = .05$, but not for power manipulation. The power of authorities had a statistically significant main effect for trust ($F(1,326) = 24.50$, $p < .01$, partial $\eta 2 = .07$) and for power scores, $F(1,326) = 493.58$, p

< .001, partial $\eta 2$ =.51. Trust in authorities had a significant main effect for trust, F (1,326) = 333.27, $p < .001$, partial $\eta 2$=.51, and for power, F (1,326) = 9.36, $p < .01$, partial $\eta 2$ =.03. Given the results, we concluded that both trust and power were successfully manipulated.

Table 1. Means, standard deviations, Cronbach's alphas and intercorrelations among variables (N=330)

Variables	*M*	*SD*	*α*	1	2	3	4	5	6
1. Intended comp.	6.20	1.87	.91	-					
2. Trust	4.22	2.53	.85	.42**	-				
3. Power	5.09	2.68	.85	.39**	.31**	-			
4. Volun-tary comp.	6.18	1.82	.87	.48**	.29**	.13*	-		
5. Enforced comp.	4.69	2.47	.92	.20**	.08	.53**	-.02	-	
6. Tax evasion	5.06	1.02	.88	-.42**	-.24**	-.13*	-.38**	.14**	-

Note: comp. = compliance. * p<.05 level; ** p<.01 (2-tailed). All means are given based on the 7-point response scale except for tax evasion which are the 9-point response scale.

To examine the effect of trust and power on intended compliance a two-way ANCOVA was run with trust and power as independent factors, intended compliance as dependent variable and controlled by gender, age and income. The interaction between power and trust was not significant, but the main effects were statistically significant, respectively F (1,225) = 27.42, $p < .001$, partial $\eta 2$ =.11 for power, and F (1,225) = 26.86, $p < .001$, partial $\eta 2$=.11 for trust. Findings suggested that both power and trust affected intention to pay taxes. Covariates were not significant.

Univariate tests were used to evaluate differences among means and they were found to be significant at .001 level for both power and trust. Respondents showed a higher intention to pay taxes when power and trust were high than when they were low. When authorities were described as both powerful and trustworthy and not corrupt respondents were more willing to pay taxes (see Tables 2 and 3).

A MANCOVA examined the influence of trust and power on the two types of compliance, with voluntary and enforced compliance as dependent variables, trust (high and low) and power (high and low) as independent factors with age, sex and income as covariates. There was no significant interaction effect of trust and power. The main effect of trust on voluntary tax compliance was significant, $F(1,225) = 10.28$, $p < .01$, partial $\eta 2 = .04$), but not on enforced compliance. Conversely, the main effect of power was significant on enforced compliance, $F(1,225) = 85.03$, $p < .001$, partial $\eta 2 = .27$, and not on voluntary compliance. For the covariates gender, age and income no significant effects were found.

The estimated mean for voluntary compliance was higher for high trust than low trust, which suggests that voluntary compliance was higher when authorities were seen as trustworthy and fair than untrustworthy and unfair. As for enforced compliance, when authorities were seen as having a strong power to detect and punish tax evasion, enforced compliance was higher than when they were seen as having weak power (see Table 2).

Table 2. Estimated means and standard errors of mean intended compliance, tax evasion, voluntary compliance and enforced compliance in the four conditions

	Power		Trust	
Dependent variables	**High power**	**Low power**	**High trust**	**Low trust**
Intended compliance	5.79 (.07)	5.27 (.07)	5.84 (.07)	5.22 (.07)
Voluntary compliance	6.41 (.16)	6.22 (.17)	6.55 (.16)	5.82 (.16)
Enforced compliance	5.98 (.19)	3.39 (.20)	4.84 (.20)	4.53 (.20)
Tax evasion	5.31 (.19)	5.91 (.20)	5.30 (.20)	5.92 (.20)

Note: Higher scores indicate higher acceptance of the items. Means are corrected for covariates gender, age and income and are significant at the .05 level. Standard errors are given in parenthesis.

Voluntary compliance was higher when authorities were described as powerful and trustworthy and lowest when trust was low and power high. For enforced tax compliance, respondents tended to report the highest intended compliance when authorities were described as powerful independently of trust. The lowest intended compliance occurred when trust and power were low (see Table 3).

A ANCOVA analyzed tax evasion intentions and trust (high and low) and power (high and low) with trust and power as independent factors, tax evasion intentions as dependent variable and gender, age and income as covariates. The interaction effect between trust and power was not significant.

However, significant effects were found for trust, $F(1,225) = 5.05$, $p < .05$, partial $\eta 2 == 02$, and power, $F(1,225) = 4.63$, $p < .05$, partial $\eta 2 = .02$. As shown in Table 3, mean differences between high and low trust were significant at the .05 level. Higher scores indicated increased evasion intentions. Respondents were less willing to evade when authorities were described as trustworthy and fair and more willing to do so in the low trust condition. Mean differences were also significant between high and low power at $p <.05$, and were lower in the condition of high power than in the condition of low power. Evasion intentions were equal in the condition of low power and low trust. The covariates age and sex significantly influenced the mean of tax evasion intentions, respectively $F(1,225) = 5.89$, $p < .05$, partial $\eta 2 =.03$ and $F(1,225) = 4.21$, $p < .05$, partial $\eta 2=.02$. Income did not affect tax evasion intentions (see Table 3).

Table 3. Estimated means and standard errors of mean intended compliance, voluntary compliance, enforced compliance, and tax evasion as a function of power and trust in the four conditions

Dependent variables	High trust High power	High trust Low power	Low trust High power	Low trust Low power
Intended compliance	6.03 (.09)	5.65 (.09)	5.55 (.09)	4.89 (.09)
Voluntary compliance	6.72 (.22)	6.39 (.24)	5.57 (.23)	6.06 (.24)
Enforced compliance	5.97 (.27)	3.71 (.29)	5.9 (.28)	3.07 (.28)
Tax evasion	5.00 (.24)	5.44 (.24)	5.65 (.24)	6.16 (.26)

Note: Higher scores indicate higher acceptance of the items. Means are corrected for covariates gender, age and income and are significant at the .05 level. Standard errors are given in parenthesis.

This study examined the influence of trust and power on tax compliance intentions within the slippery slope framework. Trust and power were successfully manipulated. Participants who were told that Varosia's politicians were trustworthy trusted the authorities more than those who were told that the politicians were untrustworthy; participants who were told that authorities were powerful perceived Varosia's authorities as more powerful than participants who were told that authorities' power was weak.

Four of the six hypotheses were fully supported. Findings suggested that tax evasion intentions were lower and tax payment intentions were higher when authorities were perceived as fair, not corrupt and trustworthy and when deterrence power (frequent audits and heavy fines) was high (hypothesis 1). Findings suggested the opposite when authorities were perceived as untrustworthy and ineffective in detecting tax evasions (hypothesis 2). Voluntary compliance was lower in the conditions of low trust and high power (hypothesis 4), and enforced compliance was lower in the condition of low trust and low power (hypothesis 6). However, voluntary compliance was not at its highest in the conditions of high trust and low power as posited in hypothesis 3, but rather when trust and power were both high. Nor was enforced compliance at its highest in conditions of low trust and high power, as posited in hypothesis 5, but rather in conditions of high power independently of whether trust was high or low.

Respondents were therefore more likely to comply when authorities were described as fair and trustworthy as well as when they were described as having the ability to detect and punish tax evasion. Furthermore, voluntary compliance diminished in the condition of high power and low trust and enforced compliance was higher when authorities were described as powerful. Given this, the current study on the whole gives support to the assumptions of slippery slope framework (Kirchler, 2007; Kirchler et al., 2008; Wahl et al., 2010). However, in this study voluntary compliance was at its highest when both power and trust were high and remained high even in the condition of low trust. Moreover, when authorities were described as powerful, respondents trusted the authorities more than in the low power condition.

In line with the slippery slope framework, it may thus be said that both power and trust are necessary to obtain tax compliance. Citizens who spontaneously feel inclined to comply will do so if they trust the authorities but those who do not feel so inclined may do so if motivated by the fear of being audited and punished. Moreover, if they can evade without being caught they will attempt to evade. On the other hand, "honest citizens" feel that non-compliers should be punished (Kirchler et al., 2008; Wahl et al., 2010). Intuitively, it seems plausible to suggest that this tendency would be more evident in times of austerity.

As Feld and Frey (2007) point out, citizens may be willing to declare their taxes honestly, even if they do not receive the equivalent social wage in return, providing that the political process is perceived as fair and legitimate. Given that power of authorities to deter tax evasion is accepted when considered legitimate, the current fiscal imbalances in many countries may well legitimize the use of such power in the eyes of citizens. This being the case, coercive power may be accepted.

Voluntary compliance scores were higher in all conditions than for enforced compliance. This could be interpreted as expressing a general potential willingness to comply. Another interesting result is the difference between tax compliance specific to the case of the hypothetical country (intended tax payment) and voluntary compliance. Here too voluntary compliance scores were higher across all four conditions.

Findings must be interpreted in the cultural and social context of the respondents. Deterrence has long been the prevalent strategy in Portugal and few campaigns have been implemented to appeal to Portuguese citizens' sense of civic duty. Deterrence has not been successful in lowering tax evasion. Tax increases collides with public resentment towards the government due to perceived profligacy in public expenditure, and well publicised reports of corruption gone unpunished. As it is usually the case in times of economic austerity, disapproval of supposed benefit-scrounging by the "undeserving poor" is more in evidence. Moreover, citizens sense a shortfall between the taxes they pay and the services they receive. To this should be added the evidence, widely accepted, that the present sovereign debt crisis was due to a huge build-up of public debt and mismanaged taxpayer contributions. Considering all this, as Alm et al. (1992) have remarked, it is to be wondered why so many citizens continue to pay their taxes.

On the other hand, the current harsh fiscal measures to reduce public debt and the budget deficit have been imposed by the IMF/EU/ECB "to save the country" from bankruptcy. So far, and in spite of some opposition, the Portuguese have appeared to accept these measures. However, at the time of writing it is still unknown whether this acceptance will prevail. Ultimately the question that Portuguese tax authorities must address is how to increase taxes and revenues at a time when the public are more than ever likely to feel that they are getting, by necessity, less in return for their taxes.

As mentioned before, surveys suggest that the Portuguese believe that corruption amongst politicians is rife. Corruption "legitimizes" tax evasion as seems to be the case in Greece.

Prior research has found inconsistent findings regarding enforcement factors. This study suggested that both trust in authorities and their deterrence power are important in securing compliance. Appeals to the common good will be effective only if all citizens comply, but "non-compliers" will always exist, either because they are resistant or disengaged (Braithwaite, 2007). This may explain the importance of power in the findings. In the long run, voluntary compliance works best, but building trust is a long process and the crisis calls for more immediate remedies.

This study focused on a student population this clearly constitutes a limitation on generalizability. With few exceptions, students do not have much experience with tax issues, but they are nonetheless fully enfranchised citizens. Students are also better educated than the average of the population and thus may not be representative of it, but their education may better enable them to understand the hypothetical scenario presented to them in this study. Moreover, there is evidence that student attitudes on the subject are not different from other adults (Torgler, 2008). In the case of Portugal, given the large number of unemployed young graduates, it is particularly interesting to know students' attitudes towards tax compliance. In any case, results should be interpreted with care and future research should extend the study to employed and self-employed adults. Another limitation is that the sample was collected using economics and management students, which may bias the results. Further research should include a more diversified student population.

This study ignored a variety of socio-demographic variables outside its scope which may be nonetheless relevant to understanding tax compliance intentions. As Lewis (1982) remarks, it is not clear that antipathy towards taxation increases as income rises. Although this study included one question about income, it did not solicit information about family income and origin (rural, urban). The importance of fiscal knowledge and awareness should also be included as variables in other studies. Another interesting research avenue would be to investigate the role played by individual dispositions towards authority in general and tax compliance.

Conclusions

Tax evasion is a particularly serious problem in times of economic austerity. The current study contributes to an increased understanding of tax compliance intentions by shedding light on the influence of trust and sanctions on tax compliance intentions. Findings allow us to conclude that trust in authorities and their capacity to deter and punish tax evaders are interrelated and both are important in securing tax compliance, as suggested by the Slippery Slope framework. However, of these factors trust is essential and since corruption erodes trust, corruption must be addressed as a pre-condition.

Results were discussed in regard to the financial crisis affecting EU and especially Portugal. The main conclusion seems to be that in a climate of distrust, high power is needed by authorities to enforce compliance and increasing fines and audit probabilities may be an effective tax policy.

References

Afonso, O. and N. Gonçalves 2009, "A Economia não Registada em Portugal", *Observatório de Economia e Gestão da Fraude (OBEGEF), Working Paper 4* (accessed March 4, 2012), http://www.up.pt/RePEc/por/obegef/files/wp004.pdf

Alm, J., G. McClelland and W. Schulze 1992, "Why do People Pay Taxes?", *Journal of Public Economics* 48, 21-38

Alm, J., T. Cherry, M. Jones and M. McKee 2010, "Taxpayer Information Assistance Services and Tax Compliance Behavior", *Journal of Economic Psychology* 31, 577-86

Andreoni, J., B. Erard and J. Feinstein 1998, "Tax Compliance", *Journal of Economic Literature* 36, 818-60

Braithwaite, V. 2003, "Dancing with Tax Authorities: Motivational Postures and Non-compliant Actions", in *Taxing Democracy: Understanding Tax Avoidance and Evasion*, 15-39. Edited by Valerie Braithwaite, Aldershot: Ashgate

—. 2007, "Responsive Regulation and Taxation", *Law & Policy*, special issue 29, 3-10

Edelman Trust Barometer, The 12th Edelman Trust Barometer Survey 2012 (accessed April 21, 2012), available from http://trust.edelman.com/ about-trust/

European Commission 2012, "Corruption Report", Special Eurobarometer No 374 (accessed May 31, 2012), http://ec.europa.eu/public_opinion/archives/ebs/ebs_374_en.pdf

Feld, L. and B. Frey 2002, "Trust Breeds Trust: How Taxpayers are Treated", *Economics of Governance* 3, 87-99

Feld, L. and B. Frey 2007, "Tax Compliance as the Result of a Psychological Tax Contract: The Role of Incentives and Responsive Regulation", *Law & Policy* 29, 102–20

Frey, B. 2003, "Deterrence and Tax Morale in the European Union", *European Review* 11(3), 385-406

Kirchler, E. 2007, *The Economic Psychology of Tax Behaviour*, Cambridge: Cambridge University Press

Kirchler, E. and I. Wahl 2010, "Tax Compliance Inventory TAX-1: Designing an Inventory for Surveys of Tax Compliance", *Journal of Economic Psychology* 31, 331-46

Kirchler, E., E. Hoelzl and I. Wahl 2008, "Enforced Versus Voluntary Tax Compliance: The 'Slippery Slope Framework'", *Journal of Economic Psychology* 29, 210-25

Lewis, A. 1982, "The Social Psychology of Taxation", *British Journal of Social Psychology* 21, 151-8

Muehlbacher, S. and K. Kirchler 2010, "Tax Compliance by Trust and Power of Authorities", *International Economic Journal* 24, 607-10

Mulder, L. B., P. Verboon and D. De Cremer 2009, "Sanctions and Moral Judgments: The Moderating Effect of Sanction Severity and Trust in Authorities", *European Journal of Social Psychology* 39, 255–69

Murphy, K. and T. Tyler 2008, "Procedural Justice and Compliance Behaviour: The Mediating Role of Emotions", *European Journal of Social Psychology* 38, 652-68

Pommerehne, W. and H. Weck-Hannemann 1996, "Tax Rates, Tax Administration and Income Tax Evasion in Switzerland", *Public Choice* 88, 161-70

Rudolph, T. 2009, "Political Trust, Ideology, and Public Support for Tax Cuts", *Public Opinion Quarterly* 73, 144-58

Slemrod, J., M. Blumenthal and C. Christian 2001, "Taxpayer Response to an Increased Probability of Audit: Evidence from a Controlled Experiment in Minnesota", *Journal of Public Economics* 79, 455–83

Tavares, J. C. and M. Iglesias 2010, "Dimensions of Causal Attributions of Tax Evasion in Portugal", *Revista de Psicología del Trabajo y de las Organizaciones* 26 (1), 73-78

The Economist 2010, "Tax Evasion: Dues and Don'ts", *The Economist* (14 August), 58

Torgler, B. 2002, "Speaking to Theorists and Searching for Facts: Tax Morale and Tax Compliance in Experiments", *Journal of Economic Surveys* 16, 657–83

—. 2003, "To Evade Taxes or not to Evade: That is the Question", *Journal of Socio-Economics* 32, 283-333

—. 2004, "Tax Morale, Trust and Corruption: Empirical Evidence from Transition Countries", *Center for Research in Economics, Management and the Arts (CREMA)*, Working Paper No. 2004–05, http://www.crema-research.ch/papers/2004-05.pdf (accessed May 4, 2012)

—. 2008, "What Do you Know About Tax Fraud", *Social Research* 75, 1239-70

Trabandt, M. and H. Uhlig 2010, "How Far are we From the Slippery Slope? The Laffer Curve Revisited", *European Central Bank Working Paper* 1174

Tyler, T. R. 1997, "The Psychology of Legitimacy: A Relational Perspective on Voluntary Deference to Authorities", *Personality and Social Psychology Review* 1, 323-45

—. 2006, "Psychological Perspectives on Legitimacy and Legitimation", *Annual Review of Psychology* 57, 375-400

Wahl, I., B. Kastlunger and E. Kirchler 2010, "Trust in Authorities and Power to Enforce Tax Compliance: An Empirical Analysis of the 'Slippery Slope Framework'", *Law & Policy* 32, 383-406

Wenzel, M. 2003a, "Tax Compliance and the Psychology of Justice", in *Taxing Democracy: Understanding Tax Avoidance and Evasion*, 41-70. Edited by Valerie Braithwaite, Aldershot: Ashgate

—. 2003b, "Motivation or rationalisation? Causal Relations Between Ethics, Norms and Tax Compliance", *Journal of Economic Psychology* 26, 491-508

—. 2007, "The Multiplicity of Taxpayer Identities and Their Implications for Tax Ethics", *Law & Policy* 29, 31–50.

Appendix

Description of Varosia (different wording of the four versions is in italics)

Please read the following description of a country:

In the last census of population in 2010 Varosia had 10,570,803 inhabitants and the territory of Varosia occupies 92,090 km^2. The unemployment rate is at an average.

Since Varosia's autonomy it has been marked with a *high/low* political stability and a *democratic/ oligarchic (authority of few)* government. *Regularly/Seldom* referenda are held, in which the citizens of Varosia can co-decide in the legislation.

The government enjoys a *good/bad* reputation in the population. It can be concluded from opinion polls that 70% of the citizens are *satisfied/not satisfied with* the current government.

Varosia's legislation *is/is not* transparent and the government offers *no/the* opportunity of free counselling on judicial subjects and tax issues in information centers. Furthermore, Varosia's public authorities are *very/little* service-oriented and *interested/not interested* in supporting Varosia's citizens.

The budget expenditures of the state are *traceable/not traceable* for Varosia's citizens, because they are *informed/not informed* about the use of tax money. In an opinion poll in October 2010 78% of Varosia's citizens indicated to have the impression that their tax money is *used/not used* reasonable.

Besides *little/a lot of* tax money is embezzled by politicians. According to an international corruption index (CPI), Varosia is one of the countries with the *lowest/highest* perceived corruption.

All these factors cause that the citizens of Varosia trust their country *a lot/a little*.

The prosecution of tax evaders is *very/not very* effective. Because of the tax legislation it is *easy/difficult* for the government to conduct audits on its citizens and therewith to chase tax evaders.

The government assigns a *high/low* budget to the tax office to punish tax evasion. With the means at hand *it is/ it is not* possible for the tax office to employ qualified tax inspectors. In addition the members of the tax office of Varosia are perceived as *very/little* present.

The chance to be audited for self-employed people is very *high/low*. This is to say that self-employed *are/are not* audited very often. Therefore, very many of the committed tax offences *can/cannot* be detected. Moreover, the fines for tax evasion are *very/not very* severe in Varosia. When tax evaders are detected, they *do have/do not have* to anticipate severe fines. The tax office *does not/does* exercise benignity.

All these factors cause that the citizens of Varosia assess their government as *very/little* powerful.

Notes

[1] A result displayed by the typical Laffer-curve (for a recent discussion see Trabandt and Uhlig, 2010).

CHAPTER FIVE

TAX MORALE DIMENSIONS ANALYSIS IN PORTUGAL

CRISTINA SÁ, ANTÓNIO MARTINS
AND CARLOS GOMES

Introduction

The challenge faced by governments to simultaneously obtain high levels of fiscal revenues, promote national economic growth, and maintain an equitable tax system renewed research interest on tax compliance. Recent research recognizes tax morale as the key to explain the levels of compliance obtained in most countries (Richardson, 2006).

Tax morale is understood as the intrinsic motivation to comply with fiscal duties (Torgler, 2003). Empirical studies found strong evidence of a negative correlation between tax morale and tax evasion (Richardson, 2006; Torgler, 2003; Torgler et al., 2008) and between tax morale and the size of shadow economy (Weck, 1983). A better understanding on individual heterogeneity in tax morale may contribute for the development of alternative mechanisms to reduce tax evasion (Riahi-Belkaoiu, 2004; Lago-Peñas and Lago-Peñas, 2010) and to improve tax compliance. Such knowledge is of particular importance because of the negative consequences that tax evasion has on public revenues, and on equity level of the tax system (Kim, 2008). Furthermore, high levels of tax compliance have an important role in shaping perceptions of potential investors and, therefore, influence competitiveness (Frey, 2003; Richardson, 2006).

Based on literature review we identified a set of factors shaping tax morale. Data provided by EVS (2010) regarding to Portugal was used to identify tax morale dimensions. We applied an exploratory factor analysis in order to analyze religiosity, trust in government and democracy, trust in public institutions and political participation as dimensions of tax morale.

Literature review

Tax evasion is probably as ancient as taxes themselves. However, it seems that the study of tax compliance and tax evasion consequences has never been, until now, topic of such intense research within the scientific community, and of interest among politicians.

Taxpayers exhibit a wide range of behaviors towards their tax obligations, justified for several reasons, ranging from an economic point of view (Allingham and Sandmo, 1972; Yitzhaki, 1974) to behavioral and psychological motivations (Andreoni et al., 1998). There are taxpayers who do not make any effort to avoid taxes, regardless of the circumstances (Torgler, 2003). Their behavior does not respond to any changes in the parameters of fiscal policy like tax rates, fines or frequency of audits. There are taxpayers who obey to the economic and rational choice (Allingham and Sandmo, 1972; Torgler, 2003). They compare the benefit of evading with the penalty if they get caught and act in accordance with this calculation. Finally, there are also taxpayers who are greatly influenced by social norms, by others' behavior, or by the institutional conditions under which they must pay their taxes (Torgler, 2003).

The puzzle of tax compliance cannot be understood using only traditional economic models. Most theoretical approaches greatly over predict non-compliance (Andreoni et al., 1998). Based only on traditional economic models, would be necessary the existence of a very high level of risk aversion to justify the high levels of compliance. Arrow-Pratt measure of more than 30 must exist. However, field evidence suggests a range value between 1 and 2 (Alm et al., 1992; Feld and Frey, 2002).

The study of this topic has received, in recent years, contributions from different academic disciplines, such as accounting, law, economics, sociology and psychology (Richardson, 2006). Erard and Feinstein (1994) express the relevance of integrating moral sentiments, like shame and guilty, to provide a satisfactory explanation about taxpayer's compliance behavior. Torgler (2003) underlines that complying or not is also a function of individual´s willingness and not only a function of deterrence factors.

Researchers argue that, among non-economic variables, tax morale has an important role in explaining the high degree of tax compliance (Güth et al., 2005; Molero and Pujol, 2012), and has a strong negative impact on the shadow economy (Weck, 1983; Alm and Torgler, 2006; Torgler and Schneider, 2009) and tax evasion (Torgler and Schneider, 2007). A reduction of tax morale diminishes the moral costs of behaving illegally and increases the incentives to work in the underground economy (Torgler and Schneider, 2007).

Research on tax morale was initiated during the 1960's by the German school "Cologne school of tax psychology" with the intent to measure tax morale among taxpayers (Schmölders, 1960; Strümpel, 1969) in order to lay the bridge between economics and social psychology. They emphasized that tax compliance should not be analyzed only from a traditional economic point of view. Earlier, in 1890, Georg von Schanz already emphasized the importance of considering the taxpayers as partners in the fiscal contract between the state and taxpayers.

Tax morale is the intrinsic motivation of individuals to pay taxes (Frey, 2003) and a civic duty which can be crucial to explain the level of acceptance of tax burden (Martinez-Vazquez and Torgler, 2009). It can be conceptualized as a set of moral principles or values that individuals have regarding the payment of their taxes (Alm and Torgler, 2006). Song and Yarbrough (1978) define it as the norms of behavior governing citizens as taxpayers in their relationship with the state. Tax morale definitions provided by the literature evidence that moral rules and feelings, equity and the relation between taxpayers and government are important factors for an understanding of the concept. In our work tax morale's definition is in line with Torgler (2005a) as being the individuals' willingness or moral obligation to pay taxes or their belief in contributing to the society by paying taxes.

Although research often considers tax morale as a black box or a residuum, recent studies search for the factors that shape or help to maintain it (Alm et al., 2006; Torgler et al., 2009; Lubian and Zarri, 2011). Empirical studies show that the intrinsic motivation of each one to pay taxes or tax morale differs from country to country (Frey, 2003; Alm and Torgler, 2006) and differs over time (for Spain see Martinez-Vazquez and Torgler, 2009; for Australia see Torgler and Murphy, 2004).

A better understanding of tax morale concept can be made in the light of the many factors that have been identified to shape it. These factors are presented into five categories: personal and demographic factors, economic factors, sociological and behavioral factors, psychological factors and political factors.

Personal and demographic factors

Taxpayers aged between 30 and 64 years old present a higher level of tax morale than younger taxpayers (Alm and Torgler, 2006). This trend reflects lower taxpayers' predisposition for risk as they get older and is the result of accumulation of social capital over life (Title, 1980). Women are usually associated with a higher level of tax morale, and are more compliant compared to men (Title, 1980; Torgler, 2003; Martinez-Vazquez and Torgler, 2009). Married individuals may be more associated with a greater propensity to comply with legal obligations (Torgler, 2003) or to a non-compliant behavior, depending on the intensity with which they are constrained by their social networks (Title, 1980; Torgler and Murphy, 2004; Torgler, 2006). Unmarried and divorced taxpayers generally have a tax morale level relatively lower compared to that of married taxpayers (Torgler, 2003; Alm and Torgler, 2006). There are also studies that found that non-compliance is more common in married taxpayers (Clotfelter, 1983; Feinstein, 1991). Empirical studies support a tendency for self-employed or unemployed citizens to have lower tax morale, compared to those who have a full time job (Frey and Torgler, 2007).

Another demographic factor with impact on tax morale is the level of education of taxpayers. In most studies, the level of education is measured by the academic qualifications of taxpayers (Lubian and Zarri, 2011, Torgler et al., 2009) representing taxpayer's knowledge about tax law (Torgler, 2006). More educated taxpayers are supposed to exhibit a better understanding of the tax system and, therefore, tend to have a higher level of tax morale (Lewis, 1982). However, it also might be possible that people with a lower education have acquired a high knowledge about taxation (Eriksen and Fallan, 1996). It is also possible that more educated citizens had acquired a deeper knowledge about tax evasion and avoidance opportunities and thus exhibit a less compliant behavior (Torgler, 2006; Torgler and Schneider, 2007). Thus, the effect of taxpayer's education on tax morale is not clear, since it depends on which of the effects identified above prevails (Torgler and Schneider, 2007).

Economic factors

Traditional compliance economic models underline the importance of deterrence variables on the explanation of taxpayers' behavior. However, when the purpose of research is to explain the level of tax morale, the consideration of deterrent factors is not so evident. It seems to be suitable only when tax morale shows to be a good tax compliance indicator (Frey and Torgler, 2007).

In countries where income tax rates are progressive, such as Portugal, taxpayers with higher incomes get a higher return for each unreported monetary unit, but they may face a lower marginal utility (Torgler and Schneider, 2005; Torgler, 2006). On the other hand, taxpayers with lower income will have fewer constraints on tax evasion, but are in a less favorable position to take risks because of high marginal utility loss associated with the chance of being detected and penalized (Jackson and Millirion, 1986). There is a trend in households with a less favorable financial condition to see the payment of tax as a strong financial constraint, which can lead to a decrease in tax compliance (Torgler, 2005b). The combination of these two effects, the economic consequences and the marginal utility associated with each unreported monetary unit makes it difficult to establish, a priori, the influence of income level in the taxpayer's tax morale. This influence is dependent on the level of risk aversion of each taxpayer and the progressiveness of the income tax schedules (Torgler and Schneider, 2005).

Sociological and behavioral factors

Every society has moral constraints, which are not formally laid down (Torgler, 2006), but nevertheless influence citizens' behavior. Many of these standards are highly influenced by religious motives (Torgler, 2006). Torgler et al. (2008) results support such previous findings in that a high sense of religiosity leads to higher tax morale. Church as an institution induces moral constraints in a community and influences people's behavior (Torgler and Schneider, 2005). In this context religiosity can be a restriction on engaging in tax evasion (Torgler et al., 2008).

Taxpayers' behavior depends on observed actions of other taxpayers. In fact, taxpayers are willing to pay their taxes conditionally (Frey and Torgler, 2007). The perception of a taxpayer about others' behavior influences his tax morale. The greater the perception by an individual that others follow tax evasion practices, the more he will tend to lower his level of tax morale (Molero and Pujol, 2012).

Psychological factors

Taxpayers' perceptions of a decrease in the level of equity are accompanied by an increase in tax evasion. Taxpayers perceived tax system unfairness leads to acting in disobedience to the tax law, as the psychological costs of non-compliance are reduced (Torgler, 2003). Fortin et al. (2007) based on experiments, support the idea that unfair taxation leads to an increase in the propensity to tax evasion. Tax system fairness includes horizontal, vertical and exchange equity. Horizontal equity refers to situations were taxpayers have the same income. Vertical equity refers to the burden of taxes for certain group compared to others. Exchange equity refers to perceived fairness between the tax paid and the government provision of public goods. Alm et al. (1992) suggest that compliance occurs because some individuals value the public goods their tax payments finance. If the amount individuals receive from a given tax payment increases, their compliance rate rises.

National pride is used as a proxy to evaluate the degree of the taxpayer's identification with the state. It influences the individual's behavior in a group, organization and society (Tyler, 2000). This feeling provides a basis for encouraging cooperative behavior. Thus, the greater the pride a person has in belonging to a country, the greater his/ her tax morale is (Torgler, 2003).

Also happiness and individual satisfaction were found to have a significant positive effect on taxpayers' tax morale in Asian countries (Torgler, 2004) and in Latin America (Torgler, 2005b).

Political factors

The level of taxpayers' satisfaction with the government could help to maintain, or even increase, their level of tax morale (Torgler, 2003). In Russia, the level of tax morale has decreased during the years of transition to market economy, due to the perception of an increased level of corruption affecting people's trust in the Parliament (Alm et al., 2006). This relationship may indicate that trust is an important value that influences taxpayers. But confidence can only be created and maintained with the government's commitment to act in accordance with people's needs and desires (Hardin, 1988). A strong democratic attitude has a positive effect on tax morale (Torgler, 2005b). Alm and Torgler (2006) justified the difference between the level of tax morale existent in the U.S. and Switzerland, compared to other European countries, with a higher political participation observed in those two countries.

A government that undertakes the rules of direct democracy imposes restraints on its own power, and thus sends a signal that taxpayers are seen as responsible persons (Levi, 1988). In fact, the more taxpayers participate in the process of formulation of political decisions through their voting rights and the "tax contract" is based on trust, the greater the level of tax morale (Torgler, 2005a). The relationship between taxpayers and tax authorities has an implicit underlying or psychological contract which involves not only strong emotional ties but also a loyal bond (Torgler, 2003; Frey, 2003).

In this context, positive actions undertaken by the government are understood as inducing tax compliance. If the government acts with integrity, taxpayers will be more willing to comply with their tax obligations (Smith, 1992). This reciprocity can be an important cause of compliance.

In this regard, Feld and Frey (2002) conducted a study in Switzerland which analyzed whether the relationship between tax authorities and taxpayers influenced the level of tax compliance and tax morale. They concluded that in the cantons where citizens' participation rights are higher, tax authorities have a more respectful and less suspicious outlook on taxpayers who report lower incomes and tax morale increases.

Methodological considerations

Instrument

Tax morale determinants have being analyzed by using either survey data (Feld and Frey, 2002; Torgler, 2006; Martinez-Vazquez and Torgler, 2009; Lago-Penãs and Lago-Penãs, 2010) or experimental results (Cummings et al., 2009). A significant part of empirical literature on tax morale and tax compliance employs survey data from the European Values Study (Frey and Torgler, 2007) or World Values Survey (Torgler, 2006) and sometimes a combination of both (Devos, 2008; Torgler and Schneider, 2007). In line with literature, we used data from EVS carried out in 2008 (EVS, 2010).

The EVS is a research project on human values in Europe that explores the differences and changes in the values of citizens. Essentially, it seeks to collect data about what Europeans think about family, work, religion, politics and society. The survey provides details about ideas, beliefs, preferences, attitudes, values and opinions of citizens across Europe. This is a research program based on surveys, with an increasing number of countries participating over time. The last survey, in 2008, covered 47 European countries.

We scanned recent literature about tax morale to identify the items to measure each one of the dimensions of tax morale identified in empirical studies. After that we extracted data regarding those items from EVS database. EVS (2010) did not have information for all items but a considerable percentage was available.

Sample and procedure

The EVS (2010) allows us to work with a representative set of, at least 1,000 individuals of Portugal. Representative multi-stage or stratified random samples of the adult population of 18 years old and older were drawn. The sampling design consists of a multi-stage, random selection of sampling points with thc number of individual observations drawn from all administrative regional units, after stratification by region and by degree of urbanization. Surveys were conducted face to face with a standardized questionnaire in 2008. The survey included about 250 questions and took about 40 minutes do answer.

This sample includes individuals aged between 18 and 98 years old with an average of 51 years old. There are no major differences between genders, 56.1% of respondents are women and 43.9% are male. Most respondents are married (63.2%) and around 18.4% have never been married or with registered partnership. There are individuals from all regions of Portugal, with emphasis for North (39.3%), Center (25.3%) and Lisbon (20.5%). Around 89.6% of respondents have up to (upper) secondary education. Around 33.00% of the respondents earn less than € 18,000 a year. However, a significant percentage of the respondents (47.4%) did not answer the question or did not know how much their annual income was. Regarding to employment status, 49.00% of the respondents are employed and 29.3% are retired or pensioned. Table 1 summarizes socio-demographic characteristics of the sample.

Data analysis

The objective of the data analysis was to assess the dimensionality of the tax morale among Portuguese taxpayers. Firstly, an exploratory factor analysis was used to extract the underlying dimensions of tax morale. Sample adequacy for all variables was assessed by Kaiser-Meyer-Olkin test. The adequacy of factor analysis was measured with Bartlett test. Secondly, we applied the analysis of variance (ANOVA) procedure, and the Tukey test to check the existence of differences among the means for socio-demographic characteristics on tax morale dimensions.

Table 1 – Sample socio-demographic characterization

Item	Frequency	%	Item	Frequency	%
Age			**Marital status**		
18 – 29	152	13.2	Married	728	63.2
30 - 49	411	35.7	Widowed	126	10.9
50 - 65	268	23.3	Divorced	72	6.3
> 65	321	27.9	Separated	14	1.2
Average: 51.16	Min: 18	Max: 98	Never married or registered partnership	212	18.4
Total	1,152	100.0	**Total**	1,152	100.0
Gender			**Education level**		
Male	506	43.9	Pre-primary education or none education	106	9.2
Female	646	56.1	Primary education or first stage of basic education	540	46.9
Total	1,152	100	Lower secondary or second stage of basic education	191	16.6
Residence			(Upper) secondary education	195	16.9
North	453	39.3	First stage of tertiary education	106	9.2
Algarve	30	2.6	Second stage of tertiary education	2	1.0
Center	292	25.3	No response	2	0.20
Lisbon	236	20.5	**Total**	1,152	100.0
Alentejo	141	12.2	**Employment status**		
Total	1,152	100.0	Employed	565	49.0

Income Year			Self employed	31	2.7
< € 6,000	118	10.2	Military Service	1	0.1
€ 6,000 to < € 12,000	169	14.7	Retired/pensioned	337	29.3
€ 12,000 to < € 18,000	93	8.1	Housewife	65	5.6
€ 18,000 to < € 36,000	98	8.5	Student	40	3.5
€ 36,000 to < € 60,000	65	5.6	Unemployed	93	8.1
€ 60,000 to < € 120,000	48	4.2	Disabled	10	0.9
€ 120,000 or <	15	1.3	Other	5	0.4
No response	546	47.4	No response	5	0.4
Total	1,152	100.0	**Total**	1,152	100.0

Results

Factor analysis results

Using the Kaiser-Meyer-Olkin test, sample adequacy for all variables was analyzed. A sample adequacy overall value of 0.869 was obtained. It represents a value considered acceptable in the literature for this type of analysis (Hair et al., 2009). The principal component method, with a Varimax rotation was used to extract relevant factors. Only factor loadings greater or equal to 0.50 are displayed. The results of the Bartlett test confirmed the appropriateness of the factor analysis procedure as used. The measure of sample adequacy (MSA) is greater than 0.68 for all variables. Based on the factor analysis procedure, a four-factor solution was extracted. This factor solution explained 60.11 percent of the total variance. The four factors extracted based on this solution are presented in Table 2.

Factor one: trust in public institutions

This factor included individual's assessment of a set of public services like education, police, armed forces, social security, health care system and civil service. It also includes a measure of trust in the parliament and one measure of trust in justice system. The level of people´s trust in the parliament allows us to measure the relationship between the state and its citizens and to analyze trust more closely at the current politico-economic level (Frey and Torgler, 2007). It is closely linked to the way taxpayers feel they are treated by the state (Martinez-Vasquez and Torgler, 2009). The relationship between taxpayers and the parliament can be maintained by positive actions and well-functioning institutions (Martinez-Vasquez and Torgler, 2009). A sustainable tax system is based on a fair tax system and responsive government, achieved with strong connection between tax payments and the supply of public goods (Bird et al., 2006). It was also possible to analyze trust at the constitutional level, e.g., trust in the justice system (Frey and Torgler, 2007). Smith (1992) shows that positive actions by the state are intended to improve taxpayers' attitudes and their commitment to the tax system and lead to compliant behavior. This factor includes the following variables:

i) Level of confidence an individual has in the education system;
ii) Level of confidence an individual has in the police;
iii) Level of confidence an individual has in the armed forces;

Table 2 – Factor Analysis Results

FACTORS	F 1	F 2	F 3	F 4	Comm[1]
(Cronbach's alpha value)	(0.868)	(0.697)	(0.683)	(0.734)	
TPI – TRUST IN PUBLIC INSTITUTIONS					
- Education System	0.702				0.525
- Police	0.738				0.548
- Armed forces	0.584				0.413
- Social Security System	0.728				0.639
- Parliament	0.593				0.597
- Health Care System	0.677				0.600
- Civil Service	0.650				0.607
- Justice System	0.662				0.618
TGD – TRUST IN GOVERNMENT AND DEMOCRACY					
- Political Parties		0.670			0.613
- Confidence in Government		0.748			0.706
- Satisfaction with Democracy		0.741			0.575
- Quality of Government		0.703			0.519
R - RELIGIOSITY					
- Importance of Religion			0.788		0.627
- Church Attendance			0.771		0.608
- Confidence in Church			0.766		0.698
- Religious Orientation			0.729		0.540
PL – POLITICAL PARTICIPATION					
- Importance of Politics				0.792	0.662
- Discuss Politics with Friends				0.805	0.654
- Interest in Politics				0.796	0.673
Eingvalues	5.755	2.605	1.801	1.260	
Percent of total variance	30.290	13.709	9.478	6.633	
Cumulative percent	30. 290	43.999	53.477	60.110	

Note: 1. communalities

iv) Level of confidence an individual has in the social security system;
v) Level of confidence an individual has in the civil service;
vi) Level of confidence an individual has in the health care system;
vii) Level of confidence an individual has in the parliament;
viii) Level of confidence an individual has in the justice system.

Factor two: trust in government and democracy

The measurement of citizens' degree of trust in government and democracy was based on a set of questions related to confidence in government and political parties. Additionally, we also use one question related to individuals' perception of democracy evolution in last years (Torgler, 2005b) and another related to individuals' perception of how the country is being governed (Torgler, 2005b). It is expected that a high level of trust is reflected in a higher level of tax morale. Cummings et al. (2009) use an experimental setting to show that tax morale increases with individual perceptions of good governance. Similarly, individuals who show satisfaction with how democracy has evolved and with the way the country is being governed, have higher levels of tax morale. Institutions that respect the preferences of the citizens will have more support from people than a state that acts as Levianthan (Prinz, 2002). This factor includes the following variables:

i) Level of confidence an individual has in political parties;
ii) Level of confidence an individual has in the government;
iii) Level of satisfaction an individual has with how democracy developed Portugal over the last years;
iv) Individuals' perception of how Portugal is being governed.

Factor three: religiosity

Religiosity has been identified as a potential factor that positively affects tax morale (Torgler, 2006). It has been used as a proxy to analyze the impact of standards imposed by non-governmental organizations or the impact of values that promote compliance and punish non-compliance (Torgler, 2007). Main measures of religiosity used are church attendance, religious education, being an active member of a church or a religious organization, perceived religiosity, religious guidance and trust in the church (Torgler, 2006). EVS data allow us to explore religiosity with four variables:

i) Level of importance an individual states that religion has on her/his life;
ii) Frequency of attending religious services, not counting weddings, funerals and christenings;
iii) Level of confidence an individual has in church;
iv) Individuals' perception of being a "religious person", "not a religious person" or a "convicted atheist".

Factor four: political participation

Based on Torgler and Valev (2010) we included indicators of political interest and participation. A higher political participation and interest is linked to an increase on levels of tax morale. This factor included the following variables:

i) Importance of politics in a citizens' life;
ii) Frequency of political matters discussion with friends;
iii) Individuals' interest on politics.

Over the years, empirical research has systematically stressed the importance of socio-demographic variables in the understanding of tax morale (Torgler and Murphy, 2004; Torgler and Schneider, 2005; Torgler, 2006; Barone e Mocetti, 2011; Lubian and Zarri, 2011) and tax compliance. However, for some variables the empirical results found were not always consistent (for education level see Torgler e Schneider, 2007; for income level see Torgler, 2004). Using EVS data we extracted information regarding to age, gender, marital status, education level, employment status and yearly income.

Based on the analysis of variance (ANOVA) procedure, and the Tukey's HSD test with p set at 0.05 all socio-demographic characteristics were significantly different across religiosity and political participation dimensions. For income level, we also found significant differences on the trust in public institutions, trust in government and democracy and political participation dimensions. It was not possible to apply analysis of variance procedure on gender and employment status variables. The results are displayed in Table 3.

Table 3: Significant differences revealed by ANOVA tests

			Sum of Squares	df	Mean Square	F	Sig.
Age	Religiosity	Between Groups	61.888	3	20.629	29.422	.000*
		Within Groups	804.924	1148	.701		
		Total	866.812	1151			
	Political participation	Between Groups	14.329	3	4.776	10.850	.000*
		Within Groups	505.371	1148	.440		
		Total	519.701	1151			
Education	Trust in government and democracy	Between Groups	13.198	5	2.640	3.734	.002*
		Within Groups	808.736	1144	.707		
		Total	821.935	1149			
	Religiosity	Between Groups	61.888	3	20.629	29.422	.000*
		Within Groups	804.924	1148	.701		
		Total	866.812	1151			
	Political participation	Between Groups	14.329	3	4.776	10.850	.000*
		Within Groups	505.371	1148	.440		
		Total	519.701	1151			
Marital Status	Religiosity	Between Groups	48.527	4	12.132	17.005	.000*
		Within Groups	818.285	1147	.713		
		Total	866.812	1151			
	Political participation	Between Groups	11.072	4	2.768	6.242	.000*
		Within Groups	508.628	1147	.443		

			Sum of Squares	df	Mean Square	F	Sig.
Age	Religiosity	Between Groups	61.888	3	20.629	29.422	.000*
		Within Groups	804.924	1148	.701		
		Total	866.812	1151			
	Political participation	Between Groups	14.329	3	4.776	10.850	.000*
		Within Groups	505.371	1148	.440		
		Total	519.701	1151			
Income	Trust in public institutions	Between Groups	12.171	11	1.106	3.740	.000*
		Within Groups	175.753	594	.296		
		Total	187.924	605			
	Trust in government and democracy	Between Groups	28.104	11	2.555	3.916	.000*
		Within Groups	387.565	594	.652		
		Total	415.669	605			
	Political participation	Between Groups	30.533	11	2.776	6.804	.000*
		Within Groups	242.320	594	.408		
		Total	272.853	605			

We found significant differences among means for age on religiosity (F = 29.422, p < .001) and political participation (F = 10.850, p < .001) dimensions. No differences in age were observed on trust in public institutions (F = 1.602, p = .187) and trust in government and democracy (F = 1.184, p = .314) dimensions. Both dimensions did not differ with respondent age. Concerning to religiosity dimension, Tukey's HSD test showed the existence of significant differences between the means of individual's age up to 29 years and citizens with more than 50 years old. A significant difference between means was also found in individuals older than 65 years and youngers. Regarding to the political participation dimension, we found significant difference between citizens with age up to 49 years and citizens with more than 65 years old. Probably these results can be explained by a higher willingness to obey rules and a higher political interest associated to older people.

Concerning to education, we found significant differences among means on religiosity (F = 29.422, p < .001) and political participation (F = 10.850, p < .001) dimensions. No differences in education were observed on trust in public institutions (F = .249, p = .940) and trust in government and democracy (F = 3.734, p = .002) dimensions. In religiosity and political participation dimensions, this difference in means was visible between citizens with first stage of tertiary education or more, and the citizens with up to primary education or first stage of basic education.

Significant difference among means for marital status was found on religiosity (F = 17.005, p < .001) and political participation (F = 6.242, p < .001) dimensions. No differences in marital status were observed on trust in public institutions (F = 1.441, p = .218) and trust in government and democracy (F = 1.736, p = .140) dimensions. Regarding religiosity, the Tukey's HSD test reveal a clear difference between means on widowed and citizens with other marital status. Another difference is significant for "never married" or "registered partnership" citizens. Regarding to political participation, a difference was found between widowed, divorced and separated people and the others.

Based on the analysis of variance (ANOVA) procedure and the Tukey's HSD test significant difference among means for income level was found on all tax morale dimensions, except for religiosity. In trust in public institutions (F = 3.740, p < .001) and trust in government and democracy (F = 3.916, p < .001) dimensions there are clear differences between the citizens with very low income (less than € 3,600.00) and the ones with a very high income level (more than € 120,000.00). Regarding to political participation (F = 6.804, p < .001) dimension there are clear differences between the individuals with less than € 12,000.00 and with more than € 12,000.00.

Conclusions

A significant number of empirical studies about tax behavior explanation have been accumulated over the last 40 years. Results of econometric methods applied to survey data or to laboratory experiments or to a combination of both, induced a significant advance in tax compliance understanding. Still, there are major gaps to be clarified (Alm, 2012).

We conducted a briefly review over recent empirical literature about taxpayers behavior and observed that compliance cannot be truly understood without the consideration of behavioral and psychological variables, namely of tax morale. The intrinsic motivation to pay taxes can be the key to provide an explanation about taxpayer's behavior over the years and in different countries, to explain tax evasion levels and the level of underground economy.

Using data from EVS (2010) regarding to Portugal, we conduct a factor analysis with the purpose of identifying tax morale dimensions. Our results indicate that taxpayer's tax morale has religiosity, trust in government and democracy, trust in public institutions and political participation dimensions. It seems that an improvement in quality of public services, a better relationship between taxpayers and public authorities can promote tax morale and taxpayers compliance.

Our results are line up with Alm and Torgler's (2006, p. 243) statement that "a sustainable tax system is based on a fair tax system and responsive government, achieved with a strong connection between tax payments and the supply of public goods. If taxpayers perceive that their preferences are adequately represented and they are supplied with public goods, their identification with the state increases, and thus the willingness to pay taxes rises".

References

Allingham, M.G. and A. Sandmo 1972, "Income tax evasion: A theoretical analysis", *Journal of Public Economics* 1: 323-338

Alm, J. 2012, "Measuring, explaining, and controlling tax evasion: lessons from theory, experiments, and field studies", *International Tax Public Finance*, 19: 54-77

Alm, J., G. McClelland and W. Schulze 1992, "Why do people pay taxes?", *Journal of Public Economics* 48: 21-38

Alm, J., J. Martinez-Vazquez and B. Torgler 2006, "The evolution of tax morale in Russia in the 90s", *National Tax Association Papers and Proceedings, Conference 2005*, 287-292

Alm, J. and B. Torgler 2006, "Culture differences and tax morale in the United States and in Europe", *Journal of Economic Psychology* 27(2): 224-246

Andreoni, J., B. Erard and J. Feinstein 1998, "Tax compliance", *Journal of Economic Literature* XXXVI: 818-860

Barone, G. and S. Mocetti 2011, "Tax morale and public spending inefficiency", *Public Finance*, 18: 724-749

Bird, R., J.Martinez-Vazquez and B. Torgler (2006), "Societal institutions and tax effort in developing countries", in J. Alm, J. Martinez-Vazquez, & M. Rider (Eds.), *The challenges of tax reform in the global economy* (pp. 283–338). New York: Springer

Clotfelter, C.T. 1983, "Tax Evasion and Tax Rates: An Analysis of Individual Returns", *Review of Economics and Statistics* 65: 363-373.

Cummings, R. G., J. Martinez-Vazquez, M. McKeec, B. Torglerd 2009, "Tax morale affects tax compliance: Evidence from surveys and an artefactual field experiment", *Journal of Economic Behaviour & Organization* 70: 447-457

Devos, K. 2008, "Tax Evasion Behavior and Demographic Factors: An Exploratory Study in Australia", *Revenue Law Journal* 18(1): 1-43

Erard, B. and J.S. Feinstein 1994, "The role of moral sentiments and audit perceptions in tax compliance", *Public Finance* 49: 70-89

Eriksen K. and L. Fallan 1996, "Tax Knowledge and Attitudes Towards Taxation: A Report on a Quasi-experiment", *Journal of Economic Psychology* 17: 387-402

EVS 2010, *European Values Study 2008*: France (EVS 2008). GESIS Data Archive, Cologne. ZA4751 Data File Version 2.0.0, doi:10.4232/1.10198

Feinstein, J. 1991. An Econometric Analysis of Income Tax Evasion and its Detection. *Journal of Economics* 22: 14-35

Feld, L.P. and B. Frey 2002, "Trust breeds trust: How taxpayers are treated", *Economics of Governance* 3: 87-99

Fortin, B., G. Lacroix, and M. Villeval 2007, "Tax evasion and social interactions", *Journal of Public Economics* 91: 2089–2112

Frey, B. 2003. "Deterrence and tax morale in the European Union" *European Review* 11(3): 385-406

Frey, B. and B. Torgler 2007, "Tax morale and conditional cooperation", *Journal of Comparative Economics* 35: 136–159

Güth, W., V. Levati, and R. Sausgruber 2005, "Tax morale and (de)centralization: An experimental study", *Public Choice* 125: 171-188

Hair, J., W. Black, B. Babin and R. Anderson 2009, *Multivariate Data Analysis* (7th ed.). Prentice Hall, New Jersey

Hardin, R. 1988, *Morality within the Limits of Reason,* University of Chicago Press, Chicago

Jackson, B. and V. Milliron 1986, "Tax Compliance research: Findings, problems and prospects", *Journal of Accounting Literature* 5: 125-166

Kim, S. 2008, "Does political intention affect tax evasion?", *Journal of Policy Modeling* 30: 401-415

Lago-Peñas, I. and S. Lago-Peñas 2010, "The determinants of tax morale in comparative perspective: evidence from European Countries", *European Journal of Political Economy* 26: 441-453

Levi, M. 1988, *Rules and Revenue.* University of California Press, Berkeley

Lewis, A. 1982, *The psychology of taxation.* Oxford, England

Lubian, D. and Zarri 2011, "Happiness and tax morale: An empirical analysis", *Journal of Economic Behavior & Organization* 80: 223-243

Martinez-Vazquez, J. and B. Torgler 2009, "The Evolution of Tax Morale in Modern Spain", *Journal of Economic Issues* 43(1): 1-28

Molero, J. and F. Pujol 2012, "Walking Inside the Potential Tax Evader's Mind: Tax Morale Does Matter", *Journal of Business Ethics*, 105 (2):151-162

Prinz, A. 2002, "A moral theory of tax evasion", Westfälische Wilhelms-Universität Münster, Unpublished paper

Riahi-Belkaoiu, A. 2004, "Relationship between tax compliance internationally and selected determinants of tax morale", *Journal of International Accounting, Auditing and Taxation* 13: 135–143

Richardson, G. 2006, "Determinants of tax evasion: A cross-country investigation", *Journal of International Accounting, Auditing and Taxation* 15: 150-169

Schmölders, G. 1960, *Das Irrationale in der öffentlichen Finanzwissenschaft.* Rowolt, Hamburg

Smith, K. 1992. Reciprocity and fairness: Positive incentives for tax compliance" In J.Slenrod (Ed), *Why people pay taxes – Tax Compliance and enforcement*, 223-258. Ann Arbor, MI: University of Michigan Press

Song, Y. and T. Yarbrough 1978, "Tax Ethics and taxpayer attitudes: A survey", *Public Administration Review* 38: 442-452

Strümpel, B. 1969, "The contribution of survey research to public finance", in A. T. Peacock (Ed.), *Quantitative analysis in public finance*, 13-38. New York: Praeger

Tittle, C. 1980, *Sanctions and social deviance: The question of deterrence.* Praeger, New York

Torgler, B. 2007, *Tax Compliance and Tax Morale: A Theoretical and Empirical Analysis*, Edward Elgar, Cheltenham, UK

Torgler, B., F. Schneider and C. Schaltegger 2009, "Local autonomy, tax morale, and the shadow economy", *Public Choice* 144: 293-321

Torgler, B. 2003, "Tax Morale, Rule-Governed Behaviour and Trust", *Behaviour* 119-140

—. 2004, "Moral suasion: An alternative tax policy strategy? Evidence from a controlled field experiment in Switzerland", *Economics of Governance* 5: 235–253

—. 2005a, "Tax morale and direct democracy", *European Journal of Political Economy* 21: 525-531

—. 2005b, "Tax morale in Latin America", *Public Choice* 122: 133-157

—. 2006, "The importance of faith: Tax morale and religiosity", *Journal of Economic Behaviour & Organization* 61: 81-109

Torgler, B., I. Demir, A. Macintyre and M. Schaffner 2008, "Causes and Consequences of Tax Morale: An Empirical Investigation", *Economic Analysis & Policy* 38: 313-340

Torgler, B. and K. Murphy 2004, "Tax morale in Australia: What shapes it and has it changed over time?", *Journal of Australian Taxation* 7(2): 298-335

Torgler, B. and N.T. Valev 2010, "Gender and Public attitudes toward corruption and tax evasion", *Journal of Australian Taxation* 28: 554-568.

Torgler, B. and F. Schneider 2005, "Attitudes Towards Paying Taxes in Austria: An Empirical Analysis", *Empirica* 32: 231-250

Torgler, B. and F. Schneider 2007, "What shapes attitudes toward paying taxes? Evidence from multicultural European countries", *Social Science Quarterly* 88: 443-470

Torgler, B. and F. Schneider 2009, "The impact of tax morale and institutional quality on the shadow economy", *Journal of Economic Psychology*, 30: 228-245

Tyler, T. 2000, "Why do people cooperate in groups?", In Van Vugt, M., Snyder, M., T.R. Tyler, A. Biel, (Eds.), *Cooperation in Modern Society. Promoting the Welfare of Communities, States and Organizations*. Routledge, London, 65–82

Weck, H. 1983, "Schattenwirtschaft: Eine Möglichkeit zur Einschränkung der öffentlichen Verwaltung? Eine ökonomische Analyse", *Finanzwissenschaftliche Schriften*, 22. Bern: Lang

Yitzhaki, S. 1974, "A note on 'Income tax evasion: A theoretical analysis", *Journal of Public Economics* 3: 201-202

CHAPTER SIX

COUNTERFEIT OF LUXURY BRANDS

NEUZA SILVA AND AURORA A.C. TEIXEIRA

Introduction

> "Counterfeiting will become the crime of the 21st century." (James Moody, former chief, FBI Organized Crime Division, International Anti-Counterfeiting Coalition, 2008)

The size of the luxury market has been growing exponentially in the last two decades insofar as the purchasing behaviour of consumers is becoming more symbolic. Research into marketing acknowledges the symbolic role of possessions in the life of consumers (Solomon, 1983; Rucker, 2009; Han et al., 2010). It is widely accepted that people draw inferences about others based on what they own (Solomon, 1983; Rucker, 2009; Han et al., 2010). Luxury goods or status goods have been defined as goods which, merely by being used or displaying a particular brand, bestow prestige on the owner, regardless of any functional usefulness (Grossman and Shapiro, 1988; Nia and Zaikowsky, 2000). Indeed, Nia and Zaikowsky (2000) believe that consumers acquire luxury goods to set themselves apart from others and express their personality.

The main purpose of brands is to distinguish between rival goods, and they generally create expectations regarding the quality and features of an item, and so they are an important information tool that consumers use to assess different products. In addition, brand choice can send symbolic social signals to other consumers about the kind of person who uses the brand (Han et al., 2010). The inappropriate use of a brand compromises and destroys its value for producers and consumers.

Brand equity has been the focus of significant academic attention since the 1990s. This is partly because of changes in international accounting standards with respect to intangible assets, including brands (Eagle et al., 2003). While most academic works on this topic have centred on definitions of brand equity and its quantification, attention has been turning to the nature of the value and factors that might threaten it (Eagle et al., 2003). And one factor that could affect brand equity is, of course, counterfeiting.

In 2008 luxury goods accounted for 175 billion US dollars in all retail sales (Truong and McColl, 2011). But it is not just the number of people buying luxury goods that is growing, so, too, is the number of those buying counterfeit goods. So the production, distribution and consumption of counterfeit goods have been growing at an alarming rate, and most investigations and lawsuits concern luxury goods (Norum and Cuno, 2011). Counterfeiting is a world-wide phenomenon that has been around for a number of years in all markets, but the problem particularly affects trademarked goods esteemed and appreciated by a large majority of consumers. This phenomenon is a violation of intellectual property rights, aggravated by the fact that the offenders keep up with the latest technology and global market trends. Currently the offenders use the same means of production as those used on the legal market, which enables them to improve both the quality and quantity of their goods. As industries have globalized their production and distribution operations counterfeiting has become easier and affects a full range of industries world-wide, that is, the consumption of counterfeit goods has grown in scope and magnitude.

According to the International Chamber of Commerce (ICC),[1] counterfeiting accounts for from 5% to 7% of the world trade and is worth nearly 600 billion US dollars a year. A new ICC report, published in February 2011, indicates that the overall social and economic impacts of counterfeiting and piracy will reach 1.7 trillion dollars in 2015, threatening 2.5 million jobs annually. The World Customs Organization,[2] meanwhile, has said that whether due to increasing incidence or to higher detection rates, the number of arrests in the European context has risen tenfold in the last 10 years. *The Economic Impact of Counterfeiting and Piracy*, a study by the OECD published in 2007, notes that there has been an alarming expansion in the kinds of counterfeit goods in recent years, from luxury articles to articles with an impact on personal health and safety. This study also sheds light on the various consequences of counterfeiting: 1) general socio-economic effects (on innovation and growth, criminal activities, the environment, employment, foreign direct investment and trade); 2) effects on rights holders (on turnover and prices, brand equity and corporate reputation, royalties, corporate investment, costs and scope of operations); 3) effects on consumers (health and safety risks), and effects on governments (tax revenues, expenses and corruption).

This study sets out to further research on the impact of counterfeiting on luxury brands. In this context it is of fundamental importance to the management of luxury brands and, more directly, to controlling the impact of counterfeiting on financial results and brand equity, that the factors determining the buying behaviour of consumers of counterfeit luxury goods should be examined, and this is the basis of the empirical research. It is essential to understand why consumers buy counterfeit goods so that the most appropriate preventive measures - legal, policy, administrative and management - can be adopted (Eisend and Schubert-Güler, 2006). Academics have in fact been interested in analyzing the effectiveness of preventive measures (Grossman and Shapiro 1988; Green and Smith, 2002). In the last few years researchers have started to pay more heed to the demand side of the counterfeit market, though most studies are still limited to the context of consumer electronics and samples of Asian (Carpenter and Lear, 2011) or American students (Eisend and Schubert-Güler, 2006), and the results have been inconclusive (Bian and Veloutsou, 2007).

We undertook a quantitative causal analysis based on the collection of primary source indicators via a direct survey of 31,043 students from Portugal's largest university. The survey was designed to gather information on the scale (relative to consumers and goods) which, according to the literature on the area, determines the intention to buy counterfeit brands of luxury goods.

The chapter is organized as follows. The next section explains certain key concepts such as 'luxury', 'luxury marketing' and 'counterfeit', followed by a literature review that pinpoints the main research contributions in these areas, particularly in the determinants of intention to buy counterfeit goods. Section 3 sets out the method used for the empirical study and describes the data collection and processing. The analysis of the data and empirical results is presented in Section 4, and the conclusions complete the chapter.

Literature review

Concepts of luxury and counterfeit

'Luxury' is derived from the Latin *luxus*, meaning indulgence of the senses regardless of cost (Nueno and Quelch, 1998). Luxury or status goods have been defined as those whose mere use or display of a particular brand assigns a cost to it. Luxury brands are those in which the ratio of functional utility and price is low while the ratio of intangible and situational utility to price is high prestige for the owner, irrespective of any functional utility (Grossman and Shapiro, 1988; Nia and Zaikowsky,

2000). Indeed, Nia and Zaikowsky (2000) believe that consumers acquire luxury goods to set themselves apart from others and express their personality. For Kapferer and Bastien (2009) effectively building and managing a luxury brand implies recognizing the fundamental principles of what luxury is and its role in modern societies. We can thus identify three functions of luxury: to recreate the social gap, to be a distinctive brand and to provide personal satisfaction. In fact the essence of luxury is to recreate social stratification. While aristocracy has been replaced by meritocracy, people still need some form of social stratification to establish their place in society. Furthermore, Kapferer and Bastien (2009) argue that luxury is clearly a social indicator, which justifies the need for brands. Since the DNA of luxury is the symbolic desire to belong to a higher class, anything that can have social significance can become a luxury. In the same way, everything that loses social significance loses the status of luxury. Finally, in addition to the social function, the luxury component must have a personal and hedonistic, otherwise it would not be luxury but merely snobbery. Referring specifically to the concept of luxury brand, Nueno and Quelch (1998) argue that this is not merely a premium price product, an ephemeral status symbol or a smart investment. These authors believe that luxury brands share these characteristics: 1) Premium quality in all the goods from the line, 2) Creator legacy, often coming from the original designer, 3) Recognized design and style; 4) Limited production to ensure exclusivity and possibly to generate a waiting list; 5) Marketing programme which, through limited distribution and premium pricing, supports a market position that combines emotional appeal with product excellence; 6) Global reputation; 7) Association with a country of origin that has a particularly strong reputation as a source of excellence in the product category in question; 8) An element of uniqueness in each product; 9) Ability to schedule design changes when the category is based on fashion, and 10) Personality and values of its creator.

Lai and Zaichkowsky (1999) see counterfeit goods as illegal replicas that resemble the genuine goods (which typically include high-value brands) but which are generally cheaper and of lower quality in terms of performance, reliability and durability. A product that uses the name or logo of a trademark without the authorization of the registered owner is a counterfeit or imitation (Lear and Carpenter, 2011). Cordell et al. (1996) define counterfeits as reproductions of a trademark identical or very similar to the genuine articles. Pirated goods, meanwhile, are exact copies of the original and typically limited to technology categories such as software, movies and music (Phau and Teah, 2009). Another distinction can be made in relation to other forms of attack on intellectual property, such as grey market products. The latter are, by definition, surplus originating from subcontracted manufacturers and distributed through unofficial channels, while counterfeiting is an illegally produced copy of an original article (Phau and Teah, 2009).

From a consumer perspective, counterfeiting can be 'deceptive' or 'not deceptive' (Grossman and Shapiro, 1988). The first happens when the consumer does not know that the product they are buying is a counterfeit, as in the case of automotive components, electronics and drugs (Grossman and Shapiro, 1988). In other categories, the consumer usually knows he/she is buying counterfeits (Wilcox et al., 2009). The OECD study, *The Economic Impact of Counterfeiting and Piracy*, follows the same classification, dividing the consumer of counterfeit goods into 2 types: those who unwittingly buy counterfeit or pirated goods, thinking they are buying genuine products; those who knowingly purchase counterfeit or pirated goods that are worth less.

This latter form of counterfeiting is particularly prevalent in the markets for luxury brands (Nia and Zaichkowsky, 2000), in which the consumer can usually distinguish counterfeits from genuine brands based on price differences, distribution channels and product quality (Wilcox et al. 2,009).

According Phau and Teah (2009), consumers are more inclined to purchase counterfeit goods with a fashion-linked component, as in the case of luxury goods. Indeed, the counterfeiting of luxury brands of fashion products is particularly fierce, with clothing, handbags, wallets, watches and pens being some of the many items copied. Most consumers of authentic luxury brands value the brand, the prestige and the benefits of the image but they may be reluctant to pay a high price (Phau et al., 2009).

Counterfeits let consumers enjoy the status, as well as the visual attributes and quality of a luxury product by paying less to acquire status and not having to pay for quality (Grossman and Shapiro, 1988; Cordell et al., 1996; Ang et al. 2001).

It is also considered that consumers prefer counterfeits of a really distinguished brand that imparts some meaning to them (Cordell et al., 1996). This bolsters the idea that only the very recognizable brands are produced illegally (Eisend and Schubert-Güler, 2006). Indeed, a somewhat perverse indicator of the power of attraction of a luxury brand is the volume of counterfeits on sale on world markets (Nueno and Quelch, 1998). In the absence of other criteria for evaluating the attractiveness of the brand, copying is an indicator of value: 'Imitation is the best form of flattery' (Hilton et al., 2004). Bian and Veloutsou (2007) believe that, given the structure of the word 'economy', it is naive to say with certainty that what is counterfeit is totally bad. These authors think that counterfeiting is a sign that the brand is a hit. Only strong, highly recognized brands that are respected and loved will be the target of counterfeiting.

But this is also one of the biggest problems that companies producing luxury goods face in a globalized market (Hilton et al., 2004). Hilton et al. (2004) argue that the problem lies with the industry. Copying designs is endemic and condoned, which raises ethical dilemmas in judging the practice of counterfeiting.

As illustrated by several reports in the press, the problem of counterfeiting is comprehensive, growing and global. As industries have globalized their production and distribution operations, counterfeiting has become easier and is a problem that affects all companies worldwide (Hilton et al., 2004).

The catalytic growth of counterfeiting can be ascribed to the growth of world trade and the emergence of new markets, not to mention the rapid advances in technology and the increase of products of interest to counterfeiters (Wee et al., 1995; Phau and Teah, 2009).

Luxury brands are easily counterfeited, since they are easy to sell and involve low production costs (Phau and Teah, 2009). In addition, consumer demand is increasing due to the demand for articles of status and desire to be in tune with fashion (and Eisend Schuchbert-Güler, 2006; Phau and Teah, 2009).

Factors determining the intention to purchase counterfeit luxury brands

Theoretical framework

In the last few years researchers have started to pay more heed to the demand side of the counterfeit market, though most studies are still limited to the context of consumer electronics and samples of Asian (Carpenter and Lear, 2011) or American students (Eisend and Schubert-Güler, 2006). As culture has been regarded by researchers as an important factor influencing the purchase of software, pirated music and movies, it is expected to have the same influence on purchases of counterfeits (Eisend and Schubert-Güler, 2006), and so a specific study on the situation in Portugal is of fundamental importance. In addition, the results of existing studies have proved inconclusive (Bian and Veloutsou, 2007).

Some studies focus solely on demographic variables (Bian and Veloutsou, 2007; Carpenter and Lear, 2011, for example), others look at personality variables (You and Lee, 2009; Wilcox et al., 2009, for example) but none can sketch a complete profile of consumers of counterfeit luxury brands. In this study we detail the different determinants identified by the authors who have worked on research on counterfeit luxury brands to give us a more global view of the factors affecting intended demand for these products.

We have divided these determinants into two areas: the 'consumer area' and the 'product area' (see Figure 1).

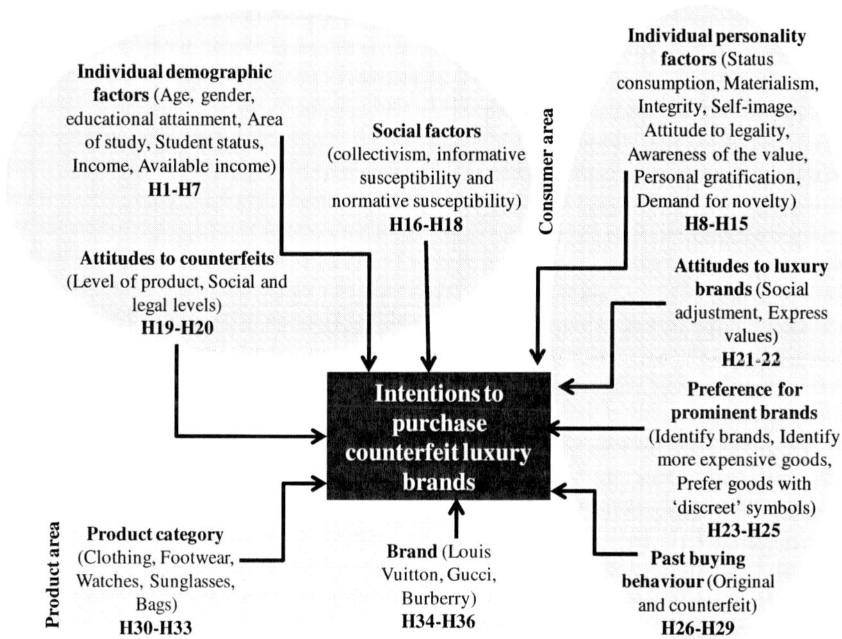

Figure 1: Theoretical framework. *Source*: Authors

Within the 'consumer area' we assess how individual demographic factors, individual personality factors, social factors, attitudes to counterfeits, attitudes to luxury brands and a preference for relatively prominent brands may have influenced past purchases of, and could influence the intention to buy counterfeit luxury brands. Moreover, we examine how actual past purchases of (buying behaviour) original and counterfeit luxury brands may influence intentions to purchase counterfeit luxury brands.

Hypotheses to be tested

Regarding the characteristics of the consumers, the evidence in studies about counterfeits demonstrates that individual demographic factors (gender, age, educational attainment and income) may influence attitudes to counterfeits and therefore to the purchase of counterfeit luxury brands. Some studies consider that these factors are not effective in distinguishing between the profile of consumers of original and counterfeit brands (Bian and Veloutsou 2007), while others consider that these factors do have an influence but a somewhat inconsistent one (Wee et al., 1995; Bian and Veloutsou 2007; Phau et al, 2009).

Veloutsou and Bian (2007) analyzed age so as to outline the demographic profile of consumers of counterfeit brands in the UK and China. They concluded that age has an influence on purchasing intention in the UK but not in China, and in Britain the young are the most receptive. Age is also considered as a control variable in studies of Carpenter and Lear (2011) and Phau and Teah (2009), for example.

H1: Younger people tend to have more intention to buy counterfeit luxury brands

Research suggests that gender is related to the intention to purchase counterfeits, with most studies reporting that men are more likely to do so (Ang. et al., 2001, Carpenter and Lear, 2011). Carpenter and Lear (2011) assessed the effect of gender on the precursors of purchase intention by looking at the effect of gender on specific precursors (attitudes to social costs, ethics and anti-big companies) of intention to purchase counterfeit luxury fashion brands. They concluded that, apparently, with regard to fashion products women have fewer concerns about the ethics of counterfeit goods, and there is no gender based difference in relation to attitudes to social costs and anti-large companies. The cross-cultural study by Bian and Veloutsou (2007) on sunglasses suggests that, with regard to the UK sample, men are more likely to buy counterfeit sunglasses for their own use and as gifts.

However, Carpenter and Lear (2011) believe that, in general, the attitudes to counterfeits are the same for men and women, except when it comes to ethics, and so gender is not a very influential determinant in counterfeiting. So, in line with the literature, we suppose that:

H2: Men tend to have more intention to buy counterfeit luxury brands

Veloutsou and Bian (2007) conclude that, for the sample studied (523 individuals randomly selected in shopping areas), educational level has a limited influence on the intention to purchase counterfeit luxury brands, although it appears that better educated people more readily admit to being likely to purchase counterfeit brands. The study by Chapa et al. (2006) shows that consumers with higher educational levels are less inclined to buy counterfeits. Some researchers believe that by being better informed about global issues, people will be less likely to put their interests above others and buy counterfeits.

H3: People with higher levels of education tend to have less intention to buy counterfeit luxury brands

According to Roeser (2006), people from different vocational areas tend to have distinct individual inclinations and personality traits. In addition, the courses will result in professions with different social statuses in society in general and Portuguese society in particular. Some studies in the area of academic integrity, notably the one by Teixeira and Rocha (2010 a,b), estimated that the magnitude of copying in examinations by students of management and economics is worrying, reaching figures of around 62% in Portugal. If we assume that buying counterfeit goods concerns the same ethical principles, it is important to inquire whether students in that area will be more likely to buy such articles.

H4: Students from the areas of economics and management tend to have more intention to buy counterfeit luxury brands

Teixeira and Rocha (2010 a,b) found that there is no statistically significant difference between students with the status of Student Union Officer and Working Students relative to students with the status 'normal'. Therefore, we assume that the status will not have any influence in the context of counterfeiting either.

H5: The status of students has no influence on the intention to buy counterfeit luxury brands

The success of counterfeit luxury brands is primarily down to the price advantages that these products offer over genuine products (Phau et al. 2009).

Indeed, consumers often buy counterfeit goods to take advantage of the benefits of brand image and prestige without paying for them (Grossman and Shapiro, 1988; Cordell et al., 1996; Carpenter and Lear, 2011).

Although (disposable) income is not regarded as crucial for studies directly related to the question of intention to purchase/purchase of counterfeit luxury products, some authors consider income as a control variable, for example Phau and Teah (2009), Han et al. (2010), Carpenter and Lear (2011). Indeed, in the study by Han et al. (2010) on brand prominence, consumers are placed into 4 groups according to their economic resources and need for status; the authors use this classification to explain consumer choice for more or less prominent brands and for counterfeits. The group that Han et al. (2010) describe as *'poseurs'* (which is French for "someone who pretends to be what they are not") are highly motivated to consume for reasons of status and, as they do not have the financial means to acquire authentic luxury goods, they are particularly motivated to buy counterfeit luxury goods as cheap substitutes for the originals.

However, other studies indicate that although at first glance it seems that counterfeit products are purchased mainly for their low price, which would be especially attractive to low-income consumers, they are also actually purchased by consumers with higher incomes (Eisend and Schubert-Güler, 2006).

H6: People with a higher income tend to have less intention to buy counterfeit luxury brands

Given that luxury goods are non-essential goods, the question of the amount available for purchases after paying all essential expenses proved important and therefore the amount available was also considered in this study.

H7: People with a higher disposable income tend to have less intention to buy counterfeit luxury brands

Social and personality precursors have long been recognized as influencing decision-making in relation to consumer intention to purchase (Phau and Teah, 2009). In terms of individual personality, status consumption, materialism and integrity are the most often-recurring factors mentioned in the literature on counterfeit luxury brands. Apart from these, some authors also consider awareness of the value, demand for novelty, personal gratification, the attitude to legality and self-image.

The consumption of status is defined as the motivational process by which an individual strives to manage to improve their social status through the explicit consumption of products that project this image (Phau et al. 2009), i.e., we are looking at the purchase, use, consumption and display of products and services as a means of acquiring status (Phau and Teah, 2009).

The demand for products that confer status at low prices has encouraged the growth of counterfeiting (Phau et al., 2009). Phau et al. (2009) studied the influence of this personality factor on the attitude to the legality of counterfeit brands and willingness to knowingly purchase counterfeit luxury brands. The results, based on a convenience sample of (202) management students at a large Australian university, demonstrate that the consumption of status does not influence the attitude to the legality of counterfeit luxury brands but it does negatively influence attitudes to the legality of purchasing counterfeit luxury brands. Nevertheless, in the study Phau et al. (2009) conclude that the consumption of status is not a determining factor in intention to buy.

Phau and Teah (2009) start out by assuming that the consumption of status negatively influences attitudes towards counterfeits. The study shows that, for a sample of 202 customers of a shopping mall in Shanghai (China), this assumption was not confirmed for the "perceptions of counterfeits" (from the standpoint of product quality) since the relationship between the consumption of status and "perceptions of counterfeits" is positive not negative, but a negative relationship with respect to attitudes towards "social consequences" was effectively confirmed.

With respect to the intention to purchase, the Phau and Teah (2009) study shows a positive relationship, i.e., consumers who buy based on status are more likely to purchase counterfeits of luxury brand goods. This is, moreover, the most significant factor in this study regarding intention to buy. Phau et al. (2009) did not identify a significant relationship between consumption of status vis-à-vis the intention to purchase, that is, in this case the negative attitude found with respect to the legality of counterfeits is not reflected in buying behaviour, which contradicts the study by Barnett, 2005, which shows that the consumption of status is a significant determinant of intention to purchase counterfeits of luxury items.

> *H8: People with a higher consumption of status tend to have more intention to buy counterfeit luxury brands*

Materialism is the importance consumers attach to worldly possessions (Belk, 1985, cit in Phau et al., 2009). According to Ritchins and Dawson (1992), materialists put their possessions and their acquisition at the centre of their lives and regard them as essential to their satisfaction and wellbeing. Materialists tend to consume in abundance, and favour status products (Wong, 1997, cit. in Phau et al. 2009).

Though they take the assumption that materialism has a positive influence on the attitude towards legality and intention to purchase counterfeit luxury brands as their starting point, Phau et al. (2009) conclude that this factor influences neither the attitude to nor the intention to purchase counterfeit luxury brands.

According to Yoo and Lee (2009), based on a sample of female students at an university in South Korea, the main goal of materialists is to impress others. From this point of view, materialism can positively affect the attitude and intention to purchase, either original brands or counterfeits, since both respond to consumer vanity through the prestigious image that they convey. Despite significant differences in quality, both products (originals and counterfeits) offer a similar look, which satisfies the materialistic mind.

H9: More materialistic people tend to have more intention to buy counterfeit luxury brands

Basic values such as integrity will influence people's judgment with respect to the acceptance of unethical activities (Steenhaut and van Kenhove, 2006 cit. in Phau et al., 2009 and Phau and Teah, 2009). Integrity is determined by personal ethical standards and obedience to the law.

If integrity is seen by consumers as fundamental, the likelihood of them seeing counterfeits of luxury brands in a positive way will be much smaller (Ang et al., 2001 cit. in Phau and Teah, 2009).

Phau and Teah (2009) start out by assuming that integrity negatively influences attitudes towards counterfeits of luxury brands. The study shows that there is no significant relationship with respect to the "perceptions of counterfeits" (from the standpoint of product quality) but a negative relationship regarding attitudes to "social consequences" is effectively confirmed. Phau et al. (2009), too, conclude that integrity has a negative influence on the attitude towards the legality of counterfeits, i.e., consumers who believe the values of honesty, upbringing and responsibility are important, are more likely to have looked unfavourably on the legality of counterfeit luxury brands.

With respect to the intention to purchase, the Phau and Teah (2009) study shows a negative relationship, i.e., consumers with high standards of integrity are less likely to purchase counterfeits of luxury brand goods.

The study by Phau et al. (2009) did not identify any significant relationship at the level of intention to purchase.

> *H10: People of higher integrity tend to have less intention to buy counterfeit luxury brands*

We also consider self-image within the personality factors, as referenced by Yoo and Lee (2009). These authors considered that consumers buy products that fit their self-image and to impress others. Thus, Yoo and Lee (2009) suggest that a high self-image positively affects the intention to purchase originals, because they convey an image of affluence and social class consistent with a high self-image (Wee et al., 1995).

> *H11: People with a high self-image tend to have less intention to buy counterfeit luxury brands*

The attitude to legality is the ultimate determinant in the context of personality factors.

Research shows that consumers who are more worried about legality have unfavourable attitudes regarding counterfeits and are less likely to purchase them (Cordell et al., 1996; Phau et al., 2009).

> *H12: People who are more concerned about legality tend to have less intention to buy counterfeit luxury brands*

Phau and Teah (2009) consider that awareness of the value might positively influence consumer attitude to counterfeiting, since counterfeits of luxury brands afford the same functional benefits as the original brands, at a fraction of the price. Indeed, most consumers of luxury brands seek genuine value associated with the brand, prestige and image benefits but may not be willing to pay a high price for them (Phau and Teah, 2009). Thus, individuals who care about the value of things and about the cost/benefit relation are more likely to buy counterfeits).

The study by Phau and Teah (2009) shows no significant relationship in terms of "perception of counterfeits" (relative to quality) and reveals a negative influence in terms of "social consequences".

Regarding intention to purchase, the study shows a positive relationship, that is, consumers who are highly value-conscious tend to have more intention to purchase counterfeits of luxury brands.

H13: People who are more value-conscious tend to have more intention to buy counterfeit luxury brands

Personal gratification is the need for achievement, social recognition and also the desire to enjoy the finer things in life (Ang et al., 2001; Phau and Teah, 2009).

Consumers with a high need for personal gratification tend to be more aware of the appearance and visibility of fashion products and are probably less likely to accept inferior quality goods, so they will appreciate the genuine version of luxury products (Phau and Teah 2009).

Phau and Teah (2009) therefore start out by assuming that personal gratification has negative effects on attitudes towards counterfeits of luxury brands. The study shows that there is no significant relationship with respect to the "perceptions of counterfeits" (from the standpoint of product quality) but a negative relationship regarding attitudes to "social consequences" is effectively confirmed. Nor did this study find any significant relationship of this variable with the intention to buy counterfeits of luxury brands.

H14: People with a high need for personal gratification tend to have less intention to buy counterfeit luxury brands

The quest for innovation is the curiosity that leads individuals to seek variety and difference (Phau and Teah, 2009).

As with the value-consciousness, Phau and Teah (2009) proposed that demand for novelty might positively influence the consumer attitude relative to counterfeiting, in this case not directly through price but because it facilitates experimentation, thereby reducing buying risk. However, the results show that it the influence is negative.

At the level of intention to purchase counterfeit luxury brands, Phau and Teah (2009) found no significant relationship.

H15: People who are keener on novelty tend to have less intention to buy counterfeit luxury brands

Social influence is related to the effect that others have on individual consumer behavior (Ang et al., 2001; Phau and Teah, 2009).

The social factors class included collectivism, informative susceptibility and normative susceptibility. Yoo and Lee (2009), Bian and Veloutsou, 2007), Phau and Teah (2009) and Phau et al. (2009) are some of the authors who have studied the influence of individual personality and social factors on the issue of counterfeits.

Collectivism was analyzed by Phau and Teah (2009) for its hypothetical positive influence on consumer attitudes to counterfeiting (following earlier studies by Ang at al., 2001), but the study did not reveal any significant relationship, either in terms attitudes or in terms of intention to purchase counterfeit luxury brands, so apparently it has no influence at these levels.

H16: Collectivism has no influence on the intention to buy counterfeit luxury brands

Two common forms of consumer susceptibility to social influences are informative susceptibility and normative susceptibility (Phau and Teah, 2009).

Normative susceptibility is related to the decision to buy based on expectations of what will impress others (Ang et al., 2001; Phau and Teah, 2009). In this case, self-image plays a key role and the bad impression that may be caused by buying counterfeit goods could mean, even in this case, that the consumer's attitude in relation to counterfeits is unfavourable. However, with regard to attitudes to counterfeits, the results of Phau and Teah (2009) show that normative susceptibility has a positive influence on "perceptions of counterfeits" (not negative, as the authors hypothesized) but does not have any significant relationship within "social consequences".

With respect to the intention to purchase, too, the Phau and Teah (2009) study shows a negative relationship, i.e., consumers with normative susceptibility are more likely to purchase counterfeits of luxury brands. This means that although consumers may have a need for luxury products to impress others, they end up (also) buying counterfeits because of the price of the original brands.

H17: People with a high normative susceptibility tend to have more intention to buy counterfeit luxury brands

Informative susceptibility relates to the purchase decision being based on the opinion of others (Ang et al., 2001; Phau and Teah, 2009). So if their peers or reference groups have a thorough understanding of the difference between originals and forgeries (especially in terms of product quality), the possible negative consequences of knowing that the consumer bought a counterfeit means the latter has a negative attitude to the counterfeits of luxury brands (Phau and Teah, 2009). This hypothesis is validated by the Phau and Teah (2009) study at the level of "perceptions of counterfeits" but not at the level of "social consequences".

With respect to the intention to purchase, the study shows a negative relationship, i.e., consumers with high informative susceptibility are less likely to purchase counterfeits of luxury brand goods.

> *H18: People with high informative susceptibility tend to have less intention to buy counterfeit luxury brands*

Several studies (Yoo and Lee, 2009; Phau and Teah, 2009; Phau et al., 2009, for example) consider the attitudes towards counterfeit goods as a determinant that affects the intention to purchase luxury brands and their corresponding counterfeits. Carpenter and Lear (2011) also considered attitudes to forgeries, specifically the attitudes to ethics, to social costs and anti-big business as precursors of intention to purchase counterfeit fashion products.

The moral assessment goes into action when the individual is faced with an ethical dilemma. Consumer choices are often influenced by behaviours held to be appropriate and consequently approved by standards, while others are considered inappropriate and therefore prohibited (Phau et al., 2009). The willingness to knowingly purchase counterfeit luxury brands is attributed to the class of non-normative consumer behaviours (Cordell et al., 1996).

Attitudes to an action, i.e., the degree to which a person favourably assesses certain behaviour favourably, positively affect behavioural intentions, according to the theory of planned behaviour (You and Lee, 2009). Thus, it is expected that positive attitudes to buying counterfeit goods positively affect the intention to buy counterfeits and vice versa. Phau and Teah (2009) also suggest that the more favourable the attitude in relation to counterfeiting the greater the likelihood of the consumer buying counterfeit brands. This assumption is based on the theory of planned behaviour, which states that the buying behaviour is determined by the intention to purchase, which in turn is determined by the attitudes (Phau and Teah, 2009).

To determine consumer attitudes, four main dimensions have been considered useful, namely, quality, economics, ethics and legality (Cordell et al., 1996; Ang et al., 2001; Phau et al., 2009). Of these, price, as the economic factor, has come to be regarded as having influence on shaping attitudes to counterfeit products (Phau et al., 2009). The low financial risks are an added benefit for consumers buying counterfeit products (Phau and

Teah, 2009). Among the biggest reasons behind the purchase of counterfeit articles are economic benefits (You and Lee, 2009).

We consider that attitudes towards counterfeit goods are of 2 types: product related, and socio-economic costs, ethics and legality related.

From the standpoint of product attributes (quality, reliability / durability, functionality), Phau et al. (2009) consider that consumer perception influences the intentions to purchase counterfeit luxury brands. In general, it has been found that if the perceived attributes of the genuine product are similar to the counterfeit product in terms of quality, the intention to buy the counterfeit product will be greater (Wee et al., 1995; Phau and Teah, 2009).

Phau and Teah (2009) conclude that buyers and non-buyers of counterfeits have different attitudes to the perception of counterfeit goods at the level of product attributes, and buyers believe that counterfeits are of similar quality, durability/reliability and functionality to the original items. Thus, in this study it is ascertained that buyers of counterfeits have more positive attitudes to counterfeits with respect to these parameters.

> *H19: People with positive attitudes to counterfeit products (quality, price, meeting needs, status) tend to have more intention to buy counterfeit luxury brands*

Regarding the socio-economic costs, ethics and legality, research suggests that consumers tend to select counterfeit goods without considering the public welfare (Cordell et al. 1996, Carpenter and Lear, 2011), although this may be due to lack of awareness (Carpenter and Lear, 2011).

While some research indicates that consumers worried about legality tend to have less favourable attitudes in relation to counterfeiting and are consequently less likely to purchase counterfeits (Cordell et al., 1996, Kim et al., 2009; Carpenter and Lear, 2011), other work suggests that the mere attitude towards the legality of counterfeit luxury brands and the legality of purchase are not valid indicators of an intention to buy (Phau et al., 2009; Carpenter and Lear, 2011). It is also claimed that consumers draw a clear distinction between legal and counterfeited goods, since almost a third of those who admit to buying counterfeits also admit to buying original brand products (Rutter and Bryce, 2008; Carpenter and Lear, 2011). Some researchers suggest that many consumers are willing to abandon their values in exchange for a cheaper price (Carpenter and Lear, 2011), including counterfeit products (Carpenter and Lear, 2011).

Phau et al. (2009) studied the effect of attitude to the legality of counterfeits on behaviour with respect to counterfeits and expected that strong convictions about the legality of counterfeits would adversely affect the consumer's willingness to knowingly purchase counterfeit luxury brands. Citing Wee et al. (1995), Phau et al. (2009) expected that the more favourable the attitude of the consumer to counterfeiting, the more likely they are to buy counterfeit luxury brands, insofar as attitudes can be considered valid factors in the prediction of intention. However, the study findings show that attitudes do not have a significant influence on intention to purchase, which may be explained by the fact that consumers think that in the general scheme of things, counterfeiting is not a major crime, when compared with other illegal acts.

Furthermore, Phau and Teah (2009) conclude that there is a significant difference between buyers and non-buyers of counterfeit articles, and both buyers and non-buyers agree that counterfeiting is a violation of intellectual property, is illegal and undermines the original manufacturers.

> *H20: The attitude to ethics/legality and the social costs of counterfeits has no influence on the intention to buy counterfeit luxury brands*

Given that the market for counterfeit brands lies in the desire of consumers for authentic luxury brands (Penz and Stottinger, 2008 a and b), then knowing the reason why consumers buy luxury brands is also very relevant to understanding the reasons behind the purchase of counterfeit brands.

Wilcox and Kim (2009) argue, based on a survey of university students, that social motivations are at the root of the propensity of individuals to consume counterfeit brands. More specifically, Wilcox and Kim (2009), based on functional theories of attitudes (Smith et al. 1956; Katz, 1960; Shavitt, 1989), show that consumers' desire for counterfeit brands and the extent to which the availability of these counterfeits alters their preference for genuine brands, are determined by the social functions underpinning their attitudes to luxury brands. Of these social functions, Wilcox and Kim (2009) emphasize self-expression (expression of values) and self-presentation (social adjustment), the first of which aims to help people communicate their beliefs, attitudes and values to others, while the second contributes to social approval.

Wilcox and Kim (2009) applied this theory to the context of luxury brands and counterfeiting and argue that the reasons behind the consumption of counterfeit lie in the social motives underlying attitudes towards luxury brands, which may be the expression of values or social adjustment. Basically, the functions served by attitudes towards one particular object (luxury brands) can influence the preference for another (counterfeit). The attitude toward luxury brands is, in itself, a determinant of attitude, and consequently of behaviour in relation to counterfeit luxury brands).

Wilcox and Kim (2009) suggest that the probability of consumers purchasing counterfeit luxury brands is greater when their attitudes to luxury brands have a social adjustment function than when their function is to express values, which is expressed in the hypotheses below.

> *H21: People whose attitudes to luxury brands serve to express values tend to have less intention to buy counterfeit luxury brands*

> *H22: People whose attitudes to luxury brands have the function of social adjustment tend to have more intention to buy counterfeit luxury brands*

Han et al. (2010), consider the prominence of the brand to be a factor to consider when analysing the preference for counterfeit luxury brands.

Based on the concept of 'brand prominence' (the extent to which a product displays clear symbols that ensure brand recognition), Han et al. (2010) propose a taxonomy that classifies consumers into 4 groups according to their economic resources and need for status. They demonstrate how the preference for relatively prominent luxury brands predictably corresponds to their desire to be associated or not associated with members of their group and other groups (social motives). Han et al. (2010) argue that consumers with high incomes and who do not need status want to be associated with members of their group and pay a premium price for 'discreet' products that only group members would recognize. Conversely, consumers with plenty of financial resources and a high need for status use 'showy' luxury products to flag their difference compared with the less affluent. Those who have a high need for status but do not have the purchasing power to buy authentic luxury goods choose 'flashy' counterfeits to be more like those they recognize as being affluent. In addition, Wee et al. (1995) argue that if status is important for a person but inaccessible, that person will be likely to purchase counterfeit products instead of the original.

This group of consumers who prefer products with 'discreet' symbols are also those who can identify the brands in the absence of their logos/symbols, and those who identify the most expensive products.

H23: People who identify brands (in the absence of their logos/symbols) tend to have less intention to buy counterfeit luxury brands

H24: People who identify more expensive goods tend to have less intention to buy counterfeit luxury brands

H25: People who prefer goods with 'discreet' symbols tend to have less intention to buy counterfeit luxury brands

Yoo and Lee (2009) consider the past behaviour (past purchases of counterfeits and originals) as a determinant that affects the intention to purchase luxury fashion brands and their corresponding forgeries.

Past behaviour is seen as a more significant predictor of later behaviour than the effects of intentions and perceptions of behavioural control (Yoo and Lee, 2009). If the circumstances are stable, past behaviour forms a habit and subsequent behaviour will depend more on past behaviour than cognitive considerations (Yoo and Lee, 2009).

Thus, past purchases of counterfeit goods is supposed to result in an intention to purchase counterfeit products, while past purchases of original products is supposed to result in an intention to buy original products (Yoo and Lee, 2009).

H26: People who bought/received original goods tend to have less intention to buy counterfeit luxury brands

H27: People who bought/received counterfeit goods tend to have more intention to buy counterfeit luxury brands

At the same time, it is important to consider to what extent the frequency of these purchases influences the (intention) purchase:

H28: People who often bought/received original luxury brands tend to have less intention to buy counterfeit luxury brands

H29: People who often bought/received counterfeit luxury brands tend to have more intention to buy counterfeit luxury brands

An important group of determinants to consider in the intention to purchase and past purchases of original luxury and counterfeit brands is that of product/brand characteristics, that is, on the one hand the product category and, on the other, the brand in question.

The propensity to buy counterfeit goods can vary according to product category (Rutter and Bryce, 2008; Carpenter and Lear, 2011), and presumably also depending on the brand (Eisend and Schubert-Güler, 2006).

According to the report *Counterfeiting Luxury: Exposing the Myths*[3] (Ledbury Research, 2007), within the luxury products, the categories most forged are clothing and footwear, followed by watches. Yoo and Lee (2009), also report that these categories have the most forgeries.

Based on the arguments above, we put the following hypothesis to be tested:

> *H30: People who bought/received original brands of clothing or footwear will tend to have more intention to buy counterfeit luxury brands*

> *H31: People who bought/received original brands of watches tend to have more intention to buy counterfeit luxury brands*

> *H32: People who bought/received original brands of sunglasses tend to have more intention to buy counterfeit luxury brands*

> *H33: People who bought/received original brands of bags tend to have more intention to buy counterfeit luxury brands*

Also thanks to the report *Counterfeiting Luxury: Exposing the Myths*, we know that the three most counterfeited brands in 2007 were Louis Vuitton, Gucci and Burberry. These brands are also identified in the study by Yoo and Lee (2009) as often being the target of such counterfeiting.

We can therefore put the following hypotheses:

> *H34: People who bought/received original brand Burberry products tend to have more intention to buy counterfeit luxury brands*

> *H35: People who bought/received original brand Louis Vuitton products tend to have more intention to buy counterfeit luxury brands*

H36: People who bought/received original brand Gucci products tend to have more intention to buy counterfeit luxury brands

Methodological considerations

Based on the literature review, we identified a set of variables that potentially explain the demand for counterfeit luxury brands, namely: 1) demographic factors; 2) personality factors; 3) social factors; 4) attitudes towards counterfeits; 5) attitudes towards luxury brands; 6) prominence of the brand; 7) purchasing behaviour; 8) product category, and 9) brand acquired. The first seven configure the consumer area and the last two the product area. We developed a set of questions/statements in the questionnaire to operationalize these determinants.

Existing studies indicate that past purchases and the product category(ies) and brand(s) purchased may influence the intention to purchase counterfeit luxury brands. Thus, the first and second parts of the questionnaire were devoted to the buying behaviour relative to luxury brands (7) and the product category and brand (8 and 9). The first part of the questionnaire identified purchasing/receiving, frequency of purchase/receipt, the purchase intention of luxury brands in the future, as well as the product category(ies) and original luxury brand(s) that the respondent purchased and/or received. In the second part the same issues were raised in relation to counterfeit luxury brands.

The variables relating to the purchase (original and counterfeit brands) were normalized by assigning a value of 1 to positive responses and 0 to the others. The variables relating to the intention to purchase luxury brands (originals and counterfeits) are the result of assigning the value 1 to the responses ‘I would certainly buy’ and ‘I would probably buy’ (the other replies, ‘I would probably not buy’, ‘I would certainly not buy’ and ‘I don’t know’ were assigned the value 0).

For the answer to questions about the frequency of purchase/receipt (original and counterfeit) a five-point scale was used (‘weekly’, ‘monthly’, ‘annually’, ‘at least once a month’, ‘never’). The variables 'Frequent Purchase/Receipt of original products’ and 'Frequent Purchase/Receipt of counterfeit products' were obtained by assigning 1 to respondents who answered 'Weekly' and 'Monthly'.

As earlier described, the product category purchased by consumers may influence the likelihood of them purchasing luxury brands. Therefore, we assign the value 1 to responses that identified the purchase or receipt of the product categories we considered in the questionnaire. The variables obtained, 'Buying/Receiving clothing/footwear', 'Purchasing/Receiving watches', 'Purchasing/Receiving sunglasses' and 'Purchasing/Receiving bags' were normalized by taking the value 1 if the respondent had purchased or received product categories in question.

Moreover, the brand acquired may also be a determining factor in the propensity of the consumer to purchase counterfeit luxury brands in the future. The most counterfeited brands are Burberry, Louis Vuitton and Gucci and so we assigned the value 1 to responses that identified the purchase or receipt of these brands. The values obtained, 'Buy/Receive original Burberry brand', 'Buy/Receive original Louis Vuitton brand' or 'Buy/Receive original Gucci brand' were normalized assuming the value 1 if the respondent had acquired or received the said brands.

Attitudes to forgeries (4) and to luxury brands (5) were included in the third and fourth parts of the questionnaire, respectively, where the respondent was asked to classify various items on a scale of 1 (strongly disagree) to 7 (fully agree).

Regarding attitudes to forgeries (4) we considered attitudes to the product on the one hand and attitudes to socio-economic costs and to the ethics/legality of counterfeits, on the other. The evidence shows that the more favourable their attitude to forgeries the more likely people are to acquire them. We thus assigned the value 1 to each attitude/behaviour of the respondent that agrees (degree of agreement of 6 or 7)[4] with the statements about counterfeits. The variable obtained ('attitude to the product') was subsequently normalized, taking the value 1 if the respondent has agreed to at least 3 of the 4 statements that reflect a favourable attitude to counterfeit products. The same method was adopted for the variables 'attitude to socio-economic costs, ethics/legality', and in the case of this last variable the value 1 is taken if the respondent has agreed to at least 5 of the 7 statements.

Regarding attitudes towards luxury brands, the literature reviewed shows that people who use luxury products with the goal of expressing values tend to buy original luxury brands. But people using luxury brands for the social adjustment function are more likely to purchase counterfeit luxury brands, compared with the previous group. In the case of luxury brands, we analyzed the determinants 'social adjustment' and 'expression of values'. We assigned the value 1 to each attitude/behaviour of the respondent that agrees (degree of agreement of 6 or 7) with the statement. The variable obtained ('expression of values' or 'social adjustment') was subsequently standardized, taking the value 1 if the respondent has agreed in part, or with a higher degree of agreement in at least 3 of the 4 statements that reflect an attitude consistent with the expression of values or social adjustment.

The fifth part of the questionnaire deals with assessment of brand prominence (6) through the variables 'identifying marks', 'identification of more expensive products' and 'preference for products with "discreet" symbols'. The authors of this theory, Han et al. (2010), considered that consumers who prefer products with 'discreet' logos/symbols prefer original luxury brands as opposed to those who prefer 'flashy' logos/symbols, who tend to feel more attracted to counterfeit marks than the first group.

These authors also say that consumers who prefer products with 'discreet' trademarks/symbols manage to recognize the brand and the price of a luxury product, regardless of the presence of symbols. Those who prefer 'showy' brands/symbols do not recognize brands in these circumstances and tend to consider that the most expensive product is the one with the more obvious logo/symbol.

Therefore, a value of 1 was assigned to respondents who correctly recognized at least 2 of the 3 brands. The same procedure was adopted for those who correctly identified at least two of the three products costing more and preferred at least 2 of the 3 products with more 'discreet' symbols.

The sixth part of the questionnaire covers the individual determinants of personality and society, namely: consumption of status, materialism, integrity, self-image, attitude to legality, value awareness, novelty seeking, personal gratification, collectivism (group spirit), normative susceptibility and informative susceptibility.

Although several authors (e.g., Phau et al., 2009, and Yoo and Lee, 2009) have included variables of this nature, no author has covered all of these variables in their study. On the whole, according to the literature, the variables that positively influence the intention to purchase/purchase of counterfeit products are consumption of status and materialism, the other negatively influence it.

For the statistical treatment of the data, we assigned the value 1 to each attitude/behaviour of the respondent who agrees (level of agreement of 6 or 7) with the statements about the respective variable. The values obtained were then normalized, taking the value 1 if the respondent has agreed to with at least 2 of the 3 statements used to assess the variables integrity and personal gratification, 1 of the 2 statements about consumption of status, materialism,[5] novelty seeking and informative susceptibility, and 1 of 1 statement used for value awareness, attitude to legality, collectivism and normative susceptibility.

The self-image was assessed based on a semantic scale and we assigned the value 1 to each attribute with a rating of 6 or 7. The variable 'self-image' obtained was subsequently normalized, taking the value 1 if the respondent has rated their self-image with 6 or 7 for at least 6 of the 11 attributes.

The last part of the questionnaire concerned the individual demographic variables: gender, age, income, money available for non-essential purchases, educational level (qualifications), areas of study/courses and student status.

According to the literature review, men, younger people, with lower disposable income and less money available value are more likely to purchase counterfeits. Furthermore, studies on academic fraud showed that students in the area of economics and management are more prone to fraud and presumably also to purchase counterfeit goods.

In terms of operationalization, the value 1 was assigned to female respondents. The age variable has a continuous distribution.

Household income was divided into 4 value scales such as the monthly cash available for spending (on non-essential goods). Under household income we have: 'low income' ('less than 250 euros' and '251-500 euros'=1); ‘medium income' (‘501 to 1000 euros’ and 'from 1001 to 1500 euros'=1); 'high income' ('1501 to 2500 euros' and 'more than 2500 euros'=1), and ‘don’t know income' (those who have not indicated any amount).

Monthly disposable cash was divided into: low ('up to 50 euros'=1); medium (‘51 to 100 euros’ and '101 to 250 euros'=1); high ('251 to 500 euros’ and 'more than 500 euros'=1) and ‘don’t know monthly amount’ (those not indicating any amount).

In terms of qualifications we considered three groups: first degree, master’s and related ('master', 'postgraduate' and 'MBA' = 1) and PhD.

The variables relating to faculties were normalized as follows: Law (‘Fac. of Law'= 1), Economics and Management ('Fac. Economics', Porto School of Management=1); Science and Technology ('Fac. Engineering' and ‘Fac. Sciences'=1); Medicine and Pharmacy ('Fac. Medicine', 'Fac. Pharmacy', 'Fac. of Dentistry', 'Fac. of Nutrition and Food Science' and 'Abel Salazar Institute of Biomedical Sciences'=1); Psychology and Arts ('Fac. Psychology and Educational Sciences' and 'Faculty of Arts’=1); and the Arts and Sport ('Fac. Sports', 'Fac. Architecture', 'Fac. Fine Arts'=1).

In terms of student status we should mention the ‘working students’ (=1 and 0 for others) and ‘student union officers’ (= 1 and 0 for others), and ‘regular/normal status students' are the default class.

The link to the questionnaire was sent to all 31,043 students of the University of Porto (target population of our study), via e-mail, at the address pmlc@fep.up.pt, created solely for the research. The University of Porto was selected as a case study for the sake of convenience (i.e., ease of contact) and because it embraces a large number of students and wide variety of courses, 26. The questionnaire was produced in Limesurvey software with the features described above and placed online on April 15, 2012.[6] The inquiry was closed on 10 May 2012, with a total of 1824 valid responses.

To gauge the demand for counterfeit luxury brands we considered two demand areas: 1) Intention to purchase counterfeit luxury brands, and 2) Purchase of counterfeit luxury brands. For each of these dimensions we transformed the variable into a dummy variable: consumers who bought or intend to buy counterfeit luxury brands take the value 1 (0 otherwise).

The binary nature of the variable to be explained/dependent variable ('intention to purchase/purchase of counterfeit luxury brands': 1 - Yes; 0 - No) restricts the choice of estimation model and, in this case, the logistic regression is presented as the regression technique suitable for modelling the occurrence (Maroco, 2010). Thus, the analysis of this study will be conducted in the context of the general framework of probabilistic models. In the logistic regression model, the parameters are estimated using the maximum likelihood method.

The overall average rate of response was 7%, with the highest response rate provided by the Faculty of Nutrition and Food Sciences with 18%, followed by the Faculty of Psychology and Educational Sciences with 12%. We generally consider that the sample is representative of the population, as regards the actual weight of the faculties in the population.

Empirical results

The University of Porto students who comprise our sample (1824) are predominantly female (69.9%), are around 23 years old and mostly taking first degrees, with the emphasis on the areas of medicine and pharmacy (21.4%) and psychology and arts (21.2%). Most have the status 'normal/regular' and have an average individual monthly income (46.8% of respondents) and low disposable cash (48.1% of respondents).

In terms of personality traits, the overwhelming majority, 87.1%, are considered to be people of integrity, they care about the cost/benefit relation of their purchases (79.8%) and value personal fulfilment/ satisfaction (68.2%). Team spirit (collectivism) and the opinion of others (informative susceptibility) are also important to the respondents.

In terms of attitudes towards counterfeits, the percentage having a favourable attitude is quite low, that is, consumers do not value the counterfeits from the standpoint of product characteristics (only 1.9% have a favourable attitude) nor do they agree with the social cost of this economic trade, and they recognize the illegality of this practice (only 2.9% are indifferent to the costs of counterfeiting).

Regarding attitudes to luxury brands, although the percentage is not very significant (2.5%), we can see that the students choose a luxury article for the sake of social adjustment, of belonging to the group, and not really to express their personality.

Most do not identify the marks unless the logo is there (only 14.8% can identify it without the logo), but a significant percentage, 40.3%, identified the more expensive brands and prefer products with 'discreet' symbols (51.4%).

Comparing the intention to buy original luxury products with the actual purchase of these products, we found that the percentages are similar, 55.2 and 56.1%, respectively. However, the difference between intention and purchase of counterfeit luxury brands (dependent variables) is remarkable, 53.0 and 37.5%, respectively.

Finally, if we look at the profile of the purchase, we found that for both original brands and counterfeit brands the clothing and footwear category is the most sought. There is very little agreement on Burberry, Gucci and Louis Vuitton within the sample and they were reported by about 2% of respondents.

The estimatcs of thc coefficients associated with each potential determinant of the intention to purchase/purchase of counterfeit luxury brands are shown in Table 1. The quality adjustment is quite acceptable, as evidenced by the quality indicators of adjustment, the percentage of observations of the dependent variables correctly estimated is high (between 63.2% and 92.5%) and the Hosmer-Lameshow test has a significance level greater than 0.10, reflecting that the null hypothesis that the model(s) represent reality is accepted.

Five specifications were considered: the A model includes only demographic, social and personality factors; the B model includes, in addition to the A model factors, attitudes (to counterfeits, and to luxury brands) and the variables related to brand prominence; the C model considers, in addition to the B model variables, purchases and frequency of purchase; the D model adds the intention to purchase original luxury brands to the variables of the C model; the E model includes the B model variables and the variables of the product area (this last model does not include variables of buying behaviour, which would trigger a full model with all possible variables, because there is a very strong correlation between some of these variables and product category variables).

In addition, people with more integrity seem to have a more positive purchase relation with the intention to buy, although this correlation may not be significant. However, this relationship is negatively and statistically significant in the case of purchases, that is, people with more integrity tend to buy fewer counterfeit luxury goods.

On analyzing the role of different groups of determinants in explaining the intention to purchase counterfeit luxury brands, we found that demographic factors are quite relevant. Indeed, we find that, all else being equal, younger men (in line with what was reported by Bian and Veloutsou, 2007) on economics or management courses and with high income and medium monthly cash are the people who tend, on average, to denote more intention to purchase counterfeit luxury brands. In contrast, students in the areas of the arts and sport as well as students with less available cash tend to have less intention to purchase counterfeit luxury brands.

Personality traits are found to be quite relevant in explaining the intention to purchase counterfeit luxury brands. People who buy certain products because these may confer status (consumption of status), those who have a strong need for personal satisfaction/fulfilment (personal gratification), who like to be up to the mark in fashion and buy the latest novelties (novelty seeking) and who have a high self-image are the ones showing more intention to purchase. From the point of view of consumption of status, these indicators confirm the study by Phau and Teah (2009), where it is the most significant factor with respect to intention to purchase. However, the variables 'personal gratification' and 'novelty seeking' are found to oppose the direction of the conclusions of these authors. Even within the personality factors, this study shows that the higher people's conviction that they must obey the law (attitude to legality), the lower their 'intention' to purchase.

In terms of social factors, no variable appears to significantly affect purchase intention. In terms of attitudes to counterfeits, only the favourable attitude to counterfeits from the standpoint that the product favourably influences both purchase intent.

'Social adjustment' proves to be a decisive factor in intention to purchase counterfeit luxury brands, as indicated by Wilcox and Kim (2009). Indeed, people who purchase luxury brands in order to achieve social approval tend to be more inclined to buy imitations and not originals.

In the sample in question, and regarding the prominence of the brand, only ‘identification of brands’ influences the intention to purchase counterfeit luxury brands. Indeed, people who can identify the make of the product in the absence of the logo are also those who express more intention to purchase counterfeits (Models B and C). It should be noted that according to the theory of Han et al. (2010), this influence would be negative rather than positive.

When considering the purchase behaviour variables, especially past purchases, we found that both the past purchases (purchase/receipt) of original luxury brands and past purchases of counterfeit luxury brands very significantly influence the intention to buy counterfeit luxury brands. This means, first, that those who purchased counterfeit luxury brands in the past were not disappointed with the product and intend to continue to buy it in future. Likewise, the fact of having acquired and having the intention to purchase original luxury brands does not exclude the possibility of acquiring (intention) and the fact of having acquired (actual purchase) counterfeit luxury brands, rather the contrary. We also found that consumers who bought original luxury brands most often (once a week or once a month) are also those with more intention to buy counterfeit luxury brands. It is noteworthy that the 'intention to purchase original luxury brands' is related to the 'intention to purchase counterfeit luxury brands' to such an extent that most of the other variables in the Model D lose significance.

Looking at the product area, we found that individuals who purchase or receive product categories of original clothing/footwear, sunglasses and bags are those who feel more tempted to buy counterfeits. As for past purchases, people who bought original clothing/footwear, watches and bags were the ones who bought more counterfeits. Thus, we can see that the product category may influence the intention to buy counterfeits. The brand bought is not seen as a determinant in the 'intention to purchase' counterfeit luxury brands.

Conclusions

The growth of the luxury market has been accompanied by the growth of counterfeit luxury goods. Clearly, counterfeiting is a complex phenomenon and one that can be characterized as a serious problem; it has even been considered to be the crime of the century (Bian and Veloutsou, 2007). The dynamics observed in terms of the growing number of publications on the subject, as well as the growing interest on the part of state authorities and business associations, are a reflection of this reality.

Table 1: Factors determining the intention to purchase counterfeit luxury brands (logistic estimates)

				A	B	C	D	E
Consumer area	**Individual - demographic factors**	Age (ln)		-1.14***	-1.159***	-1.134***	-1.171**	-1.305***
		Gender (Female=1)		-0.364***	-0.340***	-0.352***	-0.141	-0.438***
		Education (Master=1)		0.076	0.072	0.088	0.082	0.092
		Study area (default: Science and Technology	Law	0.183	0.202	0.161	0.437	0,055
			Medicine & Pharmacy	0.051	0.041	0.052	-0.041	0,003
			Economics & Management	0.354**	0.341**	0.361**	0.347	0,343**
			Psychology & Humanities	0.041	0.006	0.024	0.414	0,010
			Arts & Sports	-0.530**	-0.536**	-0.636***	0.189	-0,589***
		Student status (Default: Normal)	Part-time	-0.269	-0.242	-0.251	-0.185	-0,280
			Association member	0.407	0.435	0.466	-0.462	0,311
		Income (default: Medium)	Low	-0.059	-0.056	0.001	0.115	0,022
			High	0.370**	0.357**	0.267*	0.404	0,259
			Does not know	-0.126	-0.136	-0.175	-0.445	-0,177

	Available income (default: Medium)	Low	-0.558***	-0.570***	-0.509***	-0.133	-0,456***
		High	0.552**	0.556**	0.510**	0.325	0,511**
		Does not know	-0.065	-0.058	-0.018	0.396	-0,070
Personality factors	Status consumption		0.892***	0.837***	0.756***	0.607	0.728***
	Materialism		0.021	0.000	0.022	-0.262	0.016
	Integrity		0.046	0.070	0.086	-0.112	0.091
	Self-image		0.260**	0.265**	0.193	0.331	0.210
	Attitude towards legality		-0.180*	-0.206*	-0.175	0.035	-0.211*
	Value awareness		-0.063	-0.094	-0.060	0.167	-0.044
	Personal gratification		0.599***	0.576***	0.566***	0.213	0.528***
	Demand for novelty		0.514***	0.469***	0.396***	0.180	0.391***
Social factors	Collectivism		-0.143	-0.122	-0.130	-0.115	0.120
	Normative susceptibility		0.253	0.174	0.119	-0.117	0.191
	Informative susceptibility		-0.015	-0.022	-0.024	-0.026	-0.042
Attitude towards counterfeits	Favourable attitude – product level		-	0.225	0.212	1.330**	0.260
	Favourable attitude – social/legal levels		-	0.291	0.269	0.713	0.271
Attitude towards luxury products	Value expression		-	0.136	0.200	0.415	0.203
	Social adjustment		-	0.237*	0.197	0.037	0.242*

	Brand proiminence	Identifies brands	-	1.177**	0.965*	0.737	0.811
		Identifies the most expensive products	-	-0.151	-0.123	-0.116	-0.143
		Prefers discreet symbols	-	-0.063	-0.076	-0.318	-0.093
	Buying behaviour	Bought/Received original products	-	-	0.320***	0.065	-
		Bought/Received counterfeit products	-	-	0.359***	0.561***	-
		Intends to buy original products	-	-	-	5.155***	-
		Bought/Received original products often	-	-	1.776***	1.313**	-
		Bought/Received counterfeit products often	-	-	0.682	0.214	-
Product area	**Category of product**	Bought/Received original clothing/footwear	-	-	-	-	0.390***
		Bought/Received original watches	-	-	-	-	0.175
		Bought/Received original sunglasses	-	-	-	-	0.333**
		Bought/Received original bags	-	-	-	-	0.454***
	Brand	Bought/Received original Burberry	-	-	-	-	0.398
		Bought/Received original Louis Vuitton	-	-	-	-	-0.070

Bought/Received original Gucci	-	-	-	-	0.162
Constant	3.644	3.755	3.282	0.423	3.873
Number of cases (N)	**1824**	**1824**	**1824**	**1824**	**1824**
Intends to buy counterfeits	967	967	967	967	967
Others	857	857	857	857	857
Hosmer-Lameshow Test (*p-value*)	7,483 (0,486)	8,766 (0,362)	7,960 (0,437)	6,666 (0,573)	6,825 (0,556)
% corrects	63,2	63,8	65,3	92,5	65,8

Note 1: The grey cells represent statistically significant estimates (i.e., *p-value*<0.10); $^{***}(^{**})[^{*}]$statistically significant at 1%(5%)[10%].

By understanding the characteristics of consumers who favour buying counterfeit luxury brands, those responsible for managing the original luxury brands, the distributors and retailers, as well as the public bodies engaged in combating fraud, can identify how best to communicate with these (potential) consumers how they might instil an ethical stance in the decision-to-buy process.

The combat strategy should focus on people found, in this study, to be more likely to buy counterfeit luxury brands, given their demographic, personality and social characteristics taking into account what they value in a luxury brand and what their attitude is towards counterfeiting as well as the type of product and brands they purchase. One possible approach could be to appeal to ethical values, particularly the harm that counterfeiting does to companies owning the original luxury brands. Since many of these consumers tend to be taking courses in economics or management, they are likely to be sensitive to arguments related to the financial cost for companies. Moreover, as we are dealing with people who rate status and personal fulfilment highly, they always aim to be aware of fashion and have a high self-image, so communication should make the point that being seen wearing a counterfeit luxury brand is not good for a person's reputation. This argument is particularly important because this study also reveals that at the time of purchase these consumers are worried about what other people think and tend to buy luxury products with a view to belonging to a particular group.

Nor should it be forgotten that potential consumers of counterfeit luxury brands have also acquired and intend to again acquire authentic luxury brands. Furthermore, in contrast to the study of Han et al. (2010), these consumers recognize the make of a luxury product, even in the absence of any symbols. Thus, they are not customers to be disregarded since, by this, they demonstrate an understanding of the luxury market and, furthermore, contrary to what might be expected, these consumers are high earners. Manufacturers of brands of clothing and footwear, watches, sunglasses and bags should pay particular attention to the phenomenon of counterfeiting, since consumers of these categories show more inclination to purchase counterfeits. But the manufacturer of Burberry has reason to breathe sigh of relief, as their customers purchase fewer counterfeits than average.

Finally, it is also important to note the characteristics of consumers who tended not buy counterfeit luxury goods. Integrity and a strong belief that the law should be obeyed (and this is a characteristic of the 'intention to purchase'), are the characteristics that best distinguish them, so will be important to emphasize, in the communication that is going to be promoted to combat this threat, that buying counterfeit goods is not a correct and proper behaviour, and indeed it is an illegal transaction.

Acknowledgement

The authors are highly indebt to all students who responded to the survey as well as all the schools' directors and staff from the Marketing and External relations of the University of Porto for the valuable cooperation.

References

Ahmadi, R.; Yang, B.R. (2000), "Parallel imports: Challenges from unauthorized distribution channels", *Marketing Science*, 19 (3): 279-294

Aiello, G.; Donvito, R.; Godey, B.; Pederzoli, D.; Wiedmann, K.P.; Hennigs, N.; Siebels, A.; Chan, P.; Tsuchiya, J.; Rabino, S., Ivanovna, S.I.; Weitz, B.; Oh, H.; Singh, R. (2009), "An international perspective on luxury brand and country-of-origin effect", *Journal of Brand Management*, 16 (5/6): 323–337

Ang, S.H.; Cheng, P.S.; Lim, E.A.C.; Tambyah, S.K. (2001), "Spot the difference: Consumer responses towards counterfeits", *Journal of Consumer Marketing*, 18 (3): 219-233

Atwal, G.; Williams, A. (2009), "Luxury brand marketing - The experience is everything!", *Journal of Brand Management*, 16 (5-6): 338-346

Berthon, P.; Pitt, L.; Parent, M.; Berthon, J. P. (2009), "Aesthetics and ephemerality: Observing and preserving the luxury brand", *California Management Review,* 52 (1): 45-66+3-4

Barnett, J.M. (2005), "Shopping for Gucci on canal street: Reflections on status consumption, intellectual property, and the incentive thesis" *Virginia Law Review,* 91(6): 1381-1423

Beverland, M. (2006), "Branding authenticity in the luxury wine trade", *Journal of Business Research,* 59 (2): 251-258

Beverland, M.; Luxton, S. (2005), "The 'real thing": Managing integrated marketing communication (IMC) through strategic decoupling: How luxury wine firms retain brand leadership while appearing to be wedded to the past", *Journal of Advertising,* 34 (4): 103-116

Beverland, M.B. (2005), "Grafting brand authenticity: The case of luxury wines", *Journal of Management Studies,* 42 (5): 1003-1029

—. (2005), "Managing the design innovation-brand marketing interface: Resolving the tension between artistic creation and commercial imperatives", *Journal of Product Innovation Management,* 22 (2): 193-207

Bian, X.; Veloutsou, C. (2007), "Consumers' attitudes regarding non-deceptive counterfeit brands in the UK and China", *Journal of Brand Management*, 14 (3): 211-222

Brun, A.; Caniato, F.; Caridi, M.; Castelli, C.; Miragliotta, G.; Ronchi, S.; Sianesi, A.; Spina, G. (2008), "Logistics and supply chain management in luxury fashion retail: Empirical investigation of Italian firms", *International Journal of Production Economics,* 114 (2): 554-570

Business Action to Stop Counterfeiting and Piracy (BASCAP) (2011), *Estimating the global economic and social impacts of counterfeiting and piracy, Frontier Economics Ltd*, London

Carpenter, J.M.; Lear, K. (2011), "Consumer attitudes toward counterfeit fashion products: Does gender matter?", *Journal of Textile and Apparel, Technology and Management*, 7 (1): 1-16

Chapa, S.; Minor, M.S.; Maldonado, C. (2006), "Product Category and Origin Effects on Consumer Responses to Counterfeits: Comparing Mexico and the U.S.", *Journal of International Consumer Marketing*, 18(4): 79-99

Chiou, J.S.; Droge, C. (2006), "Service quality, trust, specific asset investment, and expertise: Direct and indirect effects in a satisfaction-loyalty framework", *Journal of the Academy of Marketing Science,* 34 (4): 613-627

Commuri, S. (2009), "The Impact of Counterfeiting on Genuine-Item Consumers' Brand Relationships", *Journal of Marketing*, 73 (3): 86-98

Cordell, V.V.; Wongtada, N.; Kieschnick Jr., R.L. (1996), "Counterfeit purchase intentions: Role of lawfulness attitudes and product traits as determinants", *Journal of Business Research*, 35 (1):. 41-53

Daun, W.; Klinger, R. (2006), "Delivering the message: How premium hotel brands struggle to communicate their value proposition", *International Journal of Contemporary Hospitality Management,* 18 (3): 246-252

Davies, I.A.; Lee, Z.; Ahonkhai, I. (2012), "Do Consumers Care About Ethical-Luxury?", *Journal of Business Ethics*, 106 (1): 37-51

De Matos, C.A.; Ituassu, C.T.; Rossi, C.A.V. (2007), "Consumer attitudes toward counterfeits: A review and extension", *Journal of Consumer Marketing,* 24 (1): 36-47

Dubois, B.; Czellar, S.; Laurent, G. (2005); "Consumer segments based on attitudes toward luxury: Empirical evidence from twenty countries", *Marketing Letters,* 16 (2): 115-128

Eagle, L.: Kitchen, P.J.; Rose, L.; Moyle, B. (2003), "Brand equity and brand vulnerability: The impact of gray marketing/parallel importing on brand equity and values", *European Journal of Marketing*, 37(10): 1332-1349

Eisend, M.; Schuchert-Güler, P. (2006), "Explaining Counterfeit Purchases: A Review and Preview", *Academy of Marketing Science Review*, 06(12): 1-25

Green, R.T.; Smith, T. (2002), "Executive insights: Countering brand counterfeiters", *Journal of International Marketing*, 10 (4) : 89-106

Grossman, G.M.; Shapiro, C. (1988) "Foreign Counterfeiting of Status Goods", *Quarterly Journal of Economics*, 103 (1): 79-100

Hahn, K.H.Y.; Kean, R. (2009), "The influence of self-construals on young Korean consumers' decision-making styles", *Journal of Fashion Marketing and Management,* 13 (1), pp. 6-19

Han, Y.J.; Nunes, J.C.; Drèze, X. (2010), "Signaling *status* with luxury goods: The role of brand prominence", *Journal of Marketing,* 74 (4): 15-30

Hauck, W.E.; Stanforth, N.S. (2007), "Cohort perception of luxury goods and services", *Journal of Fashion Marketing and Management*, 11 (2): 175-188

He, Y.; Zou, D.; Jin, L. (2010), "Exploiting the goldmine: A lifestyle analysis of affluent Chinese consumers", *Journal of Consumer Marketing,* 27 (7): 615-628

Heine, K.; Phan M. (2011), "Trading-up mass-market goods to luxury products", *Australasian Marketing Journal,* 19 (2): 108-114

Hieke, S. (2010), "Effects of counterfeits on the image of luxury brands: An empirical study from the customer perspective", *Journal of Brand Management*, 18 (2) : 159-173

Hilton, B.; Choi, C.J.; Chen, S. (2004), "The ethics of counterfeiting in the fashion industry: Quality, credence and profit issues", *Journal of Business Ethics,* 55 (4): 345-354

Hung, S. (2006), "Play in fashion: Bridging China to the west with a look at Taiwan fashion branding", *Journal of Fashion Marketing and Management,* 10 (4): 479-490

International AntiCounterfeiting Coalition, "Facts on Fakes", in http://4356049642aa3c99a6e91c99180a8219894d6198.gripelements.com/pdf/member-resources/facts_on_fakes.pdf [accessed on 24.09.2012]

International Monetary Fund (2001), "Counterfeit Goods and Income Inequality", in http://www.imf.org/external/pubs/ft/wp/2001/wp0113.pdf [accessed on 24.09.2012]

Kaigler-Walker, K.; Gilbert, Z.L. (2009), "Perception of appearance and use of appearance products among Chinese women", *Journal of Fashion Marketing and Management,* 13 (4): 553-565

Kapferer, J.N.; Bastien, V. (2009), "The specificity of luxury management: Turning marketing upside down", *Journal of Brand Management,* 16 (5-6): 311-322

Keinan, A.; Kivetz, R. (2008), "Remedying hyperopia: The effects of self-control regret on consumer behavior", *Journal of Marketing Research,* 45 (6): 676-689

Kennedy, E.J.; Lawton, L. (1996), "The effects of social and moral integration on ethical standards: A comparison of American and Ukrainian business students", *Journal of Business Ethics*, 15 (8): 901-911

Lai, K. K.-Y.; Zaichkowsky, J. L. (1999), "Brand imitation: Do the Chinese have different views?", *Asia Pacific Journal of Management,* 16 (2): 179-192

Lee, J.H.; Hwang, J. (2011), "Luxury marketing: The influences of psychological and demographic characteristics on attitudes toward luxury restaurants", *International Journal of Hospitality Management,* 30 (3): 658-669

Ling, G.; Norton, M.J.T.; Zhi-ming, Z.; Chester, K.M.T. (2009), "Potential niche markets for luxury fashion goods in China", *Journal of Fashion Marketing and Management,* 13 (4): 514-526

Maroco, J. (2010), *Análise Estatística - Com utilização do SPSS.* Lisboa: Edições Sílabo

Matthiesen, I.M.; Phau, I. (2010), "Brand image inconsistencies of luxury fashion brands: A buyer-seller exchange situation model of Hugo Boss Australia", *Journal of Fashion Marketing and Management,* 14 (2): 202-218

McCabe, M.; De Waal Malefyt, T. (2010), "Brands, interactivity, and contested fields: Exploring production and consumption in cadillac and infiniti automobile advertising campaigns", *Human Organization,* 69 (3): 252-262

Mignot, C.; Kapferer, J.N. (2009), "Is CRM for luxury brands", *Journal of Brand Management,* 16 (5-6): 406-412

Moore, C.M.; Doherty, A.M.; Doyle, S.A. (2010), "Flagship stores as a market entry method: The perspective of luxury fashion retailing", *European Journal of Marketing,* 44 (1-2): 139-161

Moore, C.M.; Doyle, S.A. (2010), "The evolution of a luxury brand: The case of Prada", *International Journal of Retail and Distribution Management,* 38 (11): 915-927

Nia, A.; Zaichkowsky, J. L. (2000), "Do counterfeits devalue the ownership of luxury brands?", *Journal of Product & Brand Management*, 9 (7): 485-497

Norum, P.S.; Cuno, A. (2011), "Analysis of the demand for counterfeit goods", *Journal of Fashion Marketing and Management*,15 (1): 27-40

Nunes, P.F.; Mulani, N.P.; Brandazza, G.; Taggart, J.M.R.; Cummings, C.S. (2008), "Can knockoffs knock out your business?", *Harvard Business Review*, 86 (10): 41-50

Nueno, J.L.; Quelch J.A. (1998), "The mass marketing of luxury", *Business Horizons*, 41 (6): 61-68

OECD (2007), "The Economic Impact of Counterfeiting and piracy" http://www.oecd.org/industry/industryandglobalisation/38707619.pdf [accessed on 24.09.2012]

Okonkwo, U. (2009), "Sustaining the luxury brand on the Internet", *Journal of Brand Management,* 16 (5-6): 302-310

Penz, E.; Stöttinger, B. (2008a), "Original brands and counterfeit brands - do they have anything in common?", *Journal of Consumer Behaviour,* 7 (2): 146-163

Penz, E.; Stöttinger, B. (2008b), "Corporate image and product similarity-assessing major demand drivers for counterfeits in a multi-country study", *Psychology and Marketing,* 25 (4): 352-381

Park, H.J.; Rabolt, N.J.; Sook, K.J. (2008), "Purchasing global luxury brands among young Korean consumers", *Journal of Fashion Marketing and Management,* 12 (2): 244-259

Phau, I.; Leng, Y.S. (2008), "Attitudes toward domestic and foreign luxury brand apparel: A comparison between *status* and non *status* seeking teenagers", *Journal of Fashion Marketing and Management,* 12 (1): 68-89

Phau, I.; Sequeira, M.; Dix, S. (2009), "Consumers' willingness to knowingly purchase counterfeit products", *Direct Marketing*, 3 (4): 262-281

Phau, I.; Teah M. (2009) "Devil wears (counterfeit) Prada: a study of antecedents and outcomes of attitudes towards counterfeits of luxury brands", *Journal of Consumer Marketing*, 26 (1): 15-27

Preiholt, H.; Hagg, C. (2006), "Growth opportunities in luxury goods and real estate", *Journal of Fashion Marketing and Management,* 10 (1): 114-119

Quelch, J.A. (1987), "Marketing the premium product", *Business Horizons,* 30 (3): 38-45

Reddy, M.; Terblanche, N.; Pitt, L.; Parent, M. (2009), "How far can luxury brands travel? Avoiding the pitfalls of luxury brand extension", *Business Horizons,* 52 (2): 187-197

Reyneke, M. (2011), "In the lap of luxury: Consumer conversation concerning online advertisements of luxury brands", *South African Journal of Business Management,* 42 (2): 27-34

Richins, M. L. ; Dawson, S. (1992), "A Consumer Values Orientation for Materialism and Its Measurement: Scale Development and Validation", *The Journal of Consumer Research*, 19(3): 303-316

Riley, F.D.; Lomax, W.; Blunden, A. (2004), "Dove vs. Dior: Extending the brand extension decision-making process from mass to luxury", *Australasian Marketing Journal,* 12 (3): 40-55

Rucker D. (2009), "Compensatory Consumption: How Threat Directs Consumers' Product Preferences", *Advances in Consumer Research,* 36: 131-134

Rutter, J. ; Bryce, J. (2008), "The consumption of counterfeit goods: 'here be pirates?'", *Sociology*, 42(6): 1146-1164

Sapra, A.; Truong V.A.; Zhang, R.Q. (2010), "How much demand should be fulfilled?", *Operations Research,* 58 (3): 719-733

Seringhaus, F.H.R (2005), "Comparison of website usage of French and Italian luxury brands", *Journal of Euromarketing,* 14 (4): 5-34

Silverstein, M.J.; Fiske, N. (2003), "Luxury for the Masses", *Harvard Business Review*, 81 (4): 48-57

Smith, A.D. (2008), "Exploring the effects of e-fashions on producers of high-end clothing", *International Journal of Business Innovation and Research,* 2 (1): 90-104

Snyder, J.C. (2008), "Needs exploitation", *Ethical Theory and Moral Practice*, 11 (4): 389-405

Solomon, M.R. (1983), "The Role of Products as Social Stimuli: A Symbolic Interactionism Perspective," *Journal of Consumer Research*, 10: 319-29

Strach, P.; Everett, A.M. (2006), "Brand corrosion: Mass-marketing's threat to luxury automobile brands after merger and acquisition", *Journal of Product and Brand Management,* 15 (2): 106-120

Teixeira, A.A.C.; Rocha, M.F. (2010a), "Academic misconduct in Portugal: results from a large scale survey to university economics/business students", *Journal of Academic Ethics*, 8 (1): 21-41

Teixeira, A.A.C.; Rocha, M.F. (2010b), "Cheating by economics and business undergraduate students. An exploratory international assessment", *Higher Education*, 59 (6): 663-701

Truong, Y.; McColl, R.; Kitchen, P.J. (2010), "Uncovering the relationships between aspirations and luxury brand preference", *Journal of Product and Brand Management,* 19 (5): 346-355

Truong, Y.; Simmons, G.; McColl, R.; Kitchen, P.J. (2008), "Status and conspicuousness - Are they related? Strategic marketing implications for luxury brands", *Journal of Strategic Marketing,* 16 (3): 189-203

Tsai, S.P. (2005), "Impact of personal orientation on luxury-brand purchase value: An international investigation", *International Journal of Market Research,* 47 (4): 429-434

Wan, W.W.N.; Luk, C.-L.; Yau, O.H.M.; Tse, A.C.B.; Sin, L.Y.M.; Kwong, K.K.; Chow, R.P.M. (2009), "Do traditional Chinese cultural values nourish a market for pirated CDs?", *Journal of Business Ethics,* 88 (1): 185-196

Wee, C.; Ta, S.; Cheok, K. (1995), "Non-price determinants of intention to purchase counterfeit goods: An exploratory study", *International Marketing Review*, 12 (6): 19-46

Weinberger, D.; Weindruch, B.; Arnold, G.; Gilmore, J.H.; Pine II, B.J.; Brackett, G. (2008),"Authenticity: Is it real or is it marketing?", *Harvard Business Review,* 86 (3): 33-43

Wilcox, K.; Kim, H.M.; Sen, S. (2009), "Why do consumers buy counterfeit luxury brands?", *Journal of Marketing Research,* 46 (2): 247-259

Wilkins, H.; Merrilees B.; Herington, C. (2007), "Towards an understanding of total service quality in hotels", *International Journal of Hospitality Management,* 26 (4): 840-853

Xiao Lu, P.; Pras, B. (2011), "Profiling mass affluent luxury goods consumers in China: A psychographic approach", *Thunderbird International Business Review,* 53 (4): 435-455

Yoo, B.; Lee, S.-H. (2009), "Buy genuine luxury fashion products or counterfeits?", *Advances in Consumer Research*, 36: 280-286

Notes

[1] http://www.iccwbo.org/ [accessed on 12.09.20].

[2] http://www.wcoomd.org/home_research_researchseries.htm [accessed on 12.09.20].

[3] http://www.a-cg.org/guest/pdf/Counterfeiting_Luxury_2007_Report.pdf [accessed on 12.09.20].

[4] In the statements "Counterfeit goods infringe intellectual property", "Counterfeit goods hurt the companies that sell the genuine products", "Buying forgeries is not ethical," "People who sell counterfeits are committing an unlawful act" and

"People who buy counterfeits are committing an unlawful act" the value 1 was assigned to respondents with a degree of agreement of 1 or 2.

[5] In the statement "People give too much importance to material goods" the valuc 1 was assigned to respondents with a degree of agreement of 1 or 2.

[6] On the same day a request to disseminate the survey was sent by email to the Vice-Chancellor and Deans of the fourteen faculties of the University of Porto and the Porto School of Management, as well as the relevant Offices of Communication and Image and Student Unions. Dissemination was by dynamic email, both via the Vice-Chancellor's office and through the Communications Offices and Student Unions of the respective faculties and, in some cases, through the Unions' websites and newsletters. In the two weeks following the sending of this email telephone calls were made to various organizations to promote dissemination of the research survey. In most cases it was possible to arrange two dissemination actions in different weeks.

Chapter Seven

Academic Fraud by Higher Education Students in Portugal: A Study of Types, Practices and Tolerance of Fraud

Filipe Almeida, Ana Seixas, Paulo Gama, Paulo Peixoto and Denise Esteves

Introduction

The world has changed significantly in recent decades. New geopolitical alignments, the spread of free trade regions, wider access to education and unprecedented technological developments have made contemporary societies more interdependent and citizens more vigilant. However, this has created as well new vulnerabilities. Freedom of communication and access to information pose increasing threats to privacy and property rights. Greater surveillance of citizens, together with demands for transparency, contrast with new forms of corruption and transgression, exemplified by recent corporate scandals involving multinational companies (Witherspoon et al., 2012). The study of ethical behaviour – whether institutional or individual – and its many ramifications within society has therefore acquired a new relevance, encompassing new challenges and problems. In the university context, the type and extent of fraud committed by students may represent an important indicator of the readiness and predisposition of societies to face these challenges by accommodating, encouraging or preventing immoral conduct, which may in turn influence future social and economic progress. Therefore, the prevailing level of (in)tolerance to fraud within a given society should be seen as both the cause and effect of academic fraud.

Academic fraud committed by students in higher education has become a widely debated subject within academia, as it is perceived as a fast growing phenomenon (Teixeira and Rocha, 2010a) and that its consequences are significantly negative in terms of institutional credibility and social progress. It is likely that this increase in fraud is related to the rise in the number of students in higher education – without any corresponding increase in the number of teachers – and to technological innovations in recent decades that offer new methods for committing fraud (Mayhew et al., 2010). On the one hand, the growing numbers of students per teacher compromise the proximity between them and weaken the moral bonds which this type of relationship naturally encourages in students. It may be argued that by ideologically promoting teaching and learning processes focusing on closer relationships between teachers and students, the Bologna model might reduce the likelihood of fraud. Paradoxically, however, by shortening the first cycle and promoting access to postgraduate training cycles, this model has led to a devaluing of the first cycle. For students, this usually translates into the assumption that graduation is instrumental, to the extent that it is seen as one stage on the path towards further training that will bring real advantages. As a means of obtaining formal recognition with increasingly lower market value, it tends to be viewed as something that does not justify extreme commitment. For teachers, it results in the imposition of mechanisms for assessment and academic recognition that increasingly have less to do with graduation and translate into growing disinvestment, specifically in terms of ensuring close and intensive pedagogical relationships with students and developing mechanisms to prevent and combat the various types of fraud. In addition, methods for overseeing and controlling the new technologies that can be used to commit fraud still do not seem to be sufficiently well developed. Teachers, who are the main agents in licensing or discouraging fraud, are showing signs of interest in this subject but are still apparently not involved in institutional policies (Jager and Brown, 2010). Given that universities still seem unprepared to deal with academic fraud (Sutherland-Smith, 2010), it is therefore imperative to investigate this phenomenon from a range of multiple perspectives in order to reach a clear understanding and combat it efficiently.

Cultural context would appear decisive in shaping the attitude of students to fraud, which is less common in countries in northern Europe and America, in contrast with the high incidences of fraud in southern and eastern Europe and Latin America (Teixeira & Rocha, 2010; Crittenden et al., 2009). This difference may be related to the permissiveness of the academic environment and to institutional features that ignore or discourage fraud. For example, the existence of a code of honour has been cited as an institutional instrument that prevents academic fraud (McCabe et al., 2002), since universities that adopt such codes have shown a more positive and assertive attitude towards fraud prevention and punishment policies (McCabe et al., 2003).

The results of recent studies seem to suggest that academic fraud amongst students is increasing throughout the world (McCabe et al., 2001), boosted by the use of new technologies (Walker, 2010; Witherspoon, 2010), and is particularly prevalent in eastern and southern Europe (Teixeira and Rocha, 2010a). In Portugal, studies on academic fraud remain rare, the most important being the recent work by Teixeira and Rocha (2010b), involving a broad national sample, and research by Rocha (2006) and Domingues (2006). This paper aims to deepen the understanding of types and practices and the reasons which cause or prevent academic fraud in Portugal. Based on a closed-question survey completed in person, in the classroom, by students in eight different degree courses in a Portuguese state university, attitudes towards 13 different types of academic fraud were analysed, in addition to the students' views on the reasons why fraud is committed and the potential means of preventing it.

Literature review

Academic fraud may seriously compromise the credibility of university institutions and the perspective of social progress in a particular country or region. Despite growing attention from researchers and political decision-makers, it remains a phenomenon whose outlines are still not clearly understood, due to a lack of consensus regarding its conceptual boundaries and the absence of any clear and comprehensive tool with which to assess it. The notion of academic fraud is rarely questioned from a conceptual point of view. In fact, there still seems to be no simple definition of academic fraud (Teixeira and Rocha, 2010a). This research therefore proposes a typology based on the following concept of academic fraud: *any conscious act or omission that may compromise the fairness of a comparative assessment of the performance, skills or knowledge of students.*

Academic fraud may therefore be committed by students, teachers, other employees in higher education institutions, outside agents, or the institution itself within the scope of its educational policy. This research focuses only on academic fraud committed by students, which is understood as any moral transgression committed by a student within the context of his/her academic relations and responsibilities to their teachers, fellow students and the institution in which they are studying.

In addition, there is still an apparent lack of any clear measurement that encompasses the various dimensions of fraud, which makes it difficult to compare studies on the matter (Walker, 2010). The most widely used measure for studying academic fraud is *copying in a written test*, usually without any analysis of whether this form of cheating involves using unauthorised materials, communication technologies or copying from a fellow student. Other common indicators, extended by the use of new technologies, include copying from unquoted sources, submitting work done by another person, asking for help from colleagues during tests and falsifying literature (Witherspoon et al., 2012; Teixeira and Rocha, 2010a). Nevertheless, this type of research lacks a theoretical model to justify the selection of practices that helps to consistently relate them. On the basis of the above definition and in order to rectify this limitation, the following typology is proposed for academic fraud:

I. Appropriation of another person's work
• appropriation with the active collaboration of others
• appropriation without the intervention of others

II. Simulation of work not produced
• self-plagiarism
• falsification of data and results

III. Facilitation of fraud committed by others
• facilitating fraud with personal gain
• facilitating fraud with personal risk
• facilitating fraud with no gain and no risk

IV. Concealment of fraud (failure to denounce fraud committed by others)

This typology envisages 4 major types of academic fraud and 13 subtypes (given that "Concealment of fraud" applies to each of the 7 subtypes). The major types I and II refer to active fraud, whereas type III covers passive practices that facilitate fraud. Type IV represents omission on the part of the observer. This theoretical model appears robust and provides a framework for most fraudulent practices involving students.

Methodological considerations

Sample and data collection

This paper describes an exploratory study aimed at establishing an initial multidisciplinary approach to investigating the Portuguese academic environment using a new research tool. A sample of students in eight undergraduate degree courses in a Portuguese state university was therefore selected, based on accessibility criteria. Data was collected through a closed-question survey answered in the classroom, in the presence of a member of the research team. 374 valid questionnaires were collected from Portuguese students, distributed as follows: *Public and Private Administration*: 48; *Education Sciences*: 48; *Computer Science*: 46; *Journalism*: 45; *Mathematics*: 32; *Sociology*: 54; *Electrotechnical Engineering*: 50; *Information Sciences*: 51.

In this sample, 45% of the participants were male, 91.4% had been educated mainly in state schools prior to university and 60% were enrolled on their first choice of degree course. With regard to student status, 88.4% were full-time students and 7.3% were working students.

The research tool

The questionnaire used in this research is a new proposal for collecting data and studying academic fraud by higher education students. The initial version was inspired by the work of Morris and Kilian (2006), with adaptations suggested by McCabe (1999) and Rennie and Rudland (2003). Discussions on academic fraud were later held with students in order to review the contents and adjust the language. A pilot version was tested with 452 students enrolled in four degree courses (Almeida et al., 2010), after which some questions were amended and added, based as well on contributions from teaching staff. The version of the questionnaire used in this research includes the following main sections: **part 1** (socio-demographic and academic information about the student); **part 2** (projective questions on nine scenarios involving academic fraud, covering the 4 types of fraud subdivided into 9 active practices and 9 situations involving concealment of - or failure to denounce - fraud); **part 3** (questions on frequency, reasons for fraud and actions that may prevent it).

In **part 2** of the questionnaire, students were asked to evaluate the seriousness of 7 practices involving appropriation and 2 involving simulation, corresponding to nine simulated scenarios, as presented in Figure 1. For each scenario, students were also asked if they would do the same and if they would denounce the act if they knew about it.

The questionnaire includes some innovations in academic fraud research. First, it does not question students directly about their practices but instead asks them about the seriousness with which they would rate the actions of a fictitious individual in a simulated scenario of possible fraud. The use of projective questions aims to reduce the risk of receiving socially acceptable answers, common in surveys that involve questioning the honesty of the respondents (Walker, 2009). Second, the practices were selected on the basis of a theory of types of fraud that incorporates the various dimensions of the concept and avoids the other common tendency to reduce the subject to one single dimension such as *plagiarism* or *copying in a written test*. Thirdly, it questions students on the reasons for fraud and how it may be prevented, thus aiming to fill another gap in this type of study which rarely asks students what they think about the causes and prevention of academic fraud (Malgwi and Rakovksi, 2009).

Types of fraud		**Fraudulent practices**
APPROPRIATION	*Appropriation WITH collaboration*	Buying work Help from relatives Copying in an exam Signing work Copying work
	Appropriation WITHOUT collaboration	Copying using a crib Copying from the Internet
SIMULATION	*Self-plagiarism*	Submitting the same work more than once
	Falsifying data and results	Inventing data
FACILITATION	*Facilitating fraud with gain*	Selling work
	Facilitating fraud with risk	Allowing work to be copied
	Facilitating fraud with no gain and no risk	Authorising authorship Lending work
CONCEALMENT	*Concealing fraud (not denouncing fraud committed by others)*	Not denouncing buying of work Not denouncing collaboration Not denouncing copying from crib during an exam Not denouncing falsification of data Not denouncing submission of same work more than once Not denouncing copying from another student during an exam Not denouncing authorship of group work without actual participation Not denouncing plagiarism of another student's work Not denouncing copying from the Internet

Figure 1 - Academic fraud – types and practices

Results

The frequency of academic fraud

Students were asked how often they thought fraud was committed in their courses and how frequently each of the 12 practices in particular occurs. The answers show that, overall, students recognised the existence of fraud (only 3.5% stated that it never happened). The Education Sciences students stood out, acknowledging a higher incidence of fraud than the Public and Private Administration, Computer Science and Mathematics students. Similarly, Information Sciences students also recorded a higher score than Public and Private Administration students.

With regard to practices, the most common method was *using unauthorised materials in written tests*, followed by *copying answers from a colleague in a written test* and *allowing answers to be copied in an exam*, showing the predominance of classic fraud in written examinations. The less frequent practices were *buying work from other students* and *buying academic work outside the institution.* Another significant result was the almost complete absence of *denouncing academic fraud committed by fellow students.* These results are presented in Table 1, showing the most frequent responses for each practice in each course (mode).

These results suggest that the classic forms of fraud in the exam room or in class remain the most frequent. It is rare for work to be bought and there appears to be a prevailing culture of tolerance towards fraud committed by fellow students, perhaps explained by the partnership that legitimises the act or allows an exchange in the future.

As for socio-demographic characteristics, the data only suggests one statistically significant difference in terms of the way in which males and females perceive fraud. In fact, although they belong to the same academic environment and are subject to the same contingencies, females tend to recognise fraud as a more frequent phenomenon than males, and are apparently more aware of these types of academic transgressions.

Table 1 - Frequency of academic fraud

	TOTAL	ADM	EDU	COM	JOUR	MAt	SOC	ELEC	INF
Copying answers from a colleague in a written test	**3**	3	3	3	2	2	3	2	3
Allowing answers to be copied in an exam	**3**	2	3	3	3	2	3	3	3
Buying academic work outside the institution	**2**	1	2	2	2	1	1	2	1
Copying work from the Internet	**3**	2	3	3	3	2	3	2	3
Copying part of work from other authors without citation	**3**	2	3	3	3	3	3	3	3
Copying work from other colleagues	**3**	2	3	3	2	3	2	3	2
Buying work from other colleagues	**1**	1	2	1	1	1	1	2	1
Submitting the same work for different courses	**2**	1	2	2	2	1	2	2	1
Submitting practical work with false data	**2**	2	2	2	1	1	2	2	1
Signing group work without having helped to produce it	**3**	3	2	3	3	2	3	2	3
Using unauthorised materials in written tests	**3**	2	4	3	3	3	4	3	4
Denouncing academic fraud committed by fellow students	**1**	1	1	1	1	1	1	1	1
SUM OF MODES	**29**	22	30	29	26	22	28	27	26

Legend: ADM: Public and Private Administration; EDUC: Education Sciences; COM: Computer Science; JOU: Journalism; MAT: Mathematics; SOC: Sociology; ELEC: Electrotechnical Engineering; INF: Information Sciences.

1 - Never; 2 – Rarely; 3 – Sometimes; 4 - Regularly

The seriousness of academic fraud

The nine scenarios in the questionnaire include nine active practices, involving appropriation or simulation, and four passive practices of facilitating fraud. The students were asked to rate the seriousness of each one. Table 2 shows the students' answers to the question of whether they considered each practice to be fraud and, if so, how serious they thought it was.

Table 2 - Seriousness of academic fraud

	N	"Yes"		"No"	"Don't know"
			Average for seriousness (from 1 to 10)		
Buying work from another student	371	95.7%	**8.60**	3%	1.3%
Selling own work to other students	371	87.6%	**7.40**	9.4%	3%
Authorised plagiarism of another student's work	371	89.5%	**7.33**	7.8%	2.7%
Help from relatives	370	88.1%	**7.25**	9.2%	2.7%
Copying answers from a colleague in a written test	371	95.1%	**6.95**	3.8%	1.1%
Using unauthorised materials in a written test	372	96.2%	**6.92**	2.7%	1.1%
Including false data in written work	373	92%	**6.80**	3.2%	4.8%
Copying work from the Internet	368	87%	**6.68**	10.6%	2.4%
Giving answers to another student in an exam	370	93.2%	**6.22**	5.7%	1.1%
Not participating in group work but benefiting from the collective mark	370	75.9%	**6.07**	17%	7%
Lending own work to other students to submit as theirs	369	74.8%	**5.72**	21.7%	3.5%
Submitting the same work for different courses	372	65.1%	**4.61**	30.4%	4.6%
Allowing a fellow student to share official authorship of work they were not involved in producing	371	62%	**4.33**	29.6%	8.4%

As can be seen, students attribute seriousness to *buying* and *selling work*, *copying work from other students* (curiously, considered more serious than *copying from the Internet*) and *getting help from a relative for work submitted in the student's own name*. Less serious practices included *submitting the same work for different courses* and *allowing a fellow student to share official authorship of work they were not involved in* (approximately 30% of the students did not even consider this to be fraud), which would appear to legitimise fraud as long as it does not involve appropriating the work of others or benefiting from sources outside the education process. The latter case may reflect the institutionalisation and rationalisation of academic fraud based on mechanisms of trust and solidarity; in other words, there is tolerance for *a fellow student sharing official authorship of work they were not involved in producing* on the understanding (or expectation) that at some time in the future the benefactor may, in turn, benefit from this practice.

The data suggests that assessment methods based on group work create the conditions for fraudulent practices which students tend not to condemn, or else consider less serious. However, this depends on how the fraud is committed: if it implies a financial transaction it is clearly condemned, whereas if it takes place within the context of the usual students' partnership, it is less serious. Therefore the introduction of this selective moral principle (non-commercial solidarity) with a view to mitigating or regularising academic fraud and its severity contains a certain irony. It should also be noted that the less common practices are also the most condemned, suggesting the existence of a principle of self-regulation or legitimisation of choices amongst students.

In the theoretical model of academic fraud presented here, it is suggested that fraudulent practices are organised according to type of fraud: appropriation, simulation, facilitation and concealment. This typology justified the selection of practices for analysis, but it may also help to understand how importance is attributed to each one. An exploratory factor analysis of the data was undertaken, in order to assess how students mentally organise fraudulent practices according to their seriousness. The results suggest that fraudulent practices are related by means of a criterion different from those arising from the proposed typology. Table 3 presents the matrix for these results.

Table 3 - Seriousness of fraud (exploratory factorial analysis)

	Main components*		
	1	**2**	**3**
Buying work from another student		.858	
Selling own work to other students		.736	
Authorised plagiarism of another student's work			
Help from relatives		.733	
Copying answers from a colleague in a written test			.868
Using unauthorised materials in a written test			.808
Including false data in written work	.504		
Copying work from the Internet	.600		
Giving answers to another student in an exam			.754
Not participating in group work but benefiting from the collective mark	.740		
Lending own work to other students to submit as theirs	.589		
Submitting the same work for different courses	.643		
Allowing a fellow student to share official authorship of work they were not involved in producing	.845		

KMO 0.835; Bartlett's Test of Sphericity *sig*. 0.000
*only weightings over 0.5 are included

The factor analysis of the main components suggests the extraction of 3 factors that explain 63% of the total variance. These may be interpreted as follows:

Factor 1 – **fraud associated with producing written assignments**
Factor 2 - **fraud based on financial or affective transactions**
Factor 3 – **fraud associated with taking written exams**

In these terms, the students seemed to distinguish between the seriousness of fraudulent practices according to the type of assessment in question: exam or assignment (i.e., individual or group work such as papers, projects and class presentations). However, it is interesting to note that if this involves a financial or affective transaction (based on family relationships), the students highlighted the seriousness of the fraud; in other words, the existence of Factor 2 appears to suggest that students perhaps tend to condemn fraud that makes use of personal economic and social advantages that are not available to all. Therefore, in assessing the seriousness of fraud, in addition to the type of assessment in question, and perhaps more importantly, the criterion students appear to elect is access to opportunities to commit fraud, which may be facilitated or hampered by the economic status or cultural background of each student. Although this may not lead to the conclusion that students condemn fraud itself less and socially and economically segmented forms of fraud more – whilst not ruling out this possibility – it at least suggests that the hierarchy of the seriousness of fraud is related to opportunities to access fraud. This analysis represents only an initial approach, providing an interesting insight into how students think about academic fraud, classifying its seriousness not only according to the active or passive stance of the individual committing the act, but also the type of assessment context in which it is committed, with the exception of situations involving the exchange of money or relationships with individuals outside the academic setting, taking advantage of cultural and socioeconomic background.

The Predisposition to Commit Fraud Indicator (IPF) and the Predisposition to Denounce Fraud Indicator (IPD)

Using the data collected with this research tool, it is possible to create an indicator of the predisposition of students to commit academic fraud: the IPF. The IPF of each student is calculated on the basis of the number of times they responded "yes" to the question of whether they would act in the same way as the offender in each of the 13 fraud scenarios presented (the indicator was later amended to operate on a scale of 0 to 10). Similarly, the data also provides an indicator of the predisposition to denounce fraud: the IPD. The IPD of each student represents the number of times they stated that they would denounce a situation if they knew about it in each of the 9 fraud scenarios (in this case no distinction was made between an active or passive practice, but only between the fraud scenarios themselves, and this indicator was also amended to operate on a scale of 0 to 10). Thus, the higher the IPD, the greater the propensity of the student to commit academic fraud, and the higher the IPD, the greater their propensity to denounce it.

These indicators are an innovative feature of this study, made possible due to the way in which the questionnaire was designed, and have proved especially interesting to deepen the analysis of students' predisposition to commit fraud and to more accurately evaluate their opinions on motivation and prevention. When the IPF and IPD of students who consider fraud acceptable in certain circumstances and those who always consider it unacceptable are compared, it can be seen that the IPF is significantly higher and the IPD insignificantly lower in the former group. This result is consistent with the reasoning underlying the construction of the indicators, thus attesting to their pertinence.

Table 4 presents a general comparison of IPF and IPD scores for the different courses. With a general average of 3.75 (out of 10), the highest IPF appears in the Computer Science degree (5.12) and the lowest in the Journalism degree (2.54). The general average of the IPD is 0.56 (out of 10), with 75.3% of students scoring an IPD of zero (273), which would appear to confirm the existence of a culture of tolerance towards fraud amongst students. It remains to be seen to what extent, within an academic context, this may be more confined to cultures based on Judeo-Christian morality – since they are based on traditions in which denunciation has, since early times, been stigmatised (see the case of Judas Iscariot) – or whether it is more transversal. Whatever the case may be, in an academic context ruled by a peer culture in which close relations and shared knowledge prevails, it is natural that the predisposition to denounce fraud would tend to be low. Brodeur and Jobard (2005) note a transversal cultural trend reflecting an aversion to denouncing fraud, but also note that this is fragmenting into different kinds of behaviour due to the emergence of social phenomena (many of which are becoming increasingly visible in academic environments), such as a guarantee of anonymity for those denouncing misdemeanours, the institutionalisation of penalties, and the dissemination of a paradigm in which citizenship is increasingly based on a propensity to denounce offences. In the courses observed as a whole, the IPD for the Information Sciences degree, although low, appears as the highest amongst the courses analysed (1.23). Perhaps, keeping this as an open question, the specific subjects and teaching methods for each course may influence students' sensitivity to fraud and their inclination to commit or denounce it. Alternatively, perhaps the opening up of formal channels to denounce fraud or the formal establishment of frameworks for sanctions may be more effective in normalising denunciations.

An analysis of the relationship between the IPF and the socio-demographic and academic status of the students showed that males had a greater propensity to commit fraud than females. This result suggests gender differentiation in the propensity to commit fraud, confirming the suspected greater female aversion to the phenomenon already identified in perceptions of the frequency with which fraud occurs. The IPF also reveals a statistically significant correlation (*sig.* 0.001), which is negative (-0.183), with the average student course mark, which suggests that the better the student's performance, the less willing they are to commit fraud. This moral inclination of the best students appears to be confirmed by the fact that the students who consider academic fraud unacceptable have higher average course marks than those who consider it acceptable in certain circumstances or who do not have an opinion on the matter. These results are consistent with the existence of a positive correlation between the average course mark and the seriousness attributed by students to fraudulent practices. Finally, the IPD is also higher for students educated mainly in private schools prior to entering university. In the case of the IPF, it was not possible to identify any statistically significant relationship with the demographic characteristics of the students.

Table 4 - Predisposition to Commit Fraud Indicator (IPF) and Predisposition to Denounce Fraud Indicator (IPD)

	TOTAL *	ADM	EDU	COM	JOUR	MAT	SOC	ELEC	INF
IPF	**3.75**	4.57	2.84	5.12	2.54	4.74	3.52	4.06	3.00
IPD	**0.56**	0.44	0.88	0.19	0.83	0.22	0.38	0.23	1.23

Legend: ADM: Public and Private Administration; EDUC: Education Sciences; COM: Computer Science; JOU: Journalism; MAT: Mathematics; SOC: Sociology; ELEC: Electrotechnical Engineering; INF: Information Sciences.
* average value for total sample (the scale for the IICF and IIDF ranged from 0 to 10)

In theoretical terms, the IPF and IPD, as indicators of attitudes towards fraud and its denunciation, may be related to perceptions of the frequency with which fraud occurs. In this sample, an analysis of the correlations between perceptions and attitudes revealed an interesting result. Only in the case of students who thought that fraud may be acceptable did their inclination to denounce it correlate with their perception of the frequency of fraud at their institution. These students appeared to have a moral attitude towards denunciation which depended on their perception of the level of fraud within the academic environment. This would seem to confirm the utilitarian criterion with which they evaluated fraud; in other words, their moral judgement depended on analysing the consequences and was therefore a flexible criterion that depended on an assessment of context. The students who thought fraud was unacceptable did not appear vulnerable to the effect of the academic environment to which they belonged in terms of deciding whether to denounce fraudulent behaviour or not. In this case, their perceptions of the frequency of fraud and their attitude towards it do not correlate and their moral criterion therefore seems to conform to a strict pre-existing principle of conduct that was independent of the specific conditions in the environment within which they acted.

Reasons for academic fraud

The students were also asked about the reasons which, in their opinion, led students to commit fraud. Table 5 summarises the results, including the average responses for each reason and their correlation with the IPF and IPD.

Table 5 - The importance of academic fraud motives and their correlation with the IPF and IPD

	Average (importance on a scale of 1 to 5)	Correlation	
		IPF	IPD
Academic workload	**3.74**	.146**	-.116*
Ensuring success in a subject failed previously	**3.71**	.101	.053
Unsure of ability to succeed in any other way	**3.28**	.115*	.004
In the habit of committing fraud since secondary school	**3.25**	.003	.164**
Type of assessment	**3.09**	.068	.003
Little practical relevance ascribed to curriculum content	**2.90**	.101	-.002
Fellow students regularly engage in fraudulent practices	**2.90**	.001	.130*
Perception that the penalty for fraud, if discovered, is not significant	**2.77**	-.101	.051
Inadequate pedagogical skills of teachers	**2.73**	.119*	-.009
Lack of understanding of what good academic conduct should be	**2.71**	-.118*	.110*
Passivity of teachers in the face of fraud	**2.68**	-.061	.114*
Lack of discussion of the subject in class with teachers	**2.59**	.032	-.016
Competitive pressure amongst fellow students	**2.51**	-.008	.023

* Spearman's correlation, with 5% significance
** Spearman's correlation, with 1% significance

In the students' opinion, the most relevant reasons are related to obstacles to achieving academic success in any other way, whether associated with the characteristics of the course or the student's lack of confidence. Curiously, competitive pressure and the attitude of teachers are ranked lower as reasons for fraud.

According to the results, as greater importance is attributed to *academic workload* as a reason for fraud, there is a parallel increase in the predisposition to commit fraud (IPF) and a reduction in the predisposition to denounce it (IPD), suggesting that academic workload functions as a rationalising mechanism in a dual sense, encouraging fraud and discouraging its denunciation. On the other hand, if greater importance is attributed to a *lack of understanding of what good academic conduct should be* as a reason for committing fraud, the IPF is lower and the IPD is higher, suggesting that students who are less likely to be offenders perhaps attribute the cause of fraud to ignorance of what good academic conduct should be and are willing to use institutional means to correct their fellow students' misdemeanours and perhaps contribute to their moral education. Conversely, students who are potentially more likely to offend appear not to accept ignorance as a reason for committing fraud. The results also show that as the IPF rises, so does the level of importance attributed to being *in the habit of committing fraud since secondary school* as a reason for fraud, which seems to suggest that the IPF tends to be higher amongst those who are already more aware of the phenomenon and acknowledge fraudulent practices since pre-university days.

The data was submitted to an exploratory factor analysis in an attempt to understand how these various motives are grouped, the results of which are shown in Table 6.

The factor analysis suggested the extraction of 3 factors which explain 54% of the total variance. These factors do not organise motives according to the importance attributed to them, but according to a criterion apparently associated with the different entities to which the students relate, identifying an inner circle of relations between self and fellow students, an intermediary circle of relations with teachers and courses, and an outer circle of relations with the institution. The factors may therefore be classified in the following terms:

Factor 1 – **academic culture of fraud (institutional level)**
Factor 2 – **educational practices (course level)**
Factor 3 – **pressure to achieve success (individual level)**

This arrangement of the way in which students organise the reasons for fraud according to their importance suggests that it may be possible, to a large extent, to combat fraud through institutional policies directed towards concrete aspects of educational policy.

Table 6 - Reasons for fraud (exploratory factor analysis)

	Main component*		
	1	2	3
Academic workload		.663	
Ensuring success in a subject failed previously			.663
Unsure of ability to succeed in any other way			.829
In the habit of committing fraud since secondary school	.683		
Type of assessment		.776	
Little practical relevance ascribed to curriculum content		.712	
Fellow students regularly engage in fraudulent practices	.636		
Perception that the penalty for fraud, if discovered, is not significant	.759		
Inadequate pedagogical skills of teachers		.702	
Lack of understanding of what good academic conduct should be	.528		
Passivity of teachers in the face of fraud	.709		
Lack of discussion of the subject in class with teachers			
Competitive pressure amongst fellow students			.688

KMO 0.783; Bartlett's Test of Sphericity, *sig.* 0.000
*only weightings over 0.5 included

Factors preventing academic fraud

The students were also asked which factors could, in their opinion, prevent academic fraud. In addition to the general importance of these factors, in this case, it was important to undertake a more detailed analysis, distinguishing between the opinions of those who think fraud is unacceptable and those who consider it acceptable in particular circumstances (whose opinions may perhaps reveal ways of preventing fraud that are potentially more effective, assuming that they are the opinions of students who are more likely to be offenders, as the correlation with the IPF for this subgroup of students confirmed). Table 7 shows these aggregated results, including the average for the responses for each prevention factor and their correlation with the IPF and IPD.

Table 7 - Importance of preventing factors and their correlation with IPF and IPD

	Average (importance on a scale of 1 to 5)				Correlation	
	Total	Acceptable	Unacceptable	*t-stat*	IPF	IPD
Heavier penalties for academic fraud	**3.37**	**2.95**	3.68	-5.10**	-.084	.097
Close relationship between teachers and students	**3.24**	**3.21**	3.20	0.04	-.002	-.020
Guarantee of anonymity when denouncing fraud by fellow students	**3.13**	**2.84**	3.36	-3.36**	-.063	.222**
Involvement of students in disseminating good academic practices	**3.06**	**2.84**	3.27	-3.17**	-.198**	.085
Regular programmes to develop academic skills	**3.00**	**2.84**	3.09	-1.76	-.167**	.095
Regular psychological and pedagogical support programmes	**2.97**	**2.90**	3.04	-0.88	-.061	-.012
Use of electronic surveillance and detection mechanisms	**2.94**	**2.50**	3.19	-4.49**	-.066	.149**
Dissemination of academic code of conduct	**2.86**	**2.55**	3.10	-3.89**	-.262**	.151**
Presentation of a statement of authorship/originality for work submitted for assessment	**2.80**	**2.70**	2.87	-1.18	-.130*	.132*
Information sessions on good academic conduct organised by departments	**2.60**	**2.30**	2.81	-3.59**	-.231**	.132*
Regular ethics courses	**2.59**	**2.26**	2.80	-3.81**	-.206**	.069
Obligatory oral tests	**2.56**	**2.39**	2.69	-2.02**	.011	.051
Public disclosure, within the institution, of the names of students committing fraud	**2.22**	**2.12**	2.31	-1.30	.019	.070

Average (t-stat): * *t-Student* statistic, with 5% significance; ** *t-Student* statistic, with 1% significance

Correlation (IPF and IPD): * Spearman's correlation, with 5% significance; ** Spearman's correlation, with 1% significance

According to the students, the main factors that prevent fraud are *heavier penalties*, a *close relationship with teachers* and a *guarantee of anonymity for denunciations*, followed by measures to ensure students are more involved with the institution. Apart from the punitive nature of heavier penalties, the remaining factors seem to suggest that a close relationship between the student and the institution may effectively discourage fraud. Here, once again, the importance of the peer culture is revealed, which explains the low inclination to denounce fraud. On the other hand, clarifying good conduct and obligatory oral tests do not seem to have a significant dissuasive effect. Interestingly, public disclosure of the names of offenders does not appear to be seen as a punishment, given the sharp distinction made by students between this and heavier penalties.

When only the opinion of the students most likely to offend is analysed (i.e., those who consider fraud acceptable), it can be seen that the main rankings in terms of importance remain unchanged, although a *close relationship with teachers* is highlighted as the most relevant means of prevention, confirming the previous interpretation for the sample as a whole. It may be the case that underlying this opinion is a complaint about distant relations between teachers and students which the new educational policies still have not managed to rectify.

As expected, the IPF relates negatively to the importance attributed to almost all the potential fraud prevention factors, confirming them as effective potential forms of discouraging offenders. In this case, the IPD suggests a more specific approach, since students with a higher IPD considered significant preventive factors to be initiatives that promote an institutional culture of intolerance to fraud that legitimises and encourages its denunciation.

As with causes, preventive factors may also be grouped into theoretically coherent categories. In order to assess this possibility, an exploratory factor analysis of the data was carried out only for the subgroup of students who considered fraud acceptable, producing the following results, as displayed in Table 8.

Table 8 - Factors preventing fraud (exploratory factor analysis)

	Main components*		
	1	2	3
Heavier penalties for academic fraud			.703
Close relationship between teachers and students		.663	
Guarantee of anonymity when denouncing fraud by fellow students			.592
Involvement of students in disseminating good academic practices	.575	.532	
Regular programmes to develop academic skills		.927	
Regular psychological and pedagogical support programmes		.894	
Use of electronic surveillance and detection mechanisms			.785
Dissemination of academic code of conduct	.888		
Presentation of a statement of authorship/originality for work submitted for assessment		.591	
Information sessions on good academic conduct organised by departments	.837		
Regular ethics courses	.859		
Obligatory oral tests			.673
Public disclosure, within the institution, of the names of students committing fraud			.683

KMO 0.794; Bartlett's Test of Sphericity, *sig*. 0.000
*only weightings over 0.5 included

Results suggested the extraction of 3 factors which explain 66.08% of the total variance (the same analysis applied to the total sample produced identical results, suggesting the universality of the interpretation of these factors). The criterion that distinguishes the grouping of these prevention factors appears to be the type of institutional strategy for combating fraud, and the 3 factors may be classified as follows:

Factor 1 – **information strategies**

Factor 2 – **involvement/commitment strategies**

Factor 3 – **dissuasion strategies**

The organisation of these 3 factors suggests that there are three possible approaches to organising the institutional fight against fraud. The first favours training and information strategies for students, focussing on good academic conduct. The second highlights the quality of the academic relationship with students, in the form of policies to reinforce closer relationships and commitment to the institution on the part of students. The third favours the creation and development of dissuasive mechanisms, based on a system of denunciation and punishment of academic fraud. If these factors are cross-referenced with the importance attributed to each of the means of prevention (Table 7), it can be seen that from amongst the measures aimed at combating fraud, the students appear to recognise coherent strategies to reinforce closer relations between teachers, students and institutions as being potentially more efficient. This may represent a relevant insight when defining institutional policies for combating fraud committed by students.

Conclusions

Academic fraud is a longstanding phenomenon with cultural roots that has recently become more visible in universities throughout the world. The rising number of students in higher education, the spread of educational institutions and new information and communications technologies, have created an environment that favours an increase in fraudulent practices committed by students within the context of the systems used to assess their work. Recent studies have confirmed this growing trend (Witherspoon et al., 2012; Teixeira and Rocha, 2010a), suggesting the need to study the phenomenon in greater depth, both in terms of its nature and its cultural specificity.

This research therefore aimed to analyse the perceptions of higher education students regarding academic fraud, its gravity and frequency, the reasons why it occurs and the possible factors that may prevent it. An empirical study was carried out, consisting of a closed-question survey completed by students in person in the classroom, involving 374 students in eight different degree courses at a Portuguese state university. The study offers several contributions. In theoretical terms, it proposes a conceptual framework for academic fraud, understood as any conscious act or omission that may compromise the fairness of a comparative assessment of the performance, skills or knowledge of students. This notion of fraud meant it could be divided into four types – *appropriation*, *simulation*, *facilitation* and *concealment* – which were then subdivided into 13 practices. In methodological terms, the tool for collecting data uses the combined approach of a direct questionnaire and projective questions for 9 possible fraud scenarios, including questions on perceptions of the frequency of fraud and opinions on the factors that cause and may prevent it. In practical terms, it was an exploratory study that enabled the general attitude of the students to be assessed, as well as an understanding of how this might differ according to the various disciplines.

The main results indicate that the majority of the students considered fraud to be a frequent practice, revealing a culture of tolerance towards academic dishonesty that neither legitimises nor encourages its denunciation. The students appeared not to categorise fraud according to its nature but in terms of the type of assessment situation in which it occurred, *exams* or *course work*, condemning more severely actions that implied access to differentiated socio-economic resources, such as buying work or getting help from relatives.

However, the perceptions and attitudes of the students varied according to the type of fraud in question, and also depended on the subject they were studying. Some results in this sample show that Journalism students consider academic fraud more serious and less acceptable, in comparison to Computer Science students, who revealed a greater inclination to commit fraud. This result may possibly be explained by the academic nature and teaching methods specific to each course, with applied sciences courses, taught on a more quantitative basis and using depersonalised teaching methods, more open to fraud.

With regard to motives, the students identified academic workload (an institutional factor) as the main reason for fraud, followed by pressure to succeed (a cultural and individual factor). In addition, initiatives that reinforce the involvement and commitment of students to the institution stand out as the factors with the greatest potential to prevent academic fraud. There appears to be an underlying complaint associated with the lack of close relations between teachers and students, which is seen as a decisive factor in combating fraud.

This study proposes two new indexes for analysing fraud: the Predisposition to Commit Fraud Indicator (IPF) and Predisposition to Denounce Fraud Indicator (IPD). When the IPF and IPD are cross-referenced with the average course mark, the results confirm that the best students are less inclined to commit fraud, although this does not mean that they are willing to denounce it. This result appears to confirm the existence of a culture of academic complicity amongst students that legitimises fraud.

Recent pedagogical trends in continuous assessment systems, involving coursework produced outside the classroom, appear to have created new opportunities for fraud. In addition, this trend demands a close relationship between teachers and students, which the latter clearly value but which has not always materialised. Rather than the opportunities afforded by new technologies, it is perhaps these two contradictory developments that are responsible for the spread of this phenomenon. Ironically, a return to investing in strategies to bring students closer to institutions would appear necessary, before fraud becomes just one of the symptoms of the fragmentation of the higher education system.

This research presents an integrated approach to the various aspects of academic fraud committed by students, proposing a wide-ranging conceptual understanding of fraud and a methodology within which it can be integrated. Comparison between subject areas represents another innovative contribution, opening up paths for new interpretations of this phenomenon and reinforcing the urgent need to develop broader studies in the future.

Acknowledgements

This work is the result of a study financed by the ERDF through the COMPETE – Competitive Factors Operational Programme and by national funds via the FCT – Foundation for Science and Technology, as part of the project "The ethics of students and the tolerance of teachers and institutions in relation to academic fraud in higher education" - PTDC/CPE-CED/115915/2009, developed by the Centro de Estudos Sociais.

References

Almeida, F., Gama, P. and Peixoto, P. 2010. La ética de los alumnos de la enseñanza superior: Un estudio exploratorio sobre el fraude académico en Portugal. Oficina do CES, 348.

Brodeur, J.-P. and Jobard, F. 2005. Citoyens et délateurs. La délation peut-elle être civique? Les Éditions Autrement, Paris.

Crittenden, V., Hanna, R., and Peterson, R. 2009. The cheating culture: A global societal phenomenon. Business Horizons, 52(4), 337-346.

Domingues, I. 2006. O copianço na Universidade. O grau zero da qualidade. Media XXI, Lisboa.

Jager, K. and Brown, C. 2010. The tangled web: Investigating academics' views of plagiarism at the University of Cape Town. Studies in Higher Education, 35(5), 513-528.

Malgwi, C. and Rakovski, C. 2009. Combating academic fraud: Are students reticent about uncovering the covert? Journal of Academic Ethics, 7, 207-221.

Mayhew, M., Seifert, T., and Pascarella, E. 2010. A multi-institutional assessment of moral reasoning development among first-year students. Review of Higher Education: Journal of the Association for the Study of Higher Education, 33(3), 357-390.

McCabe, D. 1999. Academic Dishonesty Among High School Students. Adolescence, 139(34), 681-687.

McCabe, D., Butterfield, K., and Trevino, L. 2003. Faculty and academic integrity: The influence of current honor codes and past honor code experiences. Research in Higher Education, 44(3), 367-385.

McCabe, D., Trevino, L., and Butterfield, K. 2001. Cheating in academia institutions: A decade of research. Ethics & Behavior, 11(3), 219-232.

McCabe, D., Trevino, L., and Butterfield, K. 2002. Honor codes and other contextual influences on academic integrity: A replication and extension to modified honor code settings. Research in Higher Education, 43(3), 357-378.

Morris, D. and Kilian, C. 2006. Do Accounting Students Cheat? A Study Examining Undergraduate Accounting Students' Honesty and Perceptions of Dishonest Behavior. Journal of Accounting, Ethics & Public Policy, 3(5), 375-393.

Rennie, S. and Rudland, J. 2003. Differences in Medical Students' Attitudes to Academic Misconduct and Reported Behaviour Across Years – a Questionnaire Study. Journal of Medical Ethics, 2(29), 97-102.

Rocha, M. F. 2006. Stock de Capital Humano, Fraude Académica e Corrupção. Uma Análise Intra e Inter Países. PhD thesis. University of Porto. Portugal.

Sutherland-Smith, W. 2010. Retribution, Deterrence and reform: The dilemmas of plagiarism management in universities. Journal of Higher Education Policy and Management. 32(1), 5-16.

Teixeira, A. and Rocha, M. F. 2010a. Cheating by economics and business undergraduate students: An exploratory international assessment. High Education. 59, 663-701.

Teixeira, A. and Rocha, M. F. 2010b. Academic misconduct in Portugal: results from a large scale survey to university economics/business students. Journal of Academic Ethics, 8(1), 21-41.

Walker, J. 2010. Measuring plagiarism: researching what students do, not what they say they do. Studies in Higher Education, 35(1), 41-59.

Witherspoon, M., Maldonado, N., and Lacey, C. 2012. Undergraduates and academic dishonesty. International Journal of Business and Social Science. 3(1), 76-86.

CHAPTER EIGHT

SIMILARITIES BETWEEN ENTREPRENEURSHIP AND WHITE-COLLAR CRIME: GUIDELINES FOR A TEST

JOSÉ NEVES CRUZ

Introduction

According to Baumol (1990), white-collar crime (WCC) can be viewed as destructive entrepreneurship. Innovation, recognising opportunities and risk-taking are features of entrepreneurship, but also of many types of WCC. Criminology has to date paid scant attention to this parallelism.

The definition of white-collar crime (WCC) is not consensual and diverges across different authors. In 1996, a group of criminologists who met specifically to establish the definition of WCC came up with the following formulation:

> "White collar crimes are illegal and unethical acts that violate fiduciary responsibility of public trust committed by an individual or organisation, usually during the course of legitimate occupational activity, by persons of high or respectable social status for personal or organisational gain." (Friedrichs 2010: 6)

Some elements of this definition should be highlighted: the link between WCC and professional status; the violation or abuse of trust; the goal of personal or organisational gain; the unethical as well as illegal character of the offences; their association with otherwise legitimate and respectable professions or organisations. The latter refers indirectly to the presence of specific knowledge and professional abilities normally associated with high levels of education and intelligence. Another characteristic of WCC is that it involves opportunity and risk-taking (Benson and Simpson 2009). The goal of the offender is not to conceal himself, like a conventional criminal, but to conceal the crime, which may demand some innovation and complexity so as to render it undetectable by existing control systems. Indeed, most well-known cases of WCC are intelligently prepared and use complex knowledge, innovating in relation to what had been done before. It is on this type of economic and financial offence that we focus in this study.

The perception of a parallelism between entrepreneurship and WCC led us to think that it would be interesting to apply the models used to explain entrepreneurship to the study of WCC. The personality traits model and a model of intentions based on the theory of planned behaviour (TPB) have been widely used to understand entrepreneurial behaviour. There are also a few studies where these models were applied to some types of white-collar offenses. However, none of these models - to our knowledge - has been tested on the same sample in both types of behaviour.

Thus, departing from Baumol's view that WCC might be a form of entrepreneurship, the contribution of this study is to argue that this hypothesis can be tested by comparing, for the same sample, the results of the model of personality traits applied to entrepreneurial inclination[1] (or of the model based on the TPB applied to entrepreneurial intentions[2]) with the results of each model applied to WCC inclination, or to WCC intentions, respectively.

We begin by pointing out how and in what ways WCC is similar to entrepreneurship. Next, we discuss the application of the personality traits model and intentions model (based on the TPB) to entrepreneurship and WCC, comparing similarities and differences and reviewing the results. Finally, we make suggestions for future research. This will include the empirical study of a hypothetical convergence between entrepreneurial inclination and WCC inclination and between entrepreneurial intentions and WCC intentions, based on the estimation of the two models.

Theory and evidence on the connection between entrepreneurship and white-collar crime

Baumol's approach and related literature

Economics ought to afford insights into WCC, given that the main goal of offenders is economic gain. Schumpeter (1934) revolutionised the subject by changing economic analysis from a static and equilibrium paradigm to a dynamic and evolutionary system. Technological change and innovation were henceforth understood to be the essential factors in the competition game and in the pursuit of monopoly power. The ability to make a difference to the status quo becomes the driver of economic dynamics. In this process creative destruction plays a role. Entrepreneurs are key players in this process, acting as both creators and destroyers, since the innovations they introduce make obsolete old products and ways of doing business, creating new opportunities in the process. Risk-taking and the recognition of opportunities are central to entrepreneurship. However, according to WCC literature, these two factors also characterise economic and financial crimes designed and shaped with intelligence. It is this parallelism that interests Baumol (1990), basing his work on Schumpeter's definition of entrepreneurship.

In the 1980s, following Schumpeter, the literature on entrepreneurship diversified, leading to much interdisciplinary research involving various pathways: economics, management, psychology, sociology, history, and even biology. At the beginning of the following decade, Baumol added criminology to the list (Baumol 1990). This author questioned whether entrepreneurship always creates social value. He suggested that entrepreneurs choose between productive, unproductive and destructive entrepreneurship[3] according to the expected net return on the use of their skills. Choosing the first generates social value, whereas choosing the others involves rent-seeking and illegal behaviour – e.g., white-collar and organised crime. However, it may be assumed that moral issues are factored into the cost-benefit calculus, since subjective as well as objective effects are likely to be relevant.

According to Schumpeter (1934), the entrepreneur is a unique and creative individual who develops new products, services and techniques, which renew the ways in which people operate in a given environment. The famous five forms of innovation are: (1) introduction of a new good; (2) introduction of a new method of production; (3) opening of a new market; (4) conquest of a new source of supply of raw materials or half-manufactured goods; (5) carrying out of the new organization of any industry, like the creation or breaking of a monopoly position.

Baumol (1990) indicates that each form is compatible with unproductive entrepreneurship and it is important to understand what influenced the entrepreneur's allocation of talent between the various possibilities offered by new combinations. He also argues that the forms of innovation could be expanded to include rent-seeking (such as the discovery of a legal loophole that allows pioneers to capture rents, as in the case of abusive tax-avoidance schemes) and destructive activities that are profitable for those who exploit them, despite the decrease in social value. This does not contradict Schumpeter's definition, because, for example, the creation of a monopoly position as described in item 5 may also destroy social value. Not admitting it would be reductionist: thus, according to Baumol, entrepreneurs are people "who are ingenious and creative in finding ways that add to their own wealth, power, and prestige, then it is to be expected that not all of them will be overly concerned with whether an activity that achieves these goals adds much or little to the social product or, for that matter, even whether it is an actual impediment to production." (Baumol 1990: 6).

There are of course many definitions of entrepreneurship. Some of these anticipate Baumol in pointing to the possible inclusion of WCC. Kirzner (1973), for example, defined the entrepreneur as an opportunist trader. According to this definition, the criminal needs merely to exploit the opportunity to trade to be labelled an entrepreneur.

Altogether, Smith and Gordon (2009) found sixty definitions of entrepreneurship in the literature - some of the best-known being listed in Table 1 below.

It is not hard to see that in these definitions the key terms are able to be substituted: "entrepreneur" may easily be replaced with "white-collar offender" (WCO), or "entrepreneurship" with "WCC", without doing damage to the overall sense (Table 1). The elements of exploiting opportunities, risk-taking as well as innovation are common to both entrepreneurship and to elite economic and financial crime.

According to van Duyne (1999):

> "The crime-entrepreneurship may seem confusing and look like a kind of self tormentation. Nevertheless this entrepreneur does not deviate from the more legitimate adventurer-entrepreneurial capitalists who stay (just) within the boundaries of the law." (p.3).

In 1993, the same author had pointed out that "both organized criminals and legitimate entrepreneurs operate in a similar manner." (van Duyne 1993, cit. in Smith and Gordon 2009: 257).

For Smith and Gordon (2009):

> "(…) entrepreneurial behaviour becomes visible in the planning and organizing of the crime, and in the aftermath when covering their tracks and disposing of the proceeds – manifested as trading, arbitrage and wheeling and dealing." (p. 259)

Table 1 - Definitions of entrepreneurship

Essence of definition	Author
Entrepreneurs (WCOs) attempt to predict and act upon change within markets. The entrepreneur (WCO) bears on the uncertainty of market dynamics.	(Knight, 1921, 1942)
The entrepreneur (WCO) is always a speculator. He deals with the uncertain conditions of the future. His success or failure depends on the correctness of his anticipation of uncertain events. If he fails in his understanding of things to come he is doomed.	(von Mises, 1949/1996)
The entrepreneur (WCO) is co-ordinator and arbitrageur.	(Walras, 1954)
Entrepreneurial activity (WC criminality) involves identifying opportunities within the economic system.	(Penrose, 1959/1980)
The field of entrepreneurship (WCC) involves the study of sources of opportunities; the processes of discovery, evaluation, and exploitation of opportunities; and the set of individuals who discover, evaluate, and exploit them.	(Shane and Venkataraman, 2000)
Entrepreneurship (WCC) is a context dependent social process through which individuals and teams create wealth by bringing together unique packages of resources to exploit marketplace opportunities.	(Ireland, Hitt, and Sirmon, 2003)
Entrepreneurship (WCC) is the mindset and process to create and develop economic activity by blending risk-taking, creativity and/or innovation with sound management, within a new or an existing organization.	(Commission of the European Communities, 2003)

Source: Adapted from Ahmad and Seymour (2008: 7).

These authors reviewed the literature on the relation between organised crime and entrepreneurship and concluded that the latter is embedded in the first. Based on van Duyne (1999), Smith and Gordon (2009) state that "(…) both crime and entrepreneurship emanate from learned cognitive human behaviours making them methods of operating." (p. 256).

To sum up, the notion of a correspondence between entrepreneurship and WCC behaviour is not new. It may therefore be fruitful to apply entrepreneurship models to the study of WCC, since general theories of crime fail to capture important aspects of the subject.

Some evidence on the connection between entrepreneurship and white-collar crime

Some evidence does exist on the connection between entrepreneurship and WCC. Faragó, Orhidea, and Boros (2008) compared risk-taking amongst entrepreneurs, college students and convicted criminals in hypothetical betting situations.[4] They found large differences between entrepreneurs and college students and small differences between entrepreneurs and criminals. These two groups behave similarly in winning situations or in limited losing situations. Only when faced with losing situations and the possibility of heavy losses is the behaviour of entrepreneurs and criminals significantly different. White-collar criminals were not included in the study, but it is interesting to note the affinity between entrepreneurs and criminals and the gap between these two groups from non-criminals in attitudes to risk.

Weitzel *et al.* (2010) found a significant positive relation between entrepreneurship and selfish behaviour. The authors tested the hypothesis of selfish profit-seeking entrepreneurs, that is, how far entrepreneurs would be willing to harm others to increase their profits (typical behaviour of the WCO). The results indicate that the notion of the selfish entrepreneur cannot be ruled out.

Sanders and Weitzel (2010), following Baumol (1990), formulated a model to analyse the distribution of entrepreneurial talent between productive and unproductive activities. The unproductive entrepreneur was figured as a white-collar offender who chooses crime as a way of maximising gains.

Tonoyan *et al.* (2010), using data from the World Business Environment Survey (2000), concludes that corrupt behaviour in entrepreneurs is shaped by both formal (economic and legal rules or organisations) and informal institutions (culturally embedded codes of conduct, norms and values). This result gives some support to the idea that the difference between a white-collar offender and a productive entrepreneur lies partly in the specific environment - in terms of institutions and "rules of the game".

Summing up, the idea of entrepreneurship and WCC as "two faces of the same coin" is not confined to theoretical speculation, but has some empirical support. Propensities for entrepreneurship and WCC may be reflected by applying the same models.

Stable factors determining the propensity to become entrepreneurs and to become white-collar offenders

In studying the propensity for entrepreneurial activity there are two dominant approaches. On the one hand, there is the view that entrepreneurship depends on stable personality traits, which may be mediated by inherited or genetic factors. Following this approach, individuals may have a propensity for entrepreneurship based on personality traits that are normally stable across life (entrepreneurial inclination). According to biogenetics, personality traits may be inherited and function as mediators of the influence of genes on entrepreneurial inclination (Nicolaou *et al.* 2008).

On the other hand, there is an approach based on cognitive psychology and on the theory of planned behaviour (TPB), developed by Ajzen (1985), which argues that entrepreneurship depends on less stable factors such as individual attitudes towards entrepreneurship, subjective norms and perceived behaviour control. These three dimensions may explain entrepreneurial intentions (Krueger, Reilly and Carsrud 2000).

Models based on stable factors determining entrepreneurship: genetic influence

Recently, evidence for the influence of genetic, endocrinological, biochemical, neurophysiological and neurological factors on human behaviour has been accumulating. This has largely displaced the notion of the mind as a "blank page" upon which psychosocial experiences write the determinants of behaviour. In light of these developments, entrepreneurial orientation will likely be better understood as being dependent on biological factors, mediated by personality traits.

Thus, White, Thornhill and Hampson (2006) tested testosterone levels as an index of entrepreneurial inclination, mediated by the personality trait '*risk propensity*' and concluded for a statistically significant positive relation.

Nicolaou *et al.* (2008) reported that genetic factors do not determine entrepreneurship by themselves; psychological factors and social environment are influential and may have interactive effects. Nicolaou *et al.* (2009: 109–110) referred to several studies that found a genetic basis for several psychological characteristics related to an ability to identify business opportunities: creativity; openness to experience; autonomy. They also indicated some studies that demonstrate the presence of these psychological traits in entrepreneurs. Shane *et al.* (2010: 292-293) reviewed the literature supporting the thesis that the personality trait '*openness to experience*' has a genetic component.

Almost all the research on the influence of genes is based on the comparison of monozygotic (MZ) and dizygotic (DZ) twins:

> "Comparing the similarity and difference in entrepreneurship between the two types of twins provides insight into the proportion of variance in entrepreneurship that is explained by genetic factors." (Nicolaou et al. 2008: 169)

This methodology provides no information on which genes are influential and how the interactions between genes and their mediators (e.g., personality traits) work. In the absence of such knowledge, it is not possible to produce quantitative estimates about the system of relations: genes – (phase 1) - personality traits – (phase 2) entrepreneurial inclination. Models constructed to date are solely focused in the second phase of relations (personality traits – entrepreneurial inclination).

Models based on stable factors for entrepreneurship: personality traits

The influence of personality traits on entrepreneurship attracted much attention until the end of the 1980s. However, according to Llewellyn and Wilson (2003), inconsistencies between theory and empirical results tended to reduce interest in this branch of research. Nevertheless, the relation between personality traits and entrepreneurial inclination continues to be debated.

In a review of the literature, Koh (1996) summarises the personality traits found to be most relevant to the study of entrepreneurship: internal locus of control; risk propensity; self-confidence; need for achievement; tolerance to ambiguity; and innovativeness. Individuals with high internal locus of control feel they are in control of events. Risk propensity denotes a disposition to take risks. Self-confidence characterises those who believe in their own capabilities. These traits are all predictive of entrepreneurial aptitude. The need for achievement was one of the first personality traits associated with entrepreneurs. Thus, for Kobia and Sikalieh (2010), individuals who are more oriented towards personal achievement are more likely to become entrepreneurs. Tolerance to ambiguity is related to an ability to cope with uncertainty. Innovation is the concept most associated with entrepreneurship, under the influence of Schumpeter (1934) and, later, of Drucker (1985).

Mixed empirical findings weakened the role of personality in the study of entrepreneurship, however. According to Littunen (2000), internal locus of control and need for achievement have been recognised as traits that are closely related to entrepreneurship.

Zhao and Seibert (2006) examined the role of personality traits in entrepreneurship over the last four decades and concluded that inconsistencies between theory and results stemmed from inappropriate use of personality variables, reflecting the state of personality research at time. However:

> "Two major developments that occurred in the last 15 years can help us draw more meaningful conclusions from the literature on personality and ES [*entrepreneurial status*]." "First, the emergence of the five-factor model of personality" (...) "Second, psychometric meta-analysis (e.g. Hunter and Schmidt 1990)..." (Zhao and Seibert 2006: 259)

A brief characterisation of the five-factor model (FFM) can be seen in Zhao and Seibert (2006: 260-262). The five dimensions are neuroticism; extraversion; openness to experience; agreeableness; and conscientiousness.

The authors constructed a meta-analysis of the review of the relationship between the Big Five personality dimensions and entrepreneurship and concluded that:

> "(...) entrepreneurs differ from those in managerial positions on four of the five fundamental dimensions of personality." (Zhao and Seibert 2006: 265)

The only dimension where no significant difference was found between entrepreneurs and managers was extraversion. The personality construct with the strongest relationship to entrepreneurship was conscientiousness, especially in relation to achievement motivation. This result confirms previous research in personality and entrepreneurship which concluded that the need for achievement is associated with entrepreneurship. Important also is the confirmation that innovation is associated with entrepreneurship. The results of Zhao and Seibert (2006) show:

> "(…) that entrepreneurs scored higher on *openness to experience* than did managers. Innovation, change, and creativity are at the core of recent definitions of entrepreneurship (…) and these traits evoke Schumpeter's (…) classic description of the entrepreneur as the agent of 'creative destruction'". (p. 266)

Antoncic (2009) empirically tested the FFM to technological developments by entrepreneurs and concluded that there are two personality factors, which are predictive of technological developments: openness to experience (positive impact) and neuroticism (negative impact).

An additional, widely studied, dimension of personality in entrepreneurship is, as noted above, risk propensity. According to Zhao and Seibert (2006), the inclusion of risk propensity within the FFM is controversial:

> "(…) some personality researchers argue that it forms a separate sixth dimension of personality (…) Thus, it is appropriate to examine risk propensity as a separate construct outside of the FFM (…)" (p. 259)

Stewart and Roth (2001) conducted a meta-analysis on the literature concerning risk propensity differences between entrepreneurs and managers and concluded that "(…) the risk propensity of entrepreneurs is greater than that of managers." Stewart and Roth (2001: 145)

Miner and Raju (2004) refuted this result, but Stewart and Roth (2004) reaffirmed their previous results. Caliendo, Fossen and Kritikos (2009) confirmed a positive relation between risk propensity and entrepreneurship.

In sum, it is possible to conclude that there is an association between some personality traits and entrepreneurial inclination[5]. Table 2 lists those personality traits for which the evidence for such a relation is most robust.

Table 2 - Personality traits associated to entrepreneurial inclination

FFM + RISK PROPENSITY	ENTREPRENEURSHIP LITERATURE	EVIDENCE
Openness to Experience	*Innovation*	Robust
Conscientiousness (Achievement)	*Need for Achievement*	Robust
Low Neuroticism	*Self - Confidence*	Robust
Agreeableness	----------------------	Some evidence
Extraversion	----------------------	Inconclusive
Risk Propensity	*Risk Propensity*	Robust
(a mix of several dimensions of FFM)	*Internal Locus of Control*	Robust
(a mix of several dimensions of FFM)	*Tolerance to Ambiguity*	Inconclusive

Source: Elaborated by the author.

Figure 1 shows the model used to study the influence of personality traits in entrepreneurial inclination.

Fig. 1 - Personality Traits Model for Entrepreneurial Inclination

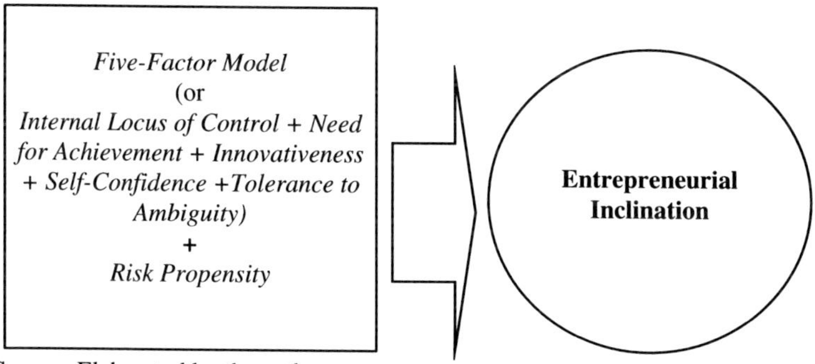

Source: Elaborated by the author.

Personality traits and white-collar crime

There has been much work on the relation between personality traits and WCC, and several studies apply the FFM, while others use alternative methodologies to measure personality. The conclusions are not as clear as in the case of entrepreneurship, and the results of different studies disagree. There are mixed results for extroversion (as in entrepreneurship studies) and for conscientiousness (some WCC studies concur with entrepreneurship studies in pointing to a higher level of that trait in WCC (e.g., Blickle *et al.* 2006). However, other studies disagree (e.g., Ragatz and Fremouw 2010). It is possible that these disagreements originate in divergence about the operationalisation of definitions and in the methodologies chosen. Nevertheless, some relation between neuroticism and agreeableness was found, indicating that WCOs are more neurotic (in contrast to the results on this personality trait obtained for entrepreneurs) and less agreeable than non-criminals.

The dimension *openness to experience* in relation to WCC has scarcely been studied. Accordingly to Elliot (2010: 274), "… those high in this trait also tend to have a broad range of interests…", and Collins and Schmidt (1993), in a study that compared the personality traits between convicted WCOs and WC non-offenders, concluded that the first are more involved in extracurricular activities[6], which may be associated with a high level of openness to experience. Nevertheless, more research has to be done on the relationship between this personality trait and WCC.

Concerning the dimension *risk propensity*, Faragó, Orhidea, and Boros (2008) concluded, as noted above, that offenders evidence higher risk behaviour than entrepreneurs when faced with unlimited loss situations. The same experiment should be applied to WCC and the results compared to the results of entrepreneurs. Although further research is needed, it is to be expected that WCOs would show a higher risk propensity than non-criminals, as is the case with entrepreneurs in relation to non-entrepreneurs.

In sum, more research is required on the relation between personality traits and WCC, with a specific focus on more complex economic and financial crimes requiring intelligence and innovative techniques. Present results (insufficient to warrant firm conclusions) indicate that the major difference in personality between entrepreneurs and WCOs is higher levels of anxiety – an element of neuroticism – exhibited by WCOs[7]. In the other personality trait constructs, no clear differences emerge between entrepreneurs and WCOs.

If in Figure 1 we replace the dependent variable "Entrepreneurial Inclination" by "WCC Inclination", we obtain the personality model for WCC inclination. The test of the model aims to capture whether there are differences between individuals who are WCC inclined and those who are not, in terms of personality traits.

"WCC inclination" could be measured asking the respondents about the probability of assuming a set of behaviours presented in the form of scenarios that constitute white-collar offenses. Then, as in Koh (1996), respondents who had a high or very high probability of committing WCC would be classified as WCC inclined; the others would be classified as non-WCC inclined. That is, WCC inclination would be measured as a dichotomous variable.

Model of intentions based on the Theory of Planned Behaviour

Ajzen and Fishbein (1977) and Gibb (2000) point out that the use of personality traits as a basis for developing a model of entrepreneurship suffer from conceptual and methodological problems. This is because personality traits tend to be stable across time and enterprise skills by contrast can be learned and developed through experience. According to Robinson *et al.* (1991), a cognitive approach based on attitudes is thus to be preferred. Attitudes are less stable than personality traits and change both across time and across situations through interaction with the environment. Several attitude models were applied to explain entrepreneurship: the Entrepreneurial Attitude Orientation model, comparing entrepreneurs to non-entrepreneurs (Robinson *et al.* 1991); the Attitude Towards Entrepreneurship model, comparing entrepreneurship potential in young people (Athayde 2009) and the Theory of Planned Behaviour (TPB), explaining entrepreneurship intentions (Krueger 1993). Krueger (2009), in charting the history of intention models as applied to entrepreneurship, argues that the theories developed by social and cognitive psychology had produced testable models, and, specifically, that intention models were already used in marketing with very robust results. Extending their application to entrepreneurship would therefore be viable. Since Krueger (1993) pioneered this approach, a large number of studies have appeared on this topic. The empirical results are robust and the model evidences high explanatory power. Krueger, Reilly and Carsrud (2000) denote that:

> "(…) existing results show that intentions are a better predictor of behaviour than personality traits or other approaches used in entrepreneurship literature." (p. 416)

Krueger, Reilly and Carsrud (2000: 411) explained the relevance of intention models to the study of entrepreneurship:

> "Why are intentions interesting to those who care about new venture formation? Entrepreneurship is a way of thinking, a way of thinking that emphasizes opportunities over threats. The opportunity identification process is clearly an intentional process, and, therefore, entrepreneurial intentions clearly merit our attention. Equally important, they offer a means to better explain—and predict—entrepreneurship. We don't start a business as a reflex, do we?" (p. 411)

If, in this quotation, we substitute the expressions related to entrepreneurship and venture creation by WCC, the text continues to make substantive sense, since WCC is a type of planned behaviour, "a way of thinking that emphasizes opportunities over threats". Identifying opportunity also plays a role on the intentional process. Indeed, "We don't *commit WCC* as a reflex, do we?".

Intention models, in particular the TPB – Theory of Planned Behaviour-, have been applied to many types of human behaviour, including unethical behaviour and some types of white-collar crime and, from what has been remarked above, it seems that there are reasonable arguments for doing so.

Theory of Planned Behaviour and entrepreneurial intentions

Krueger, Reilly and Carsrud (2000) explain that the TPB has been successfully applied to various issues and that it is derived from other intention models, configuring a robust approach to explain intentions. Guerrero, Rialp and Urbano (2008) note that the TPB stands out among several existing models. Armitage and Conner (2001: 471), in a meta-analysis of the TPB, confirm the strength of the model:

> "(...) from a database of 185 independent studies published up to the end of 1997, the TPB accounted for 27% and 39% of the variance in behaviour and intention, respectively. The perceived behavioural control (PBC) construct accounted for significant amounts of variance in intention and behaviour, independent of theory of reasoned action variables."

A summary of the TPB can be found in Ajzen (2002: 2):

> "TPB identifies three attitudinal antecedents of intention. Two reflect the perceived desirability of performing the behaviour: personal attitude toward outcomes of the behaviour and perceived social norms. The third, perceived behavioural control, reflects perceptions that the behaviour is personally controllable." (Krueger, Reilly and Carsrud 2000: 416)

When the TPB is applied to entrepreneurial intentions, *attitude* is a construct that reflects the perceived desirability of performing the behaviour – hypothesis: attitude is positively associated with entrepreneurial intentions. *Perceived social norms* (also known as subjective norms) denote a construct to measure the influence of important others on personal entrepreneurial intentions - hypothesis: exposure to perceived social norms that are conducive to entrepreneurship or being in contact with others who valorise entrepreneurial activity increase entrepreneurial intentions, and vice versa. *Perceived social norms* include the expectations of family or of friends concerning entrepreneurship, or the way they think about entrepreneurs. *Perceived behavioural control* is perceived self-efficacy, that is, the perceived ability to execute a target behaviour – hypothesis: this is positively associated with entrepreneurial intentions. According to Krueger, Reilly and Carsrud (2000):

> "Self-efficacy is linked to initiating and persisting at behaviour under uncertainty, to setting higher goals, and reducing threat-rigidity and learned helplessness (...). This is important because opportunity recognition depends on situational perceptions of controllability (…) In

addition, self efficacy has been associated with opportunity recognition and risk-taking."[8] (p. 416)

The association between *opportunity recognition* and *risk-taking* and one of the constructs of the entrepreneurial intentions model (*perceived behaviour control*) is an element of support for the adequacy of the same model to WCC intentions. Figure 2 presents a representation of the model of productive entrepreneurial intentions.

Fig. 2 - TPB and productive entrepreneurial intentions

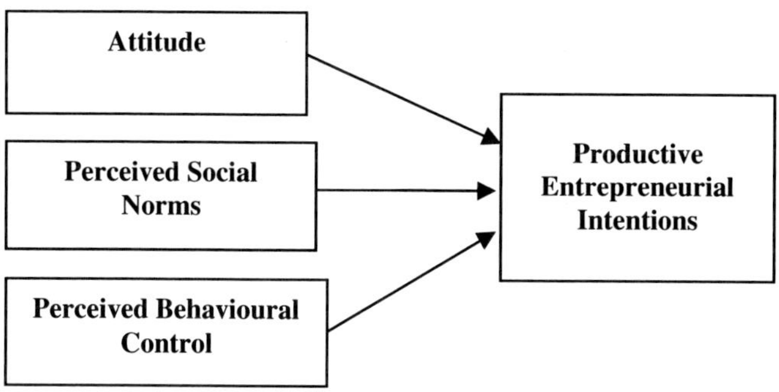

Source: Elaborated by the author.

Some examples of TPB as applied to productive entrepreneurial intentions are Krueger (1993), Krueger et al. (2000), Kolvereid and Isaksen (2006), Carr and Sequeira (2007), Liñán and Chen (2009) and Paço *et al.* (2011). Measurement of the TPB constructs was obtained by way of survey questionnaires to samples of students (mainly final year).[9] The questionnaires included several groups of questions related to demographic characteristics, personal attitudes, subjective norms, perceived behavioural control and entrepreneurial intention. According to Paço *et al.* (2011: 27) "The use of self-assessment to determine students' entrepreneurship attitudes represents well accepted practice in field of entrepreneurship research." Most studies of TPB use the methodologies of regression analysis and, more recently, structural equation modelling.

According to Liñán and Chen (2009), results indicate that this model explains about 40% of the variance in entrepreneurial intentions. Results also reveal that attitude and perceived behavioural control are statistically significant with the expected behavioural signs, with only the results for the influence of perceived social norms being inconclusive (e.g. in Krueger, Reilly and Carsrud 2000 and in Paço *et al.* 2011, relations were non-significant, whilst in Kolvereid and Isaksen 2006 and in Carr and Sequeira 2007 they were significant). Armitage and Connor (2001) in a meta-analytic review to the TPB note that:

> "Several researchers have argued that the subjective norm component of the TPB is inadequate and rarely predicts intention, and so have removed it from analysis (…) The present meta-analysis provides some support for this view: subjective norm was the TPB component most weakly related to intention." (p. 488)

Theory of Planned Behaviour and WCC intentions

The application of the TPB to WCC is challenging and somewhat complex, since measurement of the TPB constructs in relation to destructive behaviour is not easily obtained. Respondents may be unwilling to reveal WCC intentions, subjective desirability of WCC behaviour (WCC attitude) and the ability to execute it[10]. Even the perceived social norms concerning WCC may be difficult to apprehend. Nevertheless, we can find in literature several studies applying the TPB to unethical behaviour, deviance and crime, with sound results. The pioneering study is that of Beck and Ajzen (1991), who found the TPB able to predict dishonest behaviour (cheating on a test, shoplifting, and lying to get out of assignments) and "Multiple regression analyses showed that the theory of planned behaviour predicted intentions with a high degree of accuracy, and that it was moderately successful in the prediction of actual behaviour." (p. 285).

Examples of the application of the TPB to conventional crime are: Parker *et al.* (1992) - on intention to commit driving violations; Chang (1998) - on inadequate patient care; McMillan and Conner (2003) - on illicit drug use among students; Miller (2010) - on sexual offending; Kiriakidis (2010) - on young offenders' intentions to re-offend.

Moreover, there are applications of the TPB to WCC, as in Carpenter and Reimers (2005) - on unethical and fraudulent financial reporting; Bailey (2006) - on retail employee theft; Zawawi *et al.* (2008) - on behavioural intention for fraudulent reporting behaviour; Stone, Jawahar and Kisamore (2010) - on predicting academic misconduct intentions and behaviour.

However, to our knowledge, there are no studies comparing the same individuals concerning entrepreneurial intentions and WCC intentions. As noted above, according to Baumol (1990), individual differences between productive, unproductive or destructive entrepreneurs may not exist, because what matters is the maximisation of benefits in a "rules of the game" context. Thus, one who recognises an opportunity, takes risks and deploys his or her talent in innovative WCC is also a type of entrepreneur who finds in crime the best way to maximise earnings. Consequently, if perceived social norms do not influence intentions, it is expected that those who evidence entrepreneurial intentions also manifest WCC intentions. When perceived social norms are influential in the formation of individual intentions, the association between entrepreneurial intentions and WCC intentions may not exist, because when the subject's close associates (family members or peers) assign differential values to the entrepreneur or the criminal, the subject's entrepreneurial intentions (productive entrepreneurship) and WCC intentions (destructive entrepreneurship) may also diverge. However, as noted above, the construct *perceived social norms* is the component with weaker results in the TPB and, as already stated, some authors advocate its removal from the model.

If the positive relationship between entrepreneurial intentions and WCC intentions is not rejected we may establish that institutions and the contextual "rules of the game" (e.g., regulatory framework, the efficiency of the judicial system) matter and should be shaped so as to reduce the attractiveness of unproductive entrepreneurship (reducing net gains from WCC) and to incentivise productive entrepreneurship. If the influence of *perceived social norms* is not rejected, social context also becomes relevant in the choice between productive and unproductive entrepreneurship. Control variables on other individual and contextual influences could also be considered, such as morality, religious affiliation, regulatory framework, and others. If in Figure 2 we replace the dependent variable "Productive Entrepreneurial Intentions" by "WCC Intentions", we obtain the model of WCC intentions, based on the TPB.

Propositions about similarities between entrepreneurs and white-collar offenders

The above analysis has converged toward the formulation of two propositions (P_i) for the future development of empirical studies that use the models described to compare entrepreneurial behaviour with WCC.

Using the Personality Traits Model:

P_1: Individuals revealing entrepreneurial inclination are expected to show the same personality traits of those revealing WCC inclination.

Expected results: controlling for individual socio-demographic variables, we expect to find (i) a high degree of association between entrepreneurial inclination and WCC inclination, and (ii) that the results of the personality traits model for entrepreneurial inclination will be similar to the results for WCC inclination.

Using the TPB Model:

P_2. Individuals revealing entrepreneurial intentions will also reveal WCC intentions.

Expected results: controlling for individual socio-demographic variables and if the construct *perceived social norms* is not significant in the TPB model of productive entrepreneurial intentions and in the TPB model of WCC intentions, we expect to find (i) a high degree of association between entrepreneurial intentions and WCC intentions and also (ii) that the results of the application of the TPB to productive entrepreneurial intentions (in terms of explained variance of intentions and of the significance of TPB constructs) will be similar to the results of the application of the TPB to WCC intentions.

Conclusion

This study began with the presentation of the hypothesis advocated by Baumol (1990) about a parallelism between entrepreneurship and white-collar crime (WCC), taking into account the features of innovation, seizing opportunities and risk propensity engaged in WCC practices.

Next, the reviewed works served to sustain the existence of similarities between entrepreneurs and white-collar offenders.

Then, we verified from the analysis of the literature on entrepreneurial behaviour and on WCC that there are two models that have been widely applied to the study of entrepreneurship, but also to some forms of WCC: the personality traits model; and the intentions model (based on the theory of planned behaviour).

Based on these findings, we propose a way of testing Baumol's hypothesis through the integration of the empirical study of entrepreneurship and WCC. This can be done by testing each of the models with the same sample in both types of behaviour, and comparing the results. To the best of our knowledge this has never attempted before.

Finally, we draw attention to that which might be expected: that individuals revealing entrepreneurial inclination show the same personality traits as those revealing WCC inclination; and that individuals revealing entrepreneurial intentions will also reveal WCC intentions.

Acknowledgements

I am grateful to Daniela Wilks, John Wilks (in memorial), Rita Faria, Pedro Sousa and the reviewers for their helpful comments.

Bibliography

Ahmad, N. and Seymour, R. G. 2008, "Defining Entrepreneurial Activity: Definitions Supporting Frameworks for Data Collection", OECD Statistics Working Paper, 24-Jan-2008. Accessed at: http://papers.ssrn.com/sol3/papers.cfm?abstract_id=1090372, 3 September 2012

Ajzen, I. 1985, "From Intentions to Actions: A Theory of Planned Behaviour", in Julius Kuhl and Jurgen Beckmann (ed.) *Action Control: From Cognition to Behaviour*, pp. 11—39, Verlag, Berlin: Springer

—. 2002, "Perceived Behavioural Control, Self-Efficacy, Locus of Control, and the Theory of Planned Behaviour", *Journal of Applied Social Psychology* 32 (4), 665

Ajzen, I., and Fishbein, M. 1977, "Attitude. Behaviour Relations: A Theoretical Analysis and Review of Empirical Research", *Psychological Bulletin* 84 (5), 888

Antoncic, B. 2009, "The Entrepreneur's General Personality Traits and Technological Developments", *World Academy of Science, Engineering and Technology* 53 (3), 236

Armitage, C. J. and Conner, M. 2001, "Efficacy of The Theory of Planned Behaviour: A Meta--Analytic Review", *British Journal of Social Psychology* 40 (4), 471

Athayde, R. 2009, "Measuring Enterprise Potential in Young People", *Entrepreneurship Theory and Practice* 33 (2), 481

Bailey, A. 2006, "Retail Employee Theft: A Theory of Planned Behaviour Perspective", *International Journal of Retail and Distribution Management* 34 (11), 803

Baumol, W. 1990, "Entrepreneurship: Productive; Unproductive; and Destructive". *Journal of Business Venturing* 11 (1), 3

Beck, L. and Ajzen, I. 1991, "Predicting Dishonest Actions Using the Theory of Planned Behaviour", *Journal of Research in Personality* 25 (3), 285

Benson M. L. and Simpson, S. S. 2009, *White Collar Crime: An Opportunity Perspective*, New York: Routledge

Blickle, G., Schlegel, A., Fassbender, P., and Klein, U. 2006, "Some Personality Correlates of Business White--Collar Crime", *Applied Psychology: An International Review* 55 (2), 220

Caliendo, M., Fossen, F. and Kritikos, A. 2009, "Risk Attitudes of Nascent Entrepreneurs: New Evidence from an Experimentally--Validated Survey", *Small Business Economics* 32 (2), 153

Carpenter, T. D., and Reimers, J. L. 2005, "Unethical and Fraudulent Financial Reporting: Applying the Theory of Planned Behaviour", *Journal of Business Ethics* 60 (2), 115

Carr, J. C. and Sequeira, J. M. 2007, "Prior Family Business Exposure as Intergenerational Influence and Entrepreneurial Intent: A Theory of Planned Behaviour Approach", *Journal of Business Research* 60 (10), 1090

Chang, M. K. 1998, "Predicting Unethical Behaviour: A Comparison of the Theory of Reasoned Action and the Theory Of Planned Behaviour", *Journal of Business Ethics* 17 (16), 1825

Desai, S. and Acs, Z. 2007, "A Theory of Destructive Entrepreneurship", *Jena Economic Research Papers*, 0085, 43 pp.

Drucker P. 1985, *Innovation and Entrepreneurship: Practices and Principle*,. New York: Harper

Elliot, R. 2010, "Examining the Relationship between Personality Characteristics and Unethical Behaviours Resulting in Economic Crime", *Ethical Human Psychology and Psychiatry* 12 (3), 269

Faragó, K., Orhidea, K. and Boros, J. 2008, "Risk-Taking in Entrepreneurs, Compared to Criminals and Students: The Role of Uncertainty and Stakes", *The Journal of Socio-Economics* 37 (6), 2231

Finch, J. 1987, "The Vignette Technique in Survey Research", *Sociology* 21 (1), 105

Friedrichs, D. 2010, *Trusted Criminals: White Collar Crime in Contemporary Society*, (4th ed.), Belmont: Wadsworth Cengage Learning

Gibb, A. 2000, "SME Policy, Academic Research and the Growth of Ignorance: Mythical Concepts, Myths, Assumptions, Rituals and Confusions", *International Small Business Journal* 18 (3/71), 13

Guerrero M., Rialp J. and Urbano D. 2008, "The Impact of Desirability and Feasibility on Entrepreneurial Intentions: A Structural Equation Model", *International Entrepreneurship and Management Journal* 4 (1), 35

Kiriakidis, S. P. 2010, "Prediction and Explanation of Young Offenders Intentions to Re-Offend from Behavioural, Normative, and Control Beliefs", *European Psychologist* 15 (3): 211

Kirzner, I. 1973, *Entrepreneurship and Competition*, Chicago: University Of Chicago Press
Kobia, M. and Sikalieh, D. 2010, "Towards a Search for the Meaning of Entrepreneurship", *Journal of European Industrial Training* 34 (2): 110
Koh, H. C. 1996, "Testing Hypotheses of Entrepreneurial Characteristics: A Study of Hong Kong MBA Students", *Journal of Managerial Psychology* 11 (3), 12
Kolvereid L. and Isaksen E. 2006, "New Business Start-Up and Subsequent Entry into Self-Employment", *Journal of Business Venturing* 21 (6), 866
Krueger, N. 1993, "The Impact of Prior Entrepreneurial Exposure on Perceptions of New Venture Feasibility and Desirability", *Entrepreneurship Theory and Practice* 18 (1), 5
—. 2009, "Entrepreneurial Intentions Are Dead: Long Live Entrepreneurial Intentions", in Alan L. Carsrud and Malin Brannback (eds.) *Understanding the Entrepreneurial Mind: Opening the Black Box*, pp. 51-72, London: Springer.
Krueger, N., Reilly, M. D. and Carsrud, A. L. 2000, "Competing Models of Entrepreneurial Intentions", *Journal of Business Venturing* 15 (5-6), 411
Liñán, F. and Chen Y. 2009, "Development and Cross--Cultural Application of a Specific Instrument to Measure Entrepreneurial Intentions", *Entrepreneurship Theory and Practice* 33 (3), 593
Littunen, H. 2000, "Entrepreneurship and the Characteristics of the Entrepreneurial Personality", *International Journal of Entrepreneurial Behaviour and Research* 6 (6), 295
Llewellyn, D. J. and Wilson, K. M. 2003, "The Controversial Role of Personality Traits in Entrepreneurial Psychology", *Education and Training* 45 (6), 341
Mcmillan, B. and Conner, M. 2003, "Applying an Extended Version of the Theory of Planned Behaviour to Illicit Drug Use among Students", *Journal of Applied Social Psychology* 33 (8), 1662
Miller, D. 2010, "An Application of the Theory of Planned Behaviour to the Proximal and Distal Etiology of Sexual Offending", *Trauma Violence Abuse* 11 (3), 113
Miner, J. B. and Raju, N. S. 2004, "Risk Propensity Differences Between Managers and Entrepreneurs and Between Low – and High--Growth Enterprises: A Reply in a More Conservative Vein", *Journal of Applied Psychology* 89 (1), 3

Nicolaou, N., Shane, S., Cherkas, L., Hunkin, J. and Spector, T. 2008, "Is the Tendency to Engage in Entrepreneurship Genetic?", *Management Science* 54 (1), 167

Nicolaou, N., Shane, S., Cherkas, L., and Spector, T. 2009, "Opportunity Recognition and the Tendency to Be an Entrepreneur: A Bivariate Genetics Perspective", *Organizational Behaviour and Human Decision Processes* 110 (2), 108

Paço, A., Ferreira, J., Raposo, M., Rodrigues, R. and Dinis, A. 2011, "Behaviours and Entrepreneurial Intention: Empirical Findings about Secondary Students", *Journal of International Entrepreneurship* 9 (1), 20

Parker, D., Manstead, A.S.R., Stradling, S.G., Reason, J.T. and Baxter, J.S. 1992, "Intention to Commit Driving Violations: An Application of the Theory of Planned Behaviour", *Journal of Applied Psychology* 77 (1), 94

Ragatz, L., and Fremow, W. 2010, "A Critical Examination of Research on the Psychological Profiles of White--Collar Criminals", *Journal of Forensic Psychology Practice* 10 (5), 373

Robinson, P. B., Stimpson, D. V., Huefner, J. C. and Hunt, H. K. 1991, "An Attitude Approach to the Prediction of Entrepreneurship", *Entrepreneurship Theory and Practice* 15 (4), 13

Sanders, M. and Weitzel, U. 2010, "The Allocation of Entrepreneurial Talent and Destructive Entrepreneurship", *UNU--WIDER: World Institute for Development Economics Research*, Working Paper No. 2010/46: 21 pp.

Schumpeter, J. A. 1934, *The Theory of Economic Development*, Leipzig: Duncker and Humblot, 1911, (English eds.). Cambridge: Harvard University Press

Shane, S., Nicolaou, N., Cherkas, L. and Spector, T. D. 2010, "Do Openness to Experience and Recognizing Opportunities Have the Same Genetic Source?", *Human Resource Management* 49 (2), 291

Smith, R. and Gordon, R. 2009, "Understanding Entrepreneurial Behaviour in Organized Criminals", *Journal of Enterprising Communities: People and Places in the Global Economy* 3 (3), 256

Stewart Jr., Wayne H. and Roth, P. L. 2004, "Data Quality Affects Meta--Analytic Conclusions: A Response to Miner and Raju (2004) Concerning Entrepreneurial Risk Propensity", *Journal of Applied Psychology* 89 (1), 14

Stewart Jr., Wayne H. and Roth, Philip L. 2001, "Risk Propensity Differences between Entrepreneurs and Managers: A Meta--Analytic Review", *Journal of Applied Psychology* 86 (1), 145

Stone, T. H., Jawahar, I. M. and Kisamore, J. 2010, "Predicting Academic Misconduct Intentions and Behaviour Using the Theory of Planned Behaviour and Personality", *Basic and Applied Social Psychology* 32 (1), 35

Tonoyan, V., Strohmeyer, R., Habib, M. and Perlitz, M. 2010, "Corruption and Entrepreneurship: How Formal and Informal Institutions Shape Firm Behaviour in Transition and Mature Market Economies", *Entrepreneurship Theory and Practice* 34 (5), 803

van Duyne, P.C. 1999, "Mobsters are Human too", in Canter, D., Alison, L. (Ed.). *Offender Profiling Series: Profiling in Policy and Practice.* Accessed at: http://www.portill.nl/articles/Van%20Duyne/PSYCHPOL .pdf, 3 September 2012

Weitzel U., Urbig D., Desai, S.; Sanders, M. and Acs, Z. 2010, "The Good, the Bad, and the Talented: Entrepreneurial Talent and Selfish Behaviour", *Journal of Economic Behaviour and Organization* 76 (1), 64

White, R.; Thornhill, S. and Hampson, E. (2006), Entrepreneurs and Evolutionary Biology: the Relationship between Testosterone and New Venture Creation, *Organizational Behaviour and Human Decisions Processes* 100: 21--34

Zawawi, S. N. H. M., Jusoff, K., Rahman, R. A. and Idris, K. M. 2008, "Behavioural Intention for Fraudulent Reporting Behaviour Using Cognitive Theory", *Asian Social Science* 4 (7), 43

Zhang, Z. and Arvey, R. 2009, "Rule Breaking in Adolescence and Entrepreneurial Status: An Empirical Investigation", *Journal of Business Venturing* 24 (5), 436

Zhao, H. and Seibert, S. E. 2006, "The Big Five Personality Dimensions and Entrepreneurial Status: A Meta--Analytical Review", *Journal of Applied Psychology* 91 (2), 259-271

Notes

[1] The word *inclination* draws attention to the stability across life of the factors that increase the propensity for someone becoming an entrepreneur.

[2] The word *intentions* underlines the attitudinal character of the propensity for someone to become an entrepreneur. According to Krueger (2009: 51): "intentions are classically defined as the cognitive state temporally and causally prior to action".

[3] See in Desai and Acs (2007) the definition of the three types of entrepreneurship.

[4] Convicted criminals for burglary and armed robbery.

[5] Koh (1996) estimated entrepreneurial inclination by asking respondents to indicate their probability of starting a business in the next three years or so.

Respondents who had a high or very high probability of starting a business were classified as entrepreneurially inclined; the others were classified as non-entrepreneurially inclined. That is, entrepreneurial inclination was measured as a dichotomous variable.

[6] The authors did not use the FFM, but the PDI Employment Inventory.

[7] Ragatz and Fremouw (2010: 396): "(...) white-collar offenders reported higher levels of anxiety (…) than white-collar professionals." On the contrary, as mentioned above, the personality of entrepreneurs is associated to a lower level of neuroticism than that which is revealed by non-entrepreneurs.

[8] The association between opportunity recognition and risk-taking and one of the constructs of the entrepreneurial intentions model (Perceived behaviour control) is an element of support for the adequacy of the same model to WCC intentions.

[9] Usually entrepreneurs are not surveyed in questionnaires because their different past experiences may introduce a bias on their entrepreneurial attitude and intentions.

[10] In operational terms, WCC intentions can be captured by adding to the survey scenarios (or vignettes) featuring fictional white-collar offences, following the Vignette Technique as described in Finch (1987).

PART III –

PREVENTION AND ACTION

CHAPTER NINE

COULD THE LIBOR BE MANIPULATED BY A SINGLE BANK?

MARIUS-CRISTIAN FRUNZA

Introduction

The manipulation of stocks or commodity prices is considered today a criminal offense in most modern jurisdictions. Over the last decade, the losses suffered by financial institutions and the cases of violation and crime in financial markets have increased in both frequency and severity. We show through a qualitative approach that the moral hazard constitutes not only the origin of these phenomena but also amplifies the contagion of criminal activities in the institutions dealing in the financial markets. The manipulation of financial markets is considered a crime in many Western countries. Nevertheless, very few cases have been identified in the recent past and the jurisprudence is relatively scarce as is the scientific literature on the topic. This is due mainly to difficulties in tracking these occurrences and also bringing relevant proof that a violation in market efficiency is the result of an illegal action or a breach of duty towards clients by a financial agent. The nature of financial markets is far from being fully understood and the main theories resumed in the 1970s by Black & Scholes (1973) and Fama & French (1993) still constitute the foundations of modern finance. These theories, built around the market efficiency hypothesis and assumptions of non-arbitrage opportunities, do not find general consensus in the scientific community. Thus, an attempt at market manipulation is hard to detect based only on external observations since market indicators (price, volume, volatility) fail to provide relevant information. The flow of information in the process of financial market price aggregation is shown in Figure 1.

The process of information flow in the constitution of market prices starts with the empirical metrics describing the behaviour of the asset. For instance, when dealing with a stock, financial metrics are one of the most

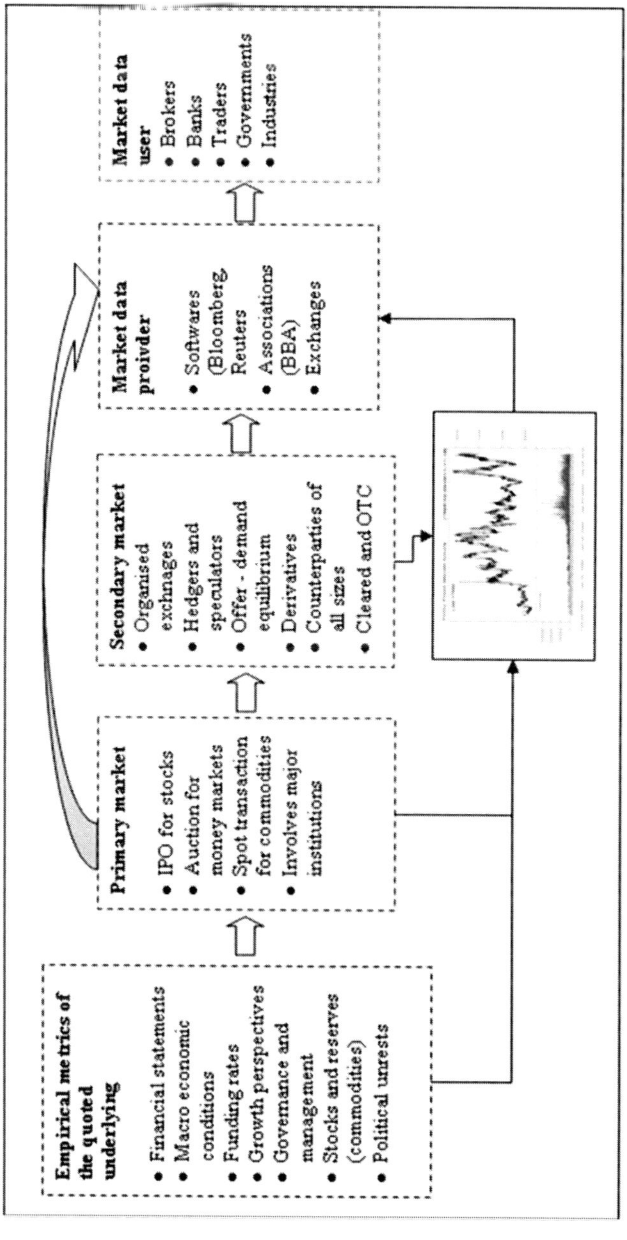

Figure 1. Information flow in the process of market price aggregation

relevant. For a commodity (i.e., oil), reserves, production and consumption are relevant. The next step is information regarding the primary markets, where initially the raw underlying data is traded from its cradle. Once bought, the underlying data is traded on secondary exchanges and this generates the price widely received by the public from market data providers.

Market manipulation can occur at each of these steps. Thus, shenanigans in the financial statements can distort the perception of markets, thereby changing the price tendency (i.e., Enron case in 2002). In the primary market, misallocation in the IPO process or attempts to corner the commodity market can obviously be cases of market manipulation (i.e., Hamanaka and the copper market case in 1990 implicating the Sumitomo Corporation). When an agent tries to alter the supply-demand equilibrium on the secondary market through misleading information, it impacts the price level in a way desired by the rogue agent. "Pump and dump" scams are a relevant case for this type of manipulation (i.e., GYMM stock scandal on NASDAQ in 1990). Once the transaction is established on the primary and secondary markets, the information is transmitted to data providers that supply institutions involved in the financial markets, and not only. The data provided is in some cases the basis for the settlement of financial instruments. Thus, if the data provided is altered, massive fluctuation in the derivatives could occur as intended by a misleading information provider. The latter case appeared in the LIBOR scandal when the information provided by some banks to calculate the LIBOR was not accurate with the underlying transaction. We will focus on an econometric study of the times series of submitted rates by the banks involved in the LIBOR. We try to assess the influence of the concerned banks on the final LIBOR figure and to evaluate the possible impact of their misrepresentation. The paper is organized as follows: Section 2 presents a literature review on capital market crime and deals with a few cases studied concerning market manipulation. Section 3 proposes a methodology to assess the LIBOR scandal through an econometric framework. Section 4 presents statistical results based on the proposed methodology, with regard to the robustness of LIBOR calculation. Section 5 develops an impact analysis of changes in bank submissions. Section 6 attempts to look backward at what could have been the real LIBOR. Section 7 concludes.

Literature review

Weiss (2003) focuses on a relevant case, the pump and dump schemes involving the use of false or misleading statements to boost microcap stocks, which are "dumped" on the public investors at inflated prices and the involvement of a New York based criminal organisation. Snider (2011) examines the challenges of detecting, punishing and preventing stock market crime in the 21st century. Fisher et al. (2011) discuss whether the parameters of criminal law are sufficiently wide to capture the conduct of financial market participants who have acted without considering the impact on the financial and economic system as a whole. We present in this section three cases of market manipulation that underline the different aspects of this crime.

Case 1. Bankia, a distressed bank

The former president of Bankia and 32 former members of the failed bank's board are to be investigated on charges of falsifying accounts, dishonest administration, price manipulation and improper appropriation. Bankia was nationalised in May 2012 at a cost of 23 billion euros for the public purse after its share price fell by 75% in less than a year. The investigators charged Bankia with carrying out "a massive fraud" on its small investors because its stock market launch was based on "the falsification of data". The Audiencia Nacional, the court that deals with serious crime, decided to investigate after the anti-corruption prosecutors said they believed there was a case to answer. The judge has also summoned the former governor of the Bank of Spain, the president of the Stock Market National Commission, the Deloitte partner who worked for Bankia and the legal representative of the Frob (Fondo de Reestructuracion Ordenada Bancaria) to testify. The Audiencia Nacional has also requisitioned from the savings banks that comprise the BFA-Bankia group details of all credits, loans and guarantees made since 2008 in favour of the board and executives and their families, as well political parties.

Case 2: Silver futures

A class action lawsuit against J.P. Morgan Chase & Co. and HSBC was filed in 2010, alleging that the banks violated federal antitrust laws by manipulating the prices of silver futures and option contracts. Beginning in early 2008, HSBC and J.P Morgan reportedly built up extremely large short positions in silver futures and options on the Commodity Exchange

Inc. (COMEX), with J.P. Morgan increasing its silver derivative holdings by over 6 billion dollars or 220 million ounces. The class action lawsuit alleges that J.P. Morgan and HSBC used a variety of tactics to artificially drive down the price of silver. The complaint alleges that HSBC and J.P. Morgan made large, coordinated trades, among other schemes, to artificially lower the price of silver at key times when the precious metal should have been trading at higher levels. By depressing the price of silver, the class action claims that the defendants made substantial illegal profits while harming investors and restraining competition in the COMEX silver futures market.

Case 3: The LIBOR scandal

The LIBOR scandal occurred in June 2012 after Barclays settled for almost 480 million US dollars when it was charged by various investigators with attempts to manipulate the LIBOR rates. Other institutions like J.P. Morgan Chase and Citibank were also cited in the affair.

A report by the Financial Security Agency (FSA) pointed to one of the Tier-one British banks. Thus, it appeared that Barclays acted inappropriately between January 2005 and July 2008 by making US dollar LIBOR and EURIBOR submissions which took into account requests made by its derivative traders motivated by profit. The bank also intended to influence the EURIBOR (and to a much lesser extent the US dollar LIBOR) submissions of other banks, contributing to the rate-setting process. Rate submissions that take into account the banks' own business needs or try to influence the submissions of other banks mean there is a real risk that the published LIBOR and EURIBOR rates can be manipulated. Thus, the bank and the submitting panel could have benefitted from this misconduct to the detriment of other market participants. In cases where the act is contrived with other banks, the risk of manipulation increases massively. Banks acted also inappropriately between September 2007 and May 2009 by submitting lower LIBOR rates than the real market conditions which took into account concerns over the negative media perception of the banks' LIBOR submissions.

Liquidity issues were a particular focus for financial institutions during the financial crisis and the banks' LIBOR submissions were seen by market analysts as a measure of their ability to raise funds to finance their assets with a highly uncertain value at that time. Senior management concerns, in turn, resulted in instructions to reduce LIBOR submissions in order to avoid negative media comment.

Regulators were also scrutinizing relationships that banks, such as HSBC, Germany's Deutsche Bank and the French banks Société Générale and Crédit Agricole, may have had with a former Barclays trader, raising questions over the allegations related to attempts to manipulate the European equivalent of LIBOR, known as EURIBOR.

Concerns about the nature of the LIBOR rates and the banks' submission are not recent. In 2008, a Wall Street Journal article stated that major banks were contributing to the erratic behaviour of a crucial global lending benchmark. The article pointed out that Citigroup Inc., WestLB, HSBC, J.P. Morgan Chase & Co. and UBS AG were among the banks that have been reporting significantly lower borrowing costs for the London interbank offered rate, or LIBOR, than that which other market measures suggested they should be. An independent research published in 2012 by Abrantes-Metz shows that some questionable patterns arise with respect to the banks' daily LIBOR quotes, especially for the period ending on August 8th, 2007, for which the intraday variance for bank quotes is not statistically different from zero. Snider (2010) presents suggestive evidence that several banks have large portfolio exposures to the LIBOR and have recently profited from the rapid descent of the LIBOR. The paper speculates that these exposures may be the source of misreporting incentives.

From the technical point of view, both LIBOR and EURIBOR are calculated as the average of submitted rates by various banks. The LIBOR definition published by the BBA is as follows: *The rate at which an individual contributor panel bank could borrow funds, were it to do so by asking for and then accepting interbank offers in reasonable market size just prior to 11:00 London time*. EURIBOR is defined by the EBF as: *The rate at which euro interbank term deposits are being offered within the EMU zone by one prime bank to another at 11:00 am Brussels time.* Thus, every day at 11:00 a.m. (CET), Thompson Reuters receives the submission from the panel and calculates an arithmetic average, eliminating the four highest and four lowest contributions.

Methodological considerations: Forensic statistics

We consider the moral hazard as a real option given for free to a financial agent in order to enhance the likelihood of generating profits. This real option is reflected amongst financial agents as a change in behaviour and conduct by exposing the institutions to unreasoned risks in order to provide higher returns. The constant pressure on financial agents to deliver profits in adverse market conditions increased the infusion of illegal liquidity sources. Thus, there is a strong shift of criminal organisations from classic activities like racketeering, shylocking and drug traffic towards "white collar" crime around financial markets.

In the current meaning introduced by Paul Krugman, moral hazard is described as a situation in which one agent makes a decision about how much risk to take, while someone else bears the cost of the undertaken risk. For instance, one trader can expose a bank to massive risk exposures in order to maximize his potential bonus indexed on the performance, without bearing the possible losses generated by the trade. Other examples of moral hazard include:

1. Brokers: (best executions: intraday options)
2. Traders: (proprietary trading: volatility option)
3. Structuring: (structured products: volatility, correlation)
4. Fund managers: (alpha seeking: style option)
5. Risk managers: (limits: P\&L option)
6. Auditors: (accounting and process review: P\&L option)
7. Regulators: (agreements: turnover options)

We focus in this chapter on the case of LIBOR manipulation and try to assess the severity of the allegations concerning the major banks with ties to the LIBOR scandal. The attempt to manipulate the rate is a consequence of the moral hazard. Thus, the bank could freely opt to submit a rate that could drive the final rate closer to an advantageous value for its business.

In order to assess the possibility that one or several banks might alter the representation of LIBOR rates, we conducted a few econometric tests. Forensic statistics is able to detect anomalies in market behaviours without having non-public, insider information, based only on the available public data. Our methodology focused on testing the following hypotheses:

1. Is the process of calculating rates robust?
2. What is the impact of individual bank submissions on the total rate and how did the contributions change over time?
3. What is the impact of a manipulation attempt coming from a single bank or from a concerted action by several banks?

In order to answer these questions, we obtained first a dataset of USD LIBOR submissions between 2005 and 2008 published by an independent analyst[1]. According to the dataset, 16 banks were submitting daily rates to the LIBOR for each maturity. If we exclude the 4 highest submissions and the 4 lowest submissions, the LIBOR was calculated with a sample of 8 submissions, that we will call S_8. We defined the following metrics:

1. $LIBObserved_M$ is the observed LIBOR for the maturity M.

2. $\boldsymbol{LIB_M}$ is the LIBOR calculated for maturity $\boldsymbol{M}$ defined as the average of the submitted rates $\boldsymbol{R_{i;M}}$ by each bank $\boldsymbol{i}$ from the panel of 8 banks $\boldsymbol{S_8}$.

$$LIB_M = \frac{1}{8}\sum_{i=1}^{8} R_{i,M} 1_{R_{i,M} \in S_8}$$

3. $\boldsymbol{LIBFS_M}$ is the full LIBOR sample for maturity $\boldsymbol{M}$ and is defined as the average of the submitted rates $\boldsymbol{R_{i;M}}$ by each bank $\boldsymbol{i}$ from the full panel of $\boldsymbol{N}$ banks.

$$LIBFS_M = \frac{1}{N}\sum_{i=1}^{N} R_{i,M}$$

4. $\boldsymbol{LIBRnd_M}$ is the LIBOR for maturity $\boldsymbol{M}$ considering the submissions from 8 banks chosen randomly amongst the panel.

$$LIBRnd_M = \frac{1}{8}\sum_{j=1}^{8} R_{,M} 1_{j \in Rnd(8,N)}$$

5. $\boldsymbol{LIBBank_{M;B}}$ is the LIBOR for maturity $\boldsymbol{M}$ calculated by the current rules considering the submission by the panel from which we exclude bank $\boldsymbol{B}$.

$$LIBBank_{M,B} = \frac{1}{8}\sum_{j=1}^{8(excluding\,B)} R_{j,M}$$

6. $\boldsymbol{LIBFSBank_{M;B}}$ is the full LIBOR sample for maturity $\boldsymbol{M}$ and is defined as the average of the submitted rates $\boldsymbol{R_{i;M}}$ by each bank $\boldsymbol{i}$ from the full panel of $\boldsymbol{N}$ banks excluding bank **B**.

$$LIBFSBank_{M,B} = \frac{1}{N-1}\sum_{j=1}^{N(excluding\,B)} R_{j,M}$$

Given these notations, we defined the following spreads:

- $\boldsymbol{FullSampleSpread_M = LIB_M - LIBFS_M}$ is the difference between the official LIBOR for maturity $\boldsymbol{M}$ and the full LIBOR sample calculated for the entire panel.
- $\boldsymbol{RandomSpread_M = LIB_M - LIBRnd_M}$ is the difference between the official LIBOR for maturity **M** and the random LIBOR calculated with 8 random submissions from the full panel.
- $\boldsymbol{PanelDistance_{M;B} = R_{M;B} - LIBFSBank_{M;B}}$ is the difference between the submitted rate for maturity $\boldsymbol{M}$ by bank $\boldsymbol{B}$ and the full LIBOR sample calculated excluding that bank.

- ***LIBORSpread**$_{M;B}$* = ***LIB**$_M$* - ***LIBBank**$_{M;B}$* is the difference between the official LIBOR for maturity ***M*** and the LIBOR calculated from a panel excluding the submissions of bank ***B***.

First, we assessed the robustness of the LIBOR calculation method by analyzing the basic statistics of the ***FullSampleSpread**$_M$* and ***RandomSpread**$_M$*. If the process were robust, we would expect an average close to zero with a small standard deviation.

We applied the structural break test of Bai and Perron (2003) for the ***PanelDistance**$_{M;B}$* metric in order to see if the submissions from an individual bank changed in pattern when compared to other institutions. We would expect to find a structural change around the crisis period in 2008, before Lehman defaulted when bank financing conditions were very difficult.

Banks	Dates for Structural Breaks
Barclays	"2007-08-27"; "2008-05-28"
Citigroup	"2007-08-14"; "2008-05-28"
JP Morgan	"2008-05-28"
UBS	"2007-08-03"; "2008-04-15"
RBS	"2008-05-28"
Bank of America	"2008-05-28"
HSBC	"2007-09-12"; "2008-05-28"
Norinchuckin	"2007-08-31"; "2008-05-28"
BTMU	"2008-05-28"
Lloyds	"2008-05-28"
Rabobank	"2008-05-28"
WestLB	"2008-05-28"
Credit Suisse	"2008-05-28"
Deutsche Bank	"2007-10-19"; "2008-05-28"

Table 1. Break points in the Panel Distance

The structural break tests show that two important moments occurred in submissions from a majority of the panel: the summer of 2007 and the spring of 2008, which correspond to the outbreak of the subprime crisis and its subsequent contagion effects, respectively (Table 1). At those moments, banks experienced changes in their funding conditions. And yet each bank reacted differently. For instance, some banks submitted rates constantly higher than the panel's (i.e., Barclays, Figure 2), some lower than the panel's (i.e., HSBC and Citigroup), while others oscillated nervously around the panel's average (i.e., BoA, UBS)

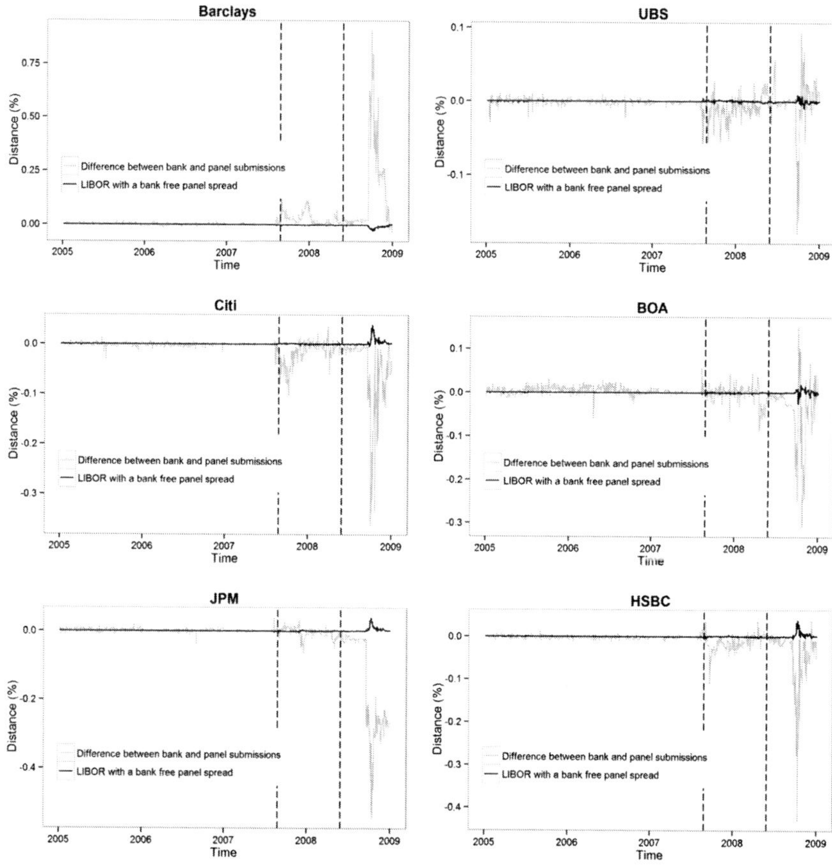

Figure 2. Panel distance and impact of bank submissions for a few banks in the panel (3-Month USD LIBOR)

Second, we assessed the manipulation attempts and analysed for each bank the difference between its submissions and those of the other banks in the panel. After the Barclays investigation, the FSA underlined that some banks showed better financing conditions than they actually had, thereby communicating a lower LIBOR to the panel. If the methodology of LIBOR's calculations is robust, the impact of one bank communicating a lower LIBOR rate should not affect the outcome, as it would be either diluted in the average or removed by the filtering of extreme submissions. Moreover, we assumed that, during the crisis period, a bank submitted a LIBOR rate 20 bp lower than its real financing at that time. We modelled the "fixing spread" as a Levy stochastic process. Based on these assumptions, we reconstructed a simulated LIBOR with the "true" rates and we considered the difference between the observed and the simulated rates. We replicated the simulation considering a concerted action between 2, 3 and 4 banks.

The third question is by far more complex and the answer is heavily dependent of the underlying assumptions. Figure 3 depicts the relationship between the 3M USD LIBOR and the 3M Treasury rates of the United States Treasury notes.

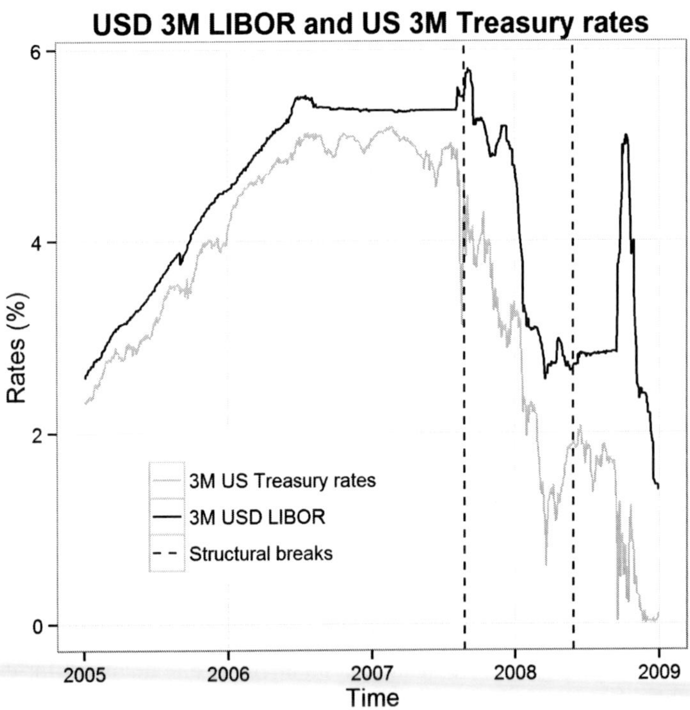

Figure 3. LIBOR vs United States Treasury rates (3 months)

The Bai and Perron test underlines two structural breaks that occurred in the nature of the relationship between the US Treasury rates and the corresponding LIBOR in August 2007 and June 2008. Curiously, the breaks appeared at the very same time as the banks in the LIBOR panel encountered changes in their submission behaviour, as emphasized by the results in the ***PanelDistance***$_{M;B}$ (Table 1). Most likely, this moment corresponds to the beginning of the credit crunch in the summer of 2007 and to the first signs of the crisis in May 2008 that culminated with Lehman's default. The capital market conditions at the time restricted the ability of banks to find liquidity, as the fear of contagion was enormous. The difference between the LIBOR and the official US Treasury rates increased, as revealed in Figure 3. Obviously, these structural changes in market conditions affected the credit markets' perception of the riskiness of banks. A high rate of funding (LIBOR) would imply a worse credit rating reflected in an inflated Credit Default Swap spread.

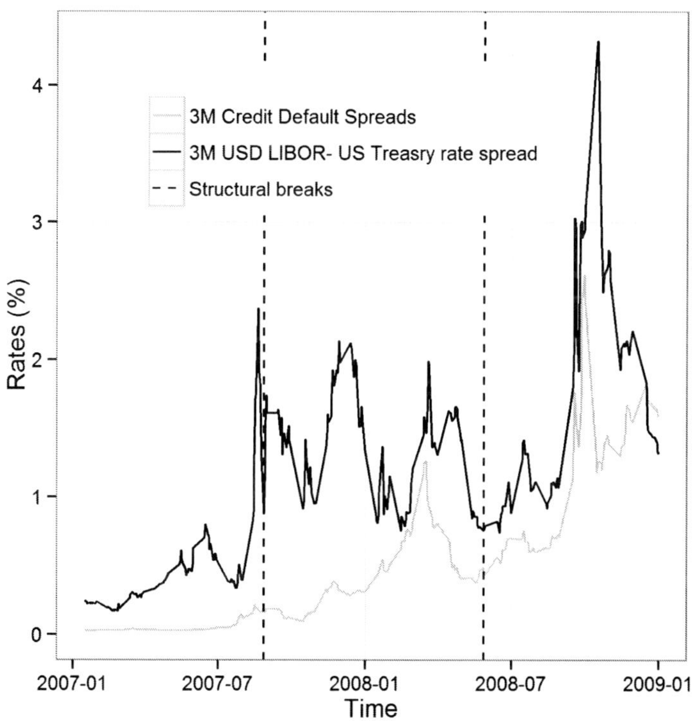

Figure 4. Average 3M CDS for the LIBOR panel banks and 3M Treasury rates vs LIBOR spread

CDS data quotes for each bank in the USD LIBOR panel were collected from CME-Markit. We computed for each bank the corresponding CDS for all maturities corresponding to LIBOR rates (1 week to 12 months). Figure 4 shows the time series of the average CDS spread corresponding to the banks included in the panel and the difference between the LIBOR and the US Treasury for a 3-month horizon. A straightforward reading of the data shows that the two times series exhibit dependency, with a Pearson correlation of 62.5% and a Spearman correlation of 71.6%, which confirms the main assumptions that LIBOR submissions and the CDS are interdependent.

Statistical results: Is the LIBOR calculation robust?

The first phase aimed to assess if the LIBOR calculation process is robust. We investigated the figure for the full LIBOR sample and for the random LIBOR compared to the observed LIBOR. Basic statistics for the difference between the full LIBOR sample and the observed LIBOR and the random LIBOR and the observed LIBOR per maturity respectively are presented in Table 2. At first glance, we can see that the differences are not significant over the entire timeframe considered.

LIBOR Maturity	Full Sample Spread Mean (%)	Full Sample Spread Standard Error (%)	Random Spread Mean (%)	Random Spread Standard Error (%)
1M	-0.001	0.013	-0.001	0.019
2M	0	0.011	0	0.017
3M	0	0.009	0	0.017
4M	-0.001	0.008	0	0.012
5M	0	0.007	0	0.013
6M	0.001	0.007	0.001	0.014
7M	0.001	0.006	0.001	0.012
8M	0	0.006	0.001	0.013
9M	0	0.006	0	0.013
10M	-0.001	0.006	0	0.012
11M	-0.001	0.007	-0.001	0.014
12M	-0.002	0.008	-0.002	0.015

Table 2. Statistics for the Full Sample and Random spreads between 2005 and 2008

LIBOR Maturity	Full Sample Spread Mean	Full Sample Spread Standard Error	Full Sample Spread Skewness	Full Sample Spread Kurtosis	Random Spread Mean	Random Spread Standard Error	Random Spread Skewness	Random Spread Kurtosis
1M	0.000	0.003	0.623	5.446	0.001	0.006	0.361	4.960
2M	0.000	0.003	-0.100	4.144	0.000	0.005	0.266	5.136
3M	0.001	0.003	0.155	5.21	0.001	0.006	0.184	5.046
4M	0.001	0.003	0.465	4.546	0.001	0.005	0.959	7.026
5M	0.001	0.003	0.695	5.647	0.001	0.005	0.787	5.309
6M	0.001	0.003	0.343	3.094	0.002	0.006	0.138	5.780
7M	0.001	0.003	-0.106	4.719	0.001	0.006	0.470	4.660
8M	0.000	0.004	-0.283	3.457	0.000	0.007	-0.042	4.093
9M	-0.001	0.005	-0.409	2.903	0	0.007	-0.136	4.015
10M	-0.002	0.006	-0.809	2.816	-0.002	0.010	-0.841	4.443
11M	-0.003	0.008	-1.009	3.015	-0.004	0.011	-1.286	4.843
12M	-0.005	0.010	-1.063	3.098	-0.004	0.013	-1.482	5.461

Table 3. Statistics for the Full Sample and Random spreads between September 2007 and May 2008

LIBOR Maturity	Theoretic Spread Mean	Theoretic Spread S.e.	Theoretic Spread Skewness	Theoretic Spread Kurtosis	Random Spread Mean	Random Spread s.e.	Random Spread Skewness	Random Spread Kurtosis
1M	-0.011	0.047	-1.543	4.551	-0.014	0.063	-1.343	7.16
2M	-0.003	0.040	-1.613	4.698	0.001	0.061	-1.075	4.886
3M	-0.003	0.032	-1.39	4.766	-0.006	0.048	-0.555	4.118
4M	-0.001	0.027	-1.44	4.466	0.009	0.05	-0.434	3.320
5M	0.004	0.023	-1.036	3.608	-0.002	0.046	-0.718	4.106
6M	0.007	0.023	-0.644	3.886	0.005	0.045	-0.361	4.434
7M	0.006	0.020	-0.57	3.909	0.007	0.039	-0.408	3.305
8M	0.004	0.018	-0.585	4.439	-0.002	0.039	-0.101	2.966
9M	0.002	0.016	-0.163	4.677	0.002	0.04	0.030	3.178
10M	0	0.016	0.131	4.767	0.007	0.035	0.012	3.672
11M	-0.003	0.015	0.660	5.039	-0.005	0.040	0.836	5.422
12M	-0.007	0.016	0.954	4.980	-0.002	0.038	-0.176	2.864

Table 4. Statistics for the Theoretical and Random spreads between June and December 2008

Table 2 shows the statistics of the Full Sample and Random spreads for the dataset of the LIBOR time series between 2005 and 2008. Both spreads are not significantly different than zero. The standard deviation of the random calculation is around 1-2 bp which shows that the process is overall stable. Table 3 and 4 compute the same statics and the third and the fourth order moments (skewness and kurtosis) for the LIBOR time series but in a particular time period. Table 3 focuses on the early period of the subprime crisis between September 2007 and May 2008, whilst Table 4 focuses on the period around Lehman's default between June and December 2008. During the early crisis, the LIBOR calculation method remained stable, but during the late phase of the crisis, it started to show signs of higher sensitivity to the underlying factors. We observe in Table 4 that the Random Spread becomes significant with higher standard deviation and with kurtosis effects.
Excluding the submissions of each bank, we can see that before 2008 the impact of individual submissions was almost zero. The impact started to gain momentum from the spring of 2008 but with limited amplitude (< 1bp). For more accuracy, we performed elaborate tests in order to prove the robustness of the LIBOR calculation. We found that the various spreads are limited in average and variance, with stationary innovations.

Proposition 1. We assess the Full Sample spread as the difference between the Full LIBOR Sample and the observed LIBOR given by the expression:

$$\left|LIBFS_M(t) - LIB_M(t)\right| = \alpha_M + \varepsilon_M(t)$$

and we cannot reject the null hypothesis, within a 95% confidence interval:

H_0: *$\alpha_M < 0.15bp$, $\varepsilon_M(t) < 1.5bp$ and $\varepsilon_M(t)$ is stationary*
H_a: *$\alpha_M \geq 0.15bp$, $\varepsilon_M(t) \geq 1.5bp$ and $\varepsilon_M(t)$ is not stationary*

Proof. Table 5 presents the results of the Phillips-Perron test for the innovation's stationarity and the one sample t-test to show the upper limit of α. For the variance of the innovation we used the one sample $\chi 2$-test for a population variance.

Maturity	Mean Chi-square test			Variance Chi-square test			Phillips-Perron test	
	α	α s.e.	p-value	$\sigma(\varepsilon)$	χ^2 value	p-value	PP value	p-value
1M	0.0038	0.0004	0	0.0129	761.94	0	-111.73	0.01
2M	0.0034	0.0003	0	0.0106	513.75	0	-123.73	0.01
3M	0.0029	0.0003	0	0.0086	341.15	0	-137.07	0.01
4M	0.003	0.0002	0	0.007	225.14	0	-170.64	0.01
5M	0.003	0.0002	0	0.0063	185.53	0	-368.58	0.01
6M	0.003	0.0002	0	0.0066	202.81	0	-442.56	0.01
7M	0.0028	0.0002	0	0.0058	153.84	0	-513.79	0.01
8M	0.0027	0.0002	0	0.0053	127.9	0	-585.73	0.01
9M	0.0028	0.0002	0	0.005	116.63	0	-698.13	0.01
10M	0.0031	0.0002	0	0.0054	132.75	0	-653.91	0.01
11M	0.0035	0.0002	0	0.006	167.55	0	-457.33	0.01
12M	0.0042	0.0002	0	0.007	228.61	0	-377.05	0.01

Table 5. Statistics for the Full Sample spreads between 2005 and 2008

Proposition 2. Considering the absolute difference between the Random LIBOR and the observed LIBOR:

$$\left|LIBRnd_M(t) - LIB_M(t)\right| = \alpha_M + \varepsilon_M(t)$$

and we cannot reject the null hypothesis, within a 95% confidence interval:

H_0: $\alpha_M < 0.15bp$, $\varepsilon_M(t) < 1.5bp$ *and* $\varepsilon_M(t)$ *is stationary*
H_a: $\alpha_M \geq 0.15bp$, $\varepsilon_M(t) \geq 1.5bp$ *and* $\varepsilon_M(t)$ *is not stationary*

Proof. Table 6 presents the results of the Phillips-Perron test for innovation's stationarity and the one sample t-test to show the upper limit of α. For the variance of the innovations we used the one sample χ^2-test for a population variance.

Proposition 3. In absolute value, the LIBOR spread $\boldsymbol{LIBORSpread_{M;B}}$ for each bank and each maturity is caped and stationary in the period before and after the crisis. We write the absolute value of the LIBOR as:

$$\left|LIB_M(t) - LIBBank_{M,B}(t)\right| = \alpha_{M,B} + \varepsilon_{M,B}(t)$$

where we cannot reject the null hypothesis in the period before the credit crisis (before July 2007):

H_0: $\alpha_{M,B} < 0.05bp$ *and* $\varepsilon_{M,B}(t)$ *is stationary*
H_a: $\alpha_{M,B} \geq 0.05bp$ *and* $\varepsilon_{M,B}(t)$ *is not stationary*

and we cannot reject the null hypothesis in the period after the beginning of the credit crisis (after July 2007):

H_0: $\alpha_{M,B} < 0.2bp$ *and* $\varepsilon_{M,B}(t)$ *is stationary*
H_a: $\alpha_{M,B} \geq 0.2bp$ *and* $\varepsilon_{M,B}(t)$ *is not stationary*

Proof. Table 7 presents for each bank, in the period before the crisis and for the 3-month LIBOR, the results of the Phillips-Perron test for the innovation's stationarity and the one sample t-test to show the upper limit of α.

Table 8 presents for each bank, in the period during the crisis and for the 3-month LIBOR, the results of the Phillips-Perron test for the innovation's stationarity and the one sample t-test to show the upper limit of α.

Maturity	Mean Chi-square test			Variance Chi-square test			Phillips-Perron test	
	α	α s.e.	p-value	$\sigma(\varepsilon)$	χ^2 value	p-value	PP value	p-value
1M	0.0062	0.0007	0	0.0218	659.09	0	-606.4	0.01
2M	0.005	0.0005	0	0.0158	617.55	0	-657.6	0.01
3M	0.0052	0.0005	0	0.015	671.14	0	-1005.1	0.01
4M	0.0047	0.0004	0	0.0124	461.98	0	-1010.7	0.01
5M	0.0046	0.0004	0	0.0119	573.98	0	-749.7	0.01
6M	0.0047	0.0004	0	0.0127	563.03	0	-1043.9	0.01
7M	0.0048	0.0003	0	0.0107	551.73	0	-910.7	0.01
8M	0.0049	0.0004	0	0.0118	639.04	0	-756.8	0.01
9M	0.0053	0.0004	0	0.0122	561.05	0	-766.3	0.01
10M	0.0057	0.0004	0	0.0117	582.03	0	-904.7	0.01
11M	0.0065	0.0004	0	0.0129	699.1	0	-694.3	0.01
12M	0.007	0.0004	0.01	0.0135	645.81	0	-878.9	0.01

Table 6. Statistics of the Random spreads between 2005 and 2008

Bank	α	α s.e.	Max(α)	χ^2 value	p-value	PP test	p-value
Barclays	0.0002	0.0004	0.0025	-21.0897	0	-590.051	0.01
Citigroup	0.0001	0.0003	0.0025	-34.1197	0	-545.719	0.01
JP Morgan	0.0002	0.0003	0.0025	-22.2895	0	-585.154	0.01
UBS	0.0001	0.0003	0.0025	-30.5261	0	-621.291	0.01
RBS	0.0002	0.0003	0.0014	-30.1817	0	-659.166	0.01
Bank of America	0.0002	0.0003	0.0025	-22.7831	0	-652.611	0.01
HSBC	0.0002	0.0003	0.0019	-27.7683	0	-640.521	0.01
Norinchuckin	0.0002	0.0003	0.0025	-23.4521	0	-637.359	0.01
BTMU	0.0002	0.0003	0.0023	-22.5111	0	-637.85	0.01
Lloyds	0.0002	0.0003	0.0025	-27.8567	0	-580.394	0.01
Rabobank	0.0002	0.0003	0.0022	-28.2372	0	-691.046	0.01
WestLB	0.0001	0.0003	0.0018	-33.035	0	-643.269	0.01
CreditSuisse	0.0001	0.0003	0.0025	-33.759	0	-614.379	0.01
Deutsche bank	0.0002	0.0003	0.0025	-28.1113	0	-556.786	0.01

Table 7. Statistics for the 3-Month LIBOR spread for each bank in the panel during the pre-crisis period

Bank	α	α s.e.	Max(α)	X^2 value	p-value	PP test	p-value
Barclays	0.0009	0.0008	0.0045	-20.7456	0	-172.406	0.01
Citigroup	0.0009	0.0007	0.0029	-24.2823	0	-140	0.01
JP Morgan	0.0008	0.0008	0.0052	-21.4354	0	-143.428	0.01
UBS	0.0009	0.0008	0.005	-21.2635	0	-178.784	0.01
RBS	0.001	0.0009	0.0052	-17.8869	0	-179.978	0.01
Bank ofAmerica	0.0008	0.0008	0.0036	-23.6429	0	-184.589	0.01
HSBC	0.001	0.0008	0.0052	-18.9898	0	-148.326	0.01
Norinchuckin	0.0008	0.0007	0.005	-25.4175	0	-196.834	0.01
BTMU	0.0007	0.0007	0.0045	-26.8654	0	-167.583	0.01
Lloyds	0.0008	0.0008	0.0052	-21.5009	0	-159.491	0.01
Rabobank	0.0009	0.0009	0.0052	-18.8297	0	-153.778	0.01
WestLB	0.0007	0.0007	0.0036	-30.1669	0	-187.627	0.01
CreditSuisse	0.0007	0.0007	0.0041	-26.9931	0	-203.626	0.01
Deutsche Bank	0.0009	0.0008	0.0041	-22.3898	0	-154.673	0.01

Table 8. Statistics for the 3-Month LIBOR spread for each bank in the panel during the crisis period

Impact analysis of changes in bank submissions

In order to answer the section question and to assess the impact of a managed manipulation attempt, we created a simulated LIBOR (3 Months) assuming that one or more banks submitted lower rates than they should have. We modelled the difference as a stochastic process with an average of 20 bp and a variance equal to the observed variance of the bank's submissions. The algorithm is resumed in equation (6).

$$LIBSim_M = \frac{1}{8}\sum_{j=1}^{8}\underbrace{(R_{j,M} + \mu + \sigma \cdot B)}_{R^{sim}{}_{j,M}} 1_{R^{sim}{}_{j,M} \in S_8} \qquad (6)$$

The simulation results of manipulation attempts on the 3-month LIBOR are shown in Figure 5, which includes the worst case impacts for the case of one bank or worst case combination. It appears that the impact of a single bank is limited with the maximum amplitude of 5bp. If the manipulation is considered as a result of concerted action, then the amplitude is considerably higher, reaching 10-15 bp for the 3-month LIBOR. During the pre-crisis period, we find that a simulated LIBOR fixing has a very low impact. Some impact occurs after the outbreak of the crisis in late 2007 and becomes significant if the fixing involves four institutions. It is thus apparently clear that a bank acting alone would not be able to operate any relevant change, as some media regulators seemed have announced. Indeed, it seems that a coordinated effort among four or more banks in an organized 'cartel-like' approach would be capable of changing the LIBOR. This event is apparently less likely in the context of the financial industry as the impact of a LIBOR fix are not genuine and could be negative even for the group of banks at the origin of the manipulation. But the crisis in 2008 also brought a lack of confidence in markets and this probably generated a fear of contagion in the interbank market that led to an alleged attempt to present a brighter side of the picture. We recall that during that period, banks were not able to refinance themselves totally in the interbank market (which generates the LIBOR) and only the intervention of the Central European Bank was able to offer some reprieve.

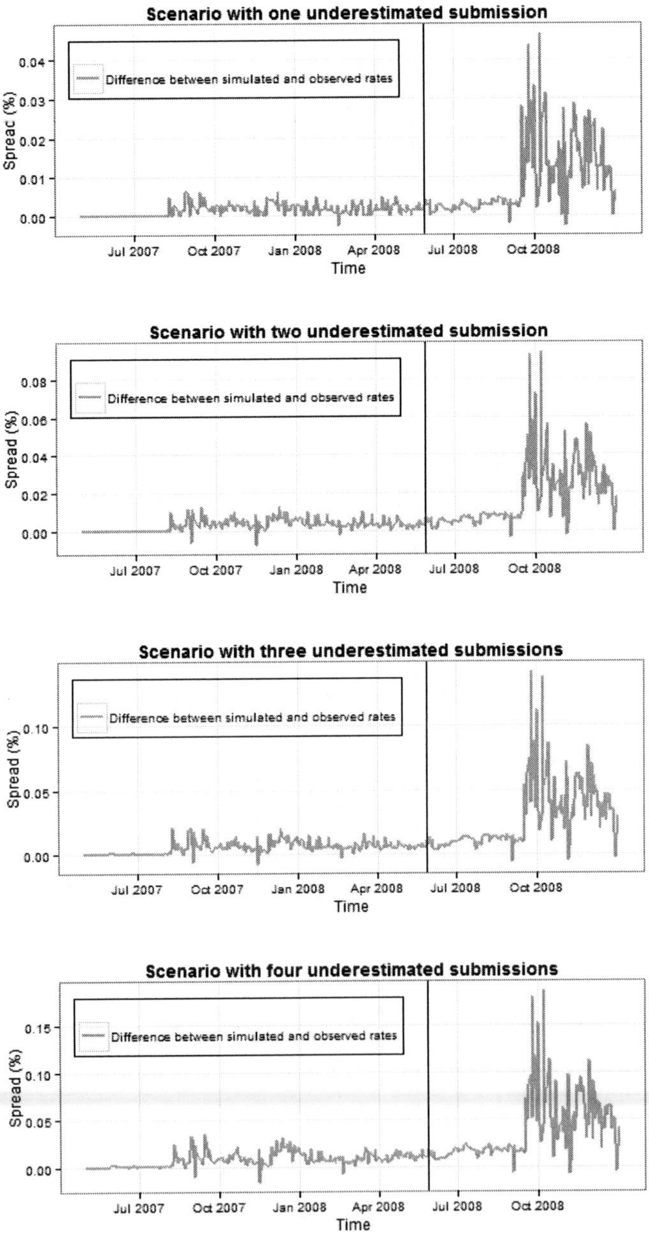

Figure 5. Simulation of manipulation attempts of the 3-Month LIBOR

Simulation: What was the true LIBOR?

The allegation of LIBOR fixing has brought much momentum around the topic, with authors claiming there is a need to change the way the rate is calculated (Garcia, 2012). In an attempt to answer the third question and to reconstitute the effect of an alleged manipulation, we will focus first on the fundamental factors that drive the LIBOR. In the previous section, we identified the US Treasury rates and the credit spreads (CDS) of the banks in the panel as potential factors. Bank ***B*** finances itself on the market for the horizon ***M*** at a rate $\boldsymbol{R_{M;B}}$, depending on the risk-free rate $\boldsymbol{r_M}$, approximated by the Treasury rates, its credit quality $\boldsymbol{CS_{M;B}}$, the available liquidity $\boldsymbol{LS_{M;B}}$ and its specific risk $\boldsymbol{IS_{M;B}}$, as exhibited in the following equation:

$$R_{M,B} = r_M + CS_{M,B} + LS_{M,B} + IS_{M,B} \qquad (7)$$

We consider here a simplified model that explains the difference between the rate of bank ***B*** and the Treasury rates for a certain maturity ***M*** that depends on the CDS of the respective bank and maturity:

$$R_{M,B} - R_{US\ Treasury\ ,M} = \alpha + \beta \cdot CDS_{M,B} + \varepsilon \qquad (8)$$

Moving further from equation (8), the relationship with the credit spread is not stationary as we showed in the structural break tests in the previous section. Following Hamilton (1989), we assume that a 2-regime switching model explains the rate of one bank with its CDS. The underlying idea is that, for a firm, there are several states in the LIBOR rate that switch following a transition matrix which is determined by a hidden factor (Guegan, 2010). This "hidden" factor could be determined by regulatory announcements, legislation or interventions by new dealers on the market. We will consider here that the "hidden" factor is in fact a fixing factor, being related to the tendency of the bank to submit the rates differently. We identify a first regime which is "normal", like in the period before the crisis, and a second regime during the crisis, when the manipulation allegedly had a significant impact. Nevertheless, as the main purpose of this paper is LIBOR modelling, we do not study the relevance of exogenous regulatory-like factors on the switching regimes, and we consider the existence of a Markov chain to explain these switches. We develop the idea in the following equation:

$$R_{M,B} - R_{US\ Treasury,M} = \alpha_i + \beta_i \cdot CDS_{M,B} + \varepsilon_i \quad i \in \{1;2\} \quad (9)$$

Using the same model as introduced in equation (8), we assume now that parameter $\boldsymbol{\beta_i}$ has the following dynamic: $\boldsymbol{\beta_i = \beta_1 S_t + \beta_2 (1 - S_t)}$, where $\boldsymbol{S_t}$

follows a 2-state Markov chain as shown in Figure 6, and $S_t = 1$, if S_t is in State 1 and $S_t = 0$ if S_t is in State 2. The switch occurs with a probability P.

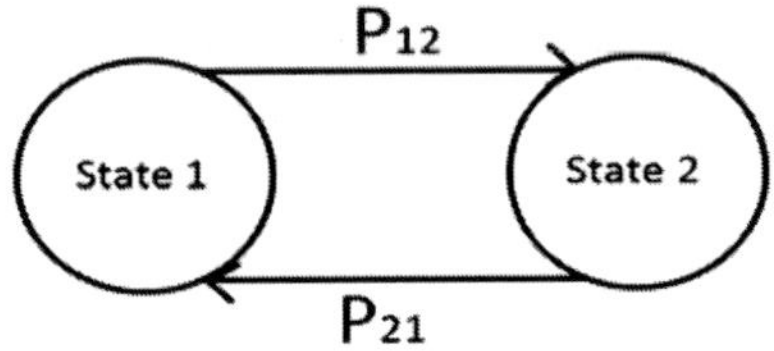

Figure 6. Switching Markov Chain

Table 9 exhibits the calibration of a Hidden Markov switching model that has two states and that allows for the flip-flops of the factors: α the intercept, β the sensitivity to the fundamental factor, σ the standard deviation of the innovations and P the probability of switch.

Following a factorial approach, we attempted to rebuild a 'true' theoretical LIBOR based on the relationship with the fundamentals (Frunza (2013)). Based on a Markov switching model calibration, we rebuilt a theoretical rate for each bank during the abnormal regime using the parameters of the normal regime. After reconstituting the theoretical submission for each bank, we recomputed the 'true' theoretical LIBOR. The results for the 3M LIBOR are presented in the Figure 7. It appears that the impact was significant in the period after July 2007 until the last quarter of 2008. The difference could be as high as 1% during certain periods. The theoretical and the observed LIBOR should be understood as two boundaries of the real financing conditions in the markets at that time.

Bank		Regime 1				Regime 2			
		Estimate	Std. Err.	z value	p-value	Estimate	Std. Err.	z value	p-value
Barclays	α	0.0047	0.0002	17.07	0.000	0.0114	0.001	10.954	0.00(
	β	0.862	0.0415	20.749	0.000	1.4097	0.1608	8.7619	0.00(
	σ	0.0022	-	-	-	0.0067	-	-	
	P	0.526	-	-	-	0.474	-	-	
HSBC	α	0.0042	0.0002	14.897	0.000	0.0095	0.0012	7.8084	(
	β	1.4311	0.0609	23.49	0.000	2.6267	0.4024	6.5275	(
	σ	0.0022	-	-	-	0.0059	-	-	
	P	0.576	-	-	-	0.424	-	-	
UBS	α	0.0038	0.0002	13.099	0.000	0.0148	0.0007	18.8654	0.00(
	β	1.6956	0.0476	35.568	0.000	0.1226	0.05695	2.1535	0.031
	σ	0.0028	-	-	-	0.0051	-	-	
	P	0.489	-	-	-	0.511	-	-	
JP Morgan	α	0.0031	0.0002	12.927	0.000	0.0108	0.0009	11.1609	(
	β	1.2699	0.2056	6.1739	0.000	1.9895	0.0561	35.421	0.00(
	σ	0.0014	-	-	-	0.0055	-	-	
	P	0.532	-	-	-	0.468	-	-	

Bank of America	α	0.0029	0.0002	13.577	0.000	0.0107	0.0008	12.1863	0
	β	1.4937	0.0583	25.604	0.000	1.5001	0.1816	8.2576	0.000
	σ	0.0012	-	-	-	0.0058	-	-	
	P	0.493	-	-	-	0.507	-	-	
Citigroup	α	0.0115	0.0008	13.134	0.000	0.0042	0.0002	19.85	0
	β	0.7031	0.0683	10.281	0.000	0.5297	0.0178	29.67	0.000
	σ	0.005				0.0018			
	P	0.438				0.562			
Credit Suisse	α	0.01	0.0015	6.5078	0.000	0.0057	0.0005	10.04	0
	β	2.7401	0.4046	6.7712	0.000	1.1715	0.0604	19.378	0.000
	σ	0.0056				0.0037			
	P	0.252				0.748			
Deutsche Bank	α	0.004	0.0002	14.07	0.000	0.0098	0.001	9.6565	0
	β	1.049	0.0516	20.334	0.000	1.5173	0.1819	8.3389	0.000
	σ	0.0018				0.0062			
	P	0.444				0.556			
Lloyds	α	0.0028	0.0001	15.537	0.000	0.0118	0.0008	13.5901	0
	β	1.8532	0.0415	44.621	0.000	0.8893	0.1458	6.0987	0.000
	σ	0.001				0.0063			
	P	0.418				0.582			

Norin	α	0.0039	0.0002	17.046	0.000	0.0117	0.0009	12.6852	0
	β	1.3191	0.0773	17.051	0.000	1.5936	0.196	8.1266	0.000
	σ	0.0018				0.0056			
	P	0.535				0.465			
RBS	α	0.004	0.0002	17.171	0.000	0.0098	0.0009	10.0266	0
	β	0.85	0.0266	31.913	0.000	1.4329	0.1545	9.2687	0.000
	σ	0.0017				0.0058			
	P	0.509				0.491			
Rabobank	α	0.0115	0.0013	8.43	0.000	0.0036	0.0006	5.7174	0
	β	0.3086	0.155	1.9903	0.000	3.0974	0.1682	18.4104	0.000
	σ	0.0045				0.0039			
	P	0.459				0.541			
WLB	α	0.0033	0.0002	13.008	0.000	0.0077	0.0008	9.1651	0
	β	1.0243	0.0345	29.67	0.000	1.9129	0.1804	10.599	0.000
	σ	0.0012				0.0057			
	P	0.397				0.603			
BTMU	α	0.0102	0.0009	11.4078	0.000	0.0040	0.0002	14.843	0
	β	2.744	0.304	9.0265	0.000	1.8065	0.0685	26.346	0.000
	σ	0.0058				0.0019			
	P	0.493				0.507			

Table 9. Switching regime regression estimates

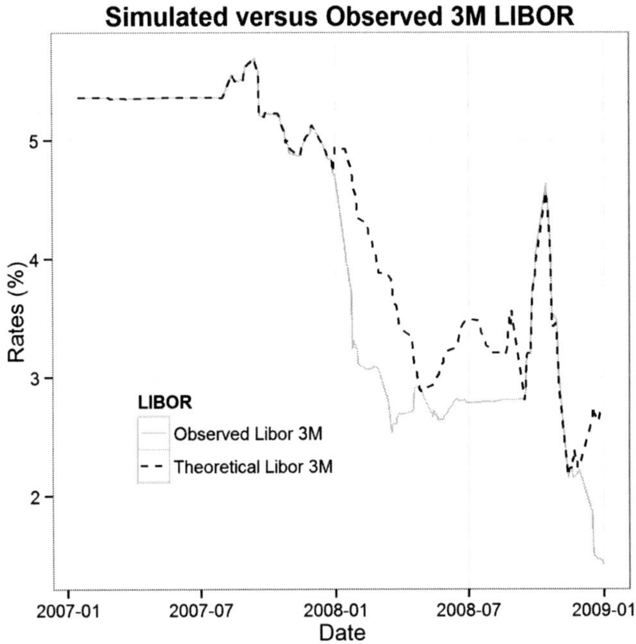

Figure 7. 'True' Theoretical versus Observed 3M LIBOR

Conclusions

Manipulation of financial markets is one of the major concerns of investigators and regulators. The recent allegation of LIBOR manipulation highlights the sensitivity of the issue. Nevertheless, LIBOR manipulation cannot be the result of an institution acting solely. Before May 2008, one bank would not be able to significantly change the LIBOR rates. An organized attempt by 2 or more banks would also have yielded non-relevant results. After 2008, under the hypothesis of a bank acting solely, the changes in LIBOR rates would have been limited. Nevertheless, an organized approach by at least four financial institutions could result in a significant manipulation of the LIBOR. The attempt to rebuild a theoretical LIBOR shows that the impact was significant in the period after July 2007 until the last quarter of 2008. The difference could be as high as 1% during certain periods. The theoretical and the observed LIBOR should be understood as two boundaries of the real financing conditions in the markets at that time.

Bibliography

Abrantes-Metz, R.M.; Kraten, M.; Metz, A.D.; Seow, G.S. (2012), "LIBOR Manipulation?", *Journal of Banking and Finance*, 36: 136 – 150.

Bai, J.; Perron, P. (2003), "Critical values for multiple structural change tests", *Econometrics Journal*, 6 (1): 72-78.

Black, F.; Scholes, M. (1973), "The pricing of options and corporate liabilities", *Journal of Political Economy*, 81(3): 637-654.

Fama, E.; French, K. (1993), "Common risk factors in the returns on stocks and bonds", *Journal of Financial Economics,* 33 (1): 3-56.

Fisher, J.; Gregan, C.; Giulio, J.; Schutze, J. (2011), "Economic crime and the global financial crisis", *Law and Financial Markets Review,* 5 (4): 276-289.

Frunza, M.C. (2013), "Aftermath of the VAT fraud on carbon emissions markets", *Journal of Financial Crime*, 20(2): 222-236.

Frunza, M.C.; Guegan, D.; Lassoudiere, A. (2010), "Forecasting strategies for carbon allowances prices: From classic arbitrage pricing theory to switching regimes", *International Review of Applied Financial Issues and Economics*, 2 (3): 576-596.

Garcia, J. (2012), " 'Fixing the Benchmark' - Wheatley considers LIBOR overhaul" (September 6, 2012). *Financial Regulation International.* Available at SSRN: http://ssrn.com/abstract=2143137.

Hamilton, J. (1989), "A new approach to the economic analysis of nonstationary time series and the business cycle", *Econometrica*, 57(2): 357-384.

Snider, C.A.; Youle, T. (2010), "Does the LIBOR reflect banks' borrowing costs?, Working Paper, Available at http://dx.doi.org/10.2139/ssrn.1569603.

Snider, L. (2012), "The technological advantages of stock market traders", in Will, S.; Handelman, S.; Brotherton, D.C. (eds.), *How They Got Away With It: White Collar Criminals and the Financial Meltdown*, Ch. 8, Columbia University Press.

Weiss, G. (2003), *Born to Steal: When the Mafia hit Wall Street*, New York: Warner Books.

Notes

[1] We used the dataset published by the English newspaper "The Guardian", available at: http://www.guardian.co.uk/news/datablog/2012/jul/03/libor-rates-set-banks.

CHAPTER TEN

PONZI SCHEMES: COMPUTER SIMULATION

MÁRIO CUNHA, HÉLDER VALENTE AND PAULO B. VASCONCELOS

Introduction

The aim of this chapter is the study of Ponzi schemes using mathematical modelling and numerical simulation. It intends to describe the mathematics of this type of scam, going beyond the simplistic explanation that its sustainability depends only on rapid (exponential) growth in the number of customers and investors. Furthermore, it aims to explore the numerical simulation of Ponzi schemes, enabling the fast evaluation of funds showing unrealistic performances.

Ponzi schemes, chain letters, pyramid schemes and bubbles are terms used, often indistinctively and inappropriately, to refer to unsustainable financial behaviour where the current and promised prices of the assets are not consistent with their value in the future. These schemes generally involve promises to pay very high interest rates. The developer of these schemes generally claims to have discovered a new secret formula that can earn large amounts of money and ensure high rates of return.

The term "Ponzi" is due to Charles Ponzi, an Italian immigrant in the USA, who operated a small deposit-taking company in a suburb of Boston in the 1920s. Since most of the economies in Europe were depressed after the First World War, he thought of buying International Reply Coupons (IRC) in Europe and selling them in the U.S. Certainly it was neither possible to buy the large amount of coupons required nor cope with the logistics to take them back to the U.S. He soon realized that the only way to become rich was by convincing others that they too could be rich if they followed his scheme and promised a 50% profit within 45 days, and soon

100% within 90 days (DeWitt, 2009). As is widely known, payments to the old investors were being paid by the new ones.

Bernard Madoff was responsible for the most infamous and long-lasting Ponzi scheme. By the time of its collapse in December 2008, reported liabilities amounted to close to 65 billion USD. Madoff kept his scheme active for approximately 20 years, affecting private and institutional investors around the world. An exhaustive description of the scheme is reported in Kindleberger and Aliber (2011).

Similar cases occurred worldwide, albeit with less visibility and dissemination by the media.

These events are becoming more and more frequent and their social and economic consequences the subject of many news reports, stories, papers and research. Fraudulent schemes take their place in the news and articles. For example, the global and well-known Madoff case is illustrated in great detail by Sander (2009) and an extensive review with recent stories of swindlers (individual and institutional) is presented in Fisher (2009).

However, there is a lack of scientific literature providing a mathematical background to these fraudulent financial instruments which could help to predict their initial success and final collapse. Two of the most prominent exceptions describing macroeconomic models of rational Ponzi games are the works of Blanchard and Weil (2001) and Bhattacharya (2003). Micro Ponzi schemes have flourished on the web or, at a smaller scale, beginning with a group of friends. These schemes are usually described by means of a simplistic explanation based on an exponential boom in the number of new investors. A mathematical model that captures the main characteristics of a Ponzi scheme was recently introduced by Artzrouni (2009).

We will briefly describe Artzrouni's model and introduce a computational approach easily adapted to new variations on the model's parameters and possibly extended to cope with other features that have not yet been considered. By considering the numerical solution of the model, an innovative approach is provided. Several simulations will be performed to assess the behaviour of a fund taking into account different perturbations on the parameters.

The aptitude of simulation in the detection of unsustainable patterns may be of interest to financial regulators and investors when confronted with situations where funds show unrealistic performances vis-à-vis economic and financial constraints.

The Artzrouni model

The model describes the dynamics of an investment fund that promises higher incomes than those it can effectively offer. At its origin, there is a promised return rate, the actual nominal rate, an unrealistic market capture rate for new investment and the rate of removal of accumulated deposits.

The fund motion equation, defining as the fund value accumulation over time, is given by

$$\frac{dS(t)}{dt} = r_n\, S(t) + s(t) - W(t) \tag{1}$$

where $S(t)$ is the amount in the fund at time t, r_n is the nominal interest rate, $s(t)$ is a continuous cash inflow (new money) and $W(t)$ the withdrawals. The inflow assumes an exponential behaviour

$$s(t) = s_0 e^{r_i t} \tag{2}$$

where r_i is the investment rate and s_0 the initial density of the deposits. For the withdrawals, the following formulation is considered

$$W(t) = r_w K e^{t(r_p - r_w)} + r_w \int_0^t s(u) e^{(r_p - r_w)(t-u)}\, du \tag{3}$$

where r_p is the promised rate and r_w a constant withdrawal rate along t. The first term refers to the density of withdrawals from those investing an initial deposit, $S(0) = K$ (or $S(0) = K + K_0$ if an in-house deposit invested at rate r_n is also considered) and the second term to those who invested $s(u)$ at time u and want to withdraw a quantity $r_w \int_0^t s(u) e^{(r_p - r_w)(t-u)}\, du$ from the beginning to time t. If $r_w < r_p$ ($r_w > r_p$) then the withdrawals increase (decrease) exponentially.

Putting (2) in (3) gives

$$W(t) = r_w e^{t(r_p - r_w)} \left(K + s_0 \frac{e^{t(r_w + r_i - r_p)} - 1}{r_w + r_i - r_p} \right) \tag{4}$$

For further details, see Artzrouni (2009). The differential equation is thus given by (1) with $W(t)$ defined by (4).

The idea behind the simulation is to tackle the solution dynamics of the model along with the dynamics resulting from a sudden parameter change at a certain moment in time. We will consider the solution path of the actual amount in the fund (its real value), $S_a(t)$, and compare it with the solution path of the promised amount (theoretical value of the fund), $S_p(t)$. The latter equation results from the former by taking the nominal interest rate equal to the promised one, $r_n = r_p$, and the initial condition $S(0) = K$.

Model calibration

For the model calibration, data available for one of the most famous fraudulent financial schemes is used: Charles Ponzi, 1920. A philanthropic version of the model is also presented for discussion, bearing in mind social security models. We follow closely DeWitt (2009) and Artzrouni (2009).

Ponzi's scheme

The model is calibrated to replicate the fraudulent scheme perpetrated by Charles Ponzi in 1920, and evaluate the effects resulting from considering the investment constant from a certain instance of time, $r_i = 0$. The data is in line with DeWitt (2009) and the time is expressed in years and the monetary values in million USD.

Since Ponzi had no funds to invest, it is assumed that $S(0) = K = 0$. Considering that he paid 100% (the money doubles) return on the invested money after 90 days (0.25 years), at an interest rate with continuous capitalization, this would result in $e^{0.25r_p} = 2$, that is, $r_p = 2.773$. The scheme worked from the 26th December to the 26th June, that is, for 213 days (0.58 years). At day 213, Ponzi collected 0.2 million USD from a total of 10 million USD invested in the fund, that is,

$$\begin{cases} s_0 e^{0.58r_i} = 0.2 * 365 \\ s_0 \left(\dfrac{e^{0.58r_i} - 1}{r_i} \right) = 10 \end{cases}$$

It can be easily shown that $s_0 = 1.130$ and $r_i = 7.187$ is the solution of this system, which represents an instantaneous rate of 7% and an initial flow of money of $\frac{1.130}{365} \cong 3.095$ USD a day. Regarding the nominal interest rate, it is assumed that $r_n = 0.01$; as mentioned by Artzrouni (2009), the profit from the IRC is negligible given the high rate of entry of new investments (one could consider r_n ranging from 0 to 5%). To compute r_w, the data available at the time of the first Ponzi trial is taken into account: he was able to pay 5 million but was still pending payment of an additional 7 million USD to investors, so $S_p(0.58) = 12$. Numerically, we can evaluate the value of $r_w = 1.470$.

From the 26th June, the growing flux of new investments had probably stopped and so, from $t = 0.58$ onwards, new parameters occurred. The daily flow remains constant and equal to 0.2 million USD, as on the last day, $r_i = 0$ and $s_0 = 0.2 * 365 = 73$. The initial values of investment are $K = S_p(0.58) = 12$ and $S(0) = S_a(0.58) \cong 7.758$ (numerically computed). The remaining parameters are kept the same (see Table 1 for a summary).

Table 1: Model parameters for the Ponzi simulation

	K	$S(0)$	s_0	r_i	r_w	r_p	r_n
$t \leq 0.58$	0	0	1.130	7.187	1.470	2.773	0.01
$t > 0.58$	12	7.758	73	0	1.470	2.773	0.01

Philanthropic scheme

The model can be easily used to mimic a philanthropic (Ponzi) scheme. Following Artzrouni (2009), let us track a manager (meritorious profile) paying 15% return on a one million dollar contribution per investor a year. It is assumed that the investors withdraw 12% of their accumulated capital (continuously), the manager can make investments at the nominal rate of 4%, and no initial investment is requested from investors. Under these conditions, the minimum value for the in-house investment needed to keep the fund solvent is $S(0) \cong 275$ (numerically computed). In the next steps, the value $S(0) = 280$ will be used for simplicity.

The philanthropic character of this fund is based on the fact that, although the actual value of the fund $S_a(t)$ and of the fund's profit, $S_a(t) - S_p(t)$ grow asymptotically at a rate equal to r_n, the lucrativeness that the manager of the fund would obtain if he had invested $S(0)$ at a rate r_n would be higher, since $S(0) > 0$.

Table 2: Model parameters for the philanthropic (Ponzi) simulation

K	$S(0)$	s_0	r_i	r_w	r_p	r_n
0	280	1	0	0.12	0.15	0.04

Model simulation and results

Simulations resulting from shocks on the parameters of the model will be presented, illustrating the impact of the success or the collapse of the investment fund.

Ponzi's scheme (1920)

Based on the parameters of the model presented in Table 1, the transition dynamics, computed numerically, are plotted in Fig. 1, for the actual $S_a\ (t)$, the promised $S_p\ (t)$ values and the difference between the two. The numerical algorithm used to solve the ordinary differential equation was the Runge-Kutta pair (4,5), embodied in the MATLAB ODE45 function (convergence criteria defined for a tolerance of 10^{-9}).

Graphically, it turns out that, at the date of Charles Ponzi's arrest, $t = 0.58$, the scheme is still sustainable, although, as expected, the real value (S_a) is growing at a lower rate than the promised one (S_p) ($S_p - S_a$ grows from $t = 0$ to $t = 0.58$) . From $t = 0.58$ onwards, with the change in the rate of investment to $r_i = 0$, the scheme starts to collapse: increases up to 0.92 years but then declines to collapse, $S_a\ (t) = 0$, 1.30 years later, that is, only 8.5 months after Ponzi is arrested.

Philanthropic scheme

Based on the parameters in Table 2, Fig. 2 depicts the time evolution of the actual and promised values for the philanthropic (Ponzi) scheme.

It can be seen that, even in the long run, a fund in these conditions is always solvent. The initial in-house entry of capital is sufficient to guarantee its sustainability. The actual value grows at a higher rate than the promised one; but it is lower than the value that the manager would earn if he had instead invested $S(0)$ at rate r_n (dotted line).

Sensitivity analysis

To illustrate the importance of $S(0)$, corresponding to the initial in-house investment, we assess what happens if it declines from 280 to 245 million USD, below the threshold of 275 (the threshold for the sustainability of the fund). Fig. 3 indicates that the scheme will collapse after about 260 years of existence.

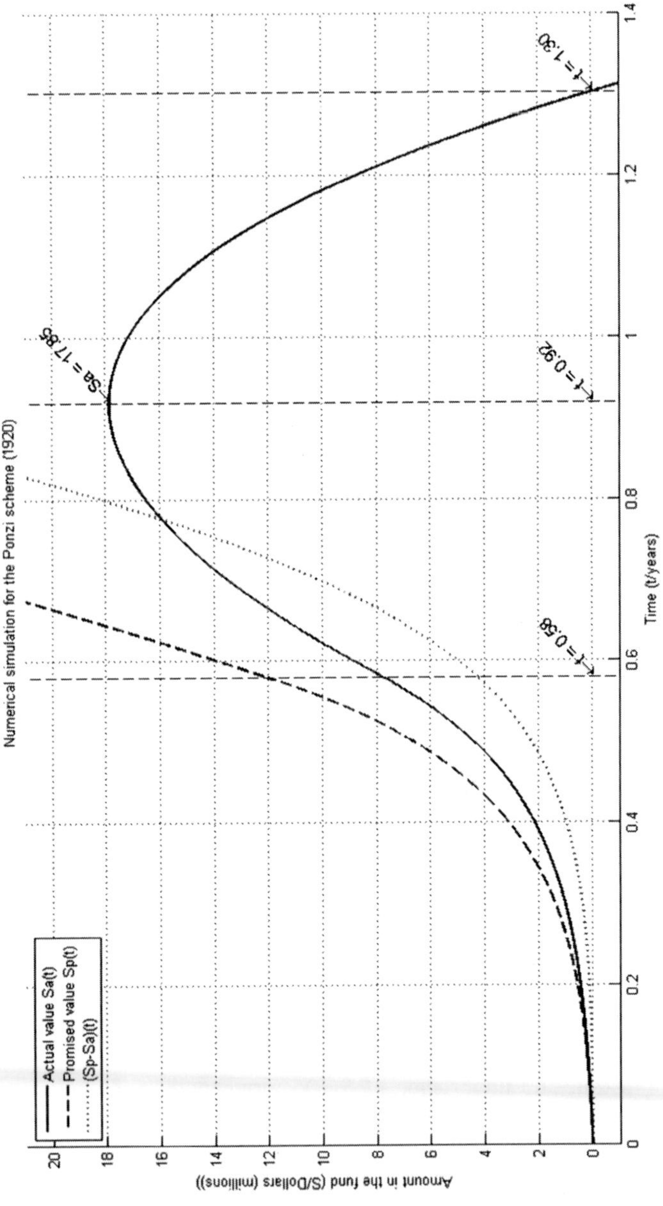

Fig. 1: Numerical simulation for the Ponzi scheme (1920)

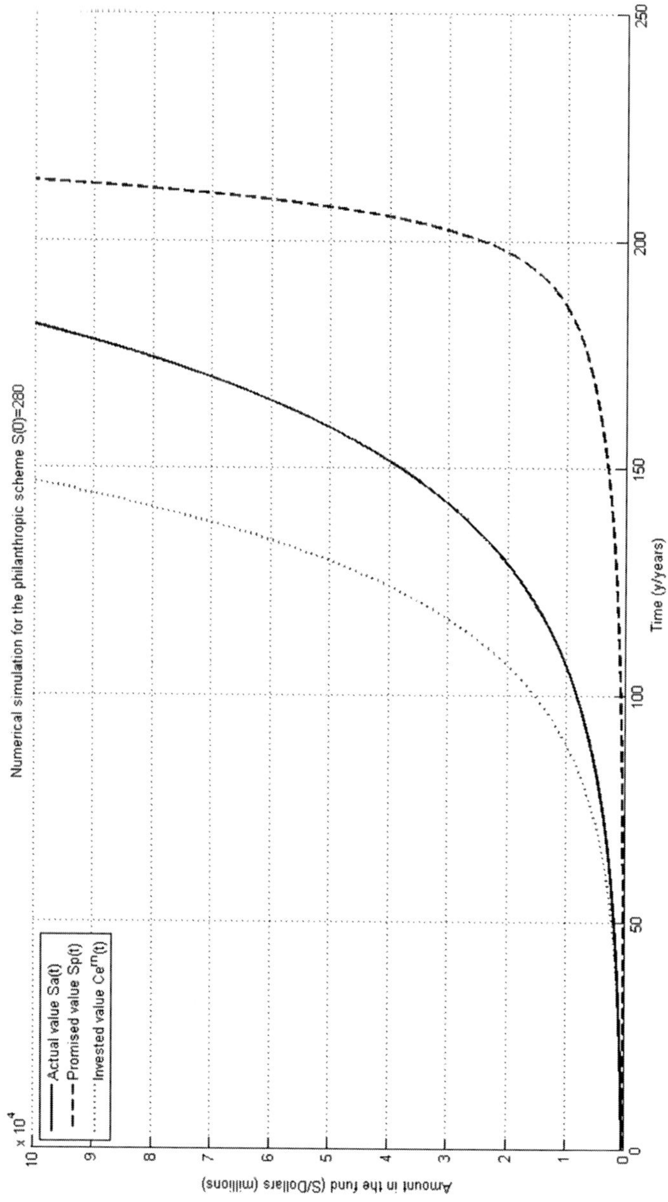

Fig. 2: Numerical simulation for the philanthropic scheme $S(0) = 280$

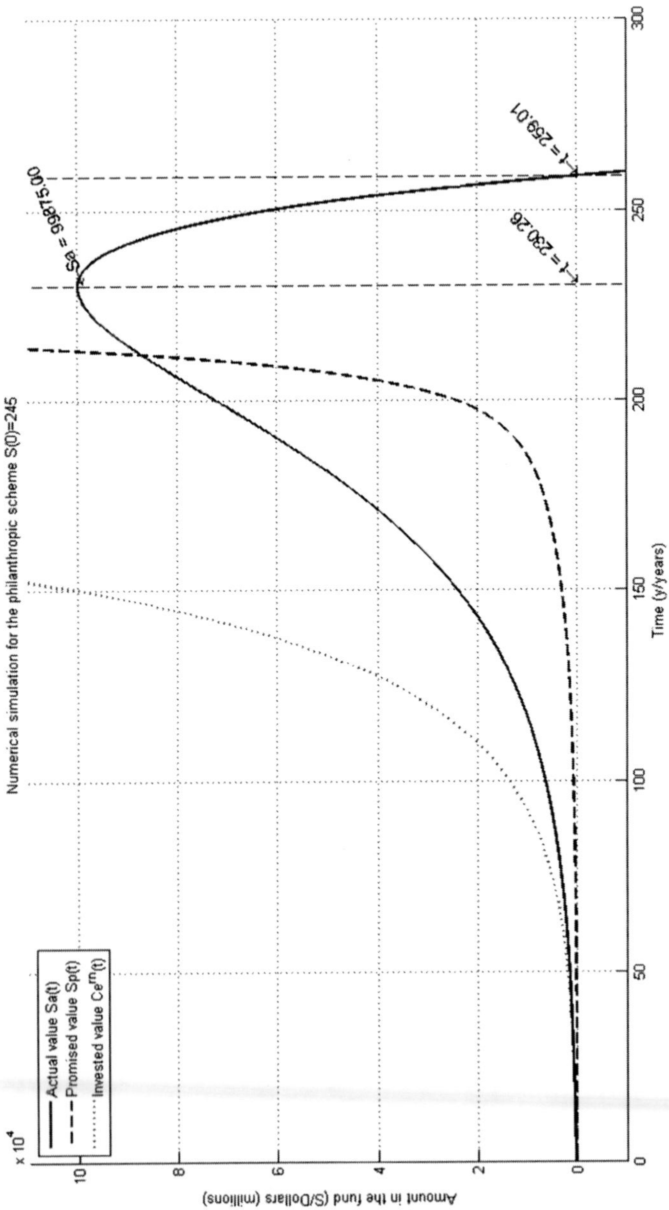

Fig. 3: Numerical simulation for the philanthropic scheme $S(0) = 245$

Table 3 shows the time it would take for several values of $S(0)$ to collapse, emphasizing that solvency depends on a philanthropic fund manager who is willing to invest a significant initial amount, giving away a share of their profits.

We extend further our sensitivity analysis by considering two additional situations, and analyse the impact on sustainability, due to changes in the initial conditions (of launch and operation).

A. *What is the effect due to changes in the rate of investment in a fund, considering the parameters in Table 4 and keeping the remaining conditions unchanged?*

Table 3: Several parameters for the philanthropic simulation (N/A means not available, N/S means not shown)

Case	K	$S(0)$	s_0	r_i	r_w	r_p	r_n	time to collapse	$max\ S_a$ reached at
Fig. 2	0	280	1	0	0.12	0.15	0.04	N/A	N/A
Fig. 3	0	245	1	0	0.12	0.15	0.04	259.01	9.99x10^{4} (t=230.26)
N/S	0	245	1	0	0.12	0.155	0.04	146.08	5.52x10^{4} (t=119.57)
N/S	0	275	1	0	0.12	0.15	0.04	N/A	N/A
N/S	0	265	1	0	0.12	0.15	0.04	368.98	2.79x10^{6} (t=340.12)
N/S	0	175	1	0	0.12	0.15	0.04	138.14	2.58x10^{3} (t=109.86)
N/S	0	100	1	0	0.12	0.15	0.04	79.78	378.79 (t=53.90)

Table 4: Parameters for scheme A (N/A means not available)

Case	K	$S(0$	s_0	r_i	r_w	r_p	r_n	time to collapse	time to recover	$min\ S_a$ reached at
1	10	10	2	14	6	5	1	N/A	N/A	0.80 (t=0.26)
2	10	10	2	10	6	5	1	0.23	0.49	-3.95 (t=0.39)
3	10	10	2	2	6	5	1	0.21	N/A	N/A

This scheme is very interesting in that, initially, the fund value decreases, reaches a minimum and then, depending on the rate of investment, can recover. Clearly, the recovery should be much faster the higher the

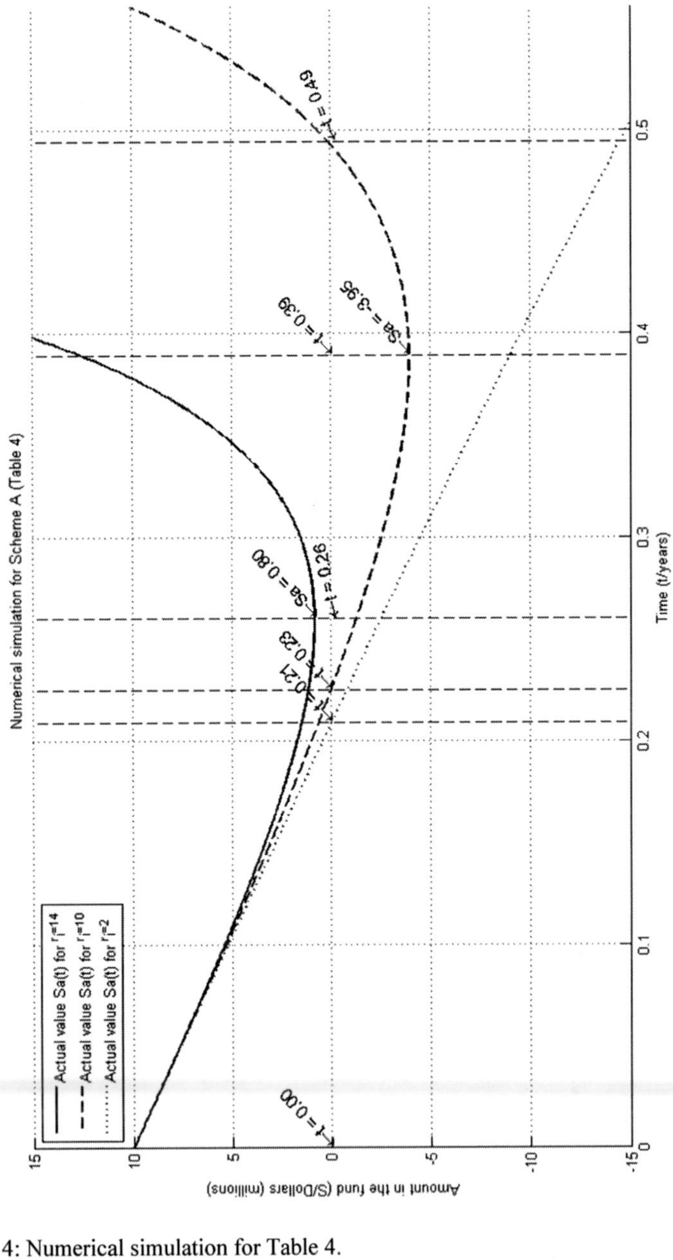

Fig. 4: Numerical simulation for Table 4.

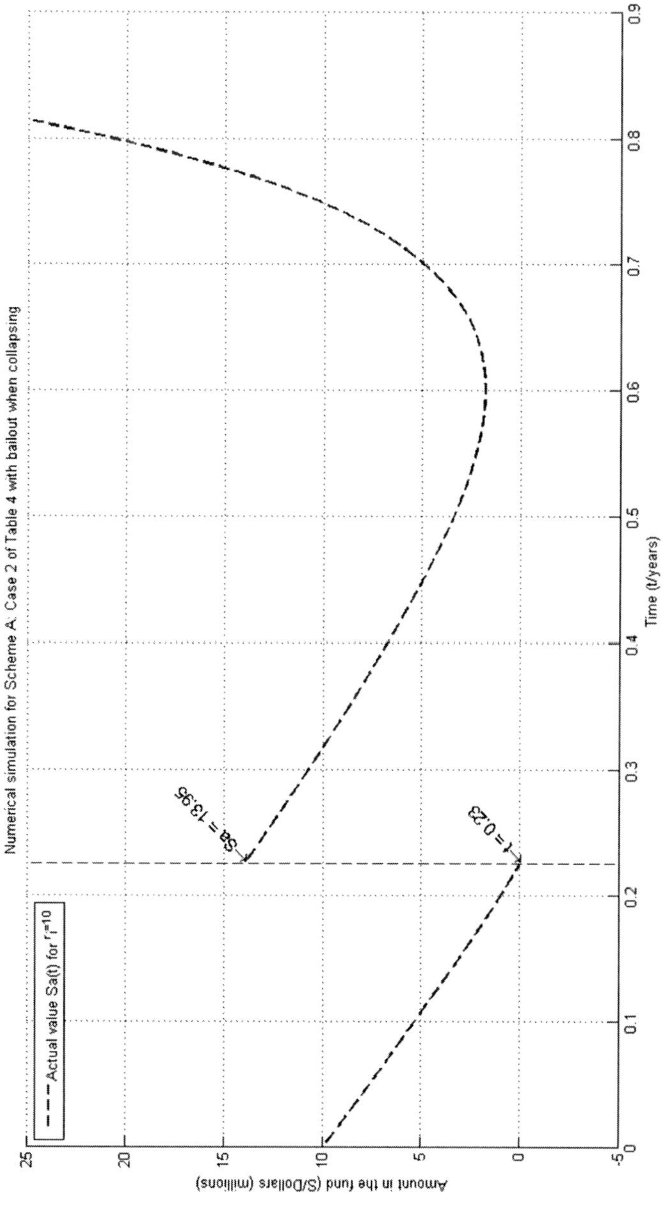

Fig. 5: Numerical simulation for bailout in case 2 of Table 4.

investment rate. If the investment rate is lower than the rate of withdrawal, the system does not retrieve and collapses shortly after its launch.

This schema also supports the idea that, although illegal ($r_p \gg r_n$), its sustainability would be ensured through an appropriate relationship between withdrawal and investment rates.

Figure 4 shows the solution paths for the cases summarized in Table 4. The dashed line depicts a fund that collapses but that can recover with a bailout equal to the value of the minimum reached. Figure 5 shows the solution path for this case.

B. *A fund offers a 10% return per month. The management entity is supposed to perform an initial investment of 50 million USD in-house. The investor's deposits are expected to increase at a 0.5 annual rate, and each investor, annually, will withdraw half of their winnings. What happens if the annual density of deposits is 12 million USD? And if it is 4 million USD?*

The conditions of the fund are summarized in Table 5.

Table 5: Parameters for scheme B

Case	K	$S(0)$	s_0	r_i	r_w	r_p	r_n	time to collapse	$max\ S_a$ reached at
1	0	50	12	0.5	0.5	1.14	0.04	3.68	69.67 (*t*=1.90)
2	0	50	4	0.5	0.5	1.14	0.04	4.41	59.32 (*t*=2.08)

If the analysis only covers the short run, 0-2 years, it seems that this scheme is sustainable. However, the combination of parameters over time, in the medium-long term, 5-6 years, means that the fund collapses. Figure 6 presents the solution path for the two cases tested (see Table 5).

Social Security systems

One of the issues currently in focus (see for example, Mandel (2008) and Buttonwood (2011)) is the easy temptation to associate Social Security systems to a Ponzi scheme. The usually short duration of Ponzi schemes, despite the longevity of the Madoff case, in counterpoint to the high longevity of Social Security systems, since 1889 in Germany or since 1935 in the United States, are motive enough for DeWitt (2009) to exclude a Ponzi oddity from Social Security systems.

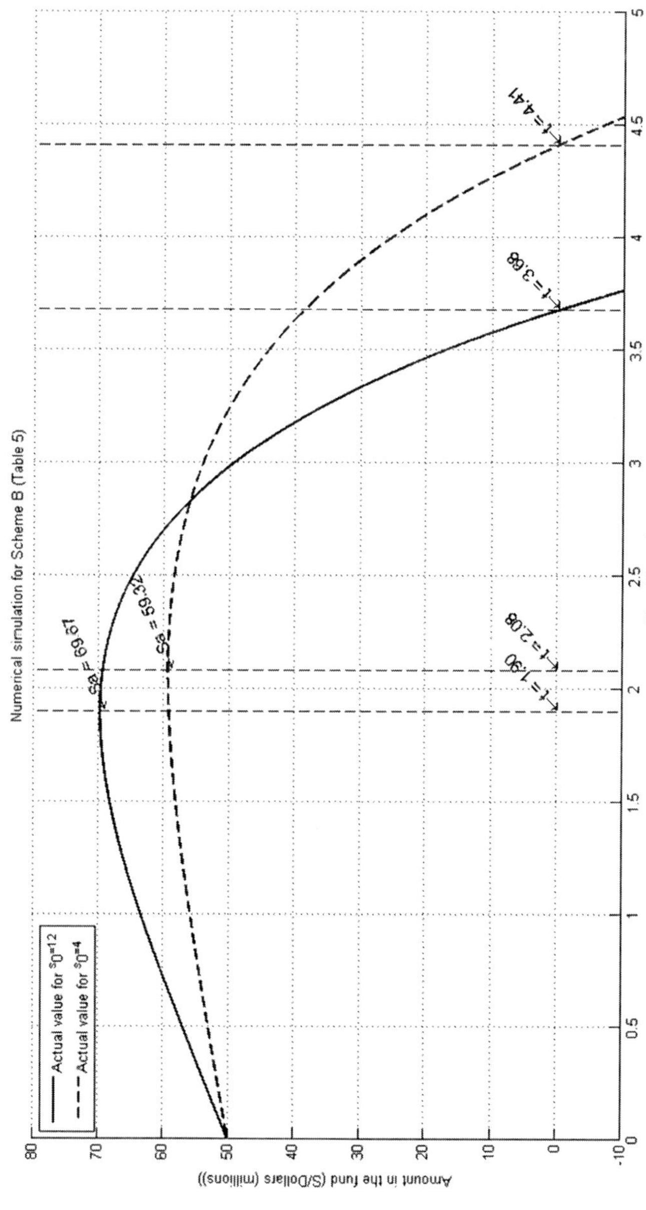

Fig. 6: Numerical simulation for Table 5.

The abovementioned philanthropic scheme clarifies some ideas on the topic, illustrating that a scheme can work sustainably "forever", provided that a high initial investment is delivered (for example, an investment in a government employment policy to create a new social security system). However, this long-term sustainability can be threatened, by investment rates, withdrawal rates and nominal rates.

We can see from Table 3 that, keeping all other parameters constant, the system is sustainable for $S(0) = 280$ and $r_p = 0.15$, whereas it collapses after 259 years for $S(0) = 245$ and $r_p = 0.15$; furthermore, for $S(0) = 245$ and $r_p = 0.155$ it collapses in almost half the time, about 146 years. The sensitivity is very high.

In periods where the beneficiaries of a social security system grow much faster than the entrance of new contributors, an operational deficit may occur. This vulnerability to demographic fluctuations has however nothing to do with Ponzi schemes or other fraudulent financial transactions.

The relationship between the model's parameters is clear. For example, fluctuations in investment withdrawal and birth rates, the rate of retirement and the presence of other individual retirement mechanisms (possibly more attractive).

Conclusions

A Ponzi scheme is a generic term to designate non-sustainable patterns of financial operations. The creators of these schemes can only fulfil their commitments to pay high interest rates if they can collect money from new loans, namely new clients and investors. The promised interest rates are so high that the sustainability of the scheme requires a continuous stream of new money and at a fast pace. Initially, many investors are so satisfied with their high returns that they allow recapitalization of their gains in the same scheme. The scheme can work and be sustainable provided that the fund's value output rate is lower than the rate of money entry of new investors. This paper describes a model that can provide some answers to financial regulators and investors when faced with situations of funds presenting themselves as having unrealistic performances regarding the economic and financial situation.

Since the model is built on continuous time, it does not allow us to carry out a follow-up of an investor situation in accordance with its position on a pyramidal structure. This may be the (only) limitation to this model.

We provide an innovative approach by considering the numerical solution of the model. Several simulations were performed to assess the behaviour of the fund by considering different perturbations in the model's parameters.

From this numerical approach to solve the model, several important model extensions can be addressed. The model can be enriched by using stochastic modelling, in line with Mayorga-Zambrano (2011). Even within this framework, further insights can be explored as well. It may be relevant to assess the model's behaviour with other inflow cash type functions rather than the exponential; or, to automatically compute the required bailout to withstand a collapsing trajectory from the first signs delivered by the model while tracking it numerically.

Bibliography

Artzrouni, M. 2009, "The Mathematics of Ponzi Schemes", *Mathematical Social Sciences* 58 (2), 190-201

Bhattacharya, U. 2003, "The Optimal Design of Ponzi Schemes in Finite Economies", *Journal of Financial Intermediation* 12 (1), 2-24

Blanchard, O. and P. Weil 2001, "Dynamic efficiency, the riskless rate, and debt Ponzi games under uncertainty", *Advances in Macroeconomics* 1(2), 1-23

Buttonwood 2011, "Pensions, Ponzis and pyramids: The retired are always supported by their children", *The Economist*, http://www.economist.com /node /21530106/print

DeWitt, L. 2009, "Ponzi Schemes vs. Social Security", *Social Security Online, Research Note #25*, http://www.ssa.gov/history/ponzi.htm

Fisher, K. L. and Hoffmans L. 2009, *How to Smell a Rat: The Five Signs of Financial Fraud*, Fisher Investments Press, published by John Wiley & Sons, Inc., Hoboken, New Jersey

Kindleberger, P. and Z. Aliber 2011, *Manias, Panics and Crashes*, London: Palgrave Macmillan

Mandel, M. 2008, "Is Social Security a Ponzi Scheme?", *Business Week*, http://www.businessweek.com/the_thread/economicsunbound/archives/2008/12/is_social_secur.html

Mayorga-Zambrano, J. 2011, "Un Modelo Matemático para Esquemas Piramidales Tipo Ponzi", *Revista Emprendedorismo y Estrategia Organizacional* 1, 1-13

Sander, P. 2009, *Madoff: Corruption, Deceit, and the Making of the World's Most Notorious Ponzi Scheme*, Lyons Press

CHAPTER ELEVEN

RISK PREVENTION IN BRAZILIAN GOVERNMENT CONTRACTS USING CREDIT SCORING

LEONARDO SALES

Introduction

The insufficient or non-existent rendering of services is one of the main problems in contracts between Brazilian public institutions and private companies. The losses it causes are always aggravated by the direct or indirect presence of public interest in these contracts.

These situations currently represent major challenges for both public administrators and government control agencies.

On the one hand, administrators need to enter into contracts with suppliers who can fulfil their obligations and provide a quality service, while ensuring the legality of the process, in compliance with a complex and inflexible legal framework.

On the other hand, the control agencies, that are frequently trying to adopt a more preventive attitude, face the challenge of anticipating risk situations that might impact on the achievement of government objectives, among them the insufficient rendering of services contracted from the private sector.

We assume in this research that it would be relevant for the government audit units to understand in advance the probability that a given contract may present problems.

Therefore, we seek to test the applicability of predictive default models used by credit institutions (usually based on multivariate data analysis) in the prevention of contract default with public agencies, defined as the private company's failure to render services.

Among the models used by financial institutions, we selected the class called Credit Scoring as the object of this research. Credit Scoring models are based on the statistical consideration of the company's characteristics (registration or historical) to calculate its probability of becoming a defaulter. These models are widely used by such institutions and have been generating good results in the prevention of defaults (Hand and Henley, 1997).

The fact that these models are based on the company's characteristics is another assumption that makes us believe that the application of these techniques to government contracts is feasible. This is because it is possible to extract a large amount of information about the suppliers from the databases used by the federal government and that are available to the control agencies.

We therefore sought to identify which of these characteristics contribute to an increased likelihood of suppliers failing to fulfil their obligations to the government, thus allowing the risk of problems to be known in advance.

We tested two statistical classification techniques used in Credit Scoring models: Logistic Regression and Decision Tree, using a database relating to a sample of government suppliers as input and divided it into two groups: those that have a history of default (called "defaulters") and those with a history of fulfilling obligations (called "compliant"). The performance of the techniques will be measured by comparing what was planned to actual ratings.

The entire research was conducted at the Office of the Comptroller General - CGU, which is the central agency of the Brazilian government's internal control system. We used the databases and the hardware and software structure of the Public Expenditure Observatory – ODP,[1] a unit that is a reference in data analysis and production of strategic information.

The results are discussed based on the evaluation of the accuracy of each technique used to predict the probability of default and the understanding of the variables that have greater predictive power.

It is hoped that the findings of this research may contribute to the CGU in building a robust methodology for contractual risk assessment, based on data analysis, which can be applied on a large scale and can increase public expenditure management and its control.

The paper is structured as follows: Section 2 presents the current literature on Credit Scoring, statistical techniques used in these models, and the Brazilian Government's experience in managing public contracts; Section 3 describes the motivation and objectives of this research; Section 4 outlines the methodology adopted; Section 5 presents the results of the constructed models; Section 6 discusses the validation of the results; and, finally, Section 7 contains the final conclusions.

Literature Review

Credit Scoring

Researchers define Credit Scoring as quantitative models employed by financial and credit institutions to measure and manage the risk of default by the borrower (Lewis, 1992). A correct understanding of this risk allows the institution to measure the amount of credit, its rate or term, and prevents difficulties in contracts in progress (Saunders, 2000).

Generally speaking, these models are based on the multivariate analysis of statistical techniques used to classify the customer into different groups according to the default risk (Hand and Henley, 1997). For this purpose, it uses information from registration and financial databases or historical records of customer transactions with the institution (Araújo and Carmona, 2007).

The idea of using quantitative models to assess and manage credit risk is directly related to the expansion and massification of credit that occurred worldwide in recent decades, which showed the need to standardize the procedures for the selection of clients and portfolio management (Marques, 2002).

Vasconcellos (2002) declares that traditional methods of credit risk assessment are based on expert opinion and are therefore subjective and individualized. Thus, it does not apply satisfactorily to large credit markets. Marques (2001) adds that although these models have evolved by aggregating scores (called credit ratings) they are still inefficient when dealing with large volumes of transactions, because they are slow and not standardized.

Therefore, the Credit Scoring models added standardization, speed and accuracy to these institutions' processes of client selection and management. The structuring of systems such as this one meant extending the process of credit risk analysis, making it less dependent on subjective factors.

Another factor that favoured the viability of these models was the development of computers, combined with the widespread use of computerized systems that made the gathering and structuring of large databases relating to transactions and customers possible. Likewise, increasing the processing capacity of computers also enabled the use of robust statistical techniques applicable to large volumes of data (Hand and Henley, 1997).

In recent studies that propose or test Credit Scoring models applied in different contexts, there is a common basis on which these systems are structured.

In general, these models are built based on three elements: a database with information about the customers (companies or individuals), another database with a structured record of negative experiences, and one or more statistical techniques that are able to learn from this experience and predict risk situations.

The steps to build the models generally involve: 1) the initial selection of samples of good and bad cases, creating two groups generally classified as "compliant" and "defaulter"; 2) the definition of variables to be used by the model to differentiate groups; and 3) the implementation of statistical processing of learning and testing accuracy.

This last step is crucial for classification. First, the statistical tool "learns" from the database, assigning "values" to the variables and revealing those most capable of separating the groups. Then, it creates a "formula" that defines the score of each company, and finally applies this formula to each case, yielding a final classification.

The usefulness of the analysis will depend on the comparison between the generated ratings and the original classification. This will allow us to calculate the percentage of correct classifications (accuracy of the model).

The classic use of Credit Scoring models is the selection of credit borrowers (Caouette et al., 1998). Furthermore, we can see examples in the literature of the use of these models in other stages of the credit life cycle. At times, it can be applied during the prospection of customers, when it is called Response Scoring; during the execution of the contract when it is called Behavioural Scoring; or even after a default has occurred when it is called Collection Scoring, to identify debtors that are more likely to pay the debt (Semedo, 2010).

As an example of the traditional use of Credit Scoring, we can cite Vasconcellos (2002), who proposes a methodology for the analysis of credit loans to individuals, using transaction records and customer registration information from a popular Brazilian bank as the object of the study. In the same vein, Gevert (2011) investigates the performance of different statistical techniques for predicting defaults in bank contracts.

Araújo and Carmona (2007), who studied a microfinance institution, also discuss the possibility of using Credit Scoring in the Behavioural Scoring model and compare the performances of two statistical techniques: Discriminant Analysis and Logistic Regression.

Statistical Techniques used in Machine Learning tools

As stated by Ghodselahi (2011), Discriminant Analysis and Logistic Regression are techniques traditionally used to create scorecards. A favourable point for the use of these techniques is that they are easily found in the available statistical packages.

Recently, other classification techniques have been used, such as Dccision Trees, Artificial Neural Networks and the Support Vector Machine.

We will discuss in more detail the technical operation of Logistic Regression and Decision Trees, which are used in this research.

Logistic Regression (LR) uses independent variables to classify elements into categorical variables and is based on a discriminant function built through the evaluation of each variable's ability to distinguish the groups. Hair et al. (1998) cite the main aspects that favour the use of this technique in relation to Discriminant Analysis (another technique which, as seen, is widely used in Credit Scoring systems): the possibility of having the dependent variable be categorical and the non-dependence of this technique on the requirement of normality for the independent variables, which also need not be numerical.

The result of the logistic function (Logit) is binomial, receiving values of 1 or 0, which indicate the presence or absence of a certain characteristic.

The function takes the following form (equation 1):

$$P(x) = \frac{1}{1 + e^{-(\propto + \sum \beta_i Y_i)}}$$

The elements that compose the logistic function are:

α = intercept (representing the minimum value of the function);

β = coefficient of each variable (Y) that determines its ability to move the function towards 1 or 0;

x = absolute value of a certain variable analyzed in the record.

According to Hair et al. (1998), the value P(x) is the probability of the function receiving the value 1 (indicating the presence of the studied characteristic).

Decision Trees are one of the most frequently used techniques worldwide to build classifiers. They consist of a simple graphical representation of the knowledge acquired through learning data analysis (Shibba et al., 2005).

Côrtes et al. (2002) compare the decision tree to a flowchart composed of the following elements: 1) nodes, which represent questions concerning attributes (predictor variables), 2) branches, which indicate answers to these questions, and 3) leaves (which are nodes without branches) that denote the distribution of records according to the response variable (dependent).

Figure 1, taken from Côrtes et al. (2002), exemplifies a Decision Tree applied to classify customers into buyers and non-buyers, based on the following variables: salary, gender, marital status and owned property.

In this classification, the technique found the variables that best divide the two groups, calculating the most effective value (referring to the variable) to separate them. This classification generates a hierarchy of divisions that will be used to classify each new record that is analyzed. Imagine that a new potential client has a salary of 3,000 and does not own a property. In this case, following the series of divisions (branches of the tree) and passing through nodes 6 and 8, he/she would be classified as a non-buyer.

Logistic Regression permeates many academic studies that propose Credit Scoring models. Among them we highlight Araujo and Carmona (2007), who compare LR with the Discriminant Analysis model in a risk management proposal for a microfinance institution, and Semedo (2010), who investigates the usefulness of the technique in market companies in Cape Verde.

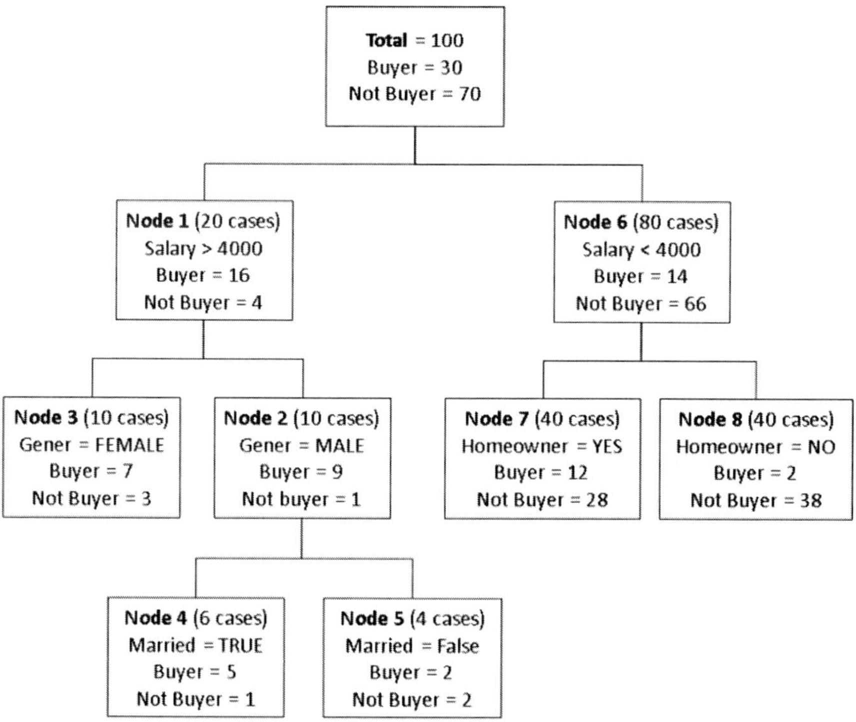

Figure 1: Decision Tree for Prospective Buyers. Source: Côrtes et al. (2002)

Vasconcellos (2002) uses decision trees to build a model of credit risk management for individuals in a Brazilian bank.

More recent studies seek to use other techniques. Semedo (2010) compares the performance of Logistic Regression with the technique of Artificial Neural Networks. Ghodeslahi (2011) and Gevert et al. (2011) test the Support Vector Machine technique, comparing its degree of accuracy with other techniques such as Neural Networks and Logistic Regression.

To the best of our knowledge, this is the first study that applies Machine Learning techniques to identify companies likely to default on public contracts. Nevertheless, there have been similar works in the government context. For instance, Carvalho et al. (2013) use a probabilistic ontology to detect and prevent procurement fraud in the Brazilian government. The main difference is that the model created in Carvalho et al. (2013) was designed by the expert instead of learned from data. Also, just a few real cases were used as a proof-of-concept.

Government Purchases

The entire process of buying products or hiring services in the federal government is governed by the rules of Law No. 8,666/1993, called the Bidding Law. Other norms complement this law such as Law No. 10,520/2005, which establishes a modality of reverse auction, and Complementary Law No. 123, which provides benefits to micro and small companies in bidding processes. Law No. 8,666/1993 details the phases of the bidding process, the bidding modalities that are allowed, the types of contracts, aspects of the qualification of companies, and also provides administrative and criminal sanctions to be applied to suppliers in case of failure to fulfil obligations.

We highlight the following parts of the Brazilian Bidding Law which defines the administrative sanctions:

> Chapter IV, Section II
>
> Administrative Sanctions
>
> Art. 87. Due to the total or partial non-performance of the contract, guaranteeing prior defence, the Administration may apply the following sanctions to the supplier:
>
> I - warning;
>
> II – fine, as provided in the bidding call or in the contract;
>
> III – temporary suspension from participating in bidding processes and impediment from celebrating contracts with the Administration, for a period no longer than 2 (two) years;
>
> IV – declaration of ineligibility to participate in bidding processes with the Public Administration while the determinant motives of the penalty

endure or until the reinstatement is executed by the authority that applied the penalty, which will be granted whenever the supplier reimburses the Administration for the resulting losses and after the period of the applied sanction, based on the previous section, has elapsed.
(Brazil, 1993)

Article 87 stipulates the penalties that the companies will face if they fail to fulfil their obligations with the government.

Sections III and IV (of Chapter IV of the law) are particularly relevant in this research. They define the companies that compose the National Registry of Ineligible and Suspended Companies - CEIS.

As foreseen in Law No. 8,666/1993, the process of acquiring and hiring in the federal government is carried out by the Integrated System for Management of General Services - SIASG. Each purchase or contract is registered in the system from the opening of the process to the commitment issuance. During the execution of contracts, public administrators can use the system to assign penalties to suppliers, if they fail to fulfil their obligations.

Established since 1994, SIASG recorded more than 400,000 contracts and nearly 4 million purchases.

Figure 2 shows the evolution of the amount of contracts published between 2000 and 2010.

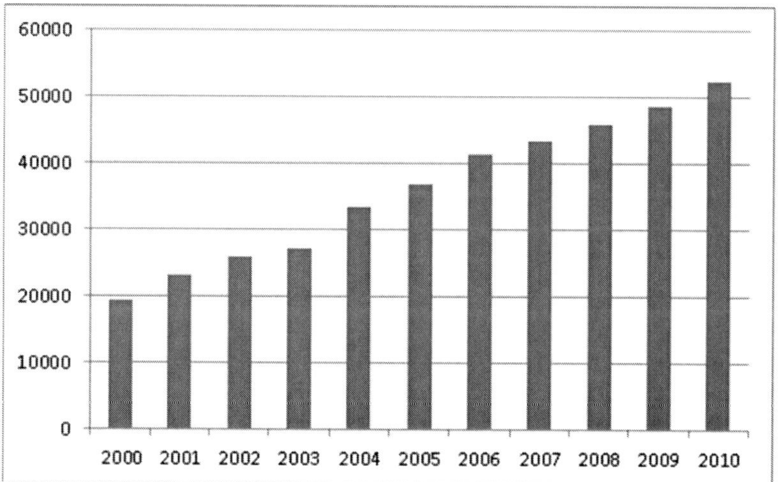

Figure 2: Amount of contracts registered in SIASG, 2000 to 2010. Source: Integrated System for Management of General Services - SIASG

Control of government acquisitions

As shown in Figure 2, more than 50,000 contracts were published in 2010 alone, exhibiting a linear growth trend. This large volume of contracts is under the supervision of government control agencies, in particular the Office of the Comptroller General - CGU, which is the central unit of the Federal Government's Internal Control System.[2]

The CGU states in its audit procedure manual that when auditing a governmental unit, each audit unit must select the contracts following criteria of materiality, severity, relevance and operational capability of the area to be audited. Then, the contracts have to be separated into three groups: exemption, unenforceability and other modalities.

The CGU also acts preventively. In 2009, it created a system to previously analyze calls for bids that looks for signs of favouritism. Usually, favouritism is related to the requirements that the supplier must fulfil in order to be hired.

Also in 2009, the CGU created the National Registry of Ineligible and Suspended Companies – CEIS,[3] fulfilling one of the goals of the National Strategy against Corruption and Money Laundering – ENCCLA. The purpose of the registry was to consolidate a list of companies that suffered sanctions by agencies and government bodies of the Public Administration (Municipal, State and Federal).

These sanctions of the Declaration of Ineligibility and Suspension (to compete in the bidding process) are foreseen in the Law 8,666/1993 and derive from the non-execution or partial execution of the contract and the existence of proven fraud at any stage of the contract or the bidding process itself.

The CEIS currently has more than 5,000 records.

Motivation and Objectives

We believe that developing statistical methodologies of data analysis, that focus on risk management and prevention on a large scale, will innovate how the CGU operates when auditing bidding processes and contracts.

There are gaps in the risk assessment process of government bidding processes by this control agency. This is because the supervision of purchasing processes always occurs in a precise manner (even when it is preventive, as in the previous analysis of calls for bids), in a number of processes that are limited to the operational capability of the audit units and the fragmentation of work by government structure. The subjective nature of assessments, as in the study of calls for bids, allows only a few of them to actually be analyzed.

This context of ad-hoc analysis which depends on expertise also exists in banking institutions and has motivated the credit risk management departments to develop Credit Scoring models. Nowadays, such models work to support the activity of the professional, who develops subjective analysis only for contracts of great materiality, attributing the largest mass of analysis to statistical tools.

This research focuses on identifying, based on statistics and data analysis, enterprises that are likely to default on public contracts. Thus, one of the expected contributions of this research is to enhance the risk management in these contracts.

The specific goals of this research are to: 1) Test the applicability and the performance of Credit Scoring models to predict the defaults caused by the supplier, and 2) Understand the characteristics of suppliers where they themselves contribute to being more prone to defaulting.

Methodology

In this study, we tested the performance of two statistical classification techniques, often used in Credit Scoring models: Logistic Regression and Decision Tree.

To be applied in the context of bidding processes, we use a database that represents two distinct groups: one with companies supposedly most likely to breach a contract and another with companies considered less prone to this type of situation. The database was also divided into groups of learning and testing.

We sought to identify and understand the variables that could best separate these two groups using classification techniques. Finally, we compared the results of each technique, calculating each accuracy percentage.

We divided the suppliers into two groups, which we call “Compliant” and “Defaulter”.

Just the fact that thc company is registered at the CEIS is enough to be classified as a “defaulter”. The fact that the supplier was registered in the CEIS means that it has committed serious errors in the execution of a contract.

To be classified as “compliant” not only must the company not be registered at the CEIS, but it also has to have had a minimum of five contracts completed with the government over the past five years.

The database used contains 2,000 companies, where 1,000 are considered to be “compliant” and 1,000 are considered to be “defaulter”. Each group contains 500 companies selected for learning and 500 for testing databases.

The 1,000 companies in the “defaulter” group were selected randomly from the CEIS database, after excluding the following cases: individuals, state-owned companies, businesses without contracts with the federal government and companies punished exclusively by municipalities or states. After these exclusions, our universe was reduced from 4,100 to 1,222 companies, and from them 1,000 selected randomly.

The constitution of the “Compliant” group was much simpler. First, since we started from a very large universe of companies, we selected those who signed contracts in the year the research was conducted, 2011. We considered that this measure would reduce the universe without the model being biased. From the new universe of 4,011 companies, we selected 1,000 also randomly.

Table 1 represents how the database was built, showing a step-by-step procedure for each category.

One of the techniques adopted to build the models was Logistic Regression because it is one of the most widely used in Credit Scoring and, moreover, it is less restrictive than the assumptions of the database used, not requiring the normality of distribution from the predictor variables nor the exclusive presence of numeric values.

This flexibility is also present in the Decision Tree. According to Meira et al. (2009), several variables in these models, numerical or categorical, could be elaborated simultaneously without damaging its performance and reliability. Moreover, this technique can graphically represent the functionality of the prediction model, which is an advantage over regression models.

To enable the construction of the models we used the STATISTICA software, from Statsoft, Inc.

The response variable used, called the dependent variable, is the group (“compliant” and “defaulter”), and will be obtained by the models through the analysis and consideration of the independent variables (predictors). Table 2 describes the predictor variables used in the models.

These variables were selected by the domain expert based on his experience and on the databases available. The rationale behind these variables is as follows:

Days until 1st contract: According to auditing and inspections performed by CGU, the longer the company is active in the private market before the first contract with the government, the better their performance in public contracts.

Campaign donations in 2010: In Brazil, there are many cases of corruption involving companies that have donated to politic parties. Even so, these companies tend to have a worse performance when executing public contracts.

Table 1: Procedure for building the database

	"Defaulter" Group	**"Compliant" Group**
Initial universe	All companies that were punished were registered at the CEIS (4,100 companies)	All suppliers with no record in CEIS, with at least five contracts completed in the previous five years (21,743 companies)
Selection criteria	Excluded: individuals, state-owned companies, businesses without contracts with the federal government and companies punished exclusively by municipalities or states.	Selected: companies with contracts signed in 2011.
New universe	1,222 companies	4,011 companies
Sample	Random	Random
Main database	1,000 companies	1,000 companies
Learning database	500 companies	500 companies
Test database	500 companies	500 companies

Incidents monitored by the CGU: One of CGU's tasks is to monitor automatically public contracts and update the alerts database (e.g., bidders of the same procurement that have an owner in common). According to the experts, the higher the number of alerts for a specific company, the more likely it is to present problems.

No. of partners and No. of employees: Also according to the experts, the higher the number of partners and employees, the better the quality of the company.

Median age of partners and employees: Although there was no previous knowledge on how the age of the partners would impact the performance of the company, the experts believed that it would have a negative correlation between the two variables.

Median salary of partners and employees: Again, according to the experts, better companies tend to pay better (higher) salaries to their partners and employees.

Table 2 – Predictor variables

Variable	Description	Source
Days until 1st contract	Number of days elapsed between the opening of the company and the first contract.	*SIASG* and Federal Revenue database
Campaign donations in 2010	Amount donated to political campaigns in 2010.	Superior Electoral Court
Incidents monitored by the CGU	Number of times the company was selected in some monitoring trail by the CGU.	*CGU*[4]
No. of partners	Number of shareholders in the company.	Federal Revenue database
No. of employees	Number of employees.	Database of Ministry of Labour and Employment
Median age of partners	Median age of the shareholders in the company.	Federal Revenue database
Median age of employees	Median age of employees.	Federal Revenue database and of the Ministry of Labour and Employment
Median salary of partners	Median salary of the shareholders in the company.	Federal Revenue database and of the Ministry of Labour and Employment
Median salary of employees	Median salary of employees.	Database of Ministry of Labour and Employment

The Logistic Regression function was built in two stages. First, using the learning database, all selected variables were used and had their coefficients of discrimination (using the Maximum Likelihood Estimation method[5]) calculated to identify those with more discriminating power. Then, only the variables that were statistically significant (at a significance level of 5%) were used together in the construction of the function.

After recalculating the best four coefficients (relative to the variables from the first round), we had enough parameters to build the classification function. This function was applied to each of the 1,000 records in the test database, giving us results according to the classification model.

To validate the results, following the usual procedures, we built a classification matrix that compares each prediction to the actual value of the dependent variable, thus achieving an accuracy rate (percentage).

The significance level of accuracy was tested according to the Press' Q test.[6]

Using the same variables and the same test database, the decision tree was built using the method of recursive partitioning, which is traditional for this technique.

The partitioning algorithm used was CART - Classification and Regression Trees,[7] which divides the distribution of each variable in order to improve the separation of groups. This division is based on the Gini coefficient (Hoffman, 1980). Partitioning creates the conditions ("if, then") for each variable and distributes them in a tree hierarchically configured according to their discriminating power.

Once the tree was constructed, the software itself classified the test database records.

Again, this classification was validated by a comparison matrix with the actual values, when we obtained a new accuracy rate.

Results

Logistic Regression

Table 3 presents the estimated parameters obtained in the first step of the Logistic Regression.

As shown in Table 3, the last four variables were significant according to the Wald test (Hair et al., 1998) state that there is significance for the variables with a p-value less than 0.05).

As already mentioned, the coefficients β determine the influence of the predictor variable on the dependent variable ("Defaulter" or "Compliant" group). The four main predictors were the age of partners, the age of employees, the salaries of partners and the salaries of employees. The negative sign of the coefficient in all of them indicates that the variable inversely contributes to the likelihood of the value of the Logit function being equal to 1 (presence of the value "Defaulter"), which supports the rationale behind each variable. In other words, the smaller the values of the variables, the closer the result of a function will be to 1. It is possible to confirm, for example, that the younger in age the partners, the higher the probability that the company will default on contracts, using the same reasoning for the other three predictors.

Besides the "direction" of influence, we must also analyze its "intensity", characterized by the absolute value of the coefficient. The closer the value is to 1, the greater the intensity of the influence of the predictor variable. In this particular case, it is clear that age (of partners and employees) has the most impact in predicting the class.

Nevertheless, the other variables did not have the expected outcome. Since their p-value was high, it was not possible to validate the expected correlation between these variables.

The next step, in order to optimize the adjustment of the model, was to rebuild it using only the significant variables (the median age and salary of partners and employees). The second step resulted in new parameters for the selected variables, as described in Table 4.

Table 3 - Estimated parameters in the first stage of Logistic Regression

Variable	β	*Wald* test	P-value
Days until 1st contract	0.000015	0.31086	0.577153
Campaign donations in 2010	0.000004	2.87676	0.089867
Incidents monitored by the CGU	0.000110	1.08392	0.297822
No. of partners	0.018996	1.03650	0.308637
No. of employees	0.000056	0.35190	0.553037
Median age of partners	-0.038611	28.78896	0.000000
Median age of employees	-0.017014	6.05829	0.013841
Median salary of partners	-0.000179	8.34594	0.003866
Median salary of employees	-0.000654	11.71519	0.000620

Table 4 - Parameters estimated in the second stage of logistic regression

Variable	β	*Wald* test	P-value
Median age of partners	-0.037118	32.86038	0.000000
Median age of employees	-0.014772	4.71279	0.029939
Median salary of partners	-0.000174	7.64116	0.005705
Median salary of employees	-0.000654	11.76702	0.005705

Thus, the Logit function was assembled using the coefficients of these four variables plus the intercept coefficient (equal to 2.688939).

Decision Tree

The tree generated from the learning database is presented in Figure 3.

As shown in Figure 3, the decision tree represents a set of rules that determines the classification of each record. These rules will be applied to the test database to validate the model.

The first division of the tree is determined by the variable number of employees. The algorithm determined the cut-off to be at the value of 8.5. Below this value the company is classified as "Compliant". Above it a new division occurs. Here, we can see that the algorithm has separated 305 companies ("Defaulters") and went in search of classifying the others.

The second division involves the median salaries of partners, where R$ 3,237.74 is the cut-off value. Above that, the company receives a rating of "Compliant" and below it new divisions occur.

The tree is dismembered until the last condition that divides the remaining 82 companies into "Compliant" to a number of monitoring instances less than 0.5, and "Defaulters" for instances above this value.

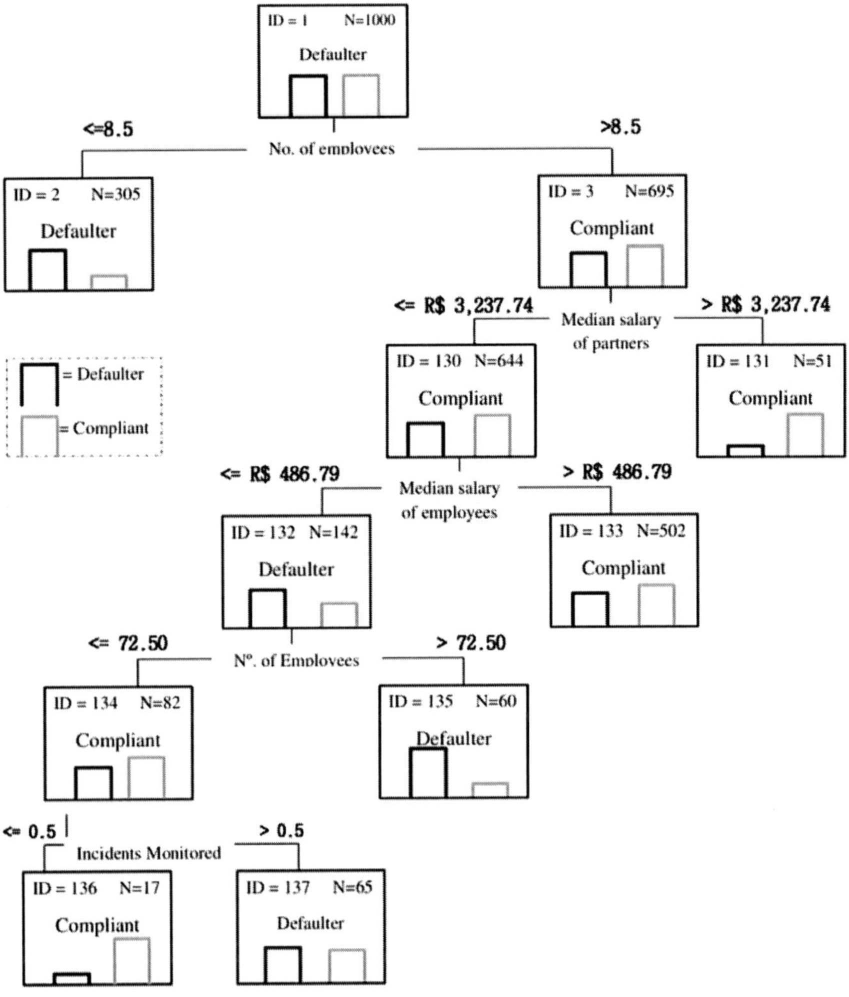

Figure 3: Results - Decision Tree

Validation of the models

The scoring matrix in Table 5 shows the degree of accuracy of the Logit model.

The Press' Q test can be used to measure the significance of the model. The formula is as follows:

$$Q = \frac{[N - (nk)]^2}{N(k-1)}$$

In this equation, "N" is the number of records in the test database, "n" is the number of correct classifications, and "k" is the number of groups.

We obtained the value of 62.5 with the use of the test, which is a result considered by Hair et al. (1998) to be the acceptable minimum to differentiate the correctness of the model than what would be obtained by the criterion of chance (randomness).

Table 5 - Classification Matrix - Logistic Regression

Accuracy Matrix	**Classification of the model**	
Real classification	**Defaulter**	**Compliant**
Defaulter	68%	32%
Compliant	43%	57%
Total accuracy	**62.5%**	

This result indicates that the model adds value to the classification, having acceptable predictive capabilities. However, it needs improvement. A positive point is that, as can be seen in the classification matrix, the performance to predict "Defaulter" companies was 68% better than that obtained in the classification of "Compliant", which is more interesting for the predictive control of bidding processes.

Another way to evaluate the consistency of the Logistic Regression is the dispersion curve of the residuals, reproduced in Figure 4.

The shape of the curve indicates the approach of residual dispersion to the normal curve, indicating that the model is suitable for the data.

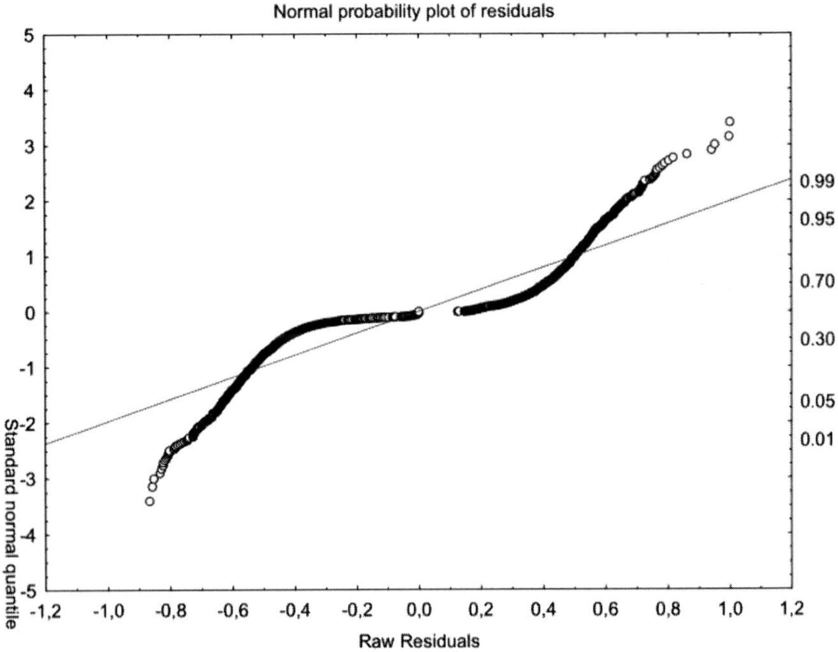

Figure 4 – Logistic Regression. Dispersion Curve of Residuals

The results of the test database on the decision tree model are shown in Table 6.

The Press' Q test once again showed an index of 67.6, slightly above that obtained for the Logistic Regression but still not an excellent result.

Table 6 - Classification Matrix - Decision Tree

Accuracy Matrix	Classification of the model	
Real classification	**Defaulter**	**Compliant**
Defaulter	56%	44%
Compliant	30%	70%
Total accuracy	**63%**	

Conclusions

In order to achieve the overall goal of this research, to contribute to building a predictive model for risk management in government contracts with private companies, we tested the applicability of statistical techniques used by financial institutions in the selection of clients.

Both models used for classification arose from an identical set of variables, selecting those most capable of separating two groups of government suppliers: those most likely to fail execution of the contracts (called “Defaulters”) and those least likely (“Compliant”). The Logistic Regression’s criterion of maximum likelihood prioritized the characteristics of salary and age of partners and employees. The CART algorithm of the Decision Tree also selected the characteristics of salary of partners and employees, but did not include aspects linked to their ages in the final model. Instead, characteristics related to the number of employees and monitoring trails of incidents were added.

The prevalence of issues linked to the “size” of companies such as major discriminating of good and bad suppliers in both models (quantity, age and salary of employees and partners) became evident. This indicates that the database used to select the group “Defaulter,” the National Registry of Ineligible and Suspended Companies - CEIS, is more populated with smaller companies, which may indicate that these companies have made commitments to the government without having sufficient structure and experience to fulfil them.

Besides these characteristics, the variable of incidents recorded in audits madc by thc CGU (monitoring trails) appears in the tree model, which gives the audit a different perspective, more focused on results.

Moreover, understanding the ability of variables to determine the potential default of suppliers is, in our opinion, the most important and immediate contribution to the context of public auditing, as well as the need for administrators of public contracts to foresee risky situations.

As a possibility in the medium term, our research confirmed the feasibility of using multivariate statistical techniques, commonly used for the evaluation of credit with financial institutions, and the prediction of problems by government administrators with their suppliers. Based on the use of two statistical techniques and only nine variables, we achieved a more representative performance than mere randomness.

However, we consider the models built here to be a starting point and not a completed solution. The prediction results were only slightly above the acceptable and they indicate a long path to search for effective forecasts. We foresee that gains in accuracy can be obtained from testing more techniques and, especially, increasing the amount of variables.

As for the use of classification models, such as Credit Scoring, we must emphasize that these cannot be used by the government in exactly the same way as they are used by financial institutions. This is because public administrators cannot reject a supplier that wants to be hired by the government based on a predictive model. The requirements to participate in bidding processes and employment are only defined by law.

However, we believe that information coming from such predictions is interesting for the government for two reasons. First of all, for administrators, it is interesting to know their suppliers and the risks they run to execute the services under their responsibility. Thus, administrative effort can be focused on those contracts that are being conducted by potentially problematic suppliers.

Secondly, regarding audit activity, besides the obvious usefulness for the selection of contracts to be audited, there is the potential of expanding the models focused on suppliers to a broader process of risk management in the provision of government services.

Bibliography

Araújo, E.A. and C.U.M. Carmona 2007, "Desenvolvimento de Modelos Credit Scoring com Abordagem de Regressão Logística para a Gestão da Inadimplência de uma Instituição de Microcrédito", *Contabilidade Vista & Revista* 18 (3), 107-131

Berry, M.J.A. and G. Linoff 1997, *Data Mining Techniques - For Marketing, Sales and Custumer Support*, Indianapolis: Computer Publishing

Brazil 2001, "Lei nº 10180 de 06 de fevereiro de 2001. Organiza e disciplina os Sistemas de Planejamento e de Orçamento Federal, de Administração Financeira Federal, de Contabilidade Federal e de Controle Interno do Poder Executivo Federal, e dá outras providências", http://www.planalto.gov.br/ccivil_03/leis/LEIS_2001/L10180.htm

—. 1993, "Lei nº 8666 de 21 de junho de 1993. Referente à regulamentação do art. nº 37, inciso XXI, da Constituição Federal, instituindo normas para licitações e contratos da administração pública", http://www.planalto.gov.br/ccivil_03/leis/LEIS_2001/L10180.htm

Caouette, J., E. Altman and P. Narayanam 1997, *Gestão do Risco de Crédito: O Grande Desafio dos Mercados Financeiros Globais*, Rio de Janeiro: Qualitymark

Carvalho, R.N., S. Matsumoto, K.B. Laskey, P.C.G. Costa, M. Ladeira and L.L. Santos 2013, "Probabilistic ontology and knowledge fusion for procurement fraud detection in Brazil", *Uncertainty Reasoning for the Semantic Web II, Lecture Notes in Computer Science* 7123, 19-40

Côrtes, S.C., R.M. Porcaro and S. Lifshitz 2002, *Mineraçao de Dados: Funcionalidades, Técnicas e Abordagens*, Rio de Janeiro: PUC-RioInf

Gevert, V.G., A.C.L. Silva, F. Gevert and V.T. Alves 2010, "Modelos de Regressão Logística, Redes Neurais e Support Vector Machine (SVM) na Análise de Crédito a pessoas jurídicas", *Revista de Ciências Exatas e Naturais* 12 (2), 269-293

Ghodselahi, A. 2011, "A Hybrid Support Vector Machine Ensemble Model for Credit Scoring", *International Journal of Computer Applications* 17 (5), 1-5

Hair, J.F., R.L. Tatham, R.E. Anderson and W. Black 1998, *Multivariate Data Analysis*, New Jersey: Prentice Hall

Hand, D.J. and W.E. Henley 1997, "Statistical Classification Methods in Consumer Credit Scoring: a review", *Journal of the Royal Statistical Society* 160 (3), 523-541

Hoffman, R. 1980, *Estatística para Economistas*, São Paulo: Pioneira

Lewis, E. 1992, *An Introduction to Credit scoring*, San Rafael: Fair Isaac

Marques, L.F.B. and G.O. Kloeckner 2002, "Gerenciamento do risco de crédito: um modelo de mercado vs. normas do Banco Central do Brasil", *Anais do Encontro Nacional da Associação Nacional de Pós-Graduação e Pesquisa em Administração*, Salvador: ANPAD

Meira, C.A.A., L.H.A. Rodrigues and S.A. Moraes 2009, "Modelos de alerta para o controle da ferrugem-do-cafeeiro em lavouras com alta carga pendente", *Pesquisa Agropecuária Brasileira* 44 (3), 233-242

Portugal, M.S. 1995, *Notas Introdutórias Sobre o Princípio da Máxima Verossimilhança: Estimação e Testes de Hipóteses*, Porto Alegre: DECON/UFRGS

Saunders, A. 2000, *Medindo o Risco de Crédito – Novas Abordagens para o Value at Risk e Outros Paradigmas*, Rio de Janeiro: Qualitymark

Semedo, D.P.V. 2010, "Credit Scoring: Aplicação da regressão logística vs redes neuronais artificiais na avaliação do risco de crédito no mercado Cabo-verdiano", http://hdl.handle.net/10362/4041

Shibba, M.H., L.R. Santos, J.A. Quintanilha and H.Y. Kim 2005, "Classificação de imagens de sensoriamento remoto pela aprendizagem por árvore de decisão: uma avaliação de desempenho", *Anais do XII Simpósio Brasileiro de Sensoriamento Remoto*, Goiânia: INPE

Vasconcellos, M.S. 2002, "Proposta de Método para Análise de Concessões de Crédito a Pessoas Físicas", http://www.teses.usp.br/teses/disponiveis/12/12138/tde-18112004-125442/pt-br.php

Notes

[1] ODP won the United Nations Public Service Awards 2011, in the category Advancing Knowledge Management in Government.

[2] Federal Law No. 10.180/2001 (BRAZIL 2001), assigned the CGU the role of central agency of the Federal Government's Internal Control System.

[3] More information at http://www.portaldatransparencia.gov.br/ceis/SaibaMais.asp

[4] CGU has an intelligence unit, called Public Expenditure Observatory (ODP), which makes use of information technology to monitor government spending at a distance. This research generates alerts that represent suspicious transactions (purchases, for example). More comments on the ODP can be found at http://www.cgu.gov.br/ODP.

[5] According to Portugal (1995), the Maximum Likelihood method is a procedure, as well as the Least Squares, which allows for the estimation of statistical parameters and testing hypotheses

[6] Details on the use of the Press' Q test in Hair et al. (1998). The equation is described in Section 6.

[7] The CART is a binary partitioning algorithm often used in the construction of Decision Trees. For more information, see Berry et al. (1997).

CHAPTER TWELVE

RETREATING INTO DOUBT: TAINTED FINANCE, CIVIL DEVICES AND THE RULE OF LAW

MICHELLE M. GALLANT

Introduction

In confronting the financial aspect of crime, states place increasing reliance on civil, in contrast to criminal, legal processes. Sometimes called non-conviction based approaches, civil devices greatly facilitate the assault on finance since they operate in accordance with conventional civil legal principles rather than the norms of the criminal law. Accordingly, since the legal ordering governing criminal manners is more exacting than the processes, rights or evidential understandings that apply to civil matters, a civil tool more ably captures tainted finance than any criminal device.[1]

Drawing principally on developments in select common law jurisdictions, particularly Canada, this article offers a critical appraisal of modern civil tools aimed at criminal finance. Part 1 locates the civil strategy within the wider global anti-criminal finance project. Part 2 introduces the central attributes of the civil mechanisms. Part 3 lays out the underlying tenets of the civil approach and Part 4 examines whether civil devices conform to the rule of law. Part 5 considers taxation as a discrete civil tool.

Tackling Criminal Finance

Reliance on civil legal processes to recover assets tainted by crime occurs as part of a global project to confront criminal activity, particularly lucrative crime, by attacking its financial underpinnings. The origins lie mainly in American struggles with illegal drugs of the 1970s when police-makers claimed that enormous revenues incapacitated control and began to introduce laws aimed specifically at the financial aspects of the drugs trade.[2] This idea of targeting finance migrated into international law to beget a global strategy that while initially drug-centric, has subsequently morphed into a generic strategy applicable to financial resources of any crime though drugs, organized crime and, latterly, terrorism, remain of central concern.[3]

The core elements of this finance-centric strategy consist of the criminalization of money laundering, the enhanced regulation of financial activity (anti-money laundering laws) and modern conviction-based forfeiture, or conviction-based confiscation of criminal earnings.[4] Anti-money laundering laws make association with the financial part of crime – the money, typically called the criminal proceeds – a criminal offence and permit the detection and interception of criminal wealth. Conviction-based forfeiture laws facilitate the garnishing of tainted wealth once a conviction for a criminal offence occurs.

The fashioning of civil devices, or civil legal approaches to criminal finance, largely began with the American re-animation of an ancient process known as civil forfeiture, sometimes confusingly identified merely as forfeiture.[5] Criminal forfeiture, or conviction-based forfeiture (sometimes called confiscation) connotes a taking of assets triggered by a criminal conviction. Civil forfeiture signifies a taking that can occur in the presence, or absence, of a criminal conviction.

Anti-money laundering regulation and conviction-based forfeiture form part of international law, part of the broader global project aimed at foreclosing upon criminal wealth. Civil forfeiture, or any other civil legal proceeding, does not. Many international treaties and related instruments speak directly to the criminalization of money laundering, to the monitoring of financial activity and to the post-conviction recovery of criminal finance but there is no specific global agreement requiring that states implement civil devices.[6] However, at the national level, individual states have been quick to embrace the promise of civil tools. South Africa, Ireland and the United Kingdom were some of the first to incorporate civil instruments into modern anti-criminal finance strategies. Australia and Canada endorsed the approach in 2002 and 2001 respectively while other jurisdictions continue to move in this direction.[7] Some states have added taxation to their civil tools.

Structural Attributes of Civil Devices

Civil forfeiture legislation is the most common civil device used to catch criminal earnings. Some jurisdictions, notably the United Kingdom, rely on the process of civil recovery while the Canadian province of Alberta relies on restitution and compensation regimes.

The structural features of the civil devices differ, at times fairly significantly, though there are a number of commonalities. The civil mechanisms contemplate the taking of assets for a connection with criminal activity without any need for a prior, or contemporaneous, criminal conviction. No model of a civil approach conditions the taking of assets upon the prior establishment of criminal culpability through a classically criminal law process. Confiscation laws, a core element of global anti-criminal finance strategy, require a conviction for an offence. The fact that the civil devices do not underscores their precise relevance to the taking of tainted assets – the procedural and substantive rights, much more generous in the context of a criminal prosecutions, simply do not apply. As a rule, this makes it easier to secure a taking of assets through reliance on a civil tool rather than through a criminal process.

Canadian civil models, which began to arrive in 2001, reflect other national civil legal regimes. As a federal state, most civil approaches have been implemented under provincial, as opposed to federal, law.[8] A federal forfeiture model was also adopted largely as a consequence of September 11, 2001.[9] Canada has not, as yet, incorporated any reliance on taxation.

Provincial law, with the exception of Alberta, relies specifically on forfeiture. Alberta law contemplates the restraint of property that subsequently may be the subject of a property disposal order.[10] Other regimes afford the seizure, restraint and subsequent forfeiture, as opposed to disposal, to the state. There is no obviously significant way in which Alberta's disposal process differs from a forfeiture process. The same appears true of the United Kingdom's reliance on civil recovery orders as opposed to forfeiture.[11] The remarkable quality of any civil legal regime is the unshackling of the taking of property tainted by association with the crime from any prosecutorial process.

The provincial models create two legal actions, one of which is common to most civil regimes. The common action is an action to forfeit the proceeds of crime; the second, more anomalous process, is an action to forfeit the instruments of crime.[12] "Proceeds of crime" has become a popular international mantra and is commonly defined as referring to any property derived directly or indirectly from a criminal offence.[13] Much of the initiative against criminal finance is often characterized as the pursuit of the proceeds of crime. Under the provincial models, the proceeds of crime liable to forfeiture include any property derived from any criminal offence acknowledged under Canadian federal or provincial law.[14] The former comprise classically criminal offences as defined by federal criminal law; the latter are usually described as regulatory, or quasi-criminal, offences, typically creatures of provincial law.

Most states embarking on this civil legal route enable the civil taking of the proceeds of crime although the scope may be framed slightly differently. The United Kingdom regime permits the civil recovery of property obtained through unlawful conduct;[15] Irish and South African law acknowledge the seizure of criminal proceeds.[16] Invariably, this action contemplates the removal of assets – whether real or personal property – derived from crime, representing the ability to seize and divest the revenues, the business profits, of illegal activity.

Provincial law permits a second civil taking of property tainted by crime, the forfeiture of the instruments of crime.[17] Neither United Kingdom nor Irish legislation entertains this concept of a property taking whereas South African and American law does.[18]

Instruments provisions permit the taking of assets that facilitate, or are otherwise linked to crime, short of the assets constituting the proceeds of crime. The province of Ontario's civil regime, for example, countenances the forfeiture of an instrument of unlawful activity which is broadly defined as any property used to engage in illegal activity, or likely to be used to engage in illegal activity.[19] Unlike a civil process aimed at revenues, or proceeds of crime, the instrument provision can reach a car used in the transport of drugs or real property used in the cultivation of illegal drugs.[20] At times, these provisions have been defined to cover the forfeiture of property upon which sexual offences occur.[21] Unlike the proceeds of, instruments are not revenues, business profits or some other reflection of criminal prosperity. Their liability to be taken hinges on their role in facilitating crime.

Other salient shared attributes of civil regulatory mechanisms include the ability to seize and hold proceeds of crime or the instruments of crime pending commencement of a civil process.[22] These prevent any pre-trial dilution of assets, fettering the ability to remove property from a jurisdiction so to diminish the impact of any civil process.

Although the incorporation of civil strategies presumes, by its language, a civil orientation, many laws implementing this initiative speak directly to the standard of proof applicable in the forfeiture process.[23] These identify the civil standard of proof, typically expressed as a balance of probabilities, as the standard that governs the action. This is somewhat curious since the standard of proof, or any other trappings of a particular mode of trial, whether civil or criminal, is usually never stated. A regime that directs civil entitlements or functions in a civil context would be governed by the norms applicable to any civil justice process.

Apart from the civil taking of the proceeds or the instruments of crime, a related dimension of non-conviction based regimes includes laws that permit the forfeiture of property for a failure to comply with declaratory export and import laws. Arising largely post-September 2001 and forming an integral part of anti-money laundering regulation, a failure to declare the import or export of certain monetary instruments entails the immediate forfeiture of that property.[24] Canadian federal law requires that the importation or exportation of any currency or financial instruments exceeding a threshold amount be reported to Canadian customs official.[25] A failure to file the declaration results in immediate seizure of the instruments. The property may be returned upon payment of a penalty unless the customs officer has reasonable grounds to believe that the property constitutes the proceeds of crime or funds for use in terrorism in the property is immediately forfeit.[26] While not generally referred to as civil forfeiture, this taking happens in the absence of any criminal conviction for any offence related to the property. In this respect, these provisions mimic civil forfeiture.

Theoretical Underpinnings

Use of civil devices is usually rationalized by the need for new tools to deal with the business of crime. Typically this rational aligns with the problem of organized crime and the related, and sometimes unrelated, concern with criminal profits, with the perils of tainted finance, with the corrosive influence of wealth, with acquisitive crime. Civil devices make sense since they facilitate the actual taking or forfeiture of property. They offer a degree of efficiency that criminal instruments – encumbered by the weighty exigencies of the prosecutorial process – do not.

Efficiency justifications are not particularly persuasive. A police state untrammeled by any rule of law may be equally efficient. The more compelling case for the civil devices are the underpinnings of civil justice, as opposed to criminal justice, systems. For the discrete tool of forfeiture, advocates tend to appeal to history. These considerations inform the analysis of whether modern civil anti-criminal finance tools conform to the rule of law.

Of Civil Proceedings

The use of civil proceedings, broadly conceived and quite apart from any new tools, targets tainted finance. An aggrieved investor, deprived of financial interests through some species of fraud, can bring a civil action to recovery lost earnings. An action for fraud involving deceit in financial dealings resembles a modern forfeiture action, a civil proceeding brought to claim property wrongfully taken.[27] A victim of theft can bring a civil action to recover their property. In the hands of the thief, that property is tainted property. There is no legal impediment to the victims of drug use, or victims of drug violence, seeking to recover compensation from a drugs dealer. In the context of regulated drugs, in contrast to prohibited substances, civil actions remove the profits of drug sales from corporations whose actions are tainted by some regulatory failing. If the state, or a state entity, is the victim of crime, it can bring a civil action to recover its losses. Fraud on a public health care system creates civil liability to repayment.

Remedies and the provision of some form of compensation, form the bedrock of civil justice system. Allegations of criminal wrongdoing, in contrast to civil wrongs, can underpin a civil action. Modern civil tools aimed at tainted finance merely assist in the latent capacity of civil justice systems to redress wrongdoing, to remedy an injustice, a wrongful, in this case unlawful, appropriate of wealth. Broadly conceived, enabling recovery of proceeds tainted by crime through civil legal mechanism accords with the traditional ends and functions of a civil justice apparatus.

Of Civil Forfeiture

As a popular vehicle through which to implement the civil strategy, civil forfeiture laws long pre-date modern anti-criminal finance initiatives. Most tie the earliest origins of forfeiture to the biblical phrase: "when an ox gore a man, the ox was forfeit …"[28] The consequences of the death, the goring, lay with the instrument of death, the ox, thus it was liable to forfeiture while no liability settled upon the ox's owner. Forfeiture, and a related doctrine known as deodands, refers loosely to this separation of liability, the fact that an object could be culpable and thereby liable to forfeiture for its wrongdoing.[29] Another version of forfeiture occurs in customs and admiralty law. Ships involved in wrongful actions on the high seas could be seized and liable to forfeiture when they arrived at a port. Goods wrongfully exported or imported have long been liable to forfeiture under customs law.[30]

In the biblical sense, and in admiralty and customs law, liability attached to the things themselves, to the property involved in the wrongful activity. Often called the "guilty property fiction," forfeiture classically affixes liability to objects, to property, without assigning any responsibility to a property owner.

Modern iterations of forfeiture share little in common with their historical forbears. Forfeiture continues, unlike other civil proceedings, to affix to things, to property, rather than individuals. Named defendants to modern forfeiture are usually the subject property, the bank accounts, the bundles of cash or the real estate seized as proceeds of crime. Yet these modern regimes are broad, reaching all manner of property including, under Canadian law, the instruments of crime. Arguably an appeal to history – the idea that states have long acknowledged the practice of civil forfeiture – as the justification for a wide array of contemporary new tools is misconceived. Rule of law considerations governing the interpretation of an uncommon process, to a peculiar strand of ancient forfeiture law, retain little cogency when applied to newly forged instruments, to expansive civil tools designed to confront the contemporary problem of inordinate criminal wealth. American law proves beholden, to a pronounced degree, to historical constructions of civil forfeiture.[31]

Civil Approaches and the Rule of Law

Adoption of the civil strategy represents perhaps one of the most profound legal developments of the past century in regards to crime control. Through the implementation of civil regimes, states acquire an unprecedented ability to sue and recover assets linked to crime. A blanket capacity to secure entitlement to assets that, on a balance of probabilities, are tainted by crime confers extraordinary power. It is true that some version of forfeiture has long formed part of common-law traditions. It is true that the victims of crime, and sometimes the state, can avail of a civil action to recover property linked to crime. Neither of these truisms captures the enormous potential of modern civil mechanisms. In the context of any type of crime having some property-based link, civil devices completely free the state from the constraints of the criminal process. Crime need no longer be proven, in any conventional criminal process, prior to securing public entitlement to any related property.

The pragmatic appeal of profound legislative developments must conform to the rule of law. The collapsing of the chase for criminal finance into a system of civil ordering proves resistant to certain challenges to its legitimacy while gently constrained by others.

Civil or Criminal Actions

The convergence of civil regulation and criminal finance prompts challenges to the proper character of civil models for the purpose of constitutional or rights-based norms. Regulation formally shaped as civil regulation may, on analysis, prove to be substantively criminal regulation and thereby, despite its formal character, attract any constitutional or rights-based constraints applicable in criminal matters. Amongst others, these would include the right to be presumed innocent and that any attribution of responsibility be suspended upon proven beyond a reasonable doubt or to some other enhanced standard of proof in contrast to standards that govern in civil matters.

In the main, the claim that civil forfeiture devices are criminal devices garbed in civil clothing has been rejected. The Canadian Supreme Court, in deciding whether, as a matter of constitutional authority, the provincial civil forfeiture regimes fell within federal jurisdiction over the criminal law, determined that inquiry in the negative.[32] The civil tools were properly characterized as civil devices not incidents of the criminal law. Other jurisdictions have researched similar conclusions in the context of whether human rights applicable in criminal matters apply in the civil taking of tainted assets.[33] As instruments of civil justice, in contrast to tools of criminal justice, the civil taking of assets need only conform to the lighter rule of law demands of civil processes.

Proportionality and Civil Devices

Proportionality is a constant of all legal systems although it assumes a variety of different forms. Constitutionally entrenched property rights can usually only be trimmed or displaced by overriding public interests, the displacement necessarily proportionate to the underlying objective. Canadian constitutional law subjects certain legal rights to a proportionality assessment, permitting the abrogation of rights if justifiable in a free and democratic society. In a conventional civil action, an award of damages, or some other remedy, constitutes a proportionate response to the underlying wrongdoing. A victim of fraud seeks to recover financial losses caused by that fraud. The remedy, an award of damages, is commensurate with that loss.

Civil forfeiture is typically thought proportionate given the tenet that the assets taken reflect the assets gained by crime. Proportionality exists between the alleged wrong – the illegal money earned – and the taking.[34] When the taking proves excessive, potentially touching on the rights of innocent property owners, the common interest in crime control, in tackling criminal finance, trumps private legal rights.[35]

There has been limited recognition of a proportionality constraint on civil regulation of tainted finance. Civil regulation is subject to the excessive fines of the US constitution.[36] This requires some proportionate relationship between scope of assets liable to forfeiture and the underlying criminal activities. A mere criminal taint, some modest association between property and crime would not suffice to justify the taking – it would be "excessive".

Some civil regimes have a proportionality component built-in. Under the United Kingdom structure access to the civil process is triggered when the tainted assets exceeds a minimum threshold.[37] In theory, this serves to tailor the civil mechanism to the particular kind of crime, or scale of criminal activity, that underpins the anti-criminal finance strategy – lucrative crime, rather than petty acquisitions, spawned the new approach. Proportionality also features under the rubric of a statutory "interests of justice" test in which the precise scope of the taking lies in the discretion of a court.[38] This yields some relief, in substance reflective of the US injunction against excessive fines.[39]

The Interaction of Civil Processes and Criminal Proceedings

Allegations of criminal activity, the source of any property liable to seizure, attract criminal prosecutions. The availability of civil mechanisms, particularly given the existence of criminal confiscation legislation, for securing title to tainted wealth invite obvious questions of the inherent fairness of simultaneous, or consecutive, civil and criminal actions evoked by the same set of circumstances.

Despite the failure to secure any constitutional, or rights-based guarantees, applicable to criminal proceedings, including double jeopardy protections, certain civil justice equivalents, constrain forfeiture actions. Classic legal doctrines such as *res judicata,* issue *estoppel* and abuse of process govern the civil actions. A civil action to recover the proceeds of crime might be precluded where the very issue of recovery was the subject of a successful, or failed, criminal legal process.[40] To the extent that these legal concepts apply, they may justify the place of the state in the position of deciding whether to pursue an individual offender or to pursue his or her assets.

Rule of Law, Instruments of Crime and the Retreat into Doubt

Overarching allusions to remedial justice and the prominence of criminal wealth coupled with the notion that civil regimes touch no more, nor less, than the proceeds of crime tends to mute opposition to the civil approach.[41] Analysis of civil regulation's congruency with the rule of law proves heavily shaped by these claims. More pernicious aspects of this trend, arguably incidents that might best be described as legislative excess, can be overlooked.

Civil regulation does not merely aim to recover criminal business revenues. The tendency is to enable the taking of assets "tainted" by crime. The instruments of crime are not criminal revenues. An instrument is tainted by its association with criminal activity and thereby liable to be seized. Further, the tainted quality catches property used in connection with offences that have nothing to do with the accumulation of resources, nothing to do with the business of crime. Under the guise of an anti-criminal finance strategy, provisions have been introduced which enable the home of an alleged sexual offender to be forfeit.[42] Such extensions and applications show that, at least in these respects, the civil approach has strayed too far from its initial moorings: proceeds, profits or material acquisitions of any kinds form no part of these offences. Worryingly, too, some aspects of the civil approach appear to unfairly allocate burdens of proof to an individual holding property liable to forfeiture. Under aspects of Canadian legislation, it appears that, once property is seized, the correctness of the taking is assumed, with the burden of proof lying with the property owner to demonstrate the lawfulness of his entitlement.[43] Rather than a civil trial in which the state must demonstrate that the property derives from, or is linked to, criminal activity, this initial task falls to the property owner.

Taxation as a Civil Tool

Finally, some states have touted, and begun to use, taxation as a tool with which to strike tainted finance. Tax occurs as a part of civil approach since it contemplates taking a piece of criminal earnings through the assessment of a tax. Revenue proceedings, with the exception of a prosecution for a tax offence, are civil processes.

Taxation of crime is not a new idea. In principle, revenues linked to criminal have a long, sometimes checkered, history of exposure to tax liability.[44] Canadian income tax law, for example, applies to particular sources of income, notably employment, property or business income. A criminal enterprise would qualify as a business, its illegal character irrelevant to its taxability as a source of business profits.[45] More intriguing questions in this regard are the scope of deductions to which the criminal entrepreneur might be entitled.[46]

In the main, the invocation of this civil device appears to deal with certain procedural or legal issues inherent in the taxability of criminal wealth rather than creating a new legal provision. Taxing criminal earnings in the United Kingdom proved somewhat difficult given the particular mechanics of the schedular-based tax system. Legislation removes those impediments, facilitating the levying of a tax assessment on a pool of allegedly criminal earnings. [47] Irish legislation equally made it easier to levy and carry out the enforcement of the taxation.[48] Rather than new approaches, taxation exists as a civil mechanism that, while available, has not been particularly vigorously deployed to ensure that criminal businesses contribute to public coffers.

Conclusion

Clearly a degree of reliance on civil tools holds some promise. It will be important, however, to monitor that reliance. Civil proceedings are not overly problematic in the context of relationships between two or more private parties. It is different when the state uses new civil devices in the context of crime. Firstly, there is the question of whether the state will in fact chose to regularly proceed with a criminal prosecution when civil liability, and its lighter procedural and substantive requirements, is at its disposal. Research might reveal an emerging preference for proceedings not merely as a mechanism for recovering tainted assets but as a mechanism that replace the criminal law. That raises profound questions about the morphing of personal criminal responsibility into some kind of compensatory justice mechanism. Underlying that potential morphing, of course, is the idea of the possible bifurcation of the justice system: compensation through the surrender of assets would apply to the high-priced criminal entrepreneurs whereas for those with nothing to forfeiture are exposed to the full force of the criminal law and criminal sanctions including potential imprisonment.

Secondly, it will be important to monitor whether the state confines reliance on civil devices to the context of profitable crimes. The legislation was originally conceived to contend with profitable crime. Any application outside of that context raises unique concerns. Civil forfeiture regulation, and other animations of the civil approach, emerged in response to an exceptional situation, that of the problem of the presence of large amounts of tainted wealth. It was clearly not about contending with assault, battery or any manner non-profit based offences. Justification such as claims that crime should not pay or allusions to the criminal origins of money underpin the shift to use of civil processes: they retain little cogency when applied to crime with little or no profit dimension.

Finally, a continuing line of inquiry is that of what these civil devices actually achieve. No doubt civil forfeiture moves money from the criminal economy into the public purse. Apart from this, there is no clear answer to any actual impact of the transfer on crime. Rationalized as a crime control strategy, not an exercise in revenue-raising, future research might aspire to determine what, if any, strategic objectives are realized.

Bibliography

Alldridge, P. and A. Mumford 2005, "Tax Evasion and the Proceeds of Crime Act 2002", *Legal Studies* 25, 353

Campbell, L. 2006, "Taxing Illegal Assets – The Revenue Work of the Criminal Assets Bureau" *Irish Law Times* 24, 316

Financial Action Task Force 2012, *International Standards on Combating Money Laundering and the Financing of Terrorism and Proliferation: The FATF Recommendations*, Paris

Gallant, M. 2005, *Money Laundering and Proceeds of Crime: Economic Crime and Civil Remedies*, Cheltenham: Edward Elgar Publications

Levy, L. 1996, *A License to Steal: The Forfeiture of Property,* Chapel Hill: University of North Carolina Press

Mumford, A. and P. Alldridge 2002, "Taxation as an Adjunct to the Criminal Justice System: the New Assets Recovery Agency Regime" *British Tax Review*, 458

Ryder, N. 2012, *Money Laundering – An Endless Cycle*, London: Routledge

Young, S. 2009, *Civil Forfeiture of Criminal Property: Legal Measures for Targeting the Proceeds of Crime*, Cheltenham: Edward Elgar Publications

Notes

[1] This difference animates civil and common-law systems though this discussion draws principally on common-law jurisdictions.
[2] M. Gallant, *Money Laundering and Proceeds of Crime: Economic Crime and Civil Remedies*, 2005, Edward Elgar 1-11.
[3] United Nations Convention Against Illicit Traffic in Narcotic Drugs and Psychotropic Substances, 1988; International Convention for the Suppression of the Financing of Terrorism, United Nations, 1999; United Nations Convention Against Transnational Organized Crime, 2000; United Nations Convention Against Corruption, 2003.
[4] These developments are ably canvassed in N. Ryder, *Money Laundering – An Endless Cycle*, 2012, Routledge, 8-39.
[5] *Supra* note 2, 74-79.
[6] An influential international actor recently recommended the adoption of civil tools: Financial Action Task Force, International Standards on Combating Money Laundering and the Financing of Terrorism and Proliferation: The FATF Recommendations, February 2012, B 4.
[7] See generally, Simon Young, Civil Forfeiture of Criminal Property: Legal Measures for Targeting the Proceeds of Crime, 2009, Edward Elgar. Italy has long had "preventative" justice measures which harken of civil forfeiture; see Raimondo v Italy (1994) 18 EHRR 237; M v Italy (1991) 70 DR 59.
[8] Civil Forfeiture Act [British Columbia], 2005; Victims Restitution and Compensation Payment Act [Alberta], 2001; Seizure of Criminal Property Act [Saskatchewan], 2005; Criminal Property Forfeiture Act [Manitoba], 2004; Civil Remedies Act [Ontario], 2001; Act Respecting the Forfeiture, Administration and Appropriation of Proceeds and Instruments of Unlawful Activity [Quebec], 2007; Civil Forfeiture Act [New Brunswick], 2010; Civil Forfeiture Act [Nova Scotia], 2007.
[9] Proceeds of Crime (Money Laundering) and Terrorist Financing Act SC 2001.
[10] Victims Restitution and Compensation Payment Act [Alberta], 2001 s 9 & 10.
[11] Proceeds of Crime Act 2002 (UK) Part 5.
[12] See Criminal Property Forfeiture Act [Manitoba] 2004 s 3.
[13] International conventions establishing the global anti-criminal framework draw on this language: see, for example, United Nations Convention against Transnational Organized Crime, art 2 e.
[14] Criminal Property Forfeiture Act [Manitoba] 2004 s 1.
[15] Proceeds of Crime Act (UK) 2002 s 240 and 241.
[16] Proceeds of Crime Act (Ireland) 1996 s 1, 2 & 4; Prevention of Organized Crime Act (South Africa) 1998 s 1 & chapter 6.
[17] Civil Remedies Act [Ontario] 2001 s 7(1). The exception is antiquated notions of civil forfeiture that continue to be scattered throughout common-law jurisdictions.
[18] Prevention of Organized Crime Act [SA] 1998 chapter 6 Part 2 & 3; 18 USC SS 981.
[19] Civil Remedies Act 2001 s 7(1).

[20] British Columbia (Director of Civil Forfeiture) v Angel Acres Recreation and Festival Property Ltd (2007) BCJ No 2475; [2009] BCCA 124; [2010] BCCA 539; Sports Car Seizure a Deep Reversal of Important Rights, CTV News, 8 September 2011; available from: http://bc.ctvnews.ca/sports-car-seizures-a-deep-reversal-of-important-rights-1.694558.

[21] Lawsuit over Man. house spurs rights concern, 30 December 2010, CBC news; available from: http://www.cbc.ca/news/canada/manitoba/story/2010/12/30/mb-skavinsky-civil-claim-reaction.html.

[22] All civil regimes contain some form of pre-trial seizure device: Proceeds of Crime Act (IR) 1996 s 2; Civil Forfeiture Act [NB] 2010 s 13.

[23] Proceeds of Crime Act (UK) 2002 s 241; Victims Restitution and Compensation Payments Act [AL] 2001 s 51.

[24] Proceeds of Crime (Money Laundering) and Terrorist Financing Act 2000 s 18.

[25] Ibid. s 12. Current threshold is $10,000: Cross-border Currency and Monetary Instruments Reporting Regulations, SOR/2002-412 s 3.

[26] Ibid s 18(2).

[27] Civil forfeiture law supplements, or supplants, securities regulation: see Director of Civil Forfeiture v Doe [2010] BCSC 1784; 661946 BC Ltd (Wellspring Capital Group Ltd) 2009 BCSCCCOM 141.

[28] Exodus 21:28.

[29] L. Levy, *A License to Steal: The Forfeiture of Property* (University of North Carolina Press, 1996) at 7-20.

[30] Supra note 2 p 57-74.

[31] See lengthy and confusing attempts to mesh new forfeiture law with the old in United States v James Daniel Good Property [1993] 510 US 43.

[32] Chatterjee v Ontario (Attorney General) [2009] 1 SCC 624.

[33] Murphy v GM, PB, PC Ltd, GH, Gilligan v CAB [2001] 4 IR 113; Gale and another v Serious Organized Crime Agency [2011] UKSC 49; United States v Ursery [1996] 518 US 267.

[34] D. Osgood (1995) 'Crime and Punishment and Punishment: Civil Forfeiture, Double Jeopardy and the War on Drugs' 71 *Washington Law Review* 489.

[35] Gilligan v CAB [1998] 3 IR 185, 237.

[36] Austin v United States [1993] 509 US 602.

[37] Proceeds of Crime Act (UK) 2002 s 287.

[38] Civil Forfeiture Act [BC] 2005 s 6.

[39] British Columbia (Director of Civil Forfeiture) v Rai [2011] BCSC 186

[40] British Columbia (Director of Civil Forfeiture) v Hyland (2010) BCCA 148

[41] It is notable that in the Canadian context only one of eight civil forfeiture initiatives elicited any significant opposition: Yukon Shelves Civil Forfeiture Act, CBC News, October 26, 2010: available from http://www.cbc.ca/news/canada/north/story/2010/10/26/yukon-civil-forfeiture-act.html.

[42] Most Canadian provincial civil forfeiture regimes allow the taking of property linked to the commission of bodily harms; Seizure of Criminal Property Act (Sask) 2005 s 2 (e) defines an instrument of unlawful activity to include "…property that

is likely to or is intended to result in the acquisition of other property or in serious bodily harm to a person."

[43] Under federal forfeiture law, once monetary instruments are seized as liable to forfeiture alleging they constitute the proceeds of crime, the burden lies with the owner, upon appeal to the Minister, to show that the resource is clean of that connection. This is not specifically stated in the regime. It flows from the ordering of administrative law; see, for example, Van Phat Hoang v Minister of National Revenue [2006] FC 182; Hui Yang v Minister of Public Safety [2008] FCA 281.

[44] P. Alldridge & A. Mumford (2005) "Tax Evasion and the Proceeds of Crime Act 2002" 25 *Legal Studies* 353 at 356-357. In Ireland, the revenues of illegal activity were held not liable to taxation, a decision which was later altered by statute: Hayes v Duggan [1929] 1 IR 406.

[45] R v Poyton [1972] CTC 411.

[46] See Neeb v R [1997] TCJ No 10 in which defendant sought to deduct the forfeiture of his drug revenues as a business expense; see also Anjaria v The Queen [2007] TCC 746.

[47] A. Mumford & P. Alldridge (2002) "Taxation as an Adjunct to the Criminal Justice System: the New Assets Recovery Agency Regime" *British Tax Review* 458 p 461-462.

[48] L. Campbell (2006) "Taxing Illegal Assets – The Revenue Work of the Criminal Assets Bureau" 24 *Irish Law Times* 316.

CHAPTER THIRTEEN

RECOVERING THE STOLEN SWEETS OF FRAUD AND CORRUPTION

JEFFREY SIMSER[1]

> … being smarter than the law enforcement agencies required the cooperation of many people. And a lot of money. Each person who dealt with the merchandise [cocaine] got a nice cut. At some point, for example, because so many people had to be paid, the minimum amount we could transport on each flight was three hundred kilos [then worth $12 million], anything less would result in a loss.[2]

Introduction

Fraud and corruption are crimes largely motivated by profit. The lucre is typically "laundered" or moved; the wrongdoer wants to place the illicit wealth beyond the reach of victims, rivals and law enforcement. Corrupt officials need a safe haven for their money (which is typically not the society they've stolen from); kleptocracies are notoriously unstable (Glenny, 2008). Money laundering is a technique that converts proceeds of crime into wealth with a patina of legitimacy. Recovering proceeds of crime is a very challenging enterprise. This paper examines fraud and corruption and asks: how do you recover the proceeds for victims?

Fraud and Corruption Combined: Allen Stanford

Allen Stanford was at the centre of a massive "Ponzi" fraud, whereby investors were promised huge returns through safe investments; in fact investments were scant and most investor returns came from the money of other investors. On March 6, 2012, Stanford was convicted of fraud and sentenced to 110 years. Gone were the days when "Sir" Allen Stanford, knighted by Antigua in 2006 for his work with the sport of cricket, enjoyed private jets and a lavish lifestyle (Roston, 2012). As with notorious convicted fraudster Bernie Madoff, Stanford's fraud was exposed following troubles in the markets. In the 2008 market meltdown, "investors" in the Ponzi sought safer positions, causing a run on the fund. There wasn't enough money to keep victims fooled (SEC, 2009).

The roots of the scheme first appeared in 1988: Stanford hired his college roommate, James M. Davis, to be the controller of his Guardian International Bank. When bank regulators in Montserrat, where Guardian was chartered, imposed heightened scrutiny Stanford closed shop and moved on to Antigua, along with Davis, creating the Stanford International Bank, Ltd. (SIB). SIB's main product was the "CD" or certificate of deposit, marketed particularly to investors in North and South America. The consumer gives their money over in exchange for a financial instrument, usually with fixed rates and fixed periods for redemption. Generally, CDs enjoy the reputation of a "safe" investment.[3] Stanford was a good salesman. By 2008, investors held $7 billion in SIB CDs. Investors were given various promises: they were told that Antigua's regulator, the Financial Services Regulatory Commission (FSRC) had oversight over SIB and that SIB's financials were subjected to outside audits (Davis Plea, 2009). One victim testified that SIB claimed, falsely, that their investments were insured by Lloyd's of London (Kaufmann, 2011). Stanford's sales pitch claimed that non-existent Antiguan income tax and the absence of an American brick and mortar operation allowed his CDs' to return 200 to 300 basis points higher than competitors (Rawl Testimony, 2011).

In fact, money invested in a "CD" was segregated by SIB into three tiers. Tier I consisted primarily of cash on hand. Tier II consisted of largely legitimate investments, but by 2008 they made up a mere 10% of the SIB portfolio. Tier III assets, illiquid and without much value, made up 80% of the portfolio and at least $2 billion in undisclosed personal loans to Stanford were hidden on the books as investments. Indeed those books were, as they say, cooked. Davis, the controller, would work with Stanford on a desired revenue number, a return on investment that would attract investors (without scaring them too much); then Davis would create false reports that backed into (or reverse engineered) those returns. As with all Ponzi schemes, an ever-widening gap between the true holdings and the lies developed: by 2008, SIB claimed $7 billion in assets, but their actual position was less than $2 billion (Davis Plea, 2009).

Stanford's scheme needed more than fraud. Stanford had left Montserrat when regulators heightened their scrutiny. Antiguan corruption made the Ponzi feasible. Leroy King, a former ambassador and bank executive, was an auditor and later CEO of Antigua's regulator, the FSRC. In 2003 King performed a "blood oath" brotherhood ceremony with

Stanford: in exchange for payments, SIB would be largely left alone by the regulator. The bribes were transferred from a numbered Swiss account to an account in Antigua. Given billions in victim losses, the bribery was cheap, costing Stanford just over $200,000. King performed for his money: he removed two FSRC employees who showed too much interest in SIB; he sent Stanford two separate confidential investigative requests from the U.S. Securities and Exchange Commission (SEC).[4]

In 2012, James Davis pled guilty and Allan Stanford was convicted on all but one of the fourteen criminal counts that he faced (AP, 2012). Just prior to being sentenced to 110 years (Madoff received 150 years), Stanford insisted that he had not defrauded any one of the purported 28,000 victims (Rushe, 2012). There are a number of aspects of the Stanford case that are beyond the scope of this paper. For example, there was clear regulatory failure. The SEC had reason to believe in 1997 that Stanford was operating a Ponzi scheme. SEC examiners were unable to convince their colleagues in enforcement to open an investigation. Apparently American diplomatic personnel were told for three years not to be photographed with Stanford, information not imparted to victims (Rushe, 2012).

Suspect Numbers

Fraud and corruption are a subset in a larger grouping of unlawful activity, crime motivated by illicit profit. Profit motivated crime is inherently difficult to quantify. Data on criminal activities and profits undermines a criminal's goal of avoiding detection. There are various attempts to quantify profit-based crime, although some numbers might be considered somewhat suspect. The global retail market for cocaine is estimated to be worth $88 billion and the opiate retail market is worth $65 billion. Trafficking in persons garners $32 billion and firearms a mere $1 billion (UNODC, 2011). A study on "occupational" fraud estimated, on a very rough measure,[5] that annual losses to companies globally could be in the order of $2.9 trillion (ACFE, 2010). One estimate suggests that each year between $1 trillion and $1.6 trillion in public assets are stolen; corrupt officials, particularly in developing countries, loot as much as $40 billion a year (Greenberg et al., 2009). Irrespective of the precise quantum, one thing links drugs, trafficking, weapons, fraud and corruption: money laundering. Money laundering is a technique used to disguise the origin of tainted property, shielding that property from law enforcement, victims and criminal predators. Estimates suggest that global money laundering involves between $500 billion and $1 trillion a year. One commentator has suggested that the most authoritative estimate is a decade old and has a massive deviation between the high and low end of the scale (Demetis, 2011).

Fraud

Fraud is a dishonest deception designed to enrich a criminal at the expense of a victim. Fraud can be understood from several different perspectives. For example, one can focus on the type of victim (individual, corporation, public bodies and so on) or one can focus on the type of fraud. Conversely, one could focus on the technique like telemarketing or the vehicle like social engineering (Rusch, 2011).[6] There are an infinite number of possibilities for a fraudster ranging from someone with insider information defrauding the securities market through to telemarketing fraud[7] and garden-variety tax fraud. This paper will look at three types of broadly practiced fraud: the advance fee scam, identity theft and ponzi schemes.

The Spanish Prisoner: Advance Fee Scams

The "Spanish Prisoner" is a confidence trick or fraud that dates back to the 16th Century. An English "con artist" would approach a victim (or mark) with the tale of an extraordinarily wealthy person who has been imprisoned in Spain under a false identity. The mark will be told that they have been chosen judiciously for their discretion and upstanding nature. Secrecy is paramount: the prisoner's family might be embarrassed if his identity was revealed. The notion of secrecy is an element of many frauds: the victim is made to feel part of the money making enterprise; more importantly, the victim is less likely to tell others about the scam and may even be too embarrassed to call law enforcement once the scam is revealed. The con artist promises various inducements to the victim (you will share in a reward, you will marry the prisoner's beautiful daughter) and seeks money to secure the prisoner's release. In time, the mark will be told that complications have arisen; more money is needed. Once the victim's money dries up, the con artist disappears (New York Times, 1898). There are numerous modern day variations on this scam. Last year a friend and colleague sent me an urgent email: while travelling in Wales, all of his possessions were stolen. The American embassy told him he could fly without a passport, but the bank was really slow in producing a replacement credit card. Could I call him at the hotel and sort out a method by which I could wire him some money? My friend's email account had been hacked, a fairly common occurrence (Fallows, 2011). Social media websites, like Facebook and the like, can similarly be manipulated by a fraudster.

In advance fee frauds, "419" scams[8], victims are invited to "invest" their money on a promise of significant return. While the invitation is unsolicited, victims are told that they were personally selected to take part in an exclusive, profitable and most importantly secret deal. Once the victim is committed to the fraud, the scammer will seek more of their money to solve unexpected problems that have arisen.[9] A typical advance fee fraud can include:

- A victim contacted by email - the fraudster often claims to represent a government agency or a solicitor;
- The email has grammatical errors and spelling mistakes; the mistakes are intended to make the victim feel superior, as though they will take advantage of the fraudster;
- A pot of gold - the victim's assistance is needed to move substantial amounts of money (inconveniently caught up by things like civil war or currency restrictions);
- Easy profit - the victim is promised an eye-popping percentage of that massive amount of money and all they need to do is allow the cash to flow through their bank account;
- Eventually a wrinkle - money is needed up front to pay taxes, storage or banking charges; and,
- A loss - the victim pays the up-front fees; when they run out of money, the con artist disappear.

While advance fee scams are popularly associated with Nigeria and West Africa, they originate in all corners of the world, including the UK, Hong Kong, Malaysia and the United Arab Emirates (Austrac, 2011).

Identity Theft

Identity theft can encompass a broad range of activities, but generally consists of the appropriation of someone's identity or the creation of a fictitious identity to facilitate fraud. The Federal Trade Commission estimates that as many as 9 million Americans have their identities stolen each year (FTC, 2012). Identities are stolen in a number of different ways:

- **Rummaging the rubbish:** fraudsters looking through garbage can find bills and other pieces of information with one's personal identity;

- **Skimming:** information on credit and debit cards can be stolen at automated teller machines or point of sale devices. The fraudster may use a skimming device which literally catches the data from the card, often in conjunction with a pinhole camera that will capture one's personal identification number or PIN. Alternatively, a bogus terminal can be used at the point of sale.
- **The Internet:** there are numerous online techniques to steal an identity. Hackers can gain access to a system using valid but stolen credentials; malware is a tool that provides remote access or control of someone's system (malware can be designed to collect information, including passwords and user names from the victim). Phishing is a social engineering technique where a fraudulent communication, often an email, is used to lure the victim into divulging information (e.g. the email purports to come from your bank seeking to correct problems with your accounts).
- **Mail Diversion:** the fraudster gives the post office a "change of address" notice and then collects the victim's mail.
- **Theft:** wallets or purses are stolen.
- **Pretexting:** false pretences are used to collect information from an unknowing third party, like a financial institution (also referred to as a social engineering technique).

Once in possession of the stolen identity, thieves have any number of options: credit card fraud, phone or utilities fraud, finance or bank fraud or government document fraud.

Ponzi Schemes

In the 1920's, Charles Ponzi induced thousands to invest in his arbitrage program involving European currencies and international reply coupons issued by European governments. In fact there was no arbitrage program. Ponzi used money from newer "investors" to pay returns to older investors. Ponzi didn't invent the scam but his name has long been associated with it. A Ponzi is fragile. There is no "real" business producing spectacular returns. This type of fraud is exposed when the fraudster cannot bring a sufficient number of new investors or when the current investors withdraw in large numbers (Smith, 2011). In scams, investors are not the only victims. For example, J.P. Morgan Chase is vigorously defending a $19 billion lawsuit launched by the trustee in the Madoff fraud (AP, 2011). A broker recently settled a lawsuit launched by the New York Attorney General, agreeing to pay over $400 million to victims of Madoff (Friefeld, 2012).

Unlike the Spanish Prisoner scam, the victim is not encouraged to adopt secrecy. Fraudsters want victims to share information and look for early marks who will influence others. Later marks invest in the Ponzi not because of the fraudster, but because their friend or neighbour or relative, who they have every reason to trust, is in fact getting paid with handsome returns. Some victims often lack the wherewithal to properly identify risk. However, very sophisticated victims can incur losses (institutional investors and sophisticated banks had money in companies like Enron).

Corruption

The Turks and Caicos Islands (TCI) is a small archipelago of islands at the eastern edge of the Caribbean (Auld, 2009).[10] TCI is also a British Overseas Territory, meaning that Westminster retains some control over the affairs of the islands. In 2008, the UK House of Commons identified concerns with corruption on TCI and a commission of inquiry was appointed. The Commissioner, Sir Robin Auld, reported on dishonesty and corruption in TCI:

- Questionable disposals of public land and payments from developers warranted criminal investigations;
- Wealthy developers donated to politicians, often through third party lawyers, without any public oversight or regulation;
- Public contracts were let in a questionable fashion;
- Assets, like jet airplanes, may have been misappropriated for personal use;
- Concessions were made where the government did not fully collect revenue and tax; and,
- Some pupils received government scholarships outside of the regular process.

The Commission made a number of observations about corruption. First, the invisibility and secrecy inherent in corrupt acts "defies discovery of proof." Second, TCI structural difficulties contributed to the problem: the economy had a narrow economic base;[11] the governance structure, between TCI and the UK did not provide for the requisite checks and balances to prevent corruption; finally, the "power and poison of politics" particularly in a system with virtually no oversight on political donations, allowed corruption to flourish unseen. Efforts to derail the inquiry through the courts were not successful.

The Commission made a number of recommendations, which included criminal investigations into a number of TCI public figures, including the former Premier. The Commission also recommended that both criminal and civil asset recovery units be created to chase down and recover the proceeds of corruption. Dedicated and independent units within the Attorney General are needed to bring cases before the courts. The Commission noted that while the notion of corruption seems "simple enough," proving corruption is very difficult to achieve. As a result of the Commission report, Britain suspended the constitution and placed TCI under direct rule.[12]

Types of Corruption

There are many forms of corruption including:

- **Bribery**: money flows from a private enterprise to a politically exposed person in exchange for a government concession (a contract, access to mineral resources and so on);
- **Extortion**: a politically exposed person demands an equity position or the split of profits from offshore investors in exchange for influence (failure to pay dooms the venture);
- **Self Dealing**: an official has a financial interest in the entity doing business in the corrupt jurisdiction; and
- **Embezzlement**: Sani Abacha, the former president, stole significant amounts of money from Nigeria's treasury. He'd issue false funding authorizations and money by the "truckload" was removed from the country's central bank (FATF, 2011).

Money Laundering

For a corrupt official or a fraudster, stealing the money is only a first step. Wrongdoers need to keep their money away from victims, rivals and law enforcement. Money well laundered accomplishes that objective. Laundering is process whereby dirty money is converted into apparently clean money with a difficult to trace provenance. Generally, money laundering is thought to have three steps: one, money enters the financial system, a step often referred to as placement (sometimes called loading); the launderer then takes steps, commonly known as layering, to obfuscate the source of the money; finally the apparently cleansed money is organized under the patina of legitimacy, a step known as integration. As we shall see, these steps are not always followed or even present. A fraudster will often take victim money from within the financial system (the victim writes a cheque or transfers money from account-to-account) and needn't worry about placement.[13]

A Sampling of Money Laundering Techniques

There are an infinite number of techniques used to hide illicit wealth. Techniques include:

- **Loading Cash:** anti-money laundering systems in many countries require reporting of large cash deposits (Simser, 2012). Evasion techniques include "smurfing" whereby a series of cash deposits below the reportable threshold are made by nominees (Welling, 1989). The money may be moved through a series of accounts, institutions and/or countries to obfuscate its source. Drug dealers typically transact in cash. By contrast, corruption and fraud corrode a system from the inside and don't necessarily involve cash payments (Simser, 2010).
- **Nominees:** practitioners of fraud and corruption often employ nominees and intermediaries, typically someone they can trust like a family member, to launder money. Following that money can be difficult for two reasons. First, the nominee will protest in the face of an inquiry that they are simply an honest business person beyond reproach. Secondly, sophisticated laundering makes following the money difficult. Consider this example: victims of an American telemarketing fraud sent cheques to a fraudster; the fraudster in turn sold the cheques at a discounted rate to a Montréal restaurant owner, who in turn sold them on to a broker, who in turn sold them to a money exchanger in Jerusalem. Following a series of further exchanges, the cheques ended up with a money exchange business in Ramallah, who presented them to U.S. financial institutions to be honoured. While law enforcement eventually unravelled the case, it was a difficult task; further there was an immense of time and space placed between the fraudster (who got his money in Montréal) and the Ramallah money exchange (Simser, 2008).
- **Trusts and Corporate Entities:** a legal trust is another nominee technique. A trust is a legal relationship: property is held by one person, generally called a trustee, for the benefit of another, generally called a beneficiary. A third person, sometimes called the settlor, can fund the trust. So for example, I could set aside money for my daughter through my personal lawyer: the lawyer is the trustee (and to the outside world may appear to be the "owner") while the daughter is the beneficiary and I am the settlor. This kind of arrangement is perfectly legitimate; however, it is not hard to see how a launderer could abuse this form of transaction. In a "peek-a-boo" trust, when the trustee is contacted by law enforcement or a

litigant (e.g. a victim or an ex-spouse), the trustee is instructed to automatically move the residue of the trust to another jurisdiction, placing one more border between the money and the victim (Simser, 2011).

- **Asset Stripping:** financial instruments and business entities can be structured to allow value to move between and amongst parties over a range of transactions. The overwhelming majority of these transactions are perfectly legal and form of the backbone of our modern economy. A clever launderer can manipulate seemingly innocuous transactions. For example, money can be moved between a business entity and the launder through dividends or loan repayments. Money can flow out of the country to pay a fictitious invoice and then be integrated back when that company "lends" money to the launderer or pays off his credit card bills. [14]
- **Insurance**: a launderer can take out a life insurance policy based on substantial initial payments and then surrender the policy later for early redemption or cash it out during the "cooling off" period. While the transaction does not make economic sense, given the penalties in the policy, the insurance company cheque appears to be a clean source of funds (FATF, 2005).
- **Trade-Based Money Laundering:** a launderer uses imports and exports to move value from party to another. By under-invoicing (or over-invoicing) the price of goods, the cash differential between the real price and the fictional price cleanses the money.

Asset Recovery

Recovering assets, particularly those secreted across borders, is a challenging enterprise. From the early 1970s to 1999, Nigeria had lost over $75.18 billion to corruption, $65 billion of which was transferred abroad (Adekoya, 2007). Only a tiny portion of those losses have been recovered. The Swiss, for example, recovered $70 million of the money stolen by the Abacha kleptocracy which was eventually repatriated to pay for healthcare, education, and infrastructure costs (Delco and Marugy, 2004). Nigeria is the world's eighth largest oil producer, but it has a crumbling infrastructure, most Nigerians lack access to basic medical treatment and education, and "poverty cripples most of the country's 140 million people" (Herskovits, 2007). Recovering assets can be a complex business. This section of the paper looks at two questions. First, how is the requisite information about the location and nature of the assets obtained? Second, what technique can be used to recover the asset?

Information Gateways

Secrecy is a key element in the crimes of fraud and corruption. The fraudster does not want their scam discovered, which can occur if the victim goes to a friend or to the police. Individuals offering bribes want to avoid prosecution. Even if the bribe is directed at an official in the developing world, the person offering the bribe can be prosecuted in their developed world home. Corrupt officials may operate in a weakened rule of law environment, thus not fearing prosecution. However, they very much desire the façade of legitimacy, to ensure that they continue to receive things like foreign aid (Spahn, 2010). Obtaining information, particularly across borders, is an inherently complicated endeavor. Without information and evidence, prosecuting those who bribe and more importantly recovering assets stolen through corruption or fraud, is impossible. Generally speaking there are several methods of procuring information, or information gateways:

- **UNCAC**: the United Nations Convention Against Corruption (UNCAC) is a global and comprehensive anti-corruption treaty. Article 56 places an affirmative duty on signatories to initiate corruption investigations without waiting for a formal request from the other country. Chapter V of UNCAC has a number of provisions respecting asset recovery. For example, states should allow other countries to bring civil recovery proceedings in their national courts and should recognize judgments from other jurisdictions. While widely subscribed, UNCAC has not been fulsomely implemented. States that are the victims of corruption often lack the wherewithal to gather information and chase assets; states that host purloined assets generally have public bodies facing growing demands and diminishing resources (Vlasic, 2010).[15]
- **MLATs**: mutual legal assistance treaties, MLATs, are bilateral treaties between nations that facilitate the gathering of involuntary evidence for use in prosecutions. So for example, a central authority in the American government could request information from their northern counterpart under their treaty with Canada. The Canadian Minister of Justice must approve the request, which is then transmitted to the requisite authority, often a provincial Attorney General, who in turn can seek a court order to compel the evidence. MLATs are generally available only to prosecuting authorities; for example, a government that brings non-conviction forfeiture proceedings cannot access the MLAT process (Podgor and Clark, 2008).

- **Letters Rogatory (letters of request)**: a party to litigation in one country can seek the assistance of the courts in another country to obtain evidence. For example, the defendant in a criminal proceeding or the plaintiff in a civil case might use this process. A letter rogatory is a formal request from the court in one country, seeking the assistance of a foreign court in taking evidence. Unlike MLATs, there is no requirement for a bilateral treaty; letters rogatory are premised on the notion of comity of nations (Blakes, 2011).
- **Hague Convention**: the Hague convention embeds the letters rogatory process for signatory countries; a litigant transmits a letter of request to a central authority in another country, which in turn can transmit same to the court for evidence taking proceedings (like a discovery). For non-compelled evidence, a litigant can ask for evidence to be gathered through a request to the diplomatic or consular office of the other country, or they can ask their own courts to appoint a commissioner to take evidence in the other state (Reufels and Kelly, 2001).
- **Civil Court Orders**: in the common law world, civil courts have devised a number of remedies that can be particularly useful in fraud and corruption cases:

▪ An ***Anton Piller*** order can issue against a defendant and in effect act like a private search warrant. Courts will only grant such an order rarely and only on clear and convincing evidence. The plaintiff must show (i) a strong prima facie case, (ii) serious damage (or potential damage) to the plaintiff as a result of the defendant's misconduct, (iii) convincing evidence that the defendant possesses incriminating documents or objects and (iv) a real possibility that such material will be destroyed before the normal court process (discoveries and so on) can operate.

▪ A ***Norwich Pharmacal*** order can be used to obtain documents, records and information from third parties (like financial institutions). The applicant must have a bona fide and reasonable claim; the respondent must somehow be involved in the acts complained of and be the only practicable source of the information; the respondent must be indemnified for the disclosure and the interests of justice must favour disclosure.

▪ Finally a ***Mareva Injunction*** is not an information gathering tool, but can be used to freeze assets. A plaintiff must: make full and frank disclosure of all facts; give particulars of their claim (including points that could be made by the defendant); provide grounds to show the assets are in the jurisdiction; give an undertaking as to damages; and show a real risk that assets will be removed or dissipated.[16]

- **NGOs and the Press**: there are a number of NGOs, including groups like Transparency International, that play an important role in publicly identifying information about corruption and hidden assets (Carr and Outhwaite, 2011). The press and websites like Wikileaks can also be sources of information.
- **MOUs**: civil asset forfeiture cases are non-conviction based proceedings brought by public bodies. For cross border cases, the MLAT process which applies to the criminal law, is not available. While letters rogatory are available, they are time consuming and resource intensive. Information can be shared bilaterally between public bodies through a memorandum of understanding.
- **FIUs**: many countries have created financial intelligence units or FIUs as part of their anti-money laundering regime. While each country is unique, generally an FIU collects information from financial institutions on transactions suspected of money laundering; that information is put to analysis and where appropriate it is shared with law enforcement and in some cases FIUs in other countries (often under bilateral MOUs).

Civil Lawsuits – the Example of Zambia

Zambia brought a lawsuit in England to recover stolen assets, culminating in a 2007 judgment of the High Court. The litigation focused primarily on the former President of Zambia, a former director of the Zambian Security and Intelligence Services and a senior officer at the Ministry of Finance. The Presidents' official salary was roughly $10,000 per annum; prior to becoming President, he held positions in the trade union movement. He had no legitimate means of amassing wealth, yet he was very wealthy. The President would take money from just about anyone, he even demanded (and received) a £30,000 kickback from his solicitors in the UK. He bought $1.2 million in clothing, a $450,000 property, and received cash payments of well over $1 million. Clothing seized from him included 349 shirts, 206 jackets and suits, and 720 pairs of shoes; most items were monogrammed.

The lawsuit against the officials highlights the complexity inherent in civil recovery litigation; that complexity also applies to the other forms of asset recovery discussed in the sections which follow. There were three main prongs to the case:

1. The "Zamtrop Conspiracy" centred around $52 million (US) that had been transferred to the Zambian National Commercial Bank in London. While some of the money was spent to meet legitimate state obligations, the court found that $25 million had been misappropriated.
2. The "MOFED" claim centered around a breach of trust; an individual, Atan Shansonga, was given a £100,000 per annum consulting contract for letting a property owned by Zambia. Ultimately, that claim was dismissed.
3. Finally, the "BK Conspiracy" involved $20 million to be paid to an arms dealer with connections to Bulgaria. The miscreants invoked the shroud of national security and used the power of the national security apparatus to hide their theft. The court ruled that there were no genuine arms sales and that the money had been misappropriated.[17]

The case required a stalwart and determined plaintiff. There were numerous complex motions. In 2005, a number of defendants argued that the UK proceedings should be stayed and reconvened in Zambia, at least against the Zambian defendants. The court denied the motion finding that the assets were in the UK and that UK solicitors had laundered funds on behalf of the Zambian defendants. The Zambian defendants then argued that prosecutors could use the evidence from the civil proceeding in a prosecution. The court responded by ordering a "ring fence" in the English proceedings; the hearings were held in private and the evidence was not to be used without prior court consent; as the Attorney General of Zambia was the plaintiff, he could (and did) give undertakings respecting prosecutions. Ironically, the main defendant broke the ring order himself by issuing a press release with documents attached to it. The Zambian defendants also moved to stay or dismiss the case on the grounds that they could not get a fair trial; some of the defendants had been arrested and as a condition of bail, they could not leave the country. The court responded in two innovative ways: the court allowed participation by video link and the trial was bifurcated, with a portion of the hearing conducted in Zambia under the oversight of a special examiner. In the trial, the initial video link was temporarily severed; the Zambian defendants refused to attend the backup link at the British High Commission and discontinued their participation in the trial.

Once the motions were dispensed with, a complex trial ensued. The judge tightly case managed the trial to a 51-day window over 2 years. Moving back and forth between Zambia and the UK required the transfer of "110 level arch files." There were expensive video links, which in the end were ignored by the Zambian defendants. Forensic accountants were retained by the Attorney General to trace funds into the London accounts and then on into various disbursements. In a civil fraud trial, like this one, the standard of proof is civil; however, as there are allegations of fraud, strong and cogent evidence is required. The court found that the evidence was overwhelming. The Zamtrop Conspiracy, for example, consisted of the Security Services running a London bank account almost exclusively for the purpose of stealing. From the plaintiff's perspective, the Attorney General of Zambia, their job was made particularly difficult by the refusal of Zambian defendants to participate. In civil trials, the plaintiff is generally permitted to disclosure from defendants. The court noted that the defendants had "nothing to say against AGZ's claim of any worth." While there were gaps in the evidence procured by the Attorney General, the court ruled that filling these gaps would not have changed the result. Finally, the litigation was grueling. One participating defendant that wanted to delay proceedings brought motions without merit (which they lost) and their "correspondence approached blizzard like proportions on occasions." All of this wrangling culminated in a massive judgment. The Zambian closing submissions on legal issues ran 1300 pages long. Legal issues ranged from the tort of conspiracy, fraud and breach of trust, through to joint and several liability issues, through to complex limitation issues.[18]

Bringing Civil Lawsuits

A number of elements are needed to successfully chase a fraudster or a corrupt official through a civil suit:

- **Deep pockets** – litigation is expensive to conduct. The Zambian case could easily have cost the plaintiff millions of pounds in legal fees;
- **Tough Decisions** – outcomes in civil litigation are never guaranteed. A judicial finding against a judgment proof defendant is a pyrrhic victory. Victims therefore need to carefully consider whether the litigation is likely to recover their losses. If it is not, they'll be spending good money to no effect;
- **Information** – some fraudsters simply dissipate their unlawful earnings through extravagant lifestyles, drugs and gambling. As a plaintiff, you need to know if the fraudster has hidden money in a nest egg. As discussed above (Information Gateways, p. 310), orders like an *Anton Piller* and *Norwich Pharamacal* are available

but difficult to obtain. Ironically the plaintiff must have adequate evidence to put before the court in order to get an order for information;

- **Dishonourable Defendants** – rules, like an *Anton Piller* order, were created out of judicial recognition that the normal rules of disclosure in civil litigation don't always work. In a garden variety civil suit both sides honourably disclose their information and ultimately the court rules on the merits. As the Zambian decision shows, corrupt officials are not always forthcoming with information required by the plaintiff;
- **Speed** – if the money is secreted away somewhere, the plaintiff needs to freeze it before it can be moved or dissipated. Some assets, like real estate, take time to move; others, like bank accounts, can be moved over borders with the stroke of a key. As noted above (Information Gateways, p. 310), a litigant can access a *Mareva Injunction* in some cases to freeze assets. While the orders are neither easy nor inexpensive to obtain, they can be granted on a worldwide basis;
- **Fortitude** – fraudsters suffer from the conceit that they can scam and fool anyone. They will try and bully and scam their way through the court system as well; and,
- **A Remedy** – can the assets be reached? Can a judgment be enforced?

Criminal Proceedings to Recover Money

Many countries have criminal confiscation measures whereby in addition to charging and prosecuting an individual for a crime, like fraud or corruption, the state can seek forfeiture of the criminal's assets, typically as part of sentencing following a conviction. As noted above, the MLAT process allows states to cooperate on cross border criminal matters. Alternatively UNCAC calls upon nations to initiate corruption investigations and inquiries without the need for a formal request. In other words, rather than investigating at the request of the victim country, an entirely domestic investigation and prosecution might occur where the wealth has been secreted. These processes generally work, although at times cooperation can be difficult to achieve (often because of resource scarcity) or slow. There are also gaps.

Consider, for example, Augusto Pinochet Ugarte, who seized power in Chile in a 1973 coup, remained as President until 1990 and Commander in Chief until 1998. A U.S. Congressional report noted:

"Since the first days of his regime, Mr. Pinochet has been accused of involvement with human rights abuses, torture, assassinations, death squads, drug trafficking, arms sales, and corruption but never convicted in a court of law" (US Senate, 2004).

In fact, the Spanish government had indicted Pinochet and sought his extradition from the UK in a widely publicized case. In 2000, the extradition was dropped and Mr. Pinochet returned to Chile. Even if Pinochet had been extradited and convicted in Spain, it is highly unlikely that a large portion of his money would have been touched.

Pinochet kept some of his money with an American financial institution, Riggs Bank. Their private banking arm accepted millions in deposits from Pinochet without any serious inquiry as to the source of funds. In 1996, Riggs established the "Ashburton Trust" in the Bahamas. While Pinochet settled the trust with his five children as beneficiaries, his name doesn't appear in the document. In 1998, the Althorp Investment Co. Ltd. was set up on a similar basis with his grandchildren as beneficiaries. Those trusts were established after the Spanish indictments were out. Following his arrest in London, Spanish courts issued an order freezing all of Pinochet's assets; Riggs Bank then moved $1.6 million of money from the UK to the U.S. Pinochet met with his Riggs bankers shortly after his return to Chile from London. He arranged a series of 38 cashier's cheques, $50,000 each, to be delivered to him in Chile between 2000 and 2002. While he told the bank he wanted to give money to descendants before he died, Pinochet cashed all of the cheques himself. As American regulators placed Riggs under greater and greater scrutiny, the Pinochet accounts were closed and the money was returned to him.

The Pinochet case revealed a number of flaws in the international system. First, there were regulatory flaws. His KYC, or "know your client," profile uncritically noted that he had family wealth in addition to his income (at $90,000 per annum). The cheques were delivered to Chile without the required regulatory filings to the US financial intelligence unit. The more fundamental flaw lies in the weakness of the criminal justice system. Spain tried to freeze his money; they also indicted him. At least a part of the money was secreted in the U.S., Bahamas, and UK; the freeze order had no effect. Further, Pinochet never faced a criminal trial, either in Spain or Chile. Even if prosecutors had managed the daunting task of convicting him, his money may not have been touched. A determined Congressional Committee, rigorously chasing down a rogue American financial institution, uncovered only part of his holdings, roughly $8 million of his estimated $50 to $100 million net worth. The family that controlled Riggs Bank agreed in 2005 to settle lawsuits by paying $9 million to victims of Pinochet (O'Hara, 2005). Pinochet's own fortune was untouched.

Civil Asset Forfeiture

Civil asset forfeiture is a statutory device that allows a state to bring a proceeding against tainted assets. In such a proceeding, the court can freeze and ultimately forfeit assets if the state proves that the provenance of the property, or its use, lies in crime. The court in essence extinguishes an unlawfully acquired title interest and forfeits that property to the state. Unlike criminal asset forfeiture, which generally requires the conviction of an individual, the defendant in a civil asset forfeiture case is the property itself. In corruption cases, which are notoriously difficult to prove, this tool can be very useful (Simser and McKeachie, 2012).

In 2011, the U.S. government launched a civil asset forfeiture case, asking the courts to seize, freeze and forfeit the assets of the son of the ruler in Equatorial Guinea ("EG"). EG is a small country on the west coast of the middle of Africa and has been governed by two men from the same family since 1968. The current ruler, President Obiang, dominates every aspect of EG life, controlling not only the government, but also key industries. In fact, this tiny, closely controlled country was considered by a group of malefactors as an ideal location in which to launch a *coup d'etat* with a small band of mercenaries. The coup did not succeed and British mercenary Simon Mann was sentenced to 34 years for his role; in 2009 he was pardoned and returned to the UK (Tremlett, 2009). Since the 1990s, EG has been awash in oil wealth; in 1998 alone, Obiang is estimated to have pocketed $96 million of the country's $130 million in oil revenues. From 1997 to 2002, three out of four people suffered from malnutrition in a country where per capita health care spending is amongst the lowest on the continent (US Senate, 2004). Despite having the largest oil reserves in Africa, most of the half million citizens of this tiny country live in poverty. Riggs Bank held $700 million in EG accounts; following U.S. hearings, the accounts were closed and the money returned to President Obiang and his cohorts. EG remains in Obiang's control, meaning the state lacks wherewithal and institutions needed to stem the kleptocracy. The Obiang regime has denied that corruption exists and has accused those who suggest otherwise of racism. In litigation still underway at the time of writing in the United States, the Department of Justice has filed for a *lis pendens* on assets of Obiang's son: luxury properties, vehicles and Michael Jackson memorabilia including "one white crystal-covered 'bad tour' glove."[19] NGOs like Transparency International and Human Rights

Watch continue to follow and report on the Obiang regime, actions which have stirred interest in a number of places including France.[20]

Liquidations and Receivers

Bernie Madoff ran a Ponzi scheme similar to the Stanford scheme discussed at the beginning of this paper; the difference was largely one of magnitude. At one point Madoff told investors that his fund held investments totalling $57.2 billion. Investigators later discovered that no securities were purchased. Madoff was treated at U.S. law as a security dealer (Stanford, by contrast, sold certificates of deposit).[21] That gave an American agency, the Securities Investment Protection Corporation (SIPC) jurisdiction. SIPC gives investors some coverage for losses. Further, SIPC commenced liquidation proceedings in respect of Madoff's fraud with a view to recovering assets and compensating victims. The liquidation was complex for a number of reasons. First of all, normally an investor recovers based on the status of their investments with a broker that has failed. In the case of Madoff, however, the investments were purely fictional. In the SIPC liquidation, victims were accounted for based on their investments, less any cash withdrawals. Further, the liquidator pursued people in the Madoff scheme who had withdrawn more than they'd invested. So for example, the owners of a New York baseball team, the Mets, settled with the liquidator agreeing to pay $162 million, which they hope to recover from their own lawsuit against Madoff (Rubin, 2012). The liquidation costs have been enormous. By October 2011, administrative costs had reached $452 million and were estimated to reach $1.094 billion by 2014. The bulk of those costs related to litigation fees, asset search and recovery costs, case administration and document review; 1,050 lawsuits had been launched to recover assets and more than 70 of the defendants were foreign. By the spring of 2012, those lawsuits had brought in recoveries of $8.7 billion (US GAO, 2012).

Opportunities

There are several opportunities to address cross border asset recovery. A number of preventative measures have and are being implemented. For example, there are efforts to generate transparency including specific proposals in the UK dealing with the extractive industry. As noted earlier, there are NGOs and investigative reporters who are dedicated to exposing stolen assets. Internationally there are various anti-money laundering initiatives, some of which are specifically designed to address politically exposed persons and discourage corruption. As the widely subscribed UNCAC becomes implemented, there will be more investigations into bribery and corruption, particularly in the developed world. There are some useful recommendations, particularly from the StAR initiative (Stolen Asset Recovery), to develop and build infrastructure, like civil asset forfeiture systems, which will improve our collective capacity to recover assets (Greenberg et al., 2009). Finally, a multilateral information gateway would strengthen that system.

Preventative Measures for Corruption

There are several strategies to recover assets. Simple transparency is critically important. In 2002, then Prime Minister Blair proposed the Extractive Industries Transparency Initiative ("EITI"), a voluntary program supported by the UK Department of International Development. The G8 supports the initiative, with 26 countries in the process of implementing it and seven reporting revenues. Nigeria was the first country to sign on to EITI and there's now interest, within Nigeria, on how oil revenues are spent. The G8, the IMF, and other multilateral organizations have all called for transparency in budgets. Non-governmental organizations have also promulgated a publish what you pay concept. If citizens in a country like EG, one of the top four oil producers in Africa, know how much money is diverted from Treasury, the legitimacy and power of the regime may be undermined. A second preventative measure is to gate-keep within Western financial systems for PEPs or politically exposed persons. Article 52 of UNCAC requires states and their financial institutions to take a number of steps to ensure that there is effective gate-keeping and record-keeping. A corrupted state is a weak one and not a desirable place to store money looted from Treasury; the money moves offshore. Reporting suspicious transactions and maintaining careful records which can be used to find the stolen money are important steps.

There are steps that private companies can take, both to comply with domestic criminal prohibitions against bribery and to recognize corporate social responsibility. Within any given company, risk assessments can be raised, identifying environments where bribery is likely to occur and internal controls can guard against bribery. For example, employee training on ethical values, a reporting system and punishment for rule breakers can all be established through company policy. Critics suggest, however, that social reporting suffers from high quantities of information that lack the requisite quality needed for action (Hess, 2012).

Anti-Money Laundering or AML Systems

Anti-money laundering or AML systems are designed with two primary goals. As noted above, attention on PEPs within most AML systems has been increasing over the past several years. Most AML systems have two pillars: prevention and enforcement (Levi and Reuter, 2006). Prevention measures are designed to deter dirty money from entering the system and to provide for transparency, through reporting, to discourage institutions from participating in money laundering. Enforcement measures are designed to investigate and punish those who manage to evade the AML barriers and launder their money. Prevention measures have four key elements: customer due diligence, reporting, regulation/supervision and sanctions. AML prevention relies on gate-keepers in the system, particularly financial institutions, to assess and disclose risks to the authorities, often through the financial investigation unit, or FIU, in the appropriate jurisdiction. Enforcement measures include disclosure to law enforcement authorities that can lead to asset recovery using civil or criminal forfeiture.

Capacity Building

The World Bank and UNODC have created the StAR or Stolen Asset recovery initiative. In 2009, they published a guide that makes a number of recommendations:

- Civil Asset Forfeiture, discussed in detail above (p. 317), is recommended as an effective device through which stolen assets can be recovered;
- The report recommends the adoption of unexplained wealth provisions whereby public officials who have significantly increased their assets would be subjected to a rebuttable presumption of unexplained wealth; and,
- Finally, a civil forfeiture statute in and of itself does nothing. A dedicated, trained and properly resourced unit is required to put such a law into operational effect (Greenberg et al., 2009).

Conclusions

Fraud and corruption may start locally, but can quickly become global. Inter-connected economies easily facilitate asset movement across borders. Further the issues of fraud, corruption and crime are, in some quarters, remarkably interlinked. One commentator has noted a trend toward "mafia states" or states in which criminals and corrupt politicians have fused their interests in places like Bulgaria, Guinea-Bissau, Montenegro, Myanmar, Ukraine and Venezuela (Naim, 2012). This paper has reviewed a number of techniques used by criminals to advance fraudulent or corrupt schemes. While a number of techniques have been listed as examples, in point of fact criminals will exploit vulnerabilities in an endless variety of creative ways. Committing the initial crime motivated by profit is merely a first step. A miscreant wants to enjoy their profits and present to the world as legitimate business person or government official. Money laundering is the technique used to advance this goal. Assets are transformed, through movement and transactions, from dirty money to apparently clean money. Recovering those assets is a challenge. Once the requisite information is obtained, there are a number of devices, ranging from court ordered forfeiture through to civil lawsuits, whereby assets can be recovered. Looking forward, there are a number of challenges to be answered. For example, how does one return assets when the kleptocrat remains in power, as Obiang does in EG? Returning recovered assets to EG today would be folly, placing them back in the pockets of the corrupt. There are opportunities as we look for better ways to prevent and deter fraud and corruption and as we seek to dispossess criminals of their loot and make victims whole.

References

ACFE (Association of Certified Fraud Examiners), 2010. Report to the Nations on Occupational Fraud and Abuse. Austin, Texas.

Adekoya, C., 2007. Renewed Battle Against Money Laundering in Nigeria. *Malawi LJ* 1:80

AP (Associated Press) June 25, 2011. Trustee Appointed to recover funds in Madoff fraud seeks billions more from JP Morgan Chase. AP, New York.

—. March 7, 2012. Texas Tycoon Guilty in Ponzi Scheme. *Toronto Star*, March 7, 2012 p. B2.

Auld, Sir Robin, 2009. Turks and Caicos Islands Commission of Inquiry 2008-2009. Cockburn Town, Turks and Caicos.

Austrac (Commonwealth of Australia), 2011. *Austrac Typologies and Case Studies Report 2011*. West Chatsford, New South Wales.

Blakes Law Firm, 2011. *Blakes Litigation and Dispute Resolution in Canada 2011*. Toronto, Ontario.

Brennan, S. and R.Vaillancourt, 2011. Money Laundering in Canada, 2009. *Statistics Canada Juristate Bulletin* Article 85-005-X.

Carr, I. and O. Outhwaite, 2011. The Role of Non-Governmental Organizations (NGOs) in Combating Corruption: Theory and Practice *Suffolk University Law Review* 44:616

Delco, F. and N. Marugy, 2004. Banks Work with Law Enforcers to Fight Terrorism and Corruption. *Intl. Fin. Law Rev.* 23:77.

Demetis, D., 2011. Unfolding Dimensions of an Anti-Money Laundering/Counter-Terrorist Financing Complex System. *LexisNexis Emerging Issues Analysis* 6019, New York.

Escobar, R. (with David Fisher), 2009. *The Accountant's Story*. Grand Central Publishing, New York.

Fallows, J. , 2011. Hacked! *Atlantic Magazine*, 308:5.

FATF, 2005. *FATF Money Laundering and Terrorist Financing Typologies*. Paris, France.

FRC (Fraud Research Centre), 2011. Top Scams of 2011. Available from URL: http://fraudresearchcenter.org/2012/02/top-scams-of-2011/

Friefeld, K., 2012. Merkin Settles Madoff Related Lawsuit, *MSN Money* June 24, 2012 available from URL: http://money.msn.com/business-news/article.aspx?feed=OBR&date=20120624&id=15258480

FTC (Federal Trade Commission), 2012. About Identity Theft. Available from http://www.ftc.gov/bcp/edu/microsites/idtheft/consumers/about-identity-theft.html

Glenny, M., 2008. *McMafia*. Random House, London.

Greenberg, T., L. Samuel, W. Grant, and L. Gray, 2009. Stolen Asset Recovery. World Bank/UNODC, Washington.

Herskovits, J., 2007. Nigeria's Rigged Democracy. Foreign Affairs 86:115.

Hess, D., 2012. Combating Corruption through Corporate Transparency: Using Enforcement Discretion to Improve Disclosure. Minnesota *Journal of International Law* 21:42.

Kaufmann, S., 2011. Testimony Before the Subcommittee on Oversight and Investigations of the Committee on Financial Services. U.S. House of Representatives, 112th Congress, 1st Session, May 13, 2011 (Serial No. 112-30).

Krauss, C., 2009. Blood Oath Sealed Stanford Deal. August 27, 2009, *New York Times*.

Levi, M. and P. Reuter, 2006. Money Laundering. *Crime & Justice* 34:289

Naim, M., 2012. Mafia State: Organized Crime Takes Office. *Foreign Affairs* 91:3.

New York Times Editorial, 1898. An Old Swindle Revived: The "Spanish Prisoner" and Buried Treasure Bait Again Being Offered to Unwary Americans. Originally published March 20, 1898 and available from

URL: http://query.nytimes.com/mem/archive-free/pdf?res=980CE5D71638E433A25753C2A9659C94699ED7CF

O'Hara, T., 2005. Allbrittons, Riggs Bank to Pay Victims of Pinochet. February 26, 2005, *Washington Post*.

Office of the Inspector General, Securities and Exchange Commission, 2010. Investigation of the SEC's Response to Concerns Regarding Robert Allen Stanford's Alleged Ponzi Scheme. SEC Case No. OIG-526, March 31, 2010.

Podgor,E. and R. Clark, 2008. Understanding International Criminal Law (2nd Ed). *LexisNexis*, New York.

Rawl, C., 2011. Testimony Before the Subcommittee on Oversight and Investigations of the Committee on Financial Services. U.S. House of Representatives, 112th Congress, 1st Session, May 13, 2011 (Serial No. 112-30).

Reufels, M. and K. Kelly, 2001. Transatlantic Discovery. *International Business Law* 29:291.

Roston, A., 2012. Bipartisanship! Republicans and Democrats both want to keep Allen Stanford's Money. *The Daily Beast*, March 7, 2012, New York.

Rubin, A., 2012. Mets End Madoff Mess with a Win. ESPN.com available from URL: http://espn.go.com/new-york/mlb/story/_/id/7709574/new-york-mets-madoff-mess-ends-amazin-win

Rusch, J., 2011. Iago's Net: Notes for an International Legal Regime to Combat Identity-Related Crime. *Georgia Journal of International Law* 42:923.

Rushe, D., 2012. Allen Stanford Sentenced to 110 Years. June 14, 2012, *The Guardian*.

Simser, J., 2011. Money Laundering: Emerging Threats and Trends. Presented to the International Symposium on Economic Crime, Jesus College, Cambridge University, September 8, 2011.

—. 2010. Asset Recovery and Kleptocracy. *Journal of Financial Crime* 17:321

—. 2011. Plata o plomo: Penetration, the Purchase of Power and the Mexican Drug Cartels. Journal of Money Laundering Control 14:266.

Simser, J. and J. McKeachie, 2012. Civil Asset Forfeiture in Canada. *Canada Law Book*, Toronto.

Simser, J., 2006. The Significance of Money Laundering: the Example of the Philippines. *Journal of Money Laundering Control* 9:293.

—. 2008. Money Laundering and Asset Cloaking Techniques. *Journal of Money Laundering Control* 11:15

Smith, F., 2011. Madoff Ponzi Scheme Exposes “The Myth of the Sophisticated Investor.” *University of Baltimore Law Review* 40:215.
Spahn, E., 2010. Discovering Secrets: Act of State Defences to Bribery Cases. *Hofstra Law Review* 38:163.
The Financial Action Task Force (FATF) 2011. Report on Laundering the Proceeds of Corruption. Paris, France.
U.S. Government Accountability Office 2012. Securities Investor Protection Corporation: Interim Report on the Madoff Liquidation Proceeding. GAO Report 12-414, March 2012, Washington.
U.S. Securities and Exchange Commission Office of Investigations 2009. Investigation of Failure of the SEC to Uncover Bernard Madoff's Ponzi Scheme. SEC Report No. OIG-509, Washington.
UNODC (United Nations Office of Drugs and Crime), 2012. World Drug Report 2012. Vienna, Austria.
—. 2004. The Global Programme Against Corruption: The UN Anti-Corruption Toolkit, 3rd Ed. Vienna, Austria.
—. 2011. World Drug Report 2011. Vienna, Austria.
—. 2012. Requesting Mutual Legal Assistance in Criminal Matters from G29 Countries. Vienna, Austria.
US Senate Permanent Subcommittee on Investigations, 2004. Money Laundering and Foreign Corruption. Congress, July 15, 2004, Washington.
Vlasic, M. and J. Noell, 2010. Fighting Corruption to Improve Global Security. *Yale Journal of International Affairs* 5:106.
Welling, S., 1989. Smurfs, Money Laundering and the Federal Criminal Law. *Florida Law Review* 41:287.

Table of Legal Cases

- *1654776 Ontario v. Stewart and the Globe and Mail*, 2012 ONSC 1991 (CanLII) (Norwich Pharmacal order)
- *Anton Piller KG v. Manufacturing Processes Ltd*, [1976] 1 All ER 779 (CA). (Anton Piller order).
- *British Columbia (Attorney General) v. Malik*, [2011] 1 SCR 657 (Anton Piller order)
- *Complex Sportivo Inc. v. Maharaj,* 2012 ONSC 2890 (CanLII) (Mareva injunction order).
- *Davis, J. M. Plea Agreement* filed August 27, 2009 with the US District Court, Southern Division of Texas, Houston Division, Criminal File Number II-09-335 (Stanford fraud).

- *Hoffmann v. Commissioner of Inquiry and Governor (Turks and Caicos Islands)*, [2012] UKPC 17; *Hoffmann v. Commissioner of Inquiry and the Governor (Turks and Caicos Islands)*, [2012] UKPC 17; *Misick,R v. Secretary of State for Foreign and Commonwealth Affairs*, [2009] EWHC 1039 (Admin); *Foley v. Ashcroft* [2012], EWCA Civ 423; *Ashcroft v. Foley*, [2011] EWHC 1710 (QB) and [2011] EWHC 292 (QB). Related Order in Council: *The Turks and Caicos Islands Constitution (Interim Amendment) (Amendment) Order 2009* was laid before Parliament on July 9, 2009 (Auld Report).
- *Mareva Compania Naviera SA* v. *International Bulkcarriers SA*, [1980] 1 All ER 213 (CA) (Mareva injunction order)
- *Mbasogu & Anor v. Logo Ltd. & Ors*, [2006] EWCA Civ 1370 (England CA) (Obiang case).
- *Motorola Credit Corporation v. Uzan & Ors* [2003] EWCA Civ 752 (Mareva injunction order across multiple jurisdictions)
- *Norwich Pharmacal Co. v. Commissioners of Customs and Excise*, [1974] AC 133 (H of L) (Norwich Pharmacal orders)
- *Re Bernard L. Madoff Investment Securities LLC*, (2011) 654 F. 3d 229 (2nd Cir CA) (Madoff fraud)
- *Federal Republic of Nigeria v. Santolina Investment Corporation*, [2007] EWHC 437 (Ch) (Nigeria corruption case with assets in England)
- *R. v. Mokelu*, [2010] EWCA Crim 288 (CA Crim Div) (advance fee fraud)
- *Securities and Exchange Commission v. Securities Investor Protection Corporation* 2012 WL 403602 (DDC, Feb 9, 2012; July 3, 2012) (Stanford fraud)
- *Serious Organized Crime Agency v. Agidi*, [2011] EWHC 175 (QB) (Nigerian corruption case with assets in England)
- *U.S. v. One White Crystal Covered "Bad Tour" Glove,* [2011 unreported] court file No. CV 11-3582 GW (Calif) (Obiang).
- *Zambia v. Meer Care Desai & Ors*, [2005] EWHC 2102 (Ch), appeal dismissed [2006] EWCA Civ 390, leave to appeal denied; [2006] EWHC 1179 and [2007] EWHC 1540 (Ch) (Zamtrop conspiracy civil lawsuit)

Notes

[1] The views expressed in this paper are the personal views of the author and do not represent the views of the Government of Ontario.

[2] A kilo of cocaine sold at that time for around $40,000, meaning a 300 kilo shipment could be worth $12 million (Escobar, 2009) at pp. 59-60 (quotation) and p. 134 (price of cocaine).

[3] Obviously this is not always so, see the SEC Bulletin on High Yield CDs at http://www.sec.gov/investor/pubs/certific.htm (last viewed June 11, 2012).

[4] The bribery included other things like Superbowl tickets and accommodations, worth about $8,000, for King and his girlfriend (Davis Plea Agreement, 2009)

[5] This number is premised on the estimate that businesses lose 5% of their revenue to fraud.

[6] Social engineering refers to the application of psychological techniques intended to influence a victim in a social setting. The fraudster identifies and then takes advantage of a vulnerability seen in the victim.

[7] One research body suggests that the majority of scams, 34.9%, are implemented through the web, followed by the telephone (29.2%), email (20.4%) or post (12.2%) (FRC, 2012).

[8] A reference to the Nigerian Penal Code prohibitions on advance fee fraud.

[9] In *Mokelu* (see Table of Cases), the victim, a consultative surgeon, was asked by email to assist in moving $300 million from Africa to the UK. In return for her assistance, she would receive between 40 and 50 percent of the money. The victim was told that money was needed for brokers' fees, legal fees, indemnity bonds, taxes and late payment penalties. She paid the fraudster £352,937. One of the three fraudsters was caught as he withdrew £20,000 from his account; his internal notes listed the victim as "miracle".

[10] Sir Robin Auld *Turks and Caicos Islands Commission of Inquiry 2008-2009* (Cockburn Town: Turks and Caicos, 2009) referred to herein as the "Auld Report" at p. 17. The report can be found online at: http://turksandcaicosislands. fco.gov. uk/resources/en/pdf/2011/commission-of-inquiry/inquiry-report.pdf (last viewed June 5, 2012).

[11] Currently tourism forms the economic base of TCI; past industries included salt extraction.

[12] Related litigation and orders in council are listed in the Table of Legal Cases (e.g. *Hoffmann v. Commissioner of Inquiry and Governor ...*).

[13] That said, converting money to cash, smuggling it and then depositing it in a jurisdiction with lax enforcement is an effective way for terrorists and criminals to obfuscate the source of cash. As long as money moves within the financial system there is a trail to follow.

[14] For example, a man named Holliday had a series of Atlanta escort agencies; he created a company in Nevada and another on the Isle of Man. Holliday had the offshore entities bill his Atlanta escort agency for fictitious services; after the invoices were paid, Holliday borrowed the money under a promissory note and used a credit card paid off by the offshore entities (Simser, 2008).

[15] UNCAC came into force in 2005 and can be found online (last viewed June 15, 2012) at http://www.unodc.org/documents/treaties/UNCAC/Publications/ Convention/08-50026_E.pdf. There are other conventions, like the 1997 OECD Convention on Combating Bribery of Foreign Public Officials in International Business Transactions as well as efforts by multilateral organizations including the World Bank, the U.N., and the African Union.
[16] See Table of Legal Cases below for legal citations.
[17] Invoking national security provides an additional weapon for a defendant trying to avoid judgment. For example, a New York defendant in a bribery case claimed that the American security establishment authorized his actions. No doubt seeking discovery and threatening to make public classified material was part of his legal strategy (Spahn, 2010).
[18] For citations, see Table of Legal Cases (Zambia).
[19] See U.S. in Table of Legal Cases.
[20] See www.transparency.org and www.hrw.org.
[21] In July 2012, the courts ruled that Stanford victims could not access the SIPC for recovery (see Table of Legal Cases).